ORGANIZATIONS IN THEORY AND PRACTICE

ORGANIZATIONS IN THEORY AND PRACTICE

CYRIL SOFER

Heinemann Educational Books · London

Heinemann Educational Books Ltd

LONDON EDINBURGH MELBOURNE AUCKLAND TORONTO
HONG KONG SINGAPORE KUALA LUMPUR
IBADAN NAIROBI JOHANNESBURG
NEW DELHI

ISBN 0 435 82878 9

Published by Heinemann Educational Books Ltd
48 Charles Street, London W1X 8AH
Printed in Great Britain by
Morrison and Gibb Ltd, London and Edinburgh

Preface

Origins of Book

This book has its immediate origins in series of lectures I have given at Cambridge for some years in the development of organizational theory. The lectures are part of a course on the sociology of organizations. The course is primarily for final year undergraduates who have already had two years of study in engineering, natural sciences, or mathematics. Apart from an eight-lecture introduction to the study of industrial society during the preceding year, this is their first experience of systematic social study. They work towards a final B.A. degree examination (a Part II Tripos Examination, in Cambridge terms) in which the sociology of organizations is one of three subject areas, the others being economics and operational research.

Plan of
the Book

The book consists of six parts.

I. The first part consists of one chapter. This chapter describes what we mean by an organization and the main attributes of large and technologically complex contemporary organizations. It argues that the large industrial organization is one of the most important social and economic phenomena of our time and explains something of its ramifications into politics and social life. It points out that the study of organizational and occupational life is interdependent. It then describes as a major trend the rationalization of work in large organizations, with special reference to the bureaucratization of administrative systems.

II. The second part consists of an exposition of certain crucial, landmark contributions to the understanding of behavior in organizations, together with a critique of each of these contributions in the light of subsequent developments and social science knowledge.

Each of the contributions I describe made a substantial advance in knowledge and thinking about organizations; or revealed some important defect in what was previously a prominent or accepted viewpoint; or opened up new ways of thinking about organizations; or precipitated criticisms that in themselves constitute advances.

This part of the book concentrates on particular individuals or groups of colleagues as contributors to organizational theory, as this makes it easier to see an attempt each time at one consistently argued viewpoint.

My choice has been guided by my teaching experience and my own personal attempts to make sense of organizational phenomena. Certain writers appear to me to convey something crucial about organizational phenomena (at any rate as I have experienced these phenomena) and to provide a stimulating starting-point for further discussion of how far they are "right" or "wrong." These include Taylor, Myers, Mayo, Lewin, Sherif, Asch, Simon, Lindblom, and the managers and consultants who have sought principles of management (including Fayol, Lee, Mooney and Reilly, Gulick, and Urwick).

These contributions are of far more than historical interest. They repay careful study both from the point of view of understanding what goes on between people within organizations and of improving their management. By examining each contribution in some detail, we can learn exactly what the nature of the contribution was and appreciate more precisely what its implications are. One also realizes as one peruses these contributions that the type of thinking that each represents (even when this has been shown to be defective) has by no means passed away but remains alive and with considerable influence over theorists and managers. This makes it all the more important that we should understand the premises of each argument, and the substantive propositions, note where the argument leads, and be alert to its implications.

I believe also that understanding of the theories and viewpoints put in the past is a necessary prelude to understanding current theory. It gives one a deeper insight into what lies behind current assumptions and propositions, and consequently a tighter grip on these.

Studying the work of past theorists gives one better perspective on what one accepts as contemporary theory. One realizes that theories are tentative statements of relations between variables; that the variables of central interest change from generation to generation; and that social theories become displaced over time as new social problems become manifest or as new technological and social forces assert themselves.

III. The chapters in Part III on the work of the Tavistock group with the British armed forces and of Samuel Stouffer and his colleagues with the Americans during the Second World War fall into a slightly different category. Like the persons and groups previously mentioned, these men made important substantive contributions to the understanding of organizational phenomena. But, more than this, they illustrate what I consider to be the major contribution possible from social sciences to management. They used the best technical apparatus available to them to analyze operational problems and to collect data bearing on those problems; they fed their analyses and information back into the organizational system; they helped discuss the practical implications of their work and the possible repercussions of alternative policies that might be followed; and, where possible, they studied as fresh theoretical sources reactions to the administrative actions eventually taken.[1]

IV. A summary statement then follows of propositions on organizational behavior which I regard as the correct assumption we can now make in approaching human problems in organizations.

I have approached this statement with some hesitation, after reflecting on the dismal fate of many attempts to generalize about organizations and to account for what happens in them.

But I have realized in the course of teaching and of writing this book that I was extracting from my consideration of each main contributor at least a few propositions or generalizations of enduring merit, and that if I could put these together in a mutually consistent way this would help to provide readers with a summary statement of where we are at present in propositions on organizations. This statement was, however, incomplete. I felt able to say with confidence more about the operation of organizations than has already been said by the contributors discussed. I could draw on two further sources. One is important to everyone in the field—that is current sociological and social psychological concepts and knowledge, whether or not directly derived from or already brought to bear on organizations. As a social science teacher in a university, I make a point of teaching some basic social science courses; these concentrate on role theory, secondary socialization, and dynamic aspects of personality and group relations. From the disciplinary point of view, these courses are combinations, in varying proportions, of sociology and social psychology. These bodies of concepts and knowledge are basic equipment for a professional level of analysis of all aspects of social life consisting primarily of interpersonal relations. It is also important, I believe, for the social scientist who studies organizations (or any other substantive research field) to be primarily a social scientist and secondarily a specialist in his field. In this way he brings to bear on his field of specialization the professional apparatus of his discipline and an analytic outlook on social institutions that puts any particular experience into a comparative perspective. To put the matter concretely, I feel more competent to study organizations because I teach basic social science in addition to organizational theory and because much of my research has been on community and family behavior.

In setting out a body of propositions I have been influenced by my personal experience of studying organizations over the past twenty years, of helping to manage them, and of advising administrators. This has given me a feel for the correctness or otherwise of organizational theories and for what is missing from them. My experience with organizations has led me to distinguish those ideas which are relevant and usable in the sorts of theoretical and practical problems I have personally confronted, from others which lack this usefulness. I hope that the inclusion of these ideas in a set of propositions on organizations will prove valuable to others whose concern is also rooted in firsthand contact with organizational phenomena. I describe my organizational experiences later in this preface so that readers can see for themselves what these have been and what they have included and excluded. To be concerte again, my experience has led me to the conclusion that there should be more recognition in organizational theory of the importance of conflict between colleagues at all levels; of career concerns as a factor in organizational developments; and of the competing ideologies accompanying organizational functioning—at one level promulgating, at other levels tempering or opposing the viewpoints of management.

V and VI. The fifth and sixth sections of the book consist of essays on selected issues endemic to the study of organizations and of the process of management. The fifth is on the way bureaucratically administered organizations actually work, the sixth on leadership, conflict, and change.

I move from being person-centered to being topic-centered. This enables me to supply a contemporary analytic viewpoint on some of the major themes which preoccupied the leading historical figures and which continue as major issues today. I have described the viewpoint as contemporary to indicate that I think most contemporary social scientists would agree with the main elements in my approach. If this were not so, the notion of there being social science at all or of professional social scientists would be misguided. At the same time, the problems and issues have my own interpretation and lead me to conclusions that will not be universally shared. This is due to the component of personal values and bias which is present in all social analysis and to my own training, background, and preoccupations. In formal training and outlook I am a sociologist with social-psychological interests and leanings. Some of the other forces that have shaped my outlook will be apparent from the later part of the preface, which describes my experiences in organizations.

Readership

In view of its provenance, the book should meet the needs of intelligent readers who are embarking on formal academic study of organizational theory or who are perhaps trying on their own to make more sense of their experiences in complex organizations.

Professionals in the field of organizational study, management studies, and industrial sociology should find some of the contents new to them. I have in mind the sections of the book which deal with the search for principles of management (especially by British scholars and managers), a subject which I found of absorbing interest as I went through the literature; the chapter on the Tavistock contributions during and since the war; the account of a study of my own on decision making; the chapter on conflict between colleagues, which includes descriptions of disputes which I observed at firsthand; and the chapter on professional interventions in organizational problems. The sections on the Tavistock contributions, on decision-making, on conflict between colleagues, and on intervention methods and theory owe a great deal to my nine years at the Tavistock Institute (1954–63). Just as poetry has been described as emotion recollected in tranquillity, so my reflections on the Tavistock work and what I did there might be regarded as action research recollected in tranquillity. I should qualify this by saying that, even though Cambridge has so far been extremely tranquil by the standards of most universities, there is little of tranquillity in the relationship between the conscientious teacher, the impatient and critical student, and an academic environment in which mathematics and physical sciences reign, and in which one's colleagues regard social sciences with attitudes compounded of ignorance, hope, and hostility. These factors have probably all influenced the style of this book, since I found that my teaching (and my research) could not deal only with their subject matter but had at the same time to demonstrate the feasibility of dealing systematically and with reasonable objectivity with social behavior. The style has also perhaps been affected by the fact that so many of my students and colleagues have been engineers or applied scientists for whom the realities of life present themselves on the one hand as physical objects and processes and on the other as individual personalities. Their first reaction to human problems is to try to establish the most rational-seeming way of relating means to ends, to attribute any deviation or loss of efficiency to the incompetence or ill will of some of the individuals involved, and to suggest that the situation be redressed by applying closer control from the top. It has fallen to me to show them that social structures, relationships, values, ideologies, and institutions are as real in their existence and effects as physical objects.

Autobiographical
Research Background

I graduated in social science at the University of Cape Town in 1945. I spent the next year as Research Officer in the School of Social Science, coding data collected in social surveys of Cape Town and Salisbury and helping in the design and execution of two sample surveys, one a study of meal patterns of Colored (mixed blood) persons and the other a study of the living costs of university teachers. During the next year I taught economics and sociology at the University of Witwatersrand and collaborated with a colleague in the Department of Sociology (Dr. H. Sonnabend) in writing an essay on the origins of the Colored people, a new "race" derived from West African, Malay, Hottentot, and European parentage.[2] I continued working on library-based studies of the Colored people of South Africa during the next two years at the London School of Economics. I then undertook my first major field study (1950 and 1951) in the township of Jinja in Uganda, first as a Colonial Social Science Research Fellow and then as a Research Fellow of the East African Institute of Social Research, Makerere College, Kampala. My colleagues and I began with a survey of the three main sections of the population (Europeans, Asians, and Africans), to obtain descriptive data on numbers in the area, age distribution, marital status, family size, household composition, earnings, employment, geographic origin, language, and so on.[3]

RACE RELATIONS
AND INDUSTRIAL OPERATIONS

With this background I went on to my first organizational study, focused on problems of race relations within local firms and government departments. These included a tobacco factory, a number of privately owned large construction companies involved in the building of the Owen Falls dam and hydroelectric works, and the Uganda Government's Public Works Department. The local situation provided a unique opportunity for the study of the beginnings of industrialization, as the small trading community of Jinja had its population approximately trebled over a matter of six to nine months by immigrant workers of every grade, from highly expert European civil and electrical engineering consultants to migrant African laborers entering their first employment of any sort.

The major problems presented by the local enterprises were (1) the inefficiency, by European and Asian standards, of the new African laborers, their lack of interest in the work, their relapse into idleness in the absence of constant supervision, their tendency to drift from job to job, or their abrupt quitting to return to their homes (thus largely vitiating investments in their training); (2) the day-to-day friction between Asian supervisors and African laborers; (3) the eagerness of Africans, after a few years of secondary schooling, to find clerical work and to avoid employment (even employment involving complex technical skills) that could be interpreted as manual work.

My observations and inquiries were partly in workplaces but largely also in the living areas of the groups involved. I spent a great deal of time in the municipal housing estate for immigrant African workers, discussing with these men their work experiences and the constructions they put on their situation. As they put it to me, they had come considerable distances from their homes partly for adventure and experience but largely to build up capital with which to return home after six to eighteen months. But the cost of living was far higher than they had expected; they had to buy much more of their food than before (food having largely been something that came 'free' from one's own plantation); they felt obliged to give part of their wages to kinsmen following them into the area; and a further large part evaporated in the face of new urban temptations, all the more attractive in the absence of their wives and families. In contrast with their own situation, the Europeans and Asians, as they saw it, had all the best things: the best houses, best food, best clothes, cars, and jobs that seemed to involve no strain—merely talking to people, writing, typing, telling others what to do, with no strenuous physical effort in the hot sun or on a factory floor. Even water (I was told) was graded; in the newly built storage tanks the best quality was for Europeans, the next for Asians, the worst for Africans. What were these other races doing here anyway? Presumably they came to take out as much as they could, if necessary at the expense of Africans. They were indifferent to the welfare of Africans or, in the case of Asians, actively hostile to Africans. They did not want to bother to teach Africans enough to make a difference to their economic position, and the Asians deliberately refrained from letting them learn things that might turn them into competitors. As far as the work day went, it was unpleasant to work hours determined by other people; to be reprimanded if one was late; to be shouted at and criticized if one did not please one's superior; to work continuously without pausing for a rest or a chat when one felt like it.

I asked what they thought to be the purposes of the work on which they were engaged. Practically none of my respondents realized that the major aim of the new acceleration of economic activity was the provision of cheap power for what was hoped would become thriving local industry providing more gainful employment for Africans and a higher standard of living and community amenities. African attitudes went further than ignorance of this to cynicism or blank disbelief that the effort they saw could be designed to bring them benefits. This was contradicted for them by the differences in power, wealth, income, and style of life between the races.

The main conclusion to which this experience led me was that it was impossible to understand events within a work enterprise except in the context of the social and community structure of which that enterprise is part. What was happening between persons within the local enterprises was largely a function of the living history of relations between the racial groups involved and of their relative political and economic power and privileges. Individual members of each racial group reacted to each other categorically, as representatives of their groups, rather than in terms of their personal characteristics. The work enterprise could not be understood as a closed social-psychological system of interpersonal or intergroup relations but reflected the society in which it was embedded.

This conception was not as obvious as it may now sound. At that time the sociology of organizations was dominated by the human relations approach which emphasized the importance of regarding the enterprise as a social system of its own; by administrative models which conceptualized the organization as a decision-making instrument; and by work emanating from Tavistock which interpreted a great deal of behavior within organizations as expressing latent needs and processes for which work arrangements provided a vehicle. Impressive though they were, all these approaches appeared to me to be limited by the fact that they stopped at the factory gate. My Jinja experience pointed unambiguously to the need to understand the social environment if one was to interpret correctly the expectations and assumptions underlying behavior in work organizations. This is not, of course, to argue that everything that happens within organizations is determined by external structures and events. Work organizations are themselves powerful initiators of social change, and educators in new skills, and play a key role in transforming the societies of which they are part. But they are subsystems within larger systems, subcultures within larger cultures, and as such are permeated with the values, ideologies, and assumptions in their social environment and constrained by the laws, customs, and conventions emanating from the outside.

My Jinja experience taught me a great deal about social research methods as well as about community structure, race relations, industrial sociology, and organizations. Our research team had combined the techniques of the sample survey, close observation of behavior, group discussion, and guided individual interviews. The surveys outlined for us the characteristics of the local population and pinpointed population groups and problem areas that merited more detailed study. The convenient unit of investigation in a survey is the individual, but individuals are not the key units in the study either of urban association or of work organizations. Our studies sprang to life only after we had spent months in workplaces, homes, and housing estates, watching, talking, and listening as people proceeded with their business. What lingers particularly in my memory is a series of discussions I conducted with African men who had left school at about sixteen or seventeen but had not gone far enough to become university students, high-grade clerks, or junior administrators. The fascinating aspect of these discussions was the light they shed on the psychological accompaniment of racially stratified communities and work groups. The nature of the local stratification system was common ground between us; what was new to me was the ambivalence of these men toward Europeans, simultaneously perceived as sources of hope and frustration, and the attribution to Europeans and Asians of a deliberate intent to subjugate Africans.

Africans were being deliberately only half-educated, said my respondents, and kept out from higher education and skilled trades so that the other races could pretend to be helping while continuing to exploit them. To an investigator like myself, coming to a country where the administration was committed to a policy of Africanization and industrialization and prepared progressively to relinquish political power to the local population, this was patently untrue and unjust. Nevertheless, these views were genuinely held, were a real part of the environment in which everyone lived and worked, helped to rationalize their situation for the people I was studying, and, one supposed, helped to perpetuate it.[4]

I left Uganda with a heightened interest in organizations, in the study of men at work, in problem-centered research, and in theoretical viewpoints and research methods that would combine understanding of both manifest and latent aspects of institutions and behavior.

STAFF RELATIONS IN
NEWLY NATIONALIZED HOSPITALS

After a year spent writing up the Jinja studies, I accepted a post at the Acton Society Trust which appeared to combine opportunities to follow up these interests. The Trust, which was centered on the study of large-scale organizations, had been making a study of the administrative changes associated with the nationalization of British hospitals in 1947. I was to study some of the implications of nationalization at the interpersonal level in three hospitals—a large general hospital formerly run by the London County Council, a smaller voluntary hospital, and a mental hospital.[5] This was a period of substantial stress, particularly for the staff of the first two hospitals and for staff groups like them. This derived from two main factors. First, power had formally been decentralized to new hospital management authorities running small groups of hospitals, and this was experienced by the hospitals as a shift to a more oppressive system. For the former London County Council hospital, power was now located just outside its own gate in a group of people constituting the local hospital management authority, to whom staff were now responsible in face-to-face relations. For the former voluntary hospital, the new situation meant that its financial problems were at an end. But the price was control from outside in accounting, appointments, promotion, ordering of medicines, admission policies, and so on. Secondly, all three hospitals were faced with an essential shift in personnel policy. The government had decided, as part of the process of nationalization, to reduce the role of hospital administration by doctors and the status of medical administrators and to bring into a position of greater equality the senior administrative, nursing, and medical staff of each hospital. There were now three streams of authority in each hospital. Nurses were responsible to the matron (head nurse) only; clerks and administrative staff, to the hospital secretary. Neither matron nor secretary was any longer to be responsible to the chief medical officer and indeed, in all but mental hospitals where legal responsibilities for patients required specification of a responsible medical officer, the role of chief medical officer was officially abolished. Greater equality was also introduced between medical officers; all consultants were now formally equal.

This situation was another illustration of the fact that work organizations are not quasi-independent entities but subsystems with mandates to perform certain limited tasks in approximately prescribed ways. It illustrated the strains of organizational change, particularly for colleagues who had worked together in one way and with particular relative status for years and were now expected or entitled to work in another way. They simply could not do so at first. In the former London County Council hospital, for instance, the former chief medical officer continued to make the main decisions, even the administrative decisions now formally in the province of the newly appointed secretary (who had previously been, in effect, only his executive officer). The rest of the staff spontaneously supported the doctor in this, partly because it seemed incredible to them that a former underling should now make major decisions and partly, it appeared to me, because in a medical organization involving life, death, and disease they felt safer or better protected from the consequences of mistakes under the wing of the professional person to whom society normally delegates these matters.

I suggested in my research report that staff members were uncomfortable unless they felt that there was a supportive senior medical person in the background, and also that the increased division of labor and responsibility in the hospital made it easier for any individual to think of himself as a cog in a system rather than a person to be singled out if anything went wrong. A whole system of thought existed to 'explain' relations with the consumers of the hospitals' services—the patients. They were represented as unreasonable, overdemanding, and insufficiently appreciative of the needs and problems of the staff. It was apparent that these viewpoints served to defend the staff against actual or potential criticism. It was also apparent that the staff of the hospitals project on to seniors, colleagues, customers, and the public attitudes and behavior that serve to legitimate their own outlook.

I found it difficult in this study consistently to remain in the role of uninvolved observer. Many of the people I was interviewing or observing were obviously under strain. They repeatedly asked me for advice or support or for my agreement that their attitudes and behavior were reasonable. If I conveyed that my role as a research worker and the necessity to remain objective prohibited this, the flow toward me of information and emotion tended to dry up. As a result I found myself deviating somewhat from the conventions of the research role in which I had been trained. I became a more empathic and sympathetic listener and more prepared to voice to my respondents tentative explanations of why difficulties were occurring, though I avoided talking about individuals or attributing blame to persons or groups. I was moving toward a quasi-interpretative role, in which I was drawing to the attention of my respondents structural forces and social processes which contributed to their feeling and behaving as they did. I did this most in the mental hospital, being propelled toward this role by the interest of the staff in the ways in which the structure of the hospital and of their own relations impinged on the psychological functioning of patients and staff and also by the expectation of the staff that as a professional social scientist I should have some therapeutic function. They would often tell me about a problem and conclude, half seriously, "Well, doctor, what's your diagnosis?" I was perhaps also influenced by the fact that for the first time in my research experience of six or seven years I was studying people much like myself in race membership, education, and cultural assumptions.

My field studies then ceased for six months which I spent as a postdoctoral student at the recently formed Harvard School of Social Relations. I exchanged experiences with other students of race relations and of hospitals and attended classes, being particularly influenced by the teaching of George Homans in industrial sociology and of Gordon Allport in social psychology.

INNOVATIVE TEACHING IN
A TECHNICAL COLLEGE

I returned to England and joined the Tavistock Institute in 1954 to lead a two to three year study of the Department of Management and Production Engineering at Acton Technical College in London and its relations with its consumer population. I had been approached by the head of that department, as he had in mind a research style similar to that of Jaques in the Glacier study mentioned later in this book and felt that my outlook was consistent with this. This was correct insofar as my conviction was growing that action research could improve the quality of research data. But I was much more concerned than Jaques had been with the impact on organizations of their environments. I planned to concentrate on analysis of formal structure and institutionalized behavior patterns, with interpretation in the social consultancy or psychoanalytic sense as a secondary, if important, aspect of my work. This intention was consistent with the nature of our research grant, which was primarily for academic study—though the members of the department being studied were naturally more interested in the help I could give them than scientific generalization. This is, of course, an endemic tension between the social research worker and his respondents. It is one that can partly be resolved through an action research arrangement—though, I feel today, at some cost in the range of data collected and in over-identification with the persons whose behavior is studied.

The Acton study encompassed several groups—the teachers in the management department, their students, the firms in the vicinity from which the students were drawn, the senior administrators of the college and of the Middlesex County Council, of whose educational services it was part.[6]

This study vividly illustrated a central dilemma of bureaucratized organizations, namely the fact that equity and accountability dictate methods involving control, uniformity, and certifiability; but those methods may frustrate the very purposes for which the organization is set up. In this instance, county council rules required a standard number of contact hours per teacher per week, personal promotion depended on devotion of the teacher's stint to formally defined "advanced" teaching, and the success of each teaching institution was judged by the number of examinations passed and certificates awarded. None of these requirements suited the need of a teaching group more concerned with effective communication and with changes in students and their employing systems. On the other hand, the teaching group did not appear to be taking full advantage of the flexibilities that could be identified in the system; this pointed again to the utility for people at work of having a superordinate structure that can be used as an explanation of why group performance does not meet the aspirations or the expectations of outside critics.

Another feature of this study was an analysis we made over a long series of meetings of the role of management studies teacher. This illustrated the variability in the way the same social role can be defined and filled by different occupants. It showed astonishing gaps in colleagues' knowledge of each others' points of view and errors in their assumptions about each other.

Strain was imparted to the teacher-student relationship by the unrealistic expectation of the students that attendance at part-time courses would transform clerks and junior technicians into effective managers; there was some pathos in the way they sat passively in classes, exhibiting the same sort of dependence on others as inhibited their personal development toward executive posts.

SOCIAL CONSULTANCY
WITH ORGANIZATIONS

Alongside this research-centered task, I was beginning, at the Tavistock, to do some social consultancy. This was first in the area of selection for management. I remember as a revelation, just before my first selection procedure the advice of E. L. Trist, that the key in understanding personality was to identify the central anxieties of the person and his main techniques for defending himself against these. Trist was then Deputy Chairman of the Institute. At the same time, I was impressed as a sociologist by the parallel concern in the Tavistock approach to selection with the social environment in which the successful candidate would be required to operate. To help give the candidate some idea of this environment, and to assist in judgments of whether he would prosper in it, the procedure provided models of situations which the entrant would encounter, including situations in which he would be required simultaneously to collaborate and compete with peers.

This has stayed in my mind as the paradigm for work in complex organizations depending, as they do, on a fine division of labor, on the concurrent coordination of the divided work, and on personal career ambition as a prime mover in economic growth and efficiency.

For some years I was a member of a Tavistock panel of advisers in the Unilever management trainees selection scheme and helped several other large companies in the recruitment, selection, and assessment of staff.

The specialty of the Tavistock house was social consultancy, action research with organizations, operationally derived from a combination of the doctor's approach to a patient and the social research worker's approach to a group of respondents. The relevance of the medical analogy lay in the idea of a professional making his knowledge and skill available to a client and sharing responsibility for whatever action was then taken; in this sense just as good an analogy might have been the work of a lawyer or engineer. I was attracted by this approach because of my own growing reservations about the conventional stance of the social research worker. I have described elsewhere the studies I have carried out on the social consultancy model.[7] At the time I was exhilarated by the way that my respondents were now actively concerned in helping me understand their situation, by the fact that my understanding of social structure, social process, and investigatory procedures helped them, and by the pleasure of seeing my ideas tried out and working.

The hospital study, the Acton study, and the new work I was doing all underlined the disparity between the high hopes with which new social schemes begin and the way these hopes are dissipated as the real problems are encountered. Organizational behavior is what it is because of a complex interplay of structural, cultural, and personality forces deeply rooted in a past and serving a number of needs, manifest and latent. When seeking to change organizations we are faced by accumulated social commitments which contain conservative elements that ensure a measure of institutional continuity, and by emotional and ideological elements that give meaning to collective effort and individual outlook. We cannot understand either organizational stability or organizational change without giving considerable weight to the personal investments by individuals in their careers and to the centrality of these investments to their personal identities. These investments and identities are predicated on the continued relevance of the person's training and expertise. Threats to these are apt to be vigorously countered both at the individual level and by groups of colleagues with similar work-life histories.

GROUP RELATIONS
TRAINING

While I was at the Tavistock, the Institute became involved for the first time in group relations training sessions open to selected members of the public. There had been continuing activity in this field before, in internal staff developments, in project work with individual firms, and in the Tavistock Clinic's work in training medical practitioners and social workers in the psychological aspects of case handling. There was also a great deal of external interest in the work. Several people in government, private industry, and social work had been impressed by the programs of the National Training Laboratories in the United States and had been interested to learn that the theoretical origins derived largely from the work of Bion and others in the Tavistock group. I joined the planning group for the first Tavistock group relations training conference (Leicester 1959) [8] and remained actively associated with this work until I left. Despite my background of theory, research, and social consultancy, I was astonished at the impact of these conferences on participants, particularly the depth of attachment that each individual developed toward whatever training subgroup he happened to be put in and at the way he became suffused with the preoccupations and values of the temporary community that we had constructed. We experienced a social microcosm in which each person became entangled, within a matter of days, in new group memberships, some complementary, some conflicting with each other. These memberships became the focus of his conscious thinking and his vehicles for the expression of love, hatred, loyalty, and aggression. Apart from the lesson in the significance of group memberships in the life space of the person, the group relations conferences vividly illustrated W. R. Bion's analysis of work group processes, particularly the way in which work groups alternate between task-centered behavior and contrasting activities which appear to be irrelevant but evidently have an expressive function or provide emotional relief. I did not feel, and still do not feel, that we understand the proceedings in these conferences well, and am uneasy that in many Western countries such events have attracted mass clienteles and serve purposes other than training and research in group behavior. At the same time, group-relations training conferences are a dramatic reminder to pay sufficient attention in organizational study to the significance for the individual of his group memberships and immediate social contacts.

CONSUMER BEHAVIOR

Finally, a substantial part of my work at the Tavistock consisted of studies of consumer behavior. Since some of the largest industrial organizations in Britain commissioned the work, I learned something of the ways in which their managements regard and use information about their environments and about the conflicts that arise around the collection and use of this type of organizational intelligence. There was not a widespread need to get to know the consumer environment better. Most administrators I met acted as if they knew what people wanted or felt that this hardly mattered to them in practice so long as their range of techniques for maintaining and stimulating demand succeeded. Only a small proportion of executives were preoccupied with questions concerning their markets in five or ten years time. Most marketing men appeared to worry almost exclusively about what to do in the short term. There were, of course, exceptions, and much of my work with two giant industrial corporations consisted of long-range consumer behavior studies or of advice on long-range studies that they were themselves carrying out.

THE USE
OF RESEARCH

One could not help but observe the strains in internal industrial research groups. There was pressure on the groups (and on me) to produce information or formulations that could be used immediately. Funds for long-range research were never quite safe. The interplay between marketing manager and research manager was always attended by impatience on the operational manager's side and bargaining for more time on the side of the research manager. The operational manager always wanted help with a current problem; the research man always argued that the management needed to think out carefully and steadily where the company was going and what their relations with consumers should become.

At the time, I was more interested in the outcomes of these recurrent debates and in the substantive research I was undertaking than in conflicts between research workers and their colleagues. But when I later left to teach and had the opportunity to comb the literature I found, of course, that I had been encountering a standard problem in the relation of research departments to colleague groups and one of crucial interest in the study of professionals and scientists in complex organizations. I refer to this topic at several points in the book.

I learned, also at firsthand, the near-impossibility for a going concern for making decisions by any but an incremental method. Often I turned up information in commissioned research which, at a purely rational level, indicated the desirability of reconsidering the whole basis of a company's marketing operations. But such information was often of little use to the man who had commissioned it, because any radical change would have required a major reorientation by several groups of colleagues and the assent of individuals very much senior to himself. The weight of the past would often be against change in approach. The manager's social environment consisted of persons who had built their careers on what was now accepted doctrine and whose relationships were based on existing premises. Those managers who did succeed in altering the approaches of their companies appeared to do so by making one move at a time and this usually only after careful and repeated consultation of peers. One saw here that decision-making was a social process, that decision-making and implementation were inseparable (new sub-decisions being repeatedly made as attempts at implementation confronted field difficulties), and that decision-making was a continuous part of organizational behavior rather than a series of discrete special events. This is discussed in detail and illustrated in Chapter 9 on decision-making.

CAREERS IN
LARGE ORGANIZATIONS

I left the Tavistock Institute in 1963 to go to Cambridge as Reader in Industrial Management and head of the University's Management Studies unit. I wanted to concentrate on a sustained social research program of my own choice. As Paul Lazarsfeld remarked in his presidential address to the American Sociological Society in 1962, working in an applied social research unit provides unique opportunities for variety, challenge, and learning.[9] It provides one with an opportunity to test the power, and to experience the limitations, of one's theoretical knowledge and research abilities. It is satisfying to know that one has professional expertise that can be deployed in dealing with practical problems. But it is difficult for a senior staff member in a research institute depending for its funding on professional practice to work on one problem of his choice in depth over a period of years. Even if one can secure a research grant from the government or a foundation, it is difficult to concentrate on one topic in the face of the new opportunities and new crises which are the staple experience of such organizations. Nevertheless I greatly value my Tavistock experience in research and social consultancy and, in helping to administer that small but complex and changeable institution.

The research program which I then developed at Cambridge was devoted to the study of careers in large organizations. A significant part of my Tavistock experience had been help to senior managements in developing personnel policies and selecting and training newly recruited management trainees and practicing middle-level managers. Because I was operating partly as a consultant, I had unusual access to these situations. I wanted to document my experience, to compare practice systematically between a few large organizations that went about these matters in different ways (if others would admit me on a pure research basis) and to tease out the assumptions about people and about organizations underlying personnel practices. At the same time, my personnel advisory experience had given me tantalizing glimpses of what a career looked like from the point of view of the applicant for a management traineeship, the man who had worked in a large company for a few years, the established manager or technical specialist, the man in mid-career. A number of questions puzzled me. Why did applicants feel that if they did not get a traineeship this was a reflection on the whole of their personalities; why did applicants feel that, however searching a selection procedure they went through, this had nothing to do with what they were like? What accounted for the rapidity with which incoming employees absorbed the values and manners of their seniors?

When people were discontented with their lot, why did more not leave to work elsewhere? Why did men fight so vehemently to justify their departments? Why were the men so absorbed in their work, so prepared to stay late and to work away from home? Why did they worry more about the economic positions of their employing organizations than about their personal finances?

I was acquainted with the scientific and semipopular literature on the industrial executive and his relations with his employers but felt that there was much more to be done and said on the subject. Much of the literature did not match my experience. Some of the accounts and discussions appeared to contain an overt or covert ideological thesis, usually connected with the "undermining" of the personality or "subversion" of the person by the large corporation. I felt that I was in a position to conduct a study which would capitalize on my applied experience. But I would try to examine the industrial career objectively from an academic base and take account of the standpoints and experiences of both the employer and employee and of their interaction.

For several years I had been studying organizations as whole systems, usually in terms of organizational change and conflict and in terms of interaction with their environments. Or I had been investigating problems as defined for or with me by one or another industrial management; that is, I had been particularly open to influence by a managerial point of view. A two-sided study of careers should correct distortions that might have been present in such a perspective. More important, the fact had been growing on me that, although we think, talk, and write abstractly in terms of organizational system, structure, and process, in the last resort we are working with individuals, people who behave in particular ways because they are moved by particular ambitions, hopes, and fears. I felt that many of the phenomena I had been observing—particularly those of departmental aggrandizement and defensiveness and of so-called resistance to change—could be better understood if we added as a dimension the careers of the individuals involved and how they converged, intersected, or clashed. What we mean by structure is the established pattern of interaction of persons. There is no such thing as an organization doing things to people. The realities consist of people doing things to or with other people, sometimes through the exercise of power, sometimes through persuasion, and sometimes by mutual agreement. It seems to me that in developing such shorthand notions as "organizational behavior," "management," "organizational change," and so on, we imply wrongly that the person is a passive or reactive object responding to impersonal forces from above. Certainly this perspective reflects much in the literature of organizational theory. This has to be corrected. I have reported elsewhere the main results of my five-year study of careers in large organizations.[10] Rather than repeat this in the present book, I have tried to demonstrate as I go the consequences of failing to recognize the importance of individual ambition, spontaneity, energy, and ingenuity even in the largest and most bureaucratized of organizations.

Teaching Background

Since 1963 I have been a university teacher in social science. Part of my teaching has been in a management studies course; part has been a contribution to a social science degree for persons who do not envisage using the teaching in subsequent managerial or professional roles. I have kept in mind the question of what would be most helpful to my students in coming to understand and cope with problems of participating in the large organizations most of them would enter and in handling their own careers. I do not see this as radically different from educating social science students. Every citizen today lives in a world in which the dominant social technology for handling big social tasks is the large organization and in which the dominant life-pattern of the educated person is that of a progressive career in some selected line of work. I have felt that the best educational help I can give is to provide both groups of students with conceptualizations of society, of organizational structure and processes, and of personality that would attempt to do justice to their complexity, and with concepts and theoretical formulations that would help in the analysis of their later experience in and with complex organizations. One way of doing this is to parade historically important contributions and dissect them; another is to take some problem like social control and leadership and to show how this can be better understood if systematically analyzed in social science terms. I have done both in my teaching and in this book.

There are commonalities running through my earlier work with experienced administrators and my later teaching of undergraduates. One major common element has been my emphasis on analysis, not blame—the need, that is, to explore how a situation has come into being and what maintains it before trying to change it. A second common element has been my recommendation to be sure each time that one has included in one's causal analysis the environmental and organizational constraints on behavior, the historical context of social processes in which the situation is embedded, the structure of institutionalized relationships in the situation, the part played in this by the technology of the tasks being performed (including the division of labor), the dominant values and ideologies of the persons involved, and the outlook and preoccupations of the leading figures. A third common element has been to give due weight to the distribution of power in the situation and to the determinants, in Lasswell's words, of who gets what, when, how.[11] A fourth element is to replace ideas of human beings as malleable objects with a notion of persons as potential adapters and transcenders of their environment.

CYRIL SOFER
Fellow of Queens' College, Cambridge
University Reader in Industrial Management

NOTES

1. I realize that this description raises the ethical problems concerning the use of social science and social scientists as servants of power which arise both in peace and war. While this is not a book on the ethics of applied social science (in whomever's service) these are problems that no social scientist can entirely avoid; and I touch on them again at several points of the book where I consider them particularly relevant.

2. H. Sonnabend and C. Sofer, *South Africa's Stepchildren,* (Johannesburg: South African Institute of Race Relations, 1946).

3. The social survey of Jinja is reported in C. Sofer and R. Ross *Jinja Transformed,* (Kampala: East African Institute of Social Research, 1955); "Characteristics of an East African European Population," *British Journal of Sociology,* 2, no. 4 (December 1951): 315–327.

4. My studies of race relations in industry are reported in C. Sofer, "Working Groups in a Plural Society," *Industrial and Labour Relations Review,* 8, no. 1 (October 1954), and "Urban African Social Structure and Working Group Behaviour," *Social Implications of Industrialization and Urbanization in Africa,* U.N.E.S.C.O. (1956).

5. Published as C. Sofer, "Reactions to Administrative Change," *Human Relations,* 8, no. 3 (1955).

6. The research report was published as C. Sofer and G. J. Hutton, *New Ways in Management Training,* (London: Tavistock Publications, 1958).

7. C. Sofer, *The Organization From Within. A Comparative Study of Social Institutions Based on a Sociotherapeutic Approach,* (London: Tavistock Publications, 1961).

8. The planning and execution of the first conference as described in E. L. Trist and C. Sofer, *Exploration in Group Relations,* (Leicester, England: University of Leicester Press, 1959).

9. P. F. Lazarsfeld, "The Sociology of Empirical Social Research," *American Sociological Review,* 27, no. 6 (December 1962): 757–767.

10. C. Sofer, *Men in Mid-Career. A Study of British Managers and Technical Specialists,* (Cambridge, England: Cambridge University Press, 1970).

11. H. D. Lasswell, *Politics: Who Gets What, When, How,* (London, New York: McGraw Hill, 1936).

Acknowledgments

During the course of writing this book I have had the benefit of the advice of several colleagues who have read one or a group of draft chapters or with whom I have discussed its overall arrangement. Readers of various sections of the book have included Chris Argyris, Irving L. Janis and Stanley H. Udy (all of Yale University), and Robert L. Kahn (of the University of Michigan), and I am indebted to them for friendly criticism and constructive suggestions.

I should especially mention Stanley Udy, who saw most of the book at a fairly advanced stage and recommended some restructuring. He insisted also that I had a theory about organizations latent in my expositions of the past masters and in discussions of current issues. It was to mollify him that I have made these manifest in Chapter 12 ("Propositions on Organizational Behavior"), and I hope that this enriches the book and links exposition with substantive discussion. Several groups of Cambridge undergraduates have listened, argued, inserted doubt, raised new questions or reacted in such a way that I have tried out a different approach with their successors.

Mrs. Heather Avedesian, Miss Julia Bagguley, and Miss Diana Cowen have borne the brunt of typing drafts and inserting alterations and corrections. Mr. John Hawley joined me in proofreading.

Contents

PART I

Introduction

PART II

Landmark Contributions

PART III

Applied Social Sciences in Wartime

PART IV

Generalizations

PART V

Bureaucracies as Working Communities

PART VI

Leadership, Change, and Conflict

PART I

Introduction

1 : Organizations and the Rationalization of Work

ORGANIZATIONS are associations of persons grouped together around the pursuit of specific goals. Through association, members of a society are able to achieve for themselves or for others objectives beyond those they could achieve individually. Because of the instrumental aspect of this association there is usually a persistent pressure from those in charge to maintain or increase the efficiency with which resources are related to ends. It also follows from the instrumental aspect that the members of the organization come together to pursue converging or overlapping interests rather than because of more diffuse sentiments or feelings of mutual belonging. These may well develop out of their association, but they are not the central reason for the persons being assembled together.

The pursuit of the specified activities that form the raison d'être of the organization is typically continuous. Most organizations have a life-span beyond the period of membership of their members; it follows from this that arrangements are made for the periodic replacement of personnel.

The organization usually has quite clear boundaries so that it is possible to say who is a member and who is not. The members are subject to a shared body of rules and procedures, and one subgroup, normally designated the managing or administrative group, is specifically empowered to make and amend rules and to see that these are carried out.

The organization usually has its own premises, its own capital, and its own technology, that is, equipment and systems for achieving organizational ends. When I speak of *its* own premises, etc., I am referring to the corporate identity of the organization, an identity which is a legal fiction and not attached to the particular persons who compose it. This entity is legally considered to own assets; seek capital; issue shares; enter into contracts with suppliers, purchasers, and employees; pay taxes; and so on. This helps to separate the personal possessions and obligations of the main body of members from those they acquire in their collective capacity and *only* in that collective capacity. We tend to refer to organizations as if they were entities differentiated from their members when we speak of such matters as their economic position, market behavior, advertising and product policies, or even when we try to characterize their atmosphere and culture as hidebound, colorful, aggressive, or dishonest. It is often convenient to refer to "organizational aims" or to the "organization trying to do" something or other. These references are accurate in the sense that we are referring to behavior that is, in an important sense, something over and above and separate from the individual acts of members. At the same time it is always the behavior of *people* we are referring to. We are using a form of shorthand when we refer to the identity or the behavior of the organization. But it is a form of shorthand that may obscure the fact that complex interaction goes into the behavior we are considering, and that outcomes attributed to the organization are often the consequences of negotiation, bargaining, and argument, and the expression of incompletely resolved conflicts between members.

The concept of an organization described here is inseparable from that of a market, of a number of persons other than those within the organization who are prepared to buy the goods or services it can provide. An organization cannot survive unless there are consequences of the processes that go on within it which make a difference to the functioning of some other subsystem of the society. In the case of a work organization, the product is likely to be a class of output or service which is either directly consumable (food, shoes, motor cars, haircuts, laundry) or one that serves as an instrument for a further phase of the production process by other organizations (potatoes for potato chips, clippers for barbers, carburetors for cars).

The Significance
of Organizations

The existence of organizations is an aspect of the division of labor in society. Organizations are subunits of the wider social structure, carrying out tasks that are wanted by or acceptable to a wider population. This means that they must, in their operations, stay within the overall legal and value framework of the larger society, though, as with any other unit in the social division of labor, there will be some social values with which they will come into conflict, which they will contest, and which they will help to change.

In the case of business organizations, there is a standing political issue as to how far they should be allowed, in the interests of their contribution to society, to pursue their functions with minimal external intervention, and how far they should be obliged to consider the needs of society more directly. Some writers have argued persuasively that with modern industrial organization we have already reached a danger point in the amount of autonomy that they exercise; that it is the producing organizations, not the consumer population, that determines what is produced and consumed, what it will be like, and what prices it will be sold at; that they have been too free to pollute the physical environment with waste and indestructible products; and that they have undermined cultural and aesthetic standards in pursuing mass markets.[1]

Organizations are especially conspicuous in Western societies where we go to great lengths to secure the advantages of specialization between and within governmental, legal, social service, educational, and economic institutions. This form of social organization is probably one of the main factors in the higher standard of living of Western than "underdeveloped" societies, where there is less differentiation of organizations with specifically economic functions.

The fact that we segregate our economic activities from others emphasizes at the same time our high expectations: if we have institutional specialization we expect greater efficiency than if the same activity were simultaneously to meet several needs. But with specialization must go interdependence and cooperation if one is to receive the benefits of specialization. We cannot reap the benefits of institutional and organizational specialization without providing adequately for subsequent integration. This is a problem at the interorganization level.

Large industrial organizations are of crucial importance in Western economies. They control much of the wealth of the leading industrialized nations and employ high proportions of the population.[2]

They play an enormous part in the economic planning processes as well as the productive processes of modern societies, significantly influencing and partly superseding the play of the market in determining the use of economic sources. Galbraith has attributed this centrally to the accumulation of capital and the growth of complex technologies within the large industrial organization. Where massive commitments are made in research and development, construction of plant, contracts for raw materials, and recruitment and deployment of specialized talents, much time elapses between investment and actual production, and firms cannot afford to leave their markets to chance. These must be controlled or at least closely influenced through monopolies, oligopolies, tacit understandings with fellow manufacturers to compete on bases other than price, public relations, and advertising efforts to determine consumer wants, or by government guarantee or direct support. As Galbraith says, many large organizations enter into reciprocally dependent relations with the state, often performing tasks for the public bureaucracy that it cannot do, or cannot do so well, for itself. In some cases "the private sector becomes, in effect, an extended arm of the public bureaucracy."[3] This echoes Eisenhower's famous warning in his presidential valedictory address against the growing powers of the military-industrial complex.

The new large industrial corporations that have come to dominate Western economies during this century have helped to bring into existence a mixed form of economy, neither socialistic in its form nor according with the tenets of the classical individual exchange economy. This has been aptly named by R. Marris "managerial capitalism," a title that draws attention to the prominence both of the organization and its managers.[4]

Large industrial organizations penetrate into a wide spectrum of social spheres other than the economic. They wield political power across as well as within national boundaries; provide social welfare services; cut across the age, sex, class, and caste distinctions of other social institutions; influence family relations, and, in the long run, the very structure of families; and affect the educational system so that it will turn out effective employees, industrial scientists, and managers.

Work organizations help to determine where their employees live, where their children go to school, what the quality is of the community life of their wives, how much contact is maintained with families of origin.

They consume a large part of our time. The working force, that is, the bulk of the adult population, spend a third or more of their waking hours in the organizations in which they are employed. This is almost equally true of the schoolchild. A great deal of leisure time is also spent within organizations. As March and Simon say, "pre-school children and non-working housewives are the only large groups of persons whose behaviour is not substantially 'organizational'." [5]

Work organizations tend to shape us more than most groupings to which we belong. This is partly because organizational influence is highly specific —in them we have relatively specific instructions or expectations about how we are expected to behave. Our organizational work roles are clearer than our other roles, the responsibilities attached to them continue over long periods, they are made explicit to us in spoken or written form, and everyone around us in the organization knows our role and puts pressure (legitimate and other) on us to carry them out. The specificity of our roles in organizations is in turn connected with the central characteristic of organizations as purposive bodies which get a payoff from multiple contributions by coordinating them toward a common end.

Work organizations have systematic training procedures to fit members for their roles. Such training procedures, combined with role obligations and rights, and with informal pressures, substantially affect personal values.

Organizational life helps shape personal identities—we incorporate the organizations to which we belong into our thinking about ourselves, and other people think of us in terms of our organizational affiliations.

The work organizations of which we are members provide us with primary membership groups, reference groups, reference persons, and reference points for evaluating our life experiences, influencing the standards by which we evaluate our careers, our families, our recreations, and our friends.

Large, centralized, specialized organizations dealing with whole countries or groups of countries have superseded smaller, more localized agencies or informal means for providing goods and services, for placing people in employment, for educating them and for nursing them when they get ill. We deal with these matters by mass methods. Hundreds, in some cases thousands, of customers, patients, potential students, and inmates are considered at a time and dealt with on a categorical basis. When they enter these institutions they are again dealt with on a block basis. Administrative, educational, and therapeutic operations are adapted to a large throughput which takes advantage of massive investment, the economies of scale, and the division of labor.

Occupations

The study of organizations is necessarily intertwined with the study of occupations.

Contemporary large organizations, operating complex technologies and divisions of labor are entirely dependent on occupational specialists whom they must recruit or train.

Since only a small proportion of people in Western society are self-employed, the work life of the majority cannot be understood except in the context of the larger systems of work to which they contribute. Certain groups of occupations are complementary to each other and have to be combined in whole organizations before they can be practiced—examples are workmen and foremen, maintenance engineers and plant managers, pupils and teachers. One cannot understand what goes on in these organizations without understanding the interplay between the occupations. Nor can one understand any one of such occupations without grasping the way in which those who follow them are normally connected with each other.

A great deal of behavior in organizations becomes explicable only after one has considered the significance of their occupations for the people following them.

One's occupation is a significant means to the ends of personal self-support, marriage and being able to raise a family.

We rank people largely by virtue of their occupations and the success they make of their occupations, and the individual's own sense of worth-whileness is associated with what this ranking is.

Occupation is also central in determining what Max Weber called one's "life-chances" and those of one's children, that is, one's supply of goods, external living conditions, and personal life experiences. Occupation is a central determinant of income, residence area, standard of living, friends, and range of possible marital partners.

As Gould and Kolb point out,

We can tell from a child's social origins as judged by the grading of his father's occupation, whether he is more or less likely to be born prematurely, to survive the first year of life, to have numerous brothers and sisters or to be the only child, to live in conditions of overcrowding, to score well in intelligence tests, to remain at school beyond the age of compulsory attendance, to go to a university and to maintain or improve on his father's occupational status, to succumb to various diseases and to enjoy a longer or shorter life.[6]

One's occupation has a profound significance for one's behavior, personal outlook, and conception of oneself. This is partly because of the high proportion of one's time spent at work, partly because one continues to be preoccupied with work matters at other times. One's occupation determines a good deal of one's immediate social experience, precipitating one into close interaction with some types of people and cutting one off from others. One's occupation affects behavior in relation to future as well as current goals. Occupation plays a significant role in determining and shaping personal identity—how one defines oneself, what one means to oneself, how others define one and what one means to them. It has been pointed out by Erikson that "identity is never gained or maintained once and for all" [7] and underlined by Becker and Strauss that "Freudian and other psychiatric formulations of personality development probably overstress childhood experiences. . . . Central to any account of adult identity is the relation of change in identity to change in social position, for it is characteristic of adult life to afford and force frequent and momentous passages from status to status." [8] These considerations are especially important in view of the fact that adoption of an occupation by recruits confers on the managements of the organizations they enter the right to mold their identities, to influence their personalities.

Bureaucracy and Bureaucratization

The literal meaning of *bureaucracy* is "rule by the office" or "rule by officials." In popular usage the term often carries a pejorative sense. In the social sciences, usage tends to follow the classic conception, with no invidious connotations, of Max Weber in his essay on bureaucracy.[9]

Weber, who lived from 1864 to 1920, was interested in formal organization as a student of the history of social organization. He wrote about varying forms of social organization through history and reasons for their emergence and decline.

He saw bureaucracy as a form of organization that had developed historically to supersede the undependable amateur with the qualified specialist. For him this was part of the trend toward cumulative technological rationalization in human affairs.

Weber regarded bureaucracy as being made rational by the fact that within it control was exercised on the basis of knowledge, expertness, and technical competence. He was especially interested in government, and in bureaucracy as a way for the state to exercise authority in a mass society where traditional authority based on close social relations was no longer effective. But he saw it as an ubiquitous form of administration in modern society and not as something purely confined to government.

Weber's analysis of bureaucracy was in 'ideal-type' terms. This means that he was trying to identify the pure form of a certain system of administration, isolating and putting together its key characteristics and showing certain logical consequences and correlates.

Under the system Weber was identifying, and whose essence he was concerned to analyze, business is conducted by a legally constituted body on a continuous basis in accordance with systematic, general, stipulated rules which define what is to be done, by whom, and for whom under what circumstances. Decisions are not made from case to case by whoever happens to be available.

The activities to be carried out are attached to specified roles, not to particular persons, as the duties of the persons in those roles irrespective of who are the persons filling those roles.

Each role has its own area of jurisdiction and responsibility.

The official having the prescribed duties is given the powers necessary to carry out these duties (for example, to make payments up to a certain amount, or approve vacation times of defined categories of staff).

The amount of formal power attached to each role and role occupant is graded into a known hierarchy of authority. The higher officers have the right and duty to supervise and, if necessary, to overrule the lower. Usually there is provision for appeal from the lower ranks.

The resources used to carry out the business of the organization are the property of the organization, not of the individuals who are employed by the organization. The officials are empowered to use those resources for the purposes of the organization but are strictly accountable to their seniors for their use. They must not use them for personal purposes. Official premises, resources, and income are segregated from private premises, resources, and income.

Offices (roles) cannot be appropriated by their holders as private property rights which can be passed on, sold, or inherited.

Official business is conducted largely on the basis of written documents. Central files are maintained, and these are the property of the organization, not the private property of the individuals. Written records are important. This enables rulings to be recorded and consulted as precedents, enables spheres of jurisdiction to be precisely defined, and keeps track of the property and income that belong to the organization.

Under a bureaucratic system all members of the public, clients, or customers must be dealt with on the same 'categorical' basis. All persons identified by previously stipulated criteria as falling in the same category must be dealt with in the way prescribed for members of that category—whether or not they are related or known to staff and whether or not they behave in a way that the staff considers meritorious.

An essential part of Weber's characterization of bureaucracy lay in the basis of authority exerted in such a system. We normally obey orders addressed to us by others only if we concede that it is right and proper for them to give us orders and for us to obey. Weber distinguished between three types of "legitimate authority" operative in different societies and types of organization. Authority is *traditional* where one accepts the orders of certain persons or groups because this is the way things have always been, this is the way things are always done, these are the people who have always been followed. Custom, precedent, and usage are central, and established practice gains a quality of sacredness. Authority is *charismatic* [10] where one accepts a leader's order as justified because of the quality and impact of his extraordinary personality. One treats him as one set apart from ordinary persons. The proper ways for people to behave are regarded as revealed or ordained by him. Under *rational-legal* or bureaucratic authority, one accepts an order as justified because it is in line with and part of a more abstract, systematic, comprehensive set of rules that one accepts as legitimate. That larger, more inclusive set of rules and practices is thought of as operating to ensure that only people in certain specified roles, qualified in specified ways, have the right to issue orders—and may do so only to specified categories of persons and within a specified area of jurisdiction. Access to the superior roles is theoretically open to all who are competent to achieve them. Those who do achieve them are assumed to control through acknowledged expertness and to be accepted as properly superior in status and power because they have greater skill, more experience, or superior perspicacity and sagacity. In this variety of authority, rights to command and demand are rationally assigned as part of a systematic scheme for relating resources to ends, and the procedures are embodied in formal or well-understood codes and rulings which have the force of local laws.[11]

Employment and
Careers in Bureaucracies

Certain characteristics of employment and career are associated with the operation of a bureaucratic system.

The individual office holder is appointed to his post, not elected to it or nominated for it by a personal sponsor. He has a contract—he is not taken on or dismissed at whim, and his tenure, duties, and rewards are specified.

His work is rewarded by a regular salary and by prospects of regular employment (probably including advancement) in a lifetime career.

His appointment, placement, and any subsequent promotion are dependent on his technical qualifications and his competence as displayed in the work and by a formal examination, or equivalent form of scrutiny of his technical proficiency.

Notionally, educational certificates and objectively ascertainable competence replace birth and privilege as the basis of recruitment. Bureaucracy is, then, in effect, administration by experts in their fields.

The work role of the employee in a bureaucracy is meant to be separated from his personal affairs.

He exercises the authority delegated to him in accordance with impersonal principles (for example, he should not favor particular people who are his subordinates, clients, or superiors for personal reasons of affection or preference).

His loyalty is to the organization and to managerial aims rather than to specific seniors or outside persons.

Bureaucratization of the Modern Organization

Most commentators feel that the scale of the modern state and the vastness of the services it offers make this form of 'expert' administration inevitable, or at any rate difficult to avoid, in government. Bureaucracy seems to be the most effective form we have been able to develop in dealing with the new mass society which has developed in the nineteenth and twentieth centuries. This form of administration provides reassurance for the electorate that technical considerations of efficiency guide the decisions made by their representatives, that the persons carrying out the decisions are appointed on the basis of their competence, and that the policies decided on will be administered without favoritism or discrimination between individuals.

The trend in government agencies towards the bureaucratization of administrative methods has been paralleled in other spheres. Industrial corporations, trade unions, churches, and social service organizations have followed in the same direction.

One cause has been sheer growth in size. As soon as an organization becomes very large, a need arises for rules to become generalized so that economy can be achieved by treating all similar cases in a similar fashion. Reference upwards becomes necessary only for the unusual cases: one can "rule by exception."

Another cause has been increase in complexity and the concomitant need for trained experts—experts either in some particular function (law, industrial relations, or computer systems) or in bringing specialist work together.

A third cause, associated with size, has been the need for accountability. When an organization is very large, all those who own rights in it, or are entitled to reports from those who work in it, cannot be kept constantly informed of every action taken in the name of the organization. They can be reassured, however, by knowing that professionals are in charge who judge their actions in terms of their effects, not in terms of whom they favor; that generalized, categorical rules are operated, and that everyone will be treated according to such principles. One can see immediately the advantages of these aspects of bureaucratization in a religious organization which has to place hundreds of new ministers every few years or a trade union responsible for the jobs of thousands of men of different ages and skills.

In the case of the privately owned industrial corporation, certain factors apply with special force. The investment involved in a modern large enterprise is so great that resources have to be drawn from thousands of investors, either individually or through intermediate lending institutions. Business must then be conducted in such a way that those who take decisions and make disbursements can, whenever called upon, demonstrate that they are using the funds systematically and logically. Their actions must be defensible in terms of the interests of investors. Just as the individual citizen is entitled to raise questions in the British House of Commons through his local member of Parliament about treatment received in a National Assistance office, so the individual shareholder is entitled to raise questions at his company's annual shareholders' meeting about why a particular branch has been opened or shut.

In private industry another effect of largeness of investment has been a separation of ownership from control.[12] Often no shareholder owns such a high proportion of the business that he can dominate the way it is run. As Galbraith puts it, the corporation has ceased to be the instrument of its owners and a projection of their personalities.[13] Separation of ownership from control fosters bureaucratization. If control cannot be exercised directly by owners, it must be delegated to professional administrators whose rewards are gained largely from their impartiality. They are expected to run the affairs of the business so far as possible on lines governed by objectivity, impartiality, and rationality. They are expected to be guided by, and to be rewarded for, doing the economically proper thing rather than what a particular part-owner or they themselves would like to see done.

In the case of the large industrial organization, its mode of operation is affected by the extent to which the interests of very powerful external or representative groups are concerned. Trade unions and other interest groups will press managements to treat similar classes of employees in similar ways; for instance, to follow the "last in, first out" principle in times of labor redundancy. The management must be able to show consistency in its treatment of individuals composing the labor force and in adhering to agreements which specify particular policies and the particular categories of persons to whom these should apply.

Under the managed-economy policies of present-day governments, those departments dealing with economic matters keep a close watch on private industrial organizations, as fluctuations in their level of operations can have important repercussions on national levels of employment, productivity, taxable income, the balance of payments, and so on. This brings business operations into the public arena. When mergers, large-scale dismissals, redeployments, or investments in new plants are contemplated, governments are expected to act, or have pressure on them from the electorate to act. All this adds to the pressure on the large privately-owned concern to rationalize its operations in the sense of taking actions that can be justified in the name of the interests of shareholders, employees, or the public interest, or of compromise between these. As soon as legitimization and public accountability is involved, an enterprise is bound to bureaucratize its administrative system in the same way, as massive capital investments are a force toward the rationalization of productive processes.

In his analysis of bureaucracy, Weber pointed to the importance of concentration of the means of administration into large organizations— governmental, economic, political parties, universities. Production, administration, and even scholarship had in the past, he pointed out, been carried out by individuals, by domestic groups, or by other small-scale units. But the resources required to conduct these activities efficiently and economically are in this century beyond the scope of individuals and small units, because they exceed their financial capacity. So they become concentrated in large organizations.

Since the resources are drawn from multiple suppliers, taxes of citizens, forced loans, and so on, they have to be managed in a formal, publicly visible way, and in a way that segregates their use from private considerations and interests.

REASONS FOR THE
ADVANCE OF BUREAUCRACY

Weber saw the reason for the advance of bureaucracy over other forms of getting large tasks done as sheer technical superiority. "The fully developed bureaucratic mechanism compares with other organizations exactly as does the machine with the non-mechanical modes of production." [14]

The advantages, he said, were:

Rationality, in terms of technical competence and specialization.

Precision in operation (everyone knowing exactly what his duties were).

Speed, since everyone knew what was to be done and by whom.

Reduction of friction between people, since each officeholder knew what was required of him and where the boundary lay between his responsibilities and those of others.

Steadiness, since the same sorts of decisions were given whenever the circumstances were the same.

Subordination of juniors to seniors in a strict and known way, so that one could get decisions at a particular level binding on all those below.

Reliability, since business was conducted according to known or calculable rules and large numbers of similar cases were methodically dealt with in the same systematic way—people connected with the organization knew where they were with it, and decisions were predictable. The process of decision-making became depersonalized in the sense of excluding love, hatred, irrational feelings, and personal discrimination between cases otherwise similar.

On the personnel side of organization, benefits were gained from labor being divided between people in an orderly way; from persons being trained to become experts in their particular fields and gaining a habitual and virtuoso-like mastery of their subjects.

Bureaucracy, Rationalization and the Occupational Structure

The emergence of the large, professionally managed, technologically complex bureaucracy as our major instrument for governing ourselves, producing goods, and distributing services has contributed to significant changes in occupational and class structure.

Several social commentators have suggested that the professionalization of management, and particularly the separation of ownership from control, has introduced new elements into the class and power structure of society.

James Burnham has suggested that the professional managers now constitute a significant new social category of technocrats, whose expertise lies in the manipulation of large organizations, and whose power and skill in this area can make them a new ruling class.[15] T. N. Whitehead has argued that the training and experience of senior industrial managers qualifies them for positions of leadership outside business and that they should seek out positions of community leadership in order to protect and advance industrial interests.[16] It has recently been argued by T. Nichols, on the basis of empirical inquiries in Britain, that propertied and non-propertied directors exhibit a similar outlook on business policies and their relation to wider social issues and in this sense "belong to the same social class."[17] The great bulk of persons in this category would, at least in western European countries, probably have been in the highest social strata already. But room has certainly been created by economic growth, the bureaucratization of industry, the rationalization of work, and the use of science, for new men to rise socially with the adoption and practice of their occupations.[18]

The modern industrial system is intellectually demanding and has helped bring into existence, to serve its administrative, scientific, and technical needs, a large community of educated men and women—though problems arise out of the educational narrowness that appears to go with occupational specialization. They can be described as a new 'middle class' of managers, clerks, salary earners, and white-collar workers. The proportion of such persons has grown five or six-fold since the beginning of this century. Regarded as a social class, persons in these occupations appear to be intermediate in position between the major groupings referred to by Marx: their emergence is certainly inconsistent with his expectation that social classes would polarize between a higher and a lower power category.

The higher level workers in this broad category may justifiably be regarded as part of the political and economic power structure. As bureaucrats, they play a substantial part in exercising power, to some extent in shaping decisions, and certainly a key role in executing them. In doing so they tend to embody and epitomize the values of the organizations they represent, more especially those prevalent at the higher levels.[19]

Some social analysts see the bureaucrats as an essentially conservative force in society, as an appendage of the ruling groups who administer and enforce rules made from above. It is suggested that in administering social and organizational rulings they thereby defend existing social values. They may become bastions against change in the sense that they become invested in their organizations, committed to existing ways of doing things, protectors of the stability of a system that holds out for them their main career opportunities. It is certainly extremely difficult to introduce changes into bureaucratized organizations without overcoming the initial inertia and resistance of the middle level of administrators. The career structures of bureaucracies within their existing organizations are probably in themselves likely to promote conservatism because movement upward is achieved through earning recognition and respect from powerful seniors in helping them to get their existing tasks done.

The conservative attitudes of bureaucrats may extend well outside their formal work spheres to society in general; persons for whom opportunities for occupational mobility are maintained are apt to be supporters of a politically stable status quo.

As a social category the bureaucrats or administrators may have become substituted for the small, independent tradesman or shopkeeper. The ambitious young man of today is more likely to see his future as a progressive series of steps up the hierarchy of a large organization than in independent entrepreneurship.

Mobility in bureaucracies is conditioned largely by the possession of formal educational qualifications, though less in the sense that the qualification secures one a higher job than that it entitles one to consideration. One side effect of this is to support a view that the major function of an education (including university education) is vocational preparation, the pursuit of a course followed by issue of a certificate which is a ticket for a particular type of career. Such views of educational institutions are held both by those wanting bureaucratic careers for themselves and their children and by prospective employers. Persons at the top of government departments or businesses depend for the efficient execution of their responsibilities on a continuous supply of expert middle-level administrators and see this supply as a major production function of universities and schools. This is one of the many ways in which the rise of bureaucracies, by changing the occupational structure of the society, ramifies through the world of work to affect other social institutions.

NOTES

1. See, for instance, the recent discussion by J. K. Galbraith in his Reith Lectures printed in *The Listener,* 66 (November 17, 25, December 1, 8, 15, 22, 1966): 711–714, 755–758, 793–795, 841–843, 853, 881–884, 915–918, and *The New Industrial State* (New York: Hamish Hamilton, 1967).

2. Nearly half of the corporate wealth of the United States is in the hands of 200 large organizations. Half the United States labor force works for big organizations and only 15 percent are self-employed. A. Etzioni, *Modern Organizations,* (Englewood Cliff, New Jersey: Prentice-Hall, 1964). In the private sector of British Industry the 100 largest companies, as measured by net assets, appear to be responsible for something like a third of total industrial profits. C. A. R. Crosland, "The Private and Public Corporation in Great Britain," *The Corporation in Modern Society,* E. S. Mason, ed. (Cambridge, Massachusetts: Harvard University Press, 1959).

3. J. K. Galbraith, "The Role of the State," *The Listener,* 66 (1964), pp. 841–843, 853.

4. R. Marris, *The Economic Theory of Managerial Capitalism,* (London: Macmillan, 1964).

5. J. G. March and H. A. Simon, *Organizations,* (New York: Wiley, 1958), p. 2.

6. J. Gould and W. L. Kolb, *A Dictionary of Social Sciences,* (London: Tavistock Publications, 1964): 390.

7. E. H. Erikson, *Childhood and Society,* (New York: Norton, 1950): 57.

8. H. S. Becker and A. L. Strauss, "Careers, Personality and Adult Socialization," *American Journal of Sociology,* 12 (November 1956): 253–263.

9. This was written between 1911 and 1913 as part of his *Wirtschaft und Gesellschaft.* H. H. Gerth and C. W. Mills, *From Max Weber: Essays in Sociology* (New York: Oxford University Press, 1946). An informative discussion of Weber and his work is also provided in R. Bendix, *Max Weber. An Intellectual Portrait,* (New York: Doubleday, 1960).

10. *Charisma* is a Greek word meaning "the gift of grace."

11. See discussion in T. Parsons, ed. *Max Weber. The Theory of Social and Economic Organization,* translated by A. M. Henderson and T. Parsons, (Glencoe, Ill.: Free Press), pp. 50–69.

12. The classic treatment of this topic is contained in A. A. Berle and G. C. Means, *The Modern Corporation,* (New York: Macmillan, 1932). Since that time this separation has been accelerated by the need for organizations based on complex technologies to be run by large groups encompassing a wide range of occupational specialties.

13. J. K. Galbraith, *The New Industrial State,* (London: Hamish Hamilton, 1967).

14. Gerth and Mills, "Bureaucracy," *From Max Weber: Essays in Sociology.*

15. J. Burnham, *The Managerial Revolution,* (New York: John Day, 1951).

16. T. N. Whitehead, *Leadership in a Free Society. A Study in Human Relations Based on an Analysis of Present-Day Industrial Civilization.* (London: Oxford University Press, 1936).

17. T. Nichols, *Ownership, Control and Ideology,* (London: Allen and Unwin, 1969).

18. See discussions of British data in C. Sofer, *Men in Mid-Career;* and of American in S. M. Lipsett and R. Bendix, *Social Mobility in Industrial Society,* (Berkeley, California: University of California Press, 1959) pp. 134–135, W. L. Warner and J. C. Abeggler, *Occupational Mobility in American Business and Industry,* (Minneapolis: University of Minnesota Press, 1955).

19. See discussion in R. Dahrendorf, "Recent Changes in the Class Structure of European Societies," *Daedalus,* 93 (1964): 244–252.

PART II

Landmark Contributions

2 : Frederick Winslow Taylor and Scientific Management

THE origins and impact of Frederick Winslow Taylor's work in the late nineteenth century and early years of this century and the influence of the "scientific management" movement in the United States (where it originated) and in Europe are best understood in the context of labor relations at that time.

During the thirty-year period beginning about 1880, the United States experienced probably the most rapid expansion of any industrial country for a comparable period of time. This expansion was accompanied by a complex of ideas emphasizing individual enterprise, self-help, and the opportunities offered by industrialization and economic expansion.[1] In the philosophical sentiments of the times, success and riches were regarded as the reward of those who had proved themselves in the struggle for survival. Business leaders emphasized the virtues of character and the Christian mission of business enterprises. Opportunity was considered to be abundantly available for those who wanted it—a slogan of the times was that the capitalists of today were the workingmen of yesterday and the workingmen of today the capitalists of tomorrow. Poverty did not constitute a ground for claiming assistance. If employees remained in humble and ill-paid positions, this was because of lack of will power and modesty of talent.

The division between employers and their men was held to illustrate the survival of the fittest and most virtuous, since the one possessed the power to originate and conduct great enterprises and the other "obviously" did not. Indeed the workers would live in squalor and want without the beneficial guidance of capital and brains.[2]

Bendix points out that an important element in the promulgation of such beliefs was the justification it appeared to provide for absolute authority for the industrial employer in his own firm, including authority to weed out the incompetent. Employers felt it especially important to assert their right to authority in the workplace in the light of the dramatic rise of trade unions. While in England the organization of workers in trade unions was well under way in the 1860s and 1870s, in the United States workers began to organize on a mass basis only in the 1890s, partly because they were hampered by the willingness of immigrants to work for lower wages. Between 1897 and 1904 trade-union membership increased four or fivefold in America. Employers' campaigns for the open shop constituted their attempt to repudiate the challenge of the unions to their central activity, the management of their own plants, in which they had regarded their authority as absolute. At the same time the growing strength of the unions forced employers to concern themselves with labor as a problem rather than to deal with labor troubles by bewailing inefficiency and dismissing the most conspicuously unfit. Now acting in association with each other, employers began to formulate principles of managerial policy that soon made it apparent that labor management "required more refined techniques than polemics against workers and the instant dismissal of the 'unfit.'"[3]

By 1910 primary emphasis was placed on the need of managers to concern themselves with the "man problem." Methods were recommended on how to increase labor productivity. Particular emphasis was laid on the theory that it was in the interest of the worker to collaborate in the plans of his managers and to seek advancement for himself within the enterprise by improving the quantity and quality of his output rather than by joining a trade union.

In England, wide awareness of new needs and potentialities in the labor relations aspects of management do not appear to have come as much earlier as one might expect in view of priority in intensive industrialization.

S. C. Pollard has pointed to the absence during the British Industrial Revolution of what we would today call more "professionalized" forms of management, which include the negotiation of agreement, delegation, holding together an able staff, inspiring loyalty, handling labor successfully, and so on.[4]

During the Industrial Revolution, emphasis was chiefly on the entrepreneur rather than the executive—on starting business concerns and innovating change rather than on maintaining continuity of operations or establishing and keeping to routines. In an age of basic structural changes of technology it was difficult to isolate managerial functions from technical supervision or commercial control. The entrepreneur tended to be capitalist, financier, works manager, merchant, and salesman combined and the problems were felt to be mainly in external relations and facilities—including building roads or docks and providing shops and banking facilities, which outside bodies handle today.

In a period dominated by pioneers and founder-managers, people were apt to emphasize the individuality of the person in charge and the uniqueness of his enterprise, rather than seek for generalizations. Labor appears to have been viewed as a residual problem and an obstacle in the path of technological advance and progress.

Pollard suggests that it was only in the last quarter of the nineteenth century, or perhaps even later, that the new notion emerged that the productivity of workers was as important as the productivity of machines, and that recognition became widespread that it might be worth investing in the development of workers.

F. W. Taylor

Frederick Winslow Taylor (1856–1917) was an eminent engineer who, apart from his interest in management, made distinguished contributions in his own technological field. He was responsible for a long series of experiments on metal-cutting, which he presented as his presidential address to the American Society of Mechanical Engineers at their meeting in December, 1906.[5] But he had already at that time been developing his ideas and methods of "scientific management" for two decades. He discusses in "Shop Management" a paper written in 1895 which describes applications at a steelworks during the preceding ten years.[6] This paper appears to be his first public pronouncement on management methods.

Taylor had been an undergraduate student of law at Harvard, gave this up to become an apprentice machinist, and rose to be chief engineer of the Midvale Steel Company. At age forty-three (1899) he organized his own firm to introduce scientific management in industrial organizations.

A close connection existed between Taylor's work on metal-cutting and on industrial organization. In company with White, an engineering colleague, Taylor had developed a mechanical way of cutting metal several times faster than before, as well as methods of treating the tools in order to maximize the amount of metal removed per unit of time. H. G. J. Aitken has suggested that scientific management, as Taylor developed it, was

essentially a method for exploiting the full productive potentialities of the new cutting tools . . . machines could now be run at from two to four times their former speeds. The organization of the machine shop and indeed of the whole factory had to be adjusted to this new level of productivity. . . . Taylor had begun his work with job analysis, time study, and incentive payments before his discovery of high-speed steel . . . without high-speed steel Taylor's managerial reforms might have been highly desirable; with high-speed steel they became well-nigh indispensable, at least in machine shops.[7]

Later, considering the introduction of high-speed steel and scientific management in the machine shop at Watertown Arsenal, Aitken adds:

The Taylor system of management . . . was essentially a way of adjusting the arsenal to the impact of high-speed steel . . . The whole arsenal had to be geared to the pace which it set . . . The limiting factor in productivity was no longer the machine but the organization.[8]

"UNDERWORKING" AND ITS CAUSES AND CURE

Taylor's *Principles of Scientific Management* was published in 1911. As the editor of the series in which it appeared stated, this book was "an argument for Mr. Taylor's Philosophy of Human Labour—an outline of the fundamental principles on which it rests." [9] In his own words, Taylor wrote

First. To point out, through a series of simple illustrations, the great loss which the whole country is suffering through inefficiency in almost all of our daily acts.

Second. To try to convince the reader that the remedy for this inefficiency lies in systematic management, rather than in searching for some extraordinary man.

Third. To prove that the best management is a true science, resting upon clearly defined laws, rules, and principles, as a foundation.[10] *

He started from the point that in a majority of cases, as he saw it, workmen deliberately planned to do as little as they safely could, to turn out less work than they were well able to do. If they did try their best they were abused by their fellow workers. This sort of "underworking," deliberately working slowly so as to avoid a full day's work, was, he said, nearly universal in industrial establishments. In his view this constituted the greatest evil with which the working people of both England and America were afflicted. He thought this situation had three causes:

1. The fallacy among workmen that a material increase in the output of each man on each machine in the trade would have the end result of throwing a large number of men out of work.

2. Defective existing systems of management which made it necessary for each workman to work slowly, in order to protect his own best interests.

3. Inefficient rule of thumb methods in which methods of work were entirely up to the workmen and they wasted a large part of their efforts.

Taylor thought that it was "the natural instinct and tendency of men to take it easy" where a number were brought together on similar work and pay. The faster, more energetic men would slow down to the pace of the slowest and least efficient. ("Why shoud I work hard when that lazy fellow gets the same pay and does half as much work?") It was also understandable, said Taylor, that, even under piece rates with bonuses, workers kept productivity down while trying to convince their employers that they were going at a reasonable pace. Employers tended to determine a maximum sum which each class of employees should earn every day, and prices per piece might well be lowered after employees had worked harder and increased their output.[11]

Taylor wished to maximize prosperity for both employers and employees and wanted to combine high wages with low labor cost.

SPECIALIZATION

He recommended specialization for management and worker, the former concentrating on planning and the latter on execution;

As far as possible the workmen, as well as the gang bosses and foremen, should be entirely relieved of the work of planning, and of all work which is more or less clerical in its nature. All possible brain work should be removed from the shop and centered in the planning or lay-out department.[12] *

He based this recommendation on the differences he thought to exist between the work that men of various kinds could do, and on the advantages derivable from division of labor.

In most cases one type of man is needed to plan ahead and an entirely different type to execute the work.[13]

The man in the planning room, whose speciality under scientific management is planning ahead, invariably finds that the work can be done better and more economically by a subdivision of the labour; each act of each mechanic, for example, should be preceded by various preparatory acts done by other men.[14]

Taking the notion of division of labor to what appeared to him to be a strictly logical conclusion, he asserted that,

If practicable, the work of every person in the organization should be confined to the performance of a single leading function.[15]

JOB ANALYSIS AND SUBSTITUTION
OF "THE ONE BEST WAY"

There should be detailed analysis of each job through time study in an effort to find "the one best way" of performing the job, that is, the way that permitted the largest average rate of production over the day. Taylor described "the accurate and scientific study of unit times" as "by far, the most important element in scientific management." [16]

The problem, as he saw it was that, in the absence of systematic training, workmen had to learn by observation or by self-instruction, and they consequently developed idiosyncratic ways of carrying out operations with varying degrees of efficiency.

The workmen in all our trades have been taught the details of their work by observation of those immediately around them, there are many different ways in use for doing the same thing . . . and . . . a great variety in implements used for each class of work . . . among the various methods and implements used in

---

* From *Shop Management* by Frederick Winslow Taylor (Harper & Row, 1911). Reprinted by permission of Harper & Row.

each element of each trade there is always one method and one implement which is quicker and better than any of the rest.[17]

Taylor and his colleagues broke up descriptions of work into minute particulars—"pick up," "tighten," "move right," "put on floor," etc. Rearrangement of these parts of the job into more efficient combinations could then become part of a set of instructions on how to do the job—that is, the "best" way.

They examined with stopwatches such tasks as shoveling, making observations of amounts of walking, types of movement, and so on, so that wasteful methods could be eliminated and required movements could be specified. Taylor suggested that one might begin by finding ten or fifteen men especially skillful in doing the work to be analyzed, study the exact series of elementary processes or motions they used and the time required for each of these, eliminate all false movements, slow movements, and useless movements, collect into one series the quickest and best movements as well as the best implements, and substitute these for those previously in use.[18] Once the new, best way was discovered,

ME WHEN I DIDN'T WANT TO CHANGE ROUTINE

> Each man must learn how to give up his own particular way of doing things, adapt his methods to the many new standards, and grow accustomed to receiving and obeying directions covering details, large and small, which in the past have been left to his individual judgment.[19]

The manager should "scientifically select and then train, teach, and develop the workman, whereas in the past he chose his own work and trained himself as best he could." [20]

PRESCRIBING TASK AND METHODS

Men should be written to detailing the tasks they were to perform and the way these were to be carried out:

PLANNING

> The work of every workman is fully planned out by the management at least one day in advance, and each man receives in most cases complete written instructions, describing in detail the tasks which he is to accomplish, as well as the means to be used in doing the work. . . . This . . . specifies not only what is to be done but how it is to be done and the exact time allowed for doing it.[21]

This would provide both workman and employer with a standard against which to measure a proper day's work.

JOB SATS.

> The average workman will work with the greatest satisfaction, both to himself and his employer, when he is given each day a definite task which he is to perform in a given time, and which constitutes a proper day's work for a good workman. This furnishes the workman with a clear-cut standard, by which he can throughout the day measure his own progress and the accomplishment of which affords him the greatest satisfaction.[22]

INCENTIVE SYSTEMS

The worker should be provided with an incentive to perform the job in the best way and at a good pace by giving him a specified bonus over day rates if he met the standard of production.

After management has specified what is to be done and the exact time allowed for doing it;

whenever the workman succeeds in doing his task right, and within the time limit specified, he receives an addition of from 30 per cent to 100 per cent to his ordinary wages.[23]

Bonuses should be large and capable of being sustained.

While many incentive and bonus schemes already existed in Taylor's day, he argued that these relied too much on the initiative of the worker, who was free to work in his own way, and suffered from rate-cutting practices which led to attempts to mislead managers.

In 1899 Taylor achieved fame by teaching a Dutchman named Schmidt to shovel forty-seven tons instead of twelve and a half tons of pig iron a day. Every detail of the man's job was specified—the size of the shovel, the bite into the pile, the weight of the scoop, the distance to walk, the arc of the swing, the rest periods. He describes in the *Principles* how this result was achieved. In another case description he showed an equally dramatic change. On a job involving inspection of bicycle ball bearings he organized the work so that thirty-five girls did the work formerly done by 120, and with greater accuracy.

INDIVIDUALIZATION
OF WORK

Taylor argued that tasks and rewards should be individualized, as group influences acted only as restraints on productivity.

When workmen are herded together in gangs, each man in the gang becomes far less efficient than when his personal ambition is stimulated . . . when men work in gangs, their individual ambition falls almost invariably down to or below the level of the worst man in the gang . . . they are all pulled down instead of being elevated by being herded together.[24]

The few misplaced drones, who do the loafing and [under group incentive schemes] share equally in the profits, with the rest, under co-operation are sure to drag the better men down toward their level.[25]

In one of his experimental changes reported in this book he separated women workers by seating them so far apart that they could not talk to each other.

He remarks that in dealing with workmen under his type of management, it is "an inflexible rule to talk to and deal with only one man at a time." [26]

When one was introducing a change,

only one workman at a time should be dealt with at the start. Until this single
man has been thoroughly convinced that a great gain has come to him from the
new method no further change should be made. Then one man after another
should be tactfully changed over.[27]

MOTIVATION
OF WORKMEN

He considered that what workers want most is high wages and that they
are motivated to pursue their own interests.[28]

What the workmen want from their employers beyond anything else is high
wages . . . workmen cannot be induced to work extra hard without receiving
extra pay.[29]

Even if the workman were to develop laws where before existed only rule-
of-thumb knowledge, his personal interest would lead him almost inevitably to
keep his discoveries secret, so that he could, by means of this special knowledge,
personally do more work than other men, and so obtain higher wages.[30]

It is impossible, through any long period of time to get workmen to work
much harder than the average men around them, unless they are assured a large
and a permanent increase in their pay.[31]

Taylor appeared to regard work as something the man would prefer to
get behind him.

When men are working on task work by the day. . . . as soon as the task is finished they should be allowed to go home.[32]

He goes on at this point to describe the difficulties of a superintendent
who encountered difficulty in getting the children he employed to do "a
fair day's work" until

he finally met with great success by assigning to each child a fair day's task and
allowing him to go home and play as soon as his task was done. Each child's
playtime was his own and highly prized while the greater part of his wages went
to his parents.[33]

Taylor seems attracted by similarities between workmen and children and
elsewhere in the same book referred to "the analogy which functional foremanship bears to the management of a large, up-to-date school." [34]

CAPACITIES
OF WORKMEN

He makes a clear distinction between the abilities of managers and
workmen:

In the higher classes of work the scientific laws which are developed are so intricate that the high-priced mechanic needs (even more than the cheap laborer)
the cooperation of men better educated than himself in finding the laws, and
then in selecting, developing, and training him to work in accordance with these
laws . . . the science which underlies each workman's art is so great and amounts

to so much that the workman who is best suited to doing the work is incapable, either through lack of education or through insufficient mental capacity, of understanding this science.[35]

Workers did not have the capacity to look ahead or wait for rewards:

The average workman (I don't say all men) cannot look forward to a profit which is six months or a year away. The nice time which they are sure to have to-day, if they take things easily, proves more attractive than hard work, with a possible reward to be shared with others six months later.[36]

Bonus

They could not cope with sharply increased income.

When workmen of this caliber are given a carefully measured task, which calls for a big day's work on their part, and . . . when in return for this extra effort they are paid wages up to 60 per cent. beyond the wages usually paid, . . . this increase in wages tends to make them not only more thrifty but better men in every way; . . . they live rather better, begin to save money, become more sober, and work more steadily. When, on the other hand, they receive much more than a 60 per cent. increase in wages, many of them will work irregularly and tend to become more or less shiftless, extravagant, and dissipated. Our experiments showed, in other words, that it does not do for most men to get rich too fast.[37]

CONVERSATION WITH

AN UNSKILLED MAN

Taylor provided an account, which has become famous, of the conversation in which he begins his effort to induce a man he calls Schmidt "to handle forty-seven tons of pig iron per day and making him glad to do it." [38]

This was done as follows. Schmidt was called out from among the gang of pig-iron handlers and talked to somewhat in this way:

"Schmidt, are you a high-priced man?"

"Vell, I don't know vat you mean."

"Oh yes, you do. What I want to know is whether you are a high-priced man or not."

"Vell, I don't know vat you mean."

"Oh, come now, you answer my questions. What I want to find out is whether you are a high-priced man or one of these cheap fellows here. What I want to find out is whether you want to earn $1.85 a day or whether you are satisfied with $1.15, just the same as all those cheap fellows are getting."

"Did I vant $1.85 a day? Vas dot a high-priced man? Vell, yes, I vas a high-priced man."

"Oh, you're aggravating me. Of course you want $1.85 a day—every one wants it! You know perfectly well that that has very little to do with your being a high-priced man. For goodness' sake answer my questions, and don't waste any more of my time. Now come over here. You see that pile of pig iron?"

"Yes."

"You see that car?"

"Yes."

"Well, if you are a high-priced man, you will load that pig iron on that car to-morrow for $1.85. Now do wake up and answer my question. Tell me whether you are a high-priced man or not."

"Vell—did I got $1.85 for loading dot pig iron on dot car to-morrow?"

"Yes, of course you do, and you get $1.85 for loading a pile like that every day right through the year. That is what a high-priced man does, and you know it just as well as I do."

"Vell, dot's all right. I could load dot pig iron on the car to-morrow for $1.85, and I get it every day, don't I?"

"Certainly you do—certainly you do."

"Vell, den, I vas a high-priced man."

"Now, hold on, hold on. You know just as well as I do that a high-priced man has to do exactly as he's told from morning till night. You have seen this man here before, haven't you?"

"No, I never saw him."

"Well, if you are a high-priced man, you will do exactly as this man tells you to-morrow, from morning till night. When he tells you to pick up a pig and walk, you pick it up and you walk, and when he tells you to sit down and rest, you sit down. You do that right straight through the day. And what's more, no back talk. Now a high-priced man does just what he's told to do, and no back talk. Do you understand that? When this man tells you to walk, you walk; when he tells you to sit down, you sit down, and you don't talk back at him. Now you come on to work here to-morrow morning and I'll know before night whether you are really a high-priced man or not."

This seems to be rather rough talk. And indeed it would be if applied to an educated mechanic, or even an intelligent laborer. With a man of the mentally sluggish type of Schmidt it is appropriate and not unkind, since it is effective in fixing his attention on the high wages which he wants and away from what, if it were called to his attention, he probably would consider impossibly hard work.[39]

RESPONSIBILITIES AND
RIGHTS OF MANAGEMENT

To Taylor, it was essential that management should acquire and exercise a distinct expertise in regard to the organization of work and the supervision of labor. He blamed managers, as we have seen, for defective work systems that resulted in "underworking" and for not maintaining adequate bonuses, and thought they should do far more in the way of recruitment, selection, job analysis and redesign, training, placement, and daily prescription of tasks.

He felt that the benefits available (for all concerned) from the new methods gave managers the right to enforce these on workmen.

It is only through *enforced* standardization of methods, *enforced* adoption of the best implements and working conditions, and enforced cooperation that this faster work can be assured.[40]

The manager who could not enforce the right methods was not up to the job.

There must be some man or men present in the organization who will . . . have brains enough to find out those of their employees who "get there" and nerve enough to make it unpleasant for those who fail, as well as to reward those who succeed.[41]

He considered that he and his managerial colleagues were entitled to judge what is good for workers in their life outside the plant and to act on those judgments to the extent of withholding their earnings for what they conceived to be their own good—even if this contradicted his notion that bonuses offered should be paid and not withheld.[42]

THE PLACE OF
TRADE UNIONS

Taylor acknowledged that he was critical of trade unions; his reasons were as follows:

He is firmly convinced that the best interests of workmen and their employers are the same; so that in his criticism of labor unions he feels that he is advocating the interests of both sides.[43]

While trade unions had rendered a great service in shortening the hours of labor and improving the conditions of wage-workers,

the writer believes the system of regulating the wages and conditions of whole classes of men by conference and agreement between the leaders of unions and manufacturers to be vastly inferior, both in the moral effect on the men and the material interests of both parties, to the plan of stimulating each workman's ambition by paying him according to his individual worth and without limiting him to the rate of work or pay of the average of his class.[44]

It was unfortunate, he said, that workers regarded their trade union dues as wasted investments unless wages were raised or hours shortened every year, that union officials felt obliged to manufacture grievances, that unions (in both England and the United States) discouraged their members from doing more than a given amount in a day.

Taylor considered that under his system much trade union activity or other forms of collective or individual opposition to management would become unnecessary or less necessary.

The men, he wrote,

must be brought to see that the new system changes their employers from antagonists to friends who are working as hard as possible side by side with them, all pushing in the same direction and all helping to bring about such an increase in the output and to so cheapen the cost of production that the men will be paid permanently from thirty to one hundred per cent and more than they have earned in the past, and that there will still be a good profit left over for the company.[45]

In Taylor's opinion, the adoption of scientific management would remove or greatly reduce disputes between employee and employer over wage rates as well as the need for collective bargaining. This was because, under his system, what constituted a fair day's work

would become a question for scientific investigation instead of a subject to be bargained and haggled over. . . . The great increase in wages which accompanies this type of management will largely eliminate the wage question as a source of dispute. . . . It is difficult for two people whose interests are the same, and who work side by side in accomplishing the same object, all day long, to keep up a quarrel . . . each workman has been systematically trained to his highest state of efficiency and has been taught to do a higher class of work than he was able to do under the old types of management; and at the same time he has acquired a friendly mental attitude toward his employers and his whole working conditions, whereas before a considerable part of his time was spent in criticism, suspicious watchfulness and sometimes in open warfare.[46]

He remarked that his methods provided a counterattraction to unionism:

The writer has seen . . . several times after the introduction of this system, the members of labor unions who were working under it leave the union in large numbers because they found that they could do better under the operation of the system than under the laws of the union.[47]

MANAGEMENT
AS A SCIENCE

It was a central tenet of Taylor's thinking that management could be made a science, that laws could be discovered, indeed that this could eliminate much friction about the way to do a job and how much to pay, since this would be made obvious by the law.

The exact percentage by which the wages must be increased to make them work to their maximum is not a subject to be theorized over, settled by boards of directors sitting in solemn conclave, nor voted upon by trade unions. It is a fact inherent in human nature and has only been determined through the slow and difficult process of trial and error.[48]

Managers could develop a science by distilling from the traditional knowledge that had been possessed by workmen and from the study of jobs a set of rules, laws, and formulas as to the best and most economical way of doing the work.[49] This constituted, or was a central part of, scientific method in management.

The best results would come, he said, when the "science of doing the work" had been properly developed and the carefully selected man trained to work in accordance with this science.[50]

In his thinking, management could come to resemble engineering:

Many of the elements which are now believed to be outside the field of exact knowledge will soon be standardised, tabulated, accepted and used, as are now many of the elements of engineering. Management will . . . rest upon well recognized, clearly defined and fixed principles instead of depending upon more or less hazy ideas received from a limited observation of the few organizations with which the individual may have come in contact.[51]

A CASE STUDY
IN SCIENTIFIC MANAGEMENT

Aitken has supplied us with a valuable detailed account of reactions in a government arsenal to the introduction of Taylor's methods.

In making his proposals for work at the Watertown arsenal, Taylor's colleague, Barth, stated that no difficulty with the workmen was to be expected; by the time the consultants reached the issues of task setting and wages, so many changes would have been to the benefit of the workman that he would no longer be suspicious but would fall in line. He began to install the Taylor system in June 1909.

Time studies were begun in June 1911, at first with no trouble except from one man who complained that it made him nervous to have someone stand over him with a stopwatch while he worked. But when time study was introduced into the molding department, a dispute occurred over the appropriate time for a job (which clearly involved guesswork by the timer). The molders met privately to draw up a petition asking for withdrawal of time studies as "humiliating," and when next day an attempt was made to time one of the men and he refused and was discharged, a whole group of the men walked out with him.

In elaborating their objections to the new system the men spoke of the indignity of time study, especially for an experienced craftsman, the disruption of traditional pay differentials, and the introduction of competition between colleagues. They regarded time study as an implicit criticism of their work and an encroachment on their personal privacy.

Alarming rumors spread at the arsenal, where it was said both before and after the strike that older workers were to be fired and younger men substituted, that wage rates would be cut as the speedup got going, that the senior consultant had publicly stated that the system would work as well with apes and gorillas as with men, and that a special housing estate was to be built close to the arsenal so that the men could go straight from their work to their beds.

Aitken suggests also that the "functionalization" of the first level of supervision at the arsenal deprived the social system of some of its most important leaders:

men who in normal circumstances could be counted on to indicate by a word, a gesture, perhaps merely a facial expression, what was the appropriate reaction to any change in the work situation.

In a survey of the Watertown position in 1913, an independent management consultant concluded that scientific management as presented by Taylor and applied at the arsenal lacked an adequate method of industrial education, an adequate recognition of the principles of democracy in industry, and an adequate conception of the aspirations of the worker. He commented that industrial training must be more than training for a particular piece of intensive production work and that conflict was inevitable if changes were forced on men regardless of their wishes.

ATTITUDES TO WORKMEN

Taylor was aware when he published *Shop Management* and the *Principles* that in some cases strikes had resulted from attempts to introduce his methods. This he attributed to undue hurry, imperfect training of the intermediary foremen, mixture of his methods with those they were intended to supersede, and misguided attempts to get men to work harder with relatively little increase in pay.[52]

He concluded that the introduction of his methods might involve casualties on the way, but he seemed to dismiss this as the cost of economic progress.

It will take time for the men to change from their old easy-going ways to a higher rate of speed, and to learn to stay steadily at their work and make every minute count. A certain percentage of them, with the best of intentions, will fail in this and find that they have no place in the new organization, while still others, and among them some of the best workers who are, however, either stupid or stubborn, can never be made to see that the new system is as good as the old, and these, too, must drop out.[53]

At the same time, many of his references to workmen are couched in terms of consideration and "encouragement." He regarded the training and placement systems he advocated as less "brutal" than the current practices of discharging or lowering a man in rank if he failed to make good at once. He thought his system better than one in which workmen were "herded in classes . . . all . . . paid the same wages, regardless of their respective efficiency."[54] His methods, he said, required "the kindly cooperation of management." He defended his work against the accusation that it made the workman "a mere automaton, a wooden man" on the grounds that his work would become no narrower than that of a surgeon. The only difference, he added, between the mechanic and the college student was that in industry the teacher went to the pupil, not the other way around.[55]

Discussion

Taylor was a pioneer in his realization that social arrangements within a firm were an important set of variables in themselves, in which it was worth investing time and money:

Very few . . . realize that the best organization is in many cases even more important than the plant. . . . The spending of money for good machinery appeals to them because they can see machines after they are bought; but putting money into anything so invisible, intangible, and to the average man so indefinite, as an organization seems almost like throwing it away.[56]

He not only saw the importance of organization but saw the potentialities in manipulating the organizational arrangements then current. His methods had great significance for the ways in which firms were organized. They involved a new type of division of labor between management and employees and within each of these groups. They involved new study and planning functions. They changed the occupational composition of the firm—specialized experts were needed to establish the various conditions surrounding the worker's task—methods, machine speeds, tasks and priorities. It was not only the workman but also the foreman and the manager who had their jobs broken up into smaller units and redistributed. This followed from the fact that work had to flow through a plant by a precisely planned route along which each process should be performed by the right person at the right time in the right way.

Taylor's methods were adopted by many firms in the United States, in Britain, and on the Continent. They were further developed by Gilbreth, Gantt, Bedaux, and others. Together they were pioneers of what became the new occupation of industrial engineering, consisting essentially of the design of jobs and of relations between jobs in production systems.

The Taylorists sometimes achieved startling results in raising production (and often earnings) and reducing costs. Key factors in this were a rethinking of the jobs and the relation between jobs involved in the production process; systematic scheduling of sequences of tasks and their routing through a plant; inspection between operations; standardization of methods and equipment; more continuous and fuller use of equipment; more systematic ways of distributing tools and materials; inventory control; identification and separating out components in a task; and simplification of tasks. Most of these approaches and techniques have become standard practice in modern times, even among firms which rejected Taylor in his day and would not, either then or now, subscribe to his conceptualization of industrial organization.

TAYLOR'S UNDERSTANDING OF CONFLICT
IN THE INDUSTRIAL FIRM

In Taylor's eyes, the worker who kept his output at a lower level than it could be was under a misapprehension (that a higher level would throw him or others out of work or that his rates would be cut) or was a victim of a shortsighted management who had let things work out this way.

His repeated theme was that the interests of the workers and his employer were identical or shared, that high wages went, or could go, with low labor cost. It was not against the interests of the worker to remove "brainwork" from him or confine him to one function, because in this way there would be an increase in the total amount available to distribute and an increased opportunity for the man to earn more directly in his own job. It was to the worker's advantage as well as that of his employer that he learn and adopt the simplest, standardized way of doing the job, and abandon the methods he had developed on his own in favor of those devised by his managers. Apart from the advantage in earnings, the worker could then monitor his progress against a known objective standard. If the worker did as he was told and took advantage of the new system open to him, he could earn much more (though his employer might have to limit this in his own interests). The employee who did not understand that his interests were served by the new system had either not had this adequately explained to him or had been subverted by his workmates or by trade union representatives trying to justify their own roles. It was in his personal interests to work with the system rather than oppose it; in this way he could get himself out of the ruck. The new system would also make for industrial peace by removing wage negotiations from an area of dispute, so that management and workers could collaborate on an objective basis of what productivity and wage levels should be.

There are many defects in this line of reasoning. Higher output per man does sometimes result in piece rates being cut or lower rates of employment either for groups or individual workers. Whether or not this is due to managerial inefficiency is irrelevant. It is in several important senses against the interests of a man to take the thinking out of his job: with it he may develop both the job and himself into something different. Specialization in one narrow set of tasks may raise productivity and earnings in the short term but make it easier to replace a man by someone less skilled (or by a machine) and reduces work to a boring, monotonous, and possibly degrading routine. The methods a man has developed on his own may suit him better than those developed by others; they may well constitute an appropriate adaptation by him to his work situation. The "right" standard to work to is not an objective matter but a matter of judgment and perception, grossly affected by whether one is considering the question from the point of view of a manager looking for promotion or a group of workers trying to combine an acceptable level of earnings with pleasant everyday working relations with each other. Correct wage rates are not a matter of objective definition but a function of market forces and of power relations in which collectivities of workmen are entitled to use pressure on an employer.

REACTIONS TO
TAYLORIST METHODS

Taylor's theories were clearly employer-centered in that they gave precedence to productivity and profit, and asserted management's right to information about jobs and their performance. At the same time employers were not unambiguously grateful or receptive to him. This was partly because of his stringent criticism of their existing methods. Bendix suggests that it was also partly because he appeared to be substituting knowledge, technique, tests, and measurements for the superior intelligence and judgment that had legitimized their roles. Other sources of opposition and doubt by management were connected with the high indirect costs involved in removing planning from the shop floor and centralizing production design.

Trade union critics saw a threat to their interests and those of their members. Taylor blamed the trade unions for encouraging restrictive practices against the workers' interests. Trade union leaders and those in political life who supported them argued that premium plans resulted in discharging men who, it was alleged, refused to do more than a proper day's work, that it was insulting to the knowledge and dignity of a skilled worker to time him, that the system speeded up work to a stressful degree that drove men beyond their normal capacity, that it reduced men to the status of machines, that it took the skill out of a job so that the better skilled could be replaced by laborers. As one union leader said of the separation of thinking from doing, "This system is wrong, because we want our heads left on us." [57]

Contemporaries of Taylor criticized his methods on the humanitarian grounds that speedup was bad for the health and well-being of workers.

Other critics have emphasized the impact on the worker of loss of meaning in his work, and of specialization that deprives the worker of the opportunity to carry out a whole task and identify either with a whole product or a collectivity of people. They see Taylorism as contributing significantly to what we have come to call the alienation of the worker from society.

TAYLOR'S UNDERSTANDING
OF HUMAN BEHAVIOR

The central motivational assumption in Taylor's thinking was that the principal objective of the employee is to secure the maximum earnings commensurate with the effort expended. He did not appreciate adequately the fact that wage payments constitute only one of a number of rewards in a work system, of which others are achievement, acceptance, recognition, and the experience of personal effectiveness; or the fact that definitions of appropriate wages are largely a matter of group norms, traditions, group structure, and individual judgment.

Nor did he appreciate adequately the subjective side of work, the personal and interactional aspects of performance, the meanings attributed to his work by the individual, and the significance for him of his social relations while at work.

Conspicuously also, Taylor erred in omitting to take into account the constructions that workers would put on to the new procedures, their reactions to being timed at work and closely supervised.

He had an inadequate understanding of group factors—of the relation of individual incentive to interaction with, and social dependence on, a group of immediate work associates. Study after study has now shown that motivation and performance are intimately affected by norms set by colleagues, that these norms compete with those set by employers, and that economic aspirations are modified because of dependence on social rewards and punishments emanating from and developed in interaction with colleagues. It is true, of course, that Taylor attributed "underworking" to group pressures, but he quite misunderstood the way these worked and their function for the worker. Nor did he realize that these might just as well keep production and morale up as down.

THE CLAIM TO
SCIENTIFIC STATUS

Taylor asserted that what constitutes a fair day's work, and at what rate work should be done could be scientifically determined and put into an area beyond dispute.

In fact, these are normative judgments, deeply affected by the evaluation system and role of the person judging. An observer can certainly determine at what rate a given job is in fact done by the average performer, or even by the best performer, or even what environmental conditions and equipment helps to facilitate better performances. But, inevitably, a subjective evaluation is involved on what the job really is, where its boundaries lie, and what actions are necessary for the job, how thoroughly each part needs to be done. What is "necessary" is not exclusively a physiological matter but largely a psychological and social psychological matter. It also varies between people. Taylor seems to have ignored the relationship of the worker to his task and his attitudes to his task, and questions of traditional and local culture—even leaving aside recognition of the importance of colleague relations as a later development. The subjective component in Taylor's timing of jobs is, in effect, illustrated by the practice of adding an allowance calculated (that is, estimated) by the observer to allow for fatigue, interruptions, and so on. At the Watertown arsenal, for instance, it was standard to add between 25 and 75 percent to the time for a job to allow for such factors.

While Taylor and his followers claimed wide applicability for their principles, it was the organization of the machine shop at shop floor level that was their main arena. It was here that they achieved their most remarkable successes. But even here little or no account is taken of market variations, of the environment in general, or of internal relations with other departments. As J. D. Thompson has said,

Scientific management achieves conceptual closure of the organization by assuming that goals are known, tasks are repetitive, output of the production process somehow disappears, and resources in uniform qualities are available.[58]

Taylor left out of his theories the probable impact of the methods he advocated.

Roethlisberger argues that it is wrong to criticize on these grounds Taylor and the subsequent industrial engineers who designed work systems on these lines.[59]. He suggests that this is a separate problem and not their concern. On the other hand, Taylor did claim his method to be scientific and one can hardly accept as scientific a theory or recommended procedure which makes such simplifying assumptions about human nature and personality, neglects the social dimensions of interpersonal behavior, and omits to take into account the certainty of hostile or ambivalent reactions to imposed managerial change. It is true that some of the major discoveries in these spheres were made only decades later. But we can hardly accept a claim that a theory is scientific if it oversimplifies and rationalizes key elements in a system (especially human behavior) to a point that distorts reality. Taylor repeatedly contended that workers misunderstood his system: it would surely be a mark of a scientific approach to events involving human beings if one understood rather than complained about misunderstanding of one's theories.

Taylor's system of thought distorted reality by denying the simple fact that a work organization is a human community as well as an economic instrument. Economic efficiency was in effect accepted as the ultimate criterion of a successful work system. The strategy was to plan according to a technical logic and to attempt to exercise controls in order to ensure conformity with the standards set and therefore with the technical logic. From this point of view, human reactions other than adaptation to the technical logic are viewed as friction, as constituting resistances. On the one hand, in this system of thinking, is "industrial organization,"—roughly speaking, the economic or "correct" way to go about managing things— and on the other "human behavior"—a set of obstacles to be surmounted or circumvented, something that must be subtracted from the positive. This way of thinking derogates the human being as organizer, searcher for, and creator of efficiency, as well as implying that any views other than those of managements must be construed as a nuisance.

RATIONALIZATION
AND HUMAN RESPONSE

Taylor brought to the sharpest focus the notions of applying rationality to the study and organization of work, of individualizing the employee on a strictly economic contract basis, and of adapting human beings to technological requirements. He took to their logical practical conclusion in industrial work the rationalist and individualist types of thinking about economic life and the individual that were dominant in the late nineteenth and early twentieth centuries.

He brought to the level of the individual on the shop floor the particular personal implications of the wider and more encompassing trend of the bureaucratization of work, its segregation for performance by special purpose instrumental associations, and its attempted segregation from other important sectors of personal, familial, and community life.

In April 1914 a set of formal hearings on scientific management were held by the United States Commission on Industrial Relations. At these hearings representatives of organized labor strongly opposed what they understood as scientific management, in strong contrast to the claims put forward by spokesmen of that movement. As a result, an investigation was undertaken in an attempt to test the validity of the opposing claims, to determine what, if anything, could be done to harmonize the relations of scientific management and labor, and to protect and promote the welfare of all concerned.

In bringing this chapter to an end it hardly seems possible to improve on the following extract from the investigators' own conclusions.

Two essential points stand forth. The first point is that scientific management, at its best and adequately applied, exemplifies one of the advanced stages of the industrial revolution which began with the invention and introduction of machinery. Because of its youth and the necessary application of its principles to a competitive state of industry, it is, in many respects, crude, many of its devices are contradictory of its announced principles, and it is inadequately scientific. Nevertheless, it is to date the latest word in the sheer mechanics of production and inherently in line with the march of events.

Our industries should adopt all methods which replace inaccuracy with accurate knowledge and which systematically operate to eliminate economic waste. Scientific management, at its best, has succeeded in creating an organic whole of the several departments of an institution, establishing a coördination of their functions which had previously been impossible, and, in this respect, it has conferred great benefits on industry. The social problem created by scientific management, however, does not lie in this field. It is in its direct and indirect effects upon labor that controversy has arisen, and it was in this field that the investigation was principally made. For the present, the introducers and appliers of scientific management have no influences to direct them, except where labor is thoroughly organized, other than their ideals, personal views, humanitarianism or sordid desire for immediate profit with slight regard for labor's welfare.

The second point is that neither organized nor unorganized labor finds in scientific management any adequate protection to its standards of living, any progressive means for industrial education, or any opportunity for industrial democracy by which labor may create for itself a progressively efficient share in efficient management. And, therefore, as unorganized labor is totally unequipped to work for these human rights, it becomes doubly the duty of organized labor to work unceasingly and unswervingly for them, and, if necessary, to combat an industrial development which not only does not contain conditions favorable to their growth, but, in many respects, is hostile soil.

Your investigator and his official experts are of the opinion that all the data focus in these two points, each in its own way equally vital, equally indestructible and equally uncompromising. On the one hand, the right of investigation, perpetual desire and experiment to find new ways of doing things, knowledge, science, efficiency—all these—advance in the apparent nature of our world, sometimes with a beneficent front, sometimes as a Frankenstein, temporarily destructive of human rights. On the other hand, these very human rights are unquenchable, for in the long run they contain the very life of true efficiency itself.[60]

NOTES

1. R. Bendix, *Work and Authority in Industry. Ideologies of Management in the Course of Industrialization.* (New York: Harper and Row, 1963).

2. Bendix, *Work and Authority in Industry,* p. 259.

3. Bendix, *Work and Authority in Industry,* p. 269.

4. S. C. Pollard, *The Genesis of Modern Management. A Study of the Industrial Revolution in Great Britain,* (London: Arnold, 1965).

5. See Foreword by H. R. Towne to F. W. Taylor, *Shop Management,* (New York: Harper and Row, 1911). The 1911 edition was published uniform with the *Principles,* a previous version of it having evidently been published in 1903 under the auspices of the American Society of Mechanical Engineers. See Editor's Preface.

6. Taylor, *Shop Management,* pp. 182 and 183.

7. H. G. J. Aitken, *Taylorism at Watertown Arsenal. Scientific Management in Action,* (Cambridge, Massachusetts: Harvard University Press, 1960), pp. 29–32.

8. Aitken, *Taylorism at Watertown Arsenal,* p. 102.

9. Taylor, *Shop Management,* preface.

10. Frederick W. Taylor, Introduction to *The Principles of Scientific Management,* (New York: Harper, 1911, rep. 1942).

11. Taylor, *Shop Management,* p. 33.

12. Taylor, *Shop Management,* pp. 98 and 99.

13. Taylor, *Principles,* p. 38.

14. Taylor, *Principles,* p. 38.

15. Taylor, *Shop Management,* p. 99.

16. Taylor, *Shop Management,* p. 58.

17. Taylor, *Principles,* pp. 24 and 25.

18. Taylor, *Principles,* pp. 24 and 25.

19. Taylor, *Shop Management,* p. 133.

20. Taylor, *Principles,* p. 36.

21. Taylor, *Principles,* p. 39.

22. Taylor, *Principles,* p. 120.

23. Taylor, *Principles,* p. 39.

24. Taylor, *Principles,* p. 73.

25. Taylor, *Principles,* p. 95.

26. Taylor, *Principles,* p. 43.

27. Taylor, *Principles,* p. 133.

28. Taylor, *Shop Management,* p. 22.

29. Taylor, *Shop Management,* p. 43.

30. Taylor, *Principles,* p. 104.

31. Taylor, *Principles,* p. 121.

32. Taylor, *Shop Management*, p. 73.

33. Taylor, *Shop Management*, p. 73.

34. Taylor, *Shop Management*, p. 109.

35. Taylor, *Principles*, p. 97.

36. Taylor, *Shop Management*, p. 39.

37. Taylor, *Principles*, p. 74.

38. Taylor, *Principles*, p. 44.

39. Taylor, *Principles*, pp. 44–46.

40. Taylor, *Principles*, p. 83. The italics are Taylor's.

41. Taylor, *Shop Management*, p. 137.

42. Taylor, *Shop Management*, p. 149.

43. Taylor, *Shop Management*, p. 185.

44. Taylor, *Shop Management*, pp. 185 and 186.

45. Taylor, *Shop Management*, p. 131.

46. Taylor, *Principles*, p. 144.

47. Taylor, *Shop Management*, p. 69.

48. Taylor, *Shop Management*, p. 25.

49. Taylor, *Principles*, p. 36.

50. Taylor, *Principles*, p. 60.

51. Taylor, *Shop Management*, p. 63.

52. Taylor, *Principles*, p. 144.

53. Taylor, *Shop Management*, p. 132.

54. Taylor, *Principles*, p. 70.

55. Taylor, *Principles*, pp. 125–127.

56. Taylor, *Shop Management*, p. 63.

57. Aitken, *Taylorism at Watertown Arsenal*, p. 173.

58. J. D. Thompson, *Organizations in Action. Social Science Bases of Administrative Theory* (New York: McGraw-Hill, 1967).

59. F. J. Reuthlisberger, *Management and Morale* (Cambridge, Massachusetts: Harvard University Press, 1947).

60. R. F. Hoxie, *Scientific Management and Labor* (New York: D. Appleton, 1915), Appendix 1.

3 : Early Days in Industrial Psychology

INDUSTRIAL psychology refers primarily to work done by persons trained in experimental psychology who have worked with industrial enterprises, usually in response to requests from industrial managers. Early fields of emphasis were selection, placement, training, vocational guidance, the study of physical working conditions, boredom, fatigue, safety, and work efficiency. But this enlarged to include the design of equipment and incentive schemes, and studies of attitudes to work, morale, accidents, and factors in job satisfaction.

England

The first applications of psychology to industry were during the five year period 1913–18.[1] There was a close early connection between the development of industrial psychology in England and the work of the Cambridge University Psychological Laboratory (established in 1897) and School of Psychology,[2] particularly through the first director of the School, C. S. Myers.[3] Myers was the leading English psychologist of his day and included among his pupils and assistants many psychologists who gained international fame, including Cyril Burt, F. C. Bartlett, C. A. Mace, and R. H. Thouless.

As a medical student at Cambridge in the early 1890s, Myers came under the influence of A. C. Haddon, who first taught human anatomy but later became reader in ethnology and anthropology, and W. H. R. Rivers, who directed a course in the special senses and experimental psychology in the Department of Psychology. Myers became interested in physical and physiological aspects of anthropology and published on this subject in 1897, two years after taking his bachelor's degree, as well as in experimental psychology. He later qualified in medicine. Few social scientists can have been so widely informed and multi-disciplinary in approach.

In Myers's teaching boundaries between scientific subjects were implicitly represented as arbitrary, like political frontiers. He flew over them and back at will.[4]

Another persisting theme in his work was the importance of personal differences, the idiosyncratic in personality and behavior, what Pear called "his respect for personality." [5]

Myers joined Haddon's Cambridge Anthropological Expedition to Torres Straits (New Guinea) and Sarawak (Borneo). Among the members were Rivers, William McDougall, and G. C. Seligman.[6] He went in 1898 and stayed a year, helping Haddon study local rites and customs and cooperating with Rivers in studies of hearing, smell, taste, reaction times, rhythm, and music. Myers was professor of psychology at King's College, London, from 1906, where he worked on the localization of sounds and on color senses. He returned to Cambridge as lecturer in experimental psychology. There he planned and contributed funds to the greatly expanded and improved University Psychological Laboratory and helped to extend teaching in psychology and anthropology.

He was closely concerned with the *British Journal of Psychology* and was editor from 1914 to 1924, except for his army service. He was deeply involved in changing the constitution of the British Psychological Society, and in 1920 was elected the first president of the reconstituted society. Myers joined the army in 1914 and afterwards returned to Cambridge where he later became reader in experimental psychology. He describes himself as having returned to Cambridge "fired with the desire to apply psychology to medicine, industry and education and becoming increasingly disgusted, after my very practical experience during the War, with the old academic atmosphere and opposition to psychology."

During 1918 and 1919 he began occasional lectures on industrial psychology, wrote his first book on the subject, and started with H. J. Welch to work toward the foundation of the National Institute of Industrial Psychology. The institute was finally incorporated in London in 1921, with Welch as chairman and Myers as principal. Myers eventually gave up his Cambridge post to devote his full time to the institute. He describes in his autobiography his conflict between applied and academic work and the fact that many of his scientific colleagues in England felt that he had taken a retrograde step by "going into business" when he gave up a secure academic position at Cambridge for the development of an institute of industrial psychology.[7]

EARLY STUDIES

The 1914–18 war brought about the mobilization of psychological manpower to work on industrial, medical, and technical problems deriving from the war.

The first industrial psychology researches of importance in England were undertaken in the First World War under the auspices of the Health of Munition Workers' Committee and its successor, the Industrial Fatigue Research Board, later Health Research Board, of which Myers was a member. These bodies were occupied with problems of how long one could go on working and remain fit, and what were the effects of various physical conditions on the output of industrial workers. They were also interested in proper selection and training of industrial workers.

Industrial psychologists emphasized the problems of the individual in carrying out his organizational role. One reason for this emphasis was that the psychology of their time was interested in explaining and measuring the difference between individuals.

E. Farmer has described some of the pioneering studies on the relations between human factors and industrial output in a way that brings out the distinctive approach of the academic industrial psychologist.[8] At the same time, his descriptions bring out some of the differences from, and advances on, Taylorism. Farmer's first investigations for the Industrial Fatigue Research Board dealt with what he called "time and movement study." As he says, practically all that was then known in this area was derived from the work of Taylor and Gilbreth. But in all their experiments, when changes in work had been made there had also been concurrent changes in methods of incentive payment, so that it was not really clear whether the changes in work method had in themselves affected output. Farmer's own work, which kept payment methods constant, showed that certain types of change in work method could by themselves result in significant increases in output, the main general principle being to lessen the effort required of the worker and so make the work easier and more pleasant. He pointed particularly to the fact that constantly repeated movements were easier to perform and postponed the onset of fatigue if they could be based on a definite rhythm. Farmer and his colleagues helped to introduce different work methods, involving changes in tools, bench layout, and worker movement; and they developed methods for measuring the human effort expended on a job.

Farmer emphasizes that all his early studies for the National Institute of Industrial Psychology were based on similar principles of movement study. The basic principle was to ease the effort required by the worker rather than to try to increase output by increased incentives.

It was always found that it was possible to do this [ease effort] that output increased, because some of the hindrances to effective work had been removed by adjusting the work more to the natural capacity of the worker.[9]

This quotation eloquently illustrates the departure made by the industrial psychologists from the Taylorist notion of the one best method.

Farmer also describes his notable subsequent work, especially with E. G. Chambers, on relations between what he describes as measured "psychological functions," variations in industrial performance, and the incidence of accidents. Five thousand young persons were tested and their subsequent industrial careers and accident records followed up. The tests included tests of intelligence, sensorimotor capacity, perception, and special aptitudes. This research showed an association between sensorimotor capacity and accident incidence. It was this series of studies that led Farmer and his colleagues to introduce the term "accident proneness," as they showed that liability to accident differed from one person to another. "Personal differences in accident proneness played an important part, and by personal study of the individual it was possible at least in part to predict those most liable to sustain an undue number of accidents." [10]

Their studies also showed over a wide variety of occupations, excluding the unskilled, a positive relation between test performance and proficiency —in other words, predictive instruments were being forged for vocational guidance and placement.

A close connection existed between factory and laboratory research. A useful illustration of this connection is afforded by the work described by Myers as carried out by two of the institute's investigators in the Psychological Laboratory of the University of Manchester, upon themes immediately arising from their investigations in a neighboring coal mine into the problem of lighting. Attention was directed to the after-effects which are produced in the miner's vision after the miner's lamp has been shining directly into their eyes. This frequently happens during a change of position, the miner passing in front of his lamp about forty times a minute, when shoveling into a tub or hutch the coal picked from the coal face, with the lamp immediately before him: Experiments were carried out by the institute's investigators using a standard electric miner's lamp in the darkroom of the laboratory. Their object was to ascertain the number and duration of the after-images, first according to the position of the miner's lamp relative to the direction of vision, and secondly when the transparent glass cylinder of the miner's lamp, which enclosed the electric bulb with its filament, was rendered slightly opaque by painting it with hydrofluoric acid. It was found that while for a given length of exposure to the glare of the ordinary lamp, with its naked filament, the average number of after-sensations was 3.4 and their average duration was 48.4 seconds, with the slightly opaque cylinder the average number of after-sensations was reduced to 1.7 and their average duration to 23.8 seconds. [11]

In the services during the 1914–18 war, the British industrial psychologists played an important role in the application of psychological tests on a mass basis to identify individual differences in intelligence and aptitudes. On the basis of this, very large numbers of soldiers were assigned to specific tasks. During the last year of the war, C. S. Myers devised and applied selection tests for men using listening devices for locating enemy submarines and this, according to Pear, was the turning point in Myers's change from academic to applied psychology.

Myers was also among the social scientists who worked on problems of war neuroses, which led to significant developments in psychotherapy during and after the war. Against majority medical opinion, Myers, then in the Army Medical Corps, "insisted on the psychological nature of what was then called 'shell shock' and practiced his own psycho-therapeutic methods of treatment." [12] These included hypnosis. Myers remarks ruefully in his autobiography of the opposition he encountered in the Army Medical Service in this sphere. "I doubt if even at the end of the war their original attitude was wholly changed that the 'shell-shocked' soldier was necessarily a coward and that a deserter must be either a certifiable lunatic or a criminal deserving only of being shot."

C. S. Myers and his colleagues and the work they did in the fields of industrial psychology and physiology during the interwar period became well known as the "human factors school."

What Myers meant by human factors is explained by the following:

Of the four main determinants of industrial and commercial efficiency—the mechanical, the physiological, the psychological, and the social and economic— the psychological is by far the most important and fundamental. Intelligence in foreseeing demands and in improving industrial conditions, and a sympathetic understanding of the standpoint of others, are much more "productive" than mere capital or mechanical labour. The physiological factors involved in purely muscular fatigue are now fast becoming negligible, compared with the effects of mental and nervous fatigue, monotony, want of interest, suspicion, hostility, etc. The psychological factor must therefore be the main consideration of industry and commerce in the future. [13]

The second to last sentence of this quotation is a reminder that, although such a distinguished proponent of experimental methods, and despite the psycho-physical and physiological influences in his background and approach, Myers was deeply interested in the emotions. Like many of his contemporaries his thinking was substantially influenced by Freud. [14] He was not, however, a Freudian or a member of any particular school. As he says in his autobiography, "I could never owe allegiance to any one of the various schools of psychoanalysis or psychotherapy, preferring to recognize the undoubted partial truths in each and to refuse acceptance of their wild and mutually antagonistic generalizations." According to Myers's own autobiographical statements and the descriptions of his associates, he was an eclectic.

Some years later Myers described the field of industrial psychology as follows:

Industrial Psychology deals with the human, as contrasted with the mechanical, aspects of occupational life. It is concerned with the study, inter alia, of—
   a) the psychological relations between labour and management
   b) the incentive to work
   c) the arrangement of the worker's material and the nature of the implements with which he works
   d) the posture and the movements of the worker
   e) the training and selection of the worker
   f) the distribution of periods of rest and work

g)   the physical environment of the worker
h)   psychological factors influencing the distribution of products, e.g. advertising, designing, salesmanship, market research, etc.[15]

THE NATIONAL INSTITUTE
OF INDUSTRIAL PSYCHOLOGY

In the same book Myers describes the functions of the National Institute of Industrial Psychology, of which he was then head:

The main work of the NIIP, established in 1921 is—

1. The study of the workers' movements, arrangement of material, hours of work and rest, lighting, ventilation, methods of payment, increase of interest, reduction of irritation and worry, personnel, organization, production, control, etc.
2. The study of the abilities required in various professional and trade occupations, and the elaboration of systematic methods including suitable tests, so as to secure more efficient selection of employees, and more reliable guidance for those choosing their occupation.
3. The provision of courses of training, partly by lectures given by the Institute's staff at the London School of Economics, and partly by applied practical work in factories, framed to meet the requirements of the School's recently established Department of Business Administration and of the examinations for the Academic Diploma in (Industrial) Psychology of the University of London.
4. Research work, e.g. on vocational psychology, on lighting, advertisements, etc.
5. The study of factors influencing the distribution of products, e.g. advertising, salesmanship, designing, market research, etc.[16]

Having started with two persons, by 1930 the N.I.I.P. numbered about thirty-five investigators and assistants and was earning fees for its investigations and advice of about £20,000 per annum. The work ranged widely through the study of jobs, devising of selection tests, vocational guidance, company organization, labor turnover, and attitude surveys.

The success of the institute was no doubt largely due to the personal stature of the director. Another consequence of that stature was to help make applied psychology respectable. Bartlett wrote, for instance,

Perhaps this is . . . due to the influence of Dr. C. S. Myers, but I am sometimes tempted to think that in a few years it may be found that those who are applying psychology to industry, to medicine, to the organization and training of a nation's fighting services, and to legal procedure have done more than any others to the advance of psychology as a science. The exigences and nature of the demands in these fields means that an investigator must hold himself aloof from hard and fast theory, while at the same time he must define his immediate problems clearly.[17]

A related stream of work was in an area of applied psychology which has now come to be called "engineering psychology." [18] Again there has been a close connection with Cambridge University in this field. First there was the interest of C. S. Myers in applying laboratory methods to the study of working efficiency, then the active interest of Bartlett as Myers's successor in 1923 as head of the Cambridge University Psychological Laboratory. Bartlett fostered the application of experimental psychology to solve problems of man-machine relationships. For some years the laboratory research program of the Cambridge University Department of Psychology and its work in engineering psychology were practically coterminous. Then in 1944 the Medical Research Council Applied Psychology Unit was formed; this brought together a number of psychologists with interests in this field but under more direct government aegis. The Applied Psychology Unit moved out of the University to its own premises in 1953.

VIEWS ON TAYLORISM

Myers stated that the National Institute had endeavored to base its ideals on sound psychology rather than on the superficial analogy of a person with a piece of engineering mechanism. It has sought, he said, not to press the worker from behind, but to ease the difficulties which may confront him.

The British industrial psychologists criticized several aspects of Taylor's work.

1. While they valued such of his methods as financial incentives and motion study they argued that a rigid "engineering" view of workers had limits—for example, different people had different optimum physical modes of work and the way they responded to financial incentives depended partly on personal fatigue, the monotony of the work, and the nature of the physical working environment (in effect, that they had different motivations and that motivations depended on circumstances).

The mental and bodily differences between workers are such that it is impossible to train, or to expect, each worker to perform the same operations in identically the same way. In all sport and in all forms of art, there are different styles, all equally good, some suited to some men, others to others. So it must be in regard to industrial work. There is no "one best way" . . . it is an egregious error to force all workers into a common mould, regardless of the individual differences between them. Gilbreth's notion of "one best way" is not only impossible strictly to carry out in practice, because no two persons can be trained to precisely the same features of rhythm and movement, but it may also be harmful to the worker because it tends to discourage initiative.[19]

2. They felt that Taylor worked without adequate consideration of the human factor.

The disrepute and disfavour into which Scientific Management fell initially was mainly due to the neglect of the human factor . . . when by his experiments on the best methods of shovelling at the Bethlehem Steel Company's Works, he was able to reduce the number of shovellers from about 500 to 140: when he

tried to drive out the less efficient workers by introducing systems of payment
which made it impossible for them to earn a living wage; when he told his workers "You know just as well as I do that a high-priced man has to do exactly as
he's told from morning to night" and that they had to "bear in mind that each
shop exists first, last and at all times for the purpose of paying dividends to its
owners"; when he endeavoured to force all workers into adopting what on false
physiological and psychological grounds was termed *"the one* best way"; when,
not without reason, they began to fear that all craft knowledge was being taken
away from them and vested in management, and that they were being reduced
to the level of mere automata, subject to the commands of numerous shop
"bosses," each a specialist in his own way—it is hardly surprising that the workers protested and rebelled against such so-called "Scientific" Management.[20]

3. They thought that excesses in applying Taylor's methods would have
deleterious effects on industrial cooperation. Although their work was also
oriented toward the increase of output they claimed they were more
mindful of workers' interests in such matters as speeding-up and fatigue.
In his book, published in 1920, Myers wrote:

There can be no doubt that Labour is rightly opposed in this country to the
introduction of the early American methods of scientific management. It was
at first conducted there with far too little regard of the worker's standpoint. The
organization of Labour in America is still far behind that in this country. Moreover, methods which may have obtained success in one part of the world cannot
be imported wholesale into another where conditions are different. The impartial
observer cannot regard with satisfaction the huge profits reported from the
early use of scientific management in America and, at the same time, the relatively insignificant advance in wages paid therefrom to the workers. The impartial observer cannot countenance motion study if its ideal is to encourage
types of workers who "more nearly resemble in their mental make-up the ox
than any other type" or if the worker is to be told—"You know just as well as
I do that a high-priced man has to do exactly as he is told from morning to
night." Nor can he deny the justice of the worker's demand for greater industrial
control in these days of government by consent, of increasing democratic spirit
in education, and of growth of personality and responsibility. Especially after
the experience of the war, for good or evil, class distinctions are everywhere
breaking down, and the former hard-and-fast line of cleavage between management and labour must disappear in the course of social evolution. Leadership
and management must continue to exist, but "respect" must be transferred from
mere social position to personal ability and efficiency.[21]

Later he pointed out a major fallacy underlying the scientific management approach, namely the error of ignoring the social and organizational
context of the rationalization of work.

Although [Taylor] recognised that Scientific Management was impossible without mutual understanding and co-operation between Management and Labour,
its early difficulties were the direct outcome of his failure to secure these essential conditions for its success.[22]

The Taylorian ideal that managers should assume "the burden of gathering together all the traditional knowledge which in the past has been possessed by the workman," was, said Myers, in diametrical opposition to the attitude of British workmen.

When the National Institute of Industrial Psychology was being established, it was obvious that the workers were straightway prejudiced against it by such terms as "efficiency" and "scientific management." By improvement in efficiency they feared speeding-up and the dismissal of their less competent comrades. The mention of scientific management made them suspect that all their craft knowledge would pass from them into the hands of their employers and that they would be degraded to the position of servile mechanisms. They could quote passages from Taylor's Principles of Scientific Management or from his Shop Management, such as his remarks, admittedly "in rather rough talk," to "the little Pennsylvania Dutchman," Schmidt. . . . Such remarks will pass muster only in conditions where labour is unorganized and where an endless stream of foreign immigrant workers is available.[23]

Myers quotes instances of negative reactions to Taylorist methods in British industry. These incidentally anticipate later accounts of what became known as informal organization on the shop floor, though Myers did not see the full implications of this. One of his cases describes the introduction of a premium bonus system that few mechanics understood and consequently feared, because it was so intricate and obviously included components based on guesswork. The men were not allowed to grind their own tools and had to exchange dulled tools at the stores. "No man was permitted to leave his machine except to obey the laws of nature, and even then he was timed!" Myers's informant adds:

A man may be perfectly competent to grind his own tools to his entire satisfaction, but no man can grind my tools as I like them ground. So, what we did was to ignore the regulations, and if we wanted to sharpen a tool, we simply cajoled the tool-room foreman to allow us to touch it up ourselves. If the time-limit on a job was excessive, we went "ca 'canny" to hang the time out, and if the time was insufficient, we also adopted "ca 'canny" and lodged a complaint with the foreman. Should the "feed and speed" man attempt to interfere, we either threatened him with, and sometimes applied (if we were big enough) physical violence, or we politely invited him to increase the speed himself, knowing full well (having provided for it) that as soon as he did so the job would be spoilt. . . . By such tactics—passive resistance and sabotage—the system was rendered almost unworkable.[24]

United States [25]

The history of industrial psychology in the United States started in 1901 with a series of publications by W. D. Scott on the psychology of advertising. In 1901 Scott was a teacher of psychology at Northwestern

University. In 1916 he became a professor in the first department of applied psychology in the United States, established in 1915 at the Carnegie Institute of Technology, and four years later he founded the first psychological consulting firm in the United States.

The new "Carnegie" Tech Department received grants from business to undertake research on salesmanship. As part of the program, the department studied employment interviews, demonstrating wide divergence in the judgments by sales managers on the potential of applicants for employment in their field. In collaboration with prominent businessmen in the area, they developed and improved selection procedures, profiting particularly from the pioneering work of a businessman, E. A. Woods, in establishing links between items in application forms and statistically differentiated groups of persons who succeeded or failed in their occupations. The Carnegie group set the pattern of subsequent personnel practice by developing procedures that included use of an application form with a personal history record, a tested letter to former employers, interviewers' rating scales, formal comparison of the traits of applicants and a "mental alertness" test.

Hugo Munsterberg was also among the first psychologists to work in the area of the psychological problems of industry. He published in 1913 a book entitled *Psychology and Industrial Efficiency* [26] and in 1915 another entitled *Business Psychology*.[27] His particular interest was in what may be described as the psychology of the worker, and he was a pioneer research worker on industrial accidents.

As in England, industrial psychology in the United States was shaped largely by the kinds of practical problems posed by World Wars I and II.

In the First World War the American Psychological Association initiated a program designed to help the army "eliminate those mentally unfit for Army duty, to classify according to their intelligence levels all or at least most of those who entered military service, and to select for promotion to officer status those of superior ability." [28] These tests were further developed in the army and contributed materially to the selection, classification, and placement of recruits. In a separate stream of work, Scott and his colleagues developed a "complete Army personnel program," [29] particularly oriented to rating officer-candidates, and conceptually related to the Carnegie work on selection of salesmen. This system included records of the qualifications of each enlisted man and officer; an index of occupations indicating which civilian occupations were valuable in which branches of military service; personnel specifications for military jobs; trade tests; and an Army Training Corps program.

Profit-making firms of psychologists played an important part in the development of industrial psychology in the United States. The first such enterprise was the Scott Company, founded in 1919, which went out of business in the 1923 depression. Several of the same people were involved as in the army personnel work, the idea being to offer the same service to industry. The Scott Company adapted for civilian use the system of qualification cards, helped develop internal personnel departments and training programs for firms, devised and installed mental alertness and trade tests and apprentice training manuals, and originated a points system of job classification and salary evaluation schemes. In describing (and praising) innovative work by the Scott Company, Ferguson gives it credit for developing the idea of Beardsley Ruml of "the philosophy . . . of the worker-in-his-work-unit." This was opposed to the approach of some (among whom one could no doubt include Taylor) that square pegs must be found to fit square holes.

In contrast, said the Scott Company, the task of the personnel department was to develop harmonious, worker-in-his-work-units, and in this to recognise the fact that any given job could change a worker and that any given worker could change a job.[30]

Scott and a colleague, Clothier, published a book on personnel management widely used for years.[31]

The second such enterprise was the Psychological Corporation, organized in 1921 by a group of prominent psychologists which included Cattell. This company is still active today.

In the United States, unlike England, the development of industrial psychology was closely associated with selling, particularly selling of life insurance. Again unlike England, retail training was important. A research bureau for retail training which was established at the Carnegie Institute and later transferred to the University of Pittsburgh, was prominent in the fields of job analysis, the diagnosis of organizational problems, and the preparation of training manuals based on procedural formulae.

One famous outcome of personnel research at Carnegie and subsequent work at Stanford was the development of what has become a standard tool of vocational guidance in the United States, the Strong Vocational Interest Blank, a questionnaire devised by Edward K. Strong, Jr. This is based on studies of the interests of persons actually engaged in a variety of occupations against which the interests of potential entrants can be compared.

In the late 1920s industrial social psychology entered the picture with investigations and theories of motivation, communication, and group behavior. This was an outcome largely of the Hawthorne studies, which are so important in organizational theory that they are discussed separately and at length in this book. But it is worth noting at this stage that these studies began in 1927 in the tradition of industrial psychology and were originally designed to ascertain the relations between conditions of work and the incidence of fatigue and monotony among employees. The work actually began with a classical industrial psychology problem: an attempt to determine the relationship between changes in plant illumination intensity and production.

Up to the Second World War, American industrial psychology was largely a matter of carrying into or adapting for industry the procedures, experiments, measurements, and tests developed in academic laboratories. The main operating link was with personnel practitioners in industry.[32] Leavitt contrasts this with the subsequent links made by clinical and social psychologists (and he could have added sociologists and anthropologists) with training managers and line managers.

American psychologists were deeply engaged in World War II in their professional capacities. Some of their work is discussed elsewhere in this book in the section on the wartime work of Stouffer and his colleagues. An important part of the psychological work done during the war was in the direct tradition of industrial psychology,[33] for instance in devising, developing, and evaluating selection, placement, and training programs for military personnel. Substantial work was done in vocational guidance and rehabilitation. Engineering psychology more or less became established during the war, with psychologists working in the design of equipment and of airplane cockpits to help improve perception, handling, and emergency responses.

Ferguson suggests that participation in the war helped to make the American psychologist more of a practitioner, interested more psychologists in doing applied work, made such work professionally more acceptable, and confronted psychologists with the influence of group processes and social structure on individual behavior.

Discussion

SIMILARITIES WITH
SCIENTIFIC MANAGEMENT MOVEMENT

There is a sense in which it is true to say that the industrial psychologists joined and enlarged the scientific management movement. They aided the deliberate rationalization of human work. Like the Taylorists they were interested in finding ways of improving productive performance. They devised tests to select the best man for the job, to find out whether he was working at full efficiency, to discover the extent of job satisfaction and to rate workers for merit increases and promotions. They also tried to discover causes of fatigue and boredom. They shared the interests of industrial engineers in the psychological effects of temperature, lighting, noise, and humidity. And, again like the Taylorists, they analyzed worker motivation in individualistic terms.

The conception of man used by industrial psychologists was still very much biological or physiological—an organism reacting to the stimulation of the environment. The emphasis was on the individual as an entity in himself. His intelligence, energy, skills, and temperament were believed to be predictive of his work behavior. The work done by industrial psychologists on identification and measurement of abilities, job analysis, monotony, and noise were all consistent with Taylor's physiological view of men.

DISSIMILARITIES

1. The industrial psychologists would claim, probably correctly, that they were more actively concerned with keeping the workers happy and satisfied. In a contribution, entitled "Industrial Psychology and Labour," to the W. van D. Bingham memorial program of 1961,[34] Ferguson takes up the accusation that industrial psychology is practically always management-centered. He argues the contrary. He quotes the Scott and Clothier writings [35] to the effect that workers were not commodities but had inalienable rights as human beings which it was industry's duty to recognize and that it had a moral obligation to help workers make as much of themselves and of their lives as possible. In the same line of thought was the notion of the worker-in-his-work-unit: this recognized that a person could change his task or that it could be changed for him.

2. They were more sensitive than the Taylorists to issues in employee-employer relations. Ferguson quotes cases in which the Scott Company urged its clients to cooperate with unions or announced that it would not wish to offer its services if the client wished to fight the unions. It is further clear from his account that the same group of industrial psychologists played an important role in helping employers' associations relate themselves effectively to labor organizations.[36]

3. They were more alive to the significance of individual differences. Again this is evident in the U.S. worker-in-his-work-unit [37] approach which was a direct counter to the implication that persons had merely to be fitted to jobs or to adapt to them. Ferguson quotes Scott and Hayes [38] as pleading for a new point of view for dealing with men in industry which would recognize the fact that workers differed in the things they were fit to do and were capable of doing, that they differed in their interests, ambitions, and the things that seemed to them desirable, and that as men of different capacities and desires they required individual adjustment to the opportunities offered them in the field of industry.

4. So far as sophistication in the understanding of personality goes, Taylor had relatively crude ideas about motivation and the place of sentiment in human working relations. The industrial psychologists had a more refined conception of the complexities of the individual human organism and were concerned to develop this. As B. von Haller Gillmer puts it:

Traditional organizational theory, which described the layout of jobs and how workers should perform their tasks, largely ignored man's psychological life. The early "scientific managers" made the erroneous assumptions that people on

the job try to satisfy only physical and economic needs, that there is automatically a similarity of goals among members of the organization, and that
people try rationally to seek the best solution to a problem.[39]

5. They had a wider view of the industrial worker in his environment;
that is, they saw him rather more clearly in his organizational and community context.

Taylor's efforts to functionalize management resulted in the worker being subject to a forbidding number of different "bosses." He established route clerks
engaged in the order of the work, instruction card men engaged in filling in
cards of the cost and time of the work, "gang bosses" engaged in setting up
machinery, "speed bosses" engaged in choosing and specifying tools and in determining other factors making for the greatest speed of work, inspectors
engaged in maintaining the quality of work, "repair bosses" engaged in the care
of machines, and others engaged in preserving shop discipline. Is it any wonder,
then that the worker rebelled against such excessive interferences, and that he
feared not only increased unemployment but undue wearing out owing to excessive speeding-up? [40]

Their observations went outside the firm as well.

Clearly, therefore, it becomes the function of the industrial psychologist not
merely to investigate methods of payment, the movements of the worker, and
the length of hours of his work, but also to attempt to improve the mental
make-up of the worker, to study his home conditions and to satisfy his native
impulses, so far as they are satisfiable under modern industrial conditions where,
despite longer education and increasing culture, industrial specialization tends
to reduce him to the status of a small wheel working in a vast machine, of the
nature of which he is too often kept in complete ignorance, and towards which
consequently he is apt to develop apathy or actual antagonism.[41]

LIMITATIONS OF
INDUSTRIAL PSYCHOLOGY

The work of the industrial psychologists was in turn criticized by Mayo
and his colleagues for what they considered its excessively behavioristic
outlook and for under-valuing social influences upon worker behavior.[42]
There are, of course, some respects in which the early industrial psychologists, even in the inter-war years, would be considered naïve by today's
standards. One example is the suggested relationship between individual
and organization implied in the following:

Extreme specialization of work has hitherto tended to produce an employee
who knows nothing of what goes on save in the small sphere of labour in which
he is engaged. Clearly the remedy lies in giving the novice some knowledge of
the history and aims of the concern, and of the previous and subsequent operations undergone by the material on which he works, from its raw state to the
finished product—in instructing him, in short, in all matters which will encourage interest in and loyalty to the concern, and will help him to realise the
particular social service to the community which he is performing.[43]

This formulation neglects the probability (some of us would say the certainty) of elements of conflict in the employee-employing organization relationship. Myers does take up the issue of conflict (mainly between colleague departments) elsewhere in the same book but seems to see it as an irritant avoidable by more efficient higher management and closer control rather than as a fact of organizational life with possibly beneficial consequences. He actually uses derogatory epithets to describe conflict behavior rather than treating human emotions as natural outcomes of specific social situations.

His attitudes on these matters seem affected by prejudice suffered in the field to the work of the N.I.I.P.

In a certain factory, the important work which my Institute could do in improving human efficiency and production was clearly recognised by one of the departments; but the true ground of the objections which the departmental manager raised was only later traced to his unwillingness for his own department to be saddled with the cost of the work. . . . In another factory, a considerable sum had been spent in lighting a shop before it was found necessary, owing to unforseen circumstances, to move benches and implements to fresh positions, so that the lighting became highly unsatisfactory, and efficiency was plainly and admittedly suffering from the now unsuitably distributed illumination. Lighting, however, was the function of the lighting department, which refused to increase its expenditure by further work.[44]

Myers's proposed remedy was uncharacteristically authoritarian.

The remedy clearly lies in a more powerful nervous system—a higher directorate which will control the inevitably selfish tendencies of the specialised organs (i.e. the highly functionalised sections) of the whole concern, and will co-ordinate their separate activities by encouraging or by enforcing closer and wiser intercommunication.[45]

In the quotations above are three elements of thinking in industrial psychology which lack the benefit of a social psychological or sociological viewpoint—over-optimism about the structure of the relationship between employee and employing organization; a view of conflict as an irritant in what could otherwise be a smooth working system instead of an inevitable concomitant of a working organization; and a conception of solutions to conflict in the form of stricter control from above.

CONCLUDING COMMENT: ACHIEVEMENTS
AND CONCEPTUAL CONSTRAINTS

Industrial psychology brought several important advances to the understanding and more effective use of persons in organizations. The psychologists contributed a more sophisticated picture of industrial workers, which challenged the Taylorist view that most workers could be reduced to a more or less common denominator. They showed that a human being is more than the sum of his physiological parts—a whole entity. They showed that people differed appreciably from each other in their aptitudes and qualities. They demonstrated the usefulness of classification systems by applying them to the processes of vocational guidance, selection, training, and placement. They did much to ease the efforts required by the worker, to improve his physical environment, and, in particular, to design task layouts that are adapted to human structure and needs rather than forcing uncomfortable methods on the person. Among other things this facilitates appropriate behavior in crisis situations. They introduced more scientific methods into industrial administration in the sense of experimentation and prediction. They drew attention to psychogenic factors in behavioral reactions to stress. They played a key role in improvement of personnel record systems and in the development of systems for comparing and rating jobs. Their work drew vividly to the attention of academic social scientists the possibility of contributing to their subject by studying behavior in work situations and opened up a new profession of applied psychology.

This approach has severe theoretical and practical limitations in that it effectively excludes consideration of dynamic aspects of personality; the relation between the person and his social environment; interpersonal relations and organizational process and structure.

The focus of industrial psychology was on measurable individual differences, partly because this was a central area of expertise of psychologists at the time that psychology started to be applied to practical problems (as for instance in Binet's work on intelligence testing). It was also largely because of the pressure on psychologists since the start of the 1914–18 war to help select and place soldiers and industrial employees. This in itself required the development of a technology of measurement, that is, of differentiating and classifying large masses of persons. It has been suggested by Argyris that this emphasis on measurement has been connected with the applied psychologist's wish to validate his scientific qualifications by demonstrating precision.[46]

In concentrating on measurement, the industrial psychologists concentrated on those personality attributes, largely aptitudes and skills, which can be elicited from a person in the presence of a tester. While it is much more difficult to ascertain through such procedures a person's emotional dispositions, his endemic conflicts, and his characteristic modes of resolving such conflicts, these may be crucially important both in explaining and predicting what he will actually do in his work.

A complementary limitation was the neglect of interpersonal and structural variables. The individual is the most convenient unit for study in social science. But whether he is the most significant entity for study is another matter. The industrial psychologists, more than any other social scientists who have studied work, have emphasized interaction between the person and his physical environment, particularly with the equipment he has to operate. But they cannot be said to have given anything like equal attention to transactions between one person and another. To take one example, in the field of personnel selection they developed techniques of analyzing key components of jobs and of rating and scoring these against each other so that the jobs can be classified and graded in regard to difficulty. But it is a far cry from this to studies of roles which take into account such factors as the expectations of seniors, peers, and subordinates; the ways in which persons in complementary positions operate; the nature of the social division of labor in which the roles are imbedded; and the characteristic pressures on the person in those roles. But these are likely to be the critical factors in determining what sort of experience is actually entailed in filling the roles and what the actual operating opportunities and constraints are.

Another example can be drawn from the area of attitude testing. The industrial psychologists showed great skill in attitude surveys and could be entrusted, for instance, to deliver an accurate picture of the attitudes of all levels of an organization. But in social life one and one do not make two, and knowledge of the attitudes of even all 500 members of an organization does not make clear the characteristic ways in which members behave toward each other, or the institutionalized areas of interaction which persist for long periods more or less independently of the attitudes of the persons involved.

Argyris has pointed out that the traditional approach of industrial psychology was to assume that the organization is in a steady state and is a constant that can be taken for granted, while the investigator examines particular tasks, layouts, and persons.[47] Insofar as the organization is in fact in a steady state this, of course, by-passes the important question of what is keeping it in such a condition. But, more likely, the organization is not in a steady state, and this is worth understanding from both the scientific and the practical point of view.

The steady state approach follows the assumption that the role of the psychologist is to relate people better to existing tasks as defined by the senior management. The crucial problem facing the organization may in fact be the stress involved in failure to change direction. Recruiting more people to act like existing staff or creating control conditions for making more certain that existing staff will do existing tasks better may exacerbate problems. It may in any case be the doubts of staff as to whether their seniors have the capacity to handle the major problems that inhibits their own capacity to contribute. In concentrating on person, task, and relation with the physical layout, the industrial psychologist may be neglecting the major explanatory variables in the situation and those that would best enable him to predict what is likely to happen.

These comments may seem too critical in view of the fact that the industrial psychologist was not usually called upon to act as organizational diagnostician. He was usually asked to solve particular problems of selection, job analysis, task layout, absenteeism, safety, effectiveness of an advertisement, and so on. One would hardly criticize an odd-job man for failing to point out or remedy the architectural designs that provide the framework within which he is employed. It must often have been the case that the industrial psychologist could see that much more was involved than the specific problem drawn to his attention but felt that the wider issues were beyond his brief or competence. Or he may have felt that they were within his competence but that he had progressively to earn the right to work on them through a step-by-step procedure of winning confidence. But it is nevertheless useful to point out that the contribution of industrial psychology to the wider understanding of organizations (and therefore to the solution of organizational problems) has in fact been closely circumscribed by attention to what are often peripheral problems or manifestations of deeper-lying processes.

Argyris has made the further interesting suggestion that the assumptions of the industrial psychologist, his acceptance of the brief put to him, have the effect of reinforcing the status quo. This is because the tasks given to industrial psychologists typically involve trying to make the existing organization work better, cutting down the immediate causes of friction, and reducing control problems by helping in the selection and training of people to fit the structure better.

NOTES

1. L. S. Hearnshaw, "Psychology in Great Britain: An Introductory Historical Essay," *Supplement to the Bulletin of the British Psychological Society on the Occasion of the International Congress of Psychology,* B. M. Foss, ed. (London, 1969).

2. The university department concerned is today known as the Department of Experimental Psychology. The Cambridge Psychological Laboratory is the building in which the department is housed, and its titular head is the professor of experimental psychology.

3. 1873–1946.

4. T. H. Pear, "Charles Samuel Myers: 1873–1946," *American Journal of Psychology,* 60, no. 2 (April 1947): 289–296.

5. T. H. Pear, "Obituary Notice, Charles Samuel Myers," *British Journal of Psychology,* 68 (September 1947): 1–6.

6. This field expedition appears to have been a turning point in Cambridge social science. As Bartlett wrote, ". . . The trip which took Rivers definitely over to anthropology brought Myers permanently within the ranks of the psychologists. This expedition did another thing. It put a social and ethnological stamp upon Cambridge

psychology and this had done more than anything else to make Cambridge psychologists human as well as scientific." (C. A. Murchison, ed. *A History of Psychology in Autobiography,* 3 [Worcester, Massachusetts: Clark University Press, 1936].)

7. This account is based on T. H. Pear in the two obituary notices cited; Murchison, ed., *History of Psychology,* "C. S. Myers," and on F. Bartlett, "Remembering Dr. Myers," *Bulletin of the British Psychological Society,* 18, no. 58 (1965): 1–10. Bartlett in effect describes Myers as the chief constructor of the Cambridge Psychological Laboratory, the N.I.I.P., and the British Psychological Society.

8. E. Farmer, "Early Days in Industrial Psychology: An Autobiographical Note," *Occupational Psychology,* 32 (1958): 264–267. Farmer was one of the first investigators of the Industrial Fatigue Research Board and of the National Institute of Industrial Psychology. He was also reader in experimental psychology at Cambridge from 1935 to 1953.

9. Farmer, "Early Days in Industrial Psychology," p. 265.

10. Farmer, "Early Days in Industrial Psychology," p. 266.

11. C. S. Myers, *Industrial Psychology in Great Britain,* (London: Jonathan Cape, Ltd., and New York: W. W. Norton & Company, Inc., 1926), pp. 24–25. Copyright held by estate of Dr. Myers.

12. Bartlett, "Remembering Dr. Myers."

13. C. S. Myers, "Mind and Work," *The Psychological Factor in Industry and Commerce,* (London: University of London Press, 1920). Copyright held by estate of Dr. Myers.

14. Bartlett, "Remembering Dr. Myers."

15. Myers, *Industrial Psychology,* p. 13.

16. Myers, *Industrial Psychology,* pp. 21 and 22.

17. Murchison, *History of Psychology,* and Bartlett, "Remembering Dr. Myers."

18. See D. Broadbent, "Engineering Psychology," in B. M. Foss, ed.

19. Myers, *Industrial Psychology,* p. 28. See also his criticism of the "one best way" in "The Efficiency Engineer and the Industrial Psychologist," *The Journal of the National Institute of Industrial Psychology,* 1, no. 3 (July 1922): 168–250.

20. C. S. Myers, *Business Rationalisation, Its Dangers and Advantages Considered from the Psychological and Social Standpoints,* (London: Sir Isaac Pitman & Sons, Ltd., 1932), pp. 36–37.

21. C. S. Myers, *Mind and Work. The Psychological Factor in Industry and Commerce,* (London: University of London Press, 1920), p. 175.

22. Myers, *Business Rationalization,* p. 39.

23. Myers, *Business Rationalization,* p. 21.

24. Myers, *Business Rationalization,* pp. 41 and 42.

25. This section is based largely on B. von H. Gilmer, et al, Industrial Psychology (New York: McGraw-Hill, 1961), also B. von H. Gilmer, ed., *Walter van Dyke Bingham,* (Pittsburgh, Carnegie Institute of Technology, 1962). In all three works cited, the contributions of L. W. Ferguson were particularly informative.

26. H. Munsterberg, *Psychology and Industrial Efficiency,* (Boston: Houghton Mifflin, 1913).

27. H. Munsterberg, *Business Psychology* (Chicago: La Salle Extension University, 1915).

28. L. W. Ferguson, "The Development of Industrial Psychology," in B. von H. Gilmer, et al, *Industrial Psychology* (New York: McGraw-Hill, 1961).

29. Ferguson, "The Development of Industrial Psychology."

30. Ferguson, "The Development of Industrial Psychology."

31. W. D. Scott and R. C. Clothier, *Personnel Management: Principles, Practices and Points of View,* First Edition (Chicago: A. W. Shaw, 1923).

32. H. J. Leavitt draws attention to this in B. H. von Gilmer, et al, 1962, and adds

that the link with personnel managers was unfortunate. "If not darn near moribund, that profession turned out to be at least disappointingly stodgy and unimaginative."

33. I am distinguishing this sort of work for the present from the more social psychological work done by Stouffer and his colleagues, in the analysis of enemy propaganda and morale, studies of leadership, and so on.

34. Gilmer, *Walter van Dyke Bingham.*

35. For instance, Scott and Clothier, *Personnel Management.*

36. Gilmer, *Walter van Dyke Bingham.*

37. Gilmer, *Walter van Dyke Bingham.*

38. In W. D. Scott and M. H. S. Hayes, *Science and Common Sense in Dealing with Men* (New York: Ronald Press, 1921).

39. Gilmer, "Industrial and Business Psychology," D. Sills, ed., *International Encyclopaedia of the Social Sciences,* 7 (1968): 222–229.

40. Myers, *Business Rationalization,* pp. 39 and 40.

41. Myers, *Business Rationalization,* p. 33.

42. Some were, however, not excessively behavioristic and increasingly by the later 1920s and early 1930s prominent industrial psychologists in Britain, for example, Miles and Drever, were becoming aware of the important influence that could be exerted by the work group on an individual's values and actions. See contribution of G. H. Miles in Lee, 1928, and J. Drever, "The Human Factor in Industrial Relations" in C. S. Myers, ed., *Industrial Psychology* (London: Butterworth, 1929).

43. Myers, *Business Rationalization,* p. 46.

44. Myers, *Business Rationalization,* pp. 43–44.

45. Myers, *Business Rationalization,* p. 44.

46. C. Argyris, "Some Problems and New Directions for Industrial Psychology," to be published in M. Dunnette, ed., *Handbook of Industrial and Organizational Psychology,* (New York: Rand McNally).

47. Argyris, "Some Problems. . . ."

4 : Elton Mayo and
His Harvard Colleagues

THE work of Elton Mayo (1880–1949) was in many ways emergent from industrial psychology, though an industrial psychology reinforced first by a clinical and then by a social anthropological orientation.

His first major study (conducted in the early 1920s) was, or began as, straight industrial psychology. It was concerned with problem of labor turnover in the mule-spinning department of a Philadelphia textile mill, and he carried it out while he was on the staff of the University of Pennsylvania. In this study he tried to examine the relations between differently arranged rest periods and productivity, as it was widely assumed at the time that appropriate rest periods would lead to increased output.

This study was first reported in 1924.[1] It is again reported, with a background review of British industrial psychological research (which impressed Mayo with its scientific standards, insight, and sophistication), in his *Human Problems of an Industrial Civilization,* published in 1933.[2] His interest by 1933 was in the complex nature of fatigue and monotony, which were at first explored in terms of physiology and intrinsic task content.

As he put it in 1933:

It is clear that before we can profitably assess the part played in industrial determinations by something called "monotony," we need to be accurately informed with respect to (a) external working conditions, (b) the social-personal situation in its relation to the individuals concerned, and (c) individual differences of capacity and temperament.[3]

The spinning department studied by Mayo had a high turnover rate in comparison with others in the same mill; to maintain a working force of forty, one hundred men were taken on every year. A nurse was put in charge of a small clinic in the mill. Her duties included encouraging spinners to talk over any personal preoccupations. In Mayo's own words, she thus created a "listening post" of high value to subsequent procedure in the inquiry.[4] At the early stages of the study, it was her finding "that the reflections or reveries of the workers in the spinning department were uniformly pessimistic." [5] Experimental rest pauses were introduced for a small section of the spinning department. Productive efficiency improved and comments of the men became less pessimistic. At one point, when rest pauses were ordered to be abandoned, improvements in morale were dissipated and pessimism revived. A return to the rest-pause system was ordered and the workers were told by management to take control of some aspects of the system and to arrange alternations and training themselves. Turnover sank by the end of the experiment to the 5 percent normal for the plant as a whole and remained at that figure until a change in work methods some years later. The results were interpreted by Mayo at the time in terms of the physiological and psychological effect of rest upon fatigue and upon what he called "pessimistic reverie." [6]

In *Human Problems,* Mayo remarks of this study that

Inquiry in such situations looks for some contributing factor or factors in external conditions, something also in the individual himself . . . there is a disequilibrium within the individual and between him and his work. In the case cited, the complicating problem was that of the mental preoccupations—pessimism and rage—induced in the workers by the conditions of their work. But neither they nor their immediate supervisors had been able to define or specify the contributory external conditions.[7]

This set the stage for his preliminary report on the series of studies carried out between 1927 and 1932 at the Western Electric Company's Hawthorne works in Chicago.[8] These studies were carried out in collaboration between the Company and Harvard University, particularly Mayo's group at the Graduate School of Business Administration. Mayo had moved to the Harvard Business School in 1926 and was director of the Western Electric program of research. He handled the relationships between the research team and the company. This must have been a tremendous task in view of the length and complexity of the research, the varying backgrounds of the research workers, and the active collaboration by company officials that was essential in this pioneering collaborative venture of social science and business. At the same time, Mayo contributed to the design of the research projects and to the interpretations of the results. A statistical analysis of the studies was published by T. N. Whitehead in 1938.[9] They were later written up in detail by Mayo's research co-workers Roethlisberger and Dickson in their celebrated *Management and the Worker.*[10]

The Hawthorne Studies

Before beginning work with the Harvard group, the company had conducted, between 1924 and 1927, a number of studies of the effects on productivity of variation in amount of illumination provided.[11] In a first group of studies, three departments, each engaged in a different type of work, were investigated. Although illumination was progressively increased, no systematic connection was found with productivity. In two departments production did increase but in an unsystematic way apparently unrelated to the increase in illumination. In the third, production varied randomly in relation to illumination. A second group of studies attempted to rule out or reduce the possible effects of differences in type of work and type of worker by confining the investigation to one department or to two groups of workers comparable in age and experience—one a control group and one an experimental group. In this case production of *both* groups increased substantially to the same level. A third group of studies again matched an experimental group against a control group but employed only artificial light and *decreased* the intensity of the illumination. In this case production in both groups rose steadily until a point where illumination for the test group became extremely low, when it fell off.

These results were extremely puzzling. While it was understandable that production should increase with increased illumination, why had it increased when illumination had remained the same or had even been reduced? Whatever the relation between illumination and productivity, it was clear that other variables were having an effect.

THE RELAY ASSEMBLY EXPERIMENTS

These experiments were conducted by Roethlisberger and Dickson in a way which, they hoped, would eliminate or control factors which could have confused the outcomes of the illumination studies. A part (relay assemblies) was chosen in which output was determined by the individual employee rather than being influenced by a machine and which had other advantages in being so standardized and produced often enough to facilitate measurement of variations in productivity.

In Period I of the first Relay Assembly Room experiment, the weekly production of six women workers not yet brought together was recorded without their knowledge in order to provide a comparison point for later possible changes. These women were then brought together into a separate test room, where their production was automatically recorded and they could be observed by a research worker who was required to keep a log of what happened and to create and maintain a friendly atmosphere.

In Period II the girls worked for five weeks in the test room and an attempt was made to measure the effect simply of the transfer.

In Period III the girls had a new method of remuneration. They were taken out of the overall departmental group incentive scheme and made into a separate group for payment purposes.

In Periods IV–VI rest pauses of various lengths were introduced. In Period VII snacks were provided during mid-morning and mid-afternoon breaks.

In Periods VIII and IX the length of the work day was reduced.

Period X reproduced Period VII.

In Period XI Saturday work was stopped.

Period XII reverted to the work schedule of Periods I to III, and Period XIII that of Periods VII and X.

The outstanding result of this twenty-six-month experiment was an almost uninterrupted rise, period by period, in average hourly and total weekly production. This was despite the fact that conditions were exactly similar in certain periods, and despite the fact that in one period the work day was substantially lengthened.

Roethlisberger, Dickson, and Whitehead made elaborate statistical checks on the relation between productivity and such variables as changes in work methods and materials, fatigue, monotony, temperature of the workroom, hours of sleep, fluctuations of weather, and results of physical examinations of the girls. None of the factors so tested proved to be statistically significant.

In reporting the experiment, Roethlisberger and Dickson described changes in the relations of the girls with each other and in their attitudes toward the company which occurred during the experiment. The girls grew increasingly friendly toward each other and saw each other outside the plant. They had been separated from former colleagues, were envied by these colleagues, and became conscious of themselves as a separate group. The log recorded their expressions of satisfaction at their increased freedom, at being consulted on the experimental changes instead of merely being told what to do, and at their relation with the research worker who acted as an observer rather than as a direct supervisor. There had, in other words, been conspicuous changes in the social characteristics of the test room and the experimental personnel during the period of the experiment.

The experimenters remained concerned that their results might be accounted for by the changes in the wage payment system. They designed two new experiments to test this. In one, selected workers were placed next to each other, though within their regular departments, and the only other altered condition was that they went through the same wage payment change as the first set of Relay Assembly workers, that is, to a small group incentive scheme. Their production increased, but by 13 percent, much less than the 30 percent achieved just before. In the other, the Mica Splitting Test Room, the research workers examined the effect of rest pauses without changing methods of pay, increasing the pauses as the experiment proceeded. After a rise in output in this case, production declined. This was connected by the research workers with new employment insecurity in the plant. Bigger differences existed between these girls and those in the original Relay Assembly Room test. This was thought to be due to the greater heterogeneity of the girls and the fact that they were never as separate and distinct a group with close personal relations.

Looking at the first Relay Assembly Room study, Roesthlisberger and Dickson concluded that the changed wage incentive method could not in itself have explained the continuous increase in production and that such effects as it did have were dependent on other factors.

They attributed the major result to a variety of social and psychological facts. These were the changed method of supervision introduced by the investigators and a change in employees' attitudes connected with a change in their overall situation during the course of the experiment.

This study did not demonstrate with absolutely convincing rigor that the main determinant of the increasing output of the employees in the Relay Assembly Room was the motivation deriving from their membership in the primary working group. Nor did it show just how much of the variation in output was a function of the group situation or how much was a result of other factors.[12] This was mainly because the experiment was set up to examine other factors (work timetables, physical conditions) and because the formation of the primary group was only a by-product of the experiment, not its purpose. Group membership was a residual variable of which the investigators became adequately aware only after they had spent a considerable time on the variables that they originally began to study. They did not reorganize the experiment or change the type of observations made once they hit on the social variables. At the same time, it was the social variables hypothesis that seemed to make the most sense of the data. This was supported by a number of impressionistic observations and pushed Mayo and his colleagues along a most significant line of thought, that is, the negative hypothesis they began to develop that psychophysical factors were not as important as they had been thought to be grew into a positive hypothesis regarding the importance of group ties in working-group behavior.

The only constant set of factors in these thirteen periods was the existence of a small social group, the relatively high stability in its membership, the feelings of mutual loyalty the women developed to each other as the experiment continued, and the special treatment of the group by management, that is, their being selected for participation in the experiment and being consulted before each change was introduced.

INTERVIEWING PROGRAM

One emergent from this series of studies was an interviewing program in the same firm, designed in part to discover the personal and social factors related to dissatisfactions of employees and to variations in their output. This program of interviews had been started before the Relay Assembly Room experiments, originally in order to supply case material for supervisory training courses, and the idea now was to shed light on the influence of employee attitudes on production.

In this program 21,000 employees were interviewed over a three-year period.

The research workers made detailed content analyses of records of these interviews. Among other things, they found that men talked more about matters affecting economic security and women about working conditions. They were struck by the fact that the comments of an individual on a topic made most sense when combined with what he said about other matters: what he said became more understandable if his expectations and personal standpoints were taken into account. Different people reacted differently to the same objective situation. The research workers developed non-directive methods of interviewing, somewhat similar in style to psychoanalytic therapeutic methods and to the counseling methods of Carl Rogers, in encouraging respondents to speak freely about whatever they liked, in the expectation that a meaningful pattern would emerge which would show both interviewer and respondent the central drift of what the latter was trying to convey. Some topics (like cafeteria facilities) were used more than others as vehicles for expressing dissatisfaction. Despite individual variations in outlook, general states of satisfaction or dissatisfaction were shared by some groups in a way apparently connected with the shared social relationships of those groups. These were referred to as "social sentiments."

It was to such social sentiments that the research workers now addressed themselves.

One approach they adopted was to seek to understand workers' perceptions by exploring the work situation more fully. They worked on this largely through discussion with junior supervisors which in itself led to a better understanding of these roles. They portrayed persons in junior supervisory positions as marginal men, too junior to be associated with management yet barred by their authority from easy membership of the main labor force.

The second approach was to conduct, in what became the celebrated Bank Wiring Observation Room study, a further detailed field study of a social group of workers in relation to output, but focusing much more deliberately now on social factors and shared definitions of a work situation. The shift of focus from individual to group was expressed in the reliance now placed on observation of behavior and interaction rather than on individual interview of selected persons. There was also a shift now—or rather an integration—in research methods. Referring back to the interview program, Mayo says that

The very anonymity of the interviews, though it may yield knowledge of personal contexts, yet deprives the research of the possibility of relating statements to their actual industrial context; that is, to the actualities of a particular industrial situation. A final innovation of method seeks accordingly to study the individuals of a working group simultaneously by interview and by direct observation.[13]

The topic to be studied, output control practiced on a group basis, had been particularly drawn to the attention of the research workers during their interview program. It appeared that output and wage incentive systems were not working as they were designed to do, that work groups adopted their own standards, that supervisors found it difficult to intervene, and that informal group leaders emerged who warded off superiors and instructed new workers how to behave in accordance with the requirements of colleagues at the same level.

THE BANK WIRING
OBSERVATION ROOM

The Bank Wiring Observation Room study was made over the period November 1931 to May 1932. As in the Relay Assembly experiment, the fourteen men who were to be studied first had their output observed before they knew they were going to be studied. In this case no changes in methods, in conditions of work or in payment were made by the research workers. The men were brought together in one room and an observer introduced into the room. It was found that the men did not fully understand the incentive system applicable to them, that they had their own standard of a day's work (the wiring of two banks per day) which was somewhat below that of which they were capable, and that most reported this output (in a straight-line pattern) even when they exceeded it or produced less. A belief was expressed in the group that to exceed this standard would in some way, not clearly specified, be dangerous.

The supervisors did not try to break up such practices among work group members but tended in general to side with them. To some extent this was a forced accommodation to the situation. The supervisors were dependent on the goodwill of the men for carrying out several aspects of their work and for amicable day-to-day contact, and did not have the authority to control them. Also, they were soon in a compromising situation by being observers of known breaches of the rules, which they tended not to report.

Although certain central beliefs about production norms were shared, the men were divided into subgroups. One consisted of those men whose actual and reported outputs were closest to the agreed norm. Another consisted of persons who produced less than that norm but reported more. A significant feature of the study was the treatment of individuals who particularly exceeded the norm ("rate-busters") or were below it ("chiselers"). The latter would have done less than their share to maintain the group incentive bonus. The deviants were criticized in hostile terms, excluded from convivial relations, and subjected to "binging"—painful blows on the arm.

This study was more directly concerned than the Relay Assembly Experiment with the fact of group membership, and the research method was more focused on this topic. The research workers made a point of observing the relationships of the workers to one another and to the supervisor, and made very detailed records of conversations. At the same time, by today's standards, the hypotheses were not formulated and tested systematically enough, and the ramifications of the situation not fully enough explored. Too little account was taken of external factors—for example, a depression was pending, hours of work were being reduced even for members of the experimental group, and union organization was not strong.

This study showed that primary groups among workers, where they do not have amicable relations with management, restrict output in accordance with an elaborate system of rules and sanctions.

Together the Relay Assembly and Bank Wiring studies broke new ground in providing very strong support for the hypothesis that primary group identification within the working team, and primary group relations with representatives of management are very important variables in the determination of the output rate in industrial work.

This is, of course, not to say that such phenomena had entirely escaped attention before this. But it was to this group of research workers that the task fell of documenting and bringing out the significance for performance of elaborate sets of relations between workers; the emergence of group norms of output and their maintenance through a systematic set of sanctions; and prescriptions for proper behavior towards representatives of management and deviant colleagues. This contrasted both with person-centered industrial psychology and with the management assumption that their workers were "simply individuals working next to one another." [14]

On the basis of their experiences in the Hawthorne plant, Roethlisberger and Dickson adumbrated the notion of the plant as a social system in which each piece of repeated social behavior was interdependent with every other piece and in which change in one part necessarily resulted in changes in others.

Absenteeism and
Labor Turnover

The approach of Elton Mayo and his colleagues can be further shown from their studies of absenteeism and labor turnover.[15] They found from a statistical study of absences and turnover in the United States aircraft industry that:

The highest incidence of absences and terminations is among those who are new to their work or to the plant, and who have not worked themselves into relationship with the job and with their fellow workers.[16]

They followed their finding with more detailed studies of firms, departments and what they called "work centers," that is, situations within departments in which individuals worked side by side every day, either on tasks that were identical or were obviously functionally related to each other. Absence rates differed markedly between work centers and "the question arose as to how these differences came about, whether by mere chance or by intelligent leadership." [17]

After detailed field study involving comparison of work centers with differing absentee records, the research workers concluded that

a lead man who achieved a good record of attendance in his work centre thinks of himself as having three activities: first, helping individual workers; second, adjusting technical difficulties; third, handling for members of the group their contacts with inspectors, time study men, even the departmental foreman, and others in the world outside his work centre; and of these three it is the first that takes the largest share of his time. He begins with a new employee by listening to him talk about his background, introduces him to his companions, and tries to get him congenial work associates. In addition, the lead man listens to the personal problems of any worker, new or old, and arranges trips to other parts of the plant so that he can see the parts which he has produced in place on finished assemblies.[18]

In other words, they saw low turnover as the result of deliberately planned and executed assimilation of individuals into the social system of the plant. This work center differed from other types studied

in that someone—with the respect and confidence of the workers and with the support of management as indicated by his selection as leadman, *has set himself deliberately, with intelligence and skill, to achieve a group integrity of association* and to order the relations of his *own integral* group with other departments in the plant.[19]

On the basis of studies of the type described, Mayo came to the conclusion that working behavior and output of workers in factories could not be explained simply by opportunities for high wages, physical conditions of work, desire for higher standard of living, or even mechanical skill. Another factor was the worker's evaluation of his work and the social situation of which it was part. This and his readiness to accept the orders of his superiors depended in turn on the extent to which he was a member of an intimate group consisting of his workmates, physically and emotionally close to him. His behavior and output depended further on whether his group was respected by management. If the worker did not feel respected by management and linked with it through a personal relationship or through some symbol or agency of management, there tended to be a lower contribution, reinforced by teammates sharing the same sentiments.

In the concluding section of *Teamwork and Labor Turnover*, Mayo and Lombard look back on the whole stream of empirical studies by this group, including the Philadelphia Textile Mill study, the Hawthorne studies, and also compare their findings briefly with those of certain other research workers.

In all these instances, attention by management to the organization of the human needs of their workers was followed by an apparently spontaneous development of teams and of mutual responsibility, diminished turnover and absenteeism, and improvement in the quality and quantity of work. The team took over, as it were, and participated with management in securing the accomplishment of some of the tasks that had previously been performed by management alone, such as, for instance, the disciplining of members of the teams as to production and attendance. Once the teams had taken over these functions successfully their performance became a source of satisfaction to the workers.[20]

Looking through attendance records for both West and East Coast plants, Mayo and Lombard were struck by "the invariable persistence of the human desire for active association in teamwork with others." [21] They concluded that the desire of individuals for association is sure to find some form of expression; that the question for industry was accordingly not whether there shall or shall not be working groups, but whether in any particular situation the attitude of these groups was hostile, wary, or cooperative and friendly. It was, they said, clearly unwise to leave the formation of such groups to chance. The formation and maintenance of cooperating work groups had to be planned and managed.

Discussion

SOCIAL COMMENTARY AND SOCIAL RESEARCH

It is important to distinguish between the theories, speculations, and social remedies of Mayo and his colleagues and the actual research carried out by them, more particularly in the Hawthorne series of studies. As Landsberger has pointed out, confusion of the two has tended to obscure the contributions and defects of both, including the fact that the classic *Management and the Worker* is predominantly a report on empirical studies and not an attempt to persuade readers into a new industrial ideology. This distinguishes it from Mayo's *Human Problems of an Industrial Civilization, Social Problems of an Industrial Civilization,* and *Political Problems of an Industrial Civilization,* Whitehead's *Leadership in a Free Society,* and Roethlisberger's *Management and Morale.*

There is, of course, no logical reason why a social research worker should feel less free than anybody else to express his ideas on the wider social and political implications of his studies.

At the same time, it is legitimate to examine both the empirical and action-oriented aspects of any research worker's writings (1) to see if the recommendations are supported by the findings and, (2) more important from the scientific point of view, to see if the results and interpretations have suffered from the adoption of a particular value standpoint. It is indeed a tribute to the work of Mayo and his colleagues as a landmark in the history of social science that it has been subjected to such exhaustive evaluations in these respects.

The work of Mayo and his colleagues has been described by Shils,[22] as reversing or halting a trend in sociological study in which writers had bewailed what was thought to be the breakdown of intimate, face-to-face-relations. A main theme of nineteenth-century and early twentieth-century sociology had been the problems attending the emergence and operation of the large-scale society. Tonnies, Durkheim, and others had pointed to dangers of moral breakdown associated with the breakup of small rural communities and the growth of large cities where people did not know each other and where interdependence was not obvious.

How, Durkheim asked, can individuals in such a situation be positively linked with the society and anarchy be avoided? [23] Durkheim's own answer was in terms of the realization of interdependence in the social division of labor. Mayo's answer was (1) through the face-to-face colleague work group and (2) through the work group to the management of the enterprise and (3) through them to the wider society.

One criticism that has been made of this line of reasoning has been that Mayo exaggerated the extent to which persons in industrial society are in fact isolated from social contact and the prevailing moral order. It has been pointed out that he based this observation on the employees of the Hawthorne works, who happened to have been disproportionately recent immigrants and therefore conspicuously unassimilated.[24]

More fundamentally, it has been argued by Kerr[25] and others that the very division of loyalties of a man in modern industrial society is a guarantee of freedom. If his attachment to his employer is only one of several important attachments, for example, to his family, to his trade union, to a political group, and to the nation, he is less likely to become imprisoned by an overriding commitment to just one of these, and less likely to fall short in his obligations to the others.

In describing an instrumentalistic orientation of a sample of British workers which is combined with satisfaction with the job and employer, J. H. Goldthorpe and his colleagues point out the low priority of social relations at work for these men. They do not agree that this makes them alienated or is linked with a disorganized or anomic state;

It is possible for work not to be a central life interest and to be given largely instrumental meaning without the individual being thereby virtually deprived of all social activities and relationships which are rewarding in themselves. Rather. . . . the readiness to adopt an orientation to work of the kind in question would appear often to indicate a commitment to the interest of one primary group—the conjugal family—which is of an over-riding kind.[26]

CONFLICT AND RELATIONS
BETWEEN MANAGERS AND WORKERS

A central criticism that has been made of Mayo, his research colleagues, and what has become known as the human relations school in general is that errors have been made in conceptualizing the interests of management and workers as identical or coincident. The problems of conflicting economic and power interests both within the plant and within society at large appear to have been bypassed, ignored, or denied.

It is not difficult to construe their interpretation of some of the results as implying that the workers in the Bank Wiring Room, for instance, were wrong or irrational in regarding their economic interest as opposed to that of management, and as implying that they were moved by emotions rather than by economic logic.

These criticisms have been directed largely to Mayo personally because he thought the solution to some of the main problems of industry as well as the wider problem of anomie could be reduced by better understanding and communication, and by cooperation based on recognition of shared interests.

Particularly pertinent is the criticism that this outlook "ignores the extent to which industrial relations are a matter of alignment of organizations" [27] in a state of standing or intermittent conflict with each other.

This viewpoint has been attributed in part to the approach which the Mayo school pioneered of studying industrial relations on the ground in much the same way as a social anthropologist would study a primitive tribe. Such an approach illuminates the pattern of everyday contact between the persons involved and reports in dramatic form their own values and definitions of the situations and processes in which they are engaged. On the other hand it tends to detract attention from features of their situation linked with wider social institutions which deeply affect the terms on which they interact—whether or not these are at the focus of their attention, and whether or not they are aware of them.

It must be remembered, though, that the Mayo group was anxious to underline and increase management's responsibilities for its actions. Their thinking implied that it would be utopian to argue that because external social structure affects industrial relations these must be left unchanged, even when they are patently defective and dissatisfying. As Mayo and Lombard correctly said in 1944, "No remedies external to a specific work situation can change a fundamental defect of organization in it." [28]

Their colleagues, Fox and Scott, had made much the same point in their earlier study of absenteeism—management must do what it can to solve the problems to which technological and economic advances contribute.

Because this study focused its attention primarily on the internal organization of the three companies involved, this should in no way be taken as a criticism of other studies dealing with the problem of absenteeism addressed to problems of transportation, housing, and the like. Such studies are important, but they fail to take into account sufficiently the continuing management responsibility. In a situation that demands intelligent adaptation, administrative capacity must itself be regarded as an important determinant of the whole problem.[29]

It is also not quite fair to say that all the studies of this group stopped at the factory door. For instance, in the labor turnover studies they make it clear that they regarded supervisory capacity as more important in California than in the East or Middle West because of the "seething restlessness of the local industrial population." And even in the earlier *Management and the Worker* they reported that the interviewing program had brought out the fact that participation outside the factory could have effects on productivity and morale within it.

Even if Mayo were right and a much higher level of collaboration achieved and identity of interest conceded, this could ultimately threaten the position of the industrial worker. Accommodation to the needs of management could mean the subordination of the less well organized. There is a misunderstanding in the notion that there is something which can be recognized as the needs of the organization separate from the felt needs of those who comprise it. Only persons can have needs, and if some needs predominate over others within an economic enterprise this is because some people have the power and authority to impose their needs on others. It is a restricted and restrictive view of the industrial worker that views his behavior as only a response or adaptation to the needs of others.

Insofar as conflict is recognized in the writings of this group, they suggest that a significant part can be played in its reduction by increasing the flow of information to workers, for example, on the reasons, timing, and organizational implications of technological changes that are to be introduced.[30] We would argue today that conflict is far too pervasive to be substantially influenced by such means.

MAYO AND HIS COLLEAGUES
AS MANAGEMENT AIDES

The writings of Mayo and his colleagues (including Roethlisberger and Dickson in the first part of *Management and the Worker*) contain several recommendations to managers.

Mayo suggested that interviews of the sort developed in the Hawthorne work could be an important, if indirect, method by which management could obtain the cooperation of the individual worker. According to Mayo, the interview could help the individual to get rid of what he regarded as useless emotional complications; could enable him to give himself good advice; could help him to associate more easily and satisfactorily with others; and could develop his desire and capacity to work better with management. The interviewer would represent the plant organization outside the worker's own group and could help him to work better with his own group. "This is the beginning of the necessary double loyalty—to his own group and to the larger organization." [31]

Other recommendations were that managements should take steps to link new entrants with colleagues to facilitate and foster the formation and maintenance of colleague groups; should guide employees away from group identifications and memberships hostile or indifferent to the employing organization; should identify informal group leaders, whom they could use as communication channels; and should bring workers into decision-making and disciplinary processes.[32]

The fact that Mayo and his colleagues offered advice to managers has been criticized on a number of grounds.

One set of grounds is scientific, that, by viewing problems of human behavior in industry from the standpoint of how the objectives of management could be better achieved, they restricted understanding of that behavior. They are said to have limited their observations to those variables that the manager could manipulate (communication, information, and induction procedures) and to have neglected other institutional and structural variables which conceivably had greater explanatory power. This could include the effects of home and neighborhood. It is said that they have produced a "managerial sociology" [33] which, precisely because it examines behavior from the standpoint of one group in a larger system, cannot explain the behavior it purports to study. They may be said to have failed to recognize the extent to which the economic enterprise is an arena for struggle between diverse and often conflicting individual and group interests. At the same time, labor organizations seem to have been relegated to a minor role as a force in industrial relations and as an alternative focus of loyalty and attachment.[34] A related scientific argument is that although the research workers were pioneers in drawing attention to the explanatory value of people's definitions of the situations in which they are involved, this distracts attention from the significance of objective aspects of those situations.

It has been said that, by indicating to management how they might win the collaboration of workers, they were abandoning the proper scientific role of social research workers and creating an image of social scientists as creators of manipulative techniques for those who hold power.[35]

Another set of criticisms is that as prescriptions the Mayo recommendations are weak. This is partly because they pay attention to relatively superficial manifestations (symptoms) of problems and neglect underlying, more widely ramifying schisms and conflicts. An example is the counseling program which has been described as a measure for draining off hostility rather than a means of obtaining and acting on information about the system that produced the hostility.[36]

A third set of criticisms is that the Mayo prescriptions are essentially contemptuous of the industrial worker since they tend to represent him as weak, passive, manipulable, emotional, and as a means to ends more important than his own welfare. Bell has been one of the most pungent critics of this aspect of the work, which he calls "cow-sociology." [37] The central tenet, he avers, is to create a situation in which workers will feel satisfied, esteemed, and contented with what they are doing, and will therefore produce more.

THE ROLE OF
THE INDUSTRIAL MANAGER

Mayo assigned a central place to the industrial manager in the successful working of contemporary society. As a solution to the problems of modern society, he and some of his colleagues suggested that the relation of individuals to society (conceived by Mayo as damaged by industrialization and urbanization) can be restored through managing of industrial organizations in such a way that there is spontaneous collaboration for a common purpose.

Mayo thought it an urgent problem of the present to train administrators to take proper account of "the human and social aspects of industrial organization." The immediate social and industrial problem, as he saw it, was to restore effective human collaboration. Administrators should be qualified as listeners in the sense that they should be able to relate to each other items they heard in conversation. Further, they should become acquainted with the findings and implications of studies of workers and organizations.

Just as the British colonial official was required to study anthropology, so the manager should study industrial researches.[38]

Mayo extended his argument to administration in general, the tenor being that it was essential to understand emotional as well as rational aspects of behavior.

> If at all the critical posts in communal activity we had intelligent persons capable of analyzing an individual or group attitude in terms of, first, the degree of logical understanding manifest; second, the nonlogic of social codes in action; and third, the irrational exasperations symptomatic of conflict and baffled effort; if we had an *élite* capable of such analysis, very many of our difficulties would dwindle to vanishing point. Our leaders tend to state these problems in terms of systematic economics, and since the gravamen of the issue is human and social and not primarily economic, their statements are not relevant.[39]

T. N. Whitehead makes an explicit argument for business organizations and their individual managers taking leading roles in wider social and community affairs.

> . . . it is largely to the business and industrial organizations that we must look in the immediate future for leadership in initiating and guiding the social activity made possible by their technical achievements. This applies equally to the social activity involved in the work of industry and to that outside its walls.[40]

This should be done partly because industry had to shoulder its social responsibilities.

> . . . no society can be vital in which its principal organizations do not conceive their responsibilities in social terms.[41]

But he also had in mind the involvement in communities of business for the purpose of self-protection.

> If the local fire brigade or the local church is inadequately run, the result is apt to be some form of town meeting, or its more informal equivalent. The community feels the deficiency to be its immediate concern. But if the local factory or department store is going downhill, in spite of the obvious loss to the community, the loyalty and concern of the community is not involved. . . . Managers of enterprises should take their place as leaders of their communities; then their organizations would be the centres of local activity and so become indispensable institutions whose continued existence would be a matter of general interest.[42]

Not only should the manager become a social leader in the interests of society and of his company, but he was well fitted to do so.

> As a leader the business executive has obvious qualifications. In general, the executives are responsible men, selected largely for their ability to undertake and carry through complex practical affairs; they are well trained in the techniques of organization. In the running of community activities, executives have under their control firms accustomed to the use of skilled techniques, and with the necessary local prestige to undertake a job and see it through.[43]

For him, it was industry that had brought about the modern revolution in standards of living and it was the right and duty of the industrialist to become a community leader. Whitehead did not appreciate the need for multiple power centers in complex societies.

THE SIGNIFICANCE OF SOCIAL
RELATIONS WITHIN THE PLANT

We have seen that Mayo and his colleagues repeatedly emphasized the importance of social relations within the plant for worker satisfaction, for morale, for stability of the labor force, and for productivity. In Dubin's words:

> Industrial research of the human relations school has emphasized that man is a social creature and that even at work his learned dependence on social interaction must find fulfilment.[44]

Several writers and research workers have challenged this view. In an investigation of his own, Dubin showed that in a sample drawn from three different plants in the Middle West of the United States, job and workplace were not central life interests for the majority. Most found their preferred human associations and preferred areas of behavior outside their employment.[45]

But the fact that people seek or find their significant social relations mainly outside the plant does not necessarily imply that significant social relations inside the plant are not important to them. It may be that the men in the Dubin study sought but did not find such relations there, or that they had become accommodated to a life situation of this sort.

In their study in England, J. H. Goldthorpe and his colleagues report on a field study of skilled and semiskilled workers in three companies to the effect that:

There is no evidence that within our sample any association exists between job satisfaction (or deprivation) in terms of workers' immediate shop-floor experience and their attachment to their present employment. This attachment appears rather to be based upon predominantly extrinsic—that is to say, economic—considerations . . . Only a small number of workers in our sample appeared to be members of solidary work groups . . . there was no indication that the majority of our respondents were greatly concerned to maintain close relationships with their workmates, either within or without the workplace . . . for the most part, the workers we studied were reasonably satisfied with their firms as employers . . . in the main, these workers saw their relationships with their firms as an almost exclusively contractural one, founded upon a bargain of money for effort.[46]

Later, in comment, they add that

where men are oriented toward their employment in an essentially instrumental way, situations which from the point of view of 'human relations' theory would appear potentially pathological do not prove to be so . . . The absence of solidary work groups or of employee-centered supervision is unlikely to produce any marked degree of frustration or discontent on the part of employees; and the fact that they do not identify very closely with the enterprise or feel any sense of moral commitment towards it need in no way betoken a breakdown in organizational coherence or effectiveness.[47]

The authors are, of course, not arguing that all relations of workers with workmates and employers are only or mainly instrumental, but that a wide range of possible alternative orientations to work exist. In their particular case they make plain the fact that a large proportion of the work force they studied had come expressly from other parts of the country and from other jobs (sometimes from jobs with higher status) for the purpose of raising their earnings. In other words, to return to the Dubin quotation at the beginning of this section, wanting to associate on the job and to have meaningful relations with colleagues and employers does not in fact appear to be a universal need. As both this group and Landsberger point out, Mayo and his colleagues may well have exaggerated this point in their reaction against the strongly individualistic emphasis of classical economics and early industrial psychology.

The important point has been made that Mayo and his colleagues have greatly exaggerated the economic value of teamwork in the modern factory. Dubin makes the assertion:

There is no significant body of evidence to support the conclusion that the social structuring of work to take into account the sociability of people at work succeeded in maximising productivity or output.[48]

At first sight this seems unduly bold. But the word "maximizing" renders it of course both true and yet so inexact as to lack meaning. Probably no action "maximizes" productivity since targets can be infinite. At the same time Dubin is correct in implying that the variability in production contingent on changing human relationships (for example, styles of supervision) has seldom been shown to be more than about 15–30 percent.[49] This is high and worthwhile in itself, but economically unimportant when contrasted with changes achievable through alterations in work methods.

THE MAYO HERITAGE

The Mayo heritage is vast.

First, he and his colleagues were pioneers in research methods. They used an extremely wide range of research techniques, including statistical analysis, case studies, field experiments, interviews and direct observations. The combination of non-directive interviews with field observation was unique. Mayo adapted the interviewing methods of clinical psychologists to the field methods of anthropologists and brought them to bear on studies of industrial organization. Systematic content analysis was applied for the first time to large batches of interview protocols of industrial workers. Mayo put small industrial groups under close professional scrutiny and in so doing virtually created a new field in the sociology of work. He and his colleagues afforded a scientific demonstration *in vivo* of the behavior of social groups, showing that a group had a life of its own, complete with customs, norms, and effective social controls on its members.

Homans rightly points out that Mayo's contribution was much wider in its methodological implications for sociology than its application in an industrial context. In his words, "For empirical investigation, Elton Mayo was to sociology what Lewin was to psychology." [50]

As far as the impact of the Mayo group on conceptions of the industrial worker and his immediate environment was concerned:

The conclusions of Mayo and his co-workers completely upset the commonly held notions of how workers react to authority and how production can be stimulated. Instead, a social model of the worker was put forward to oppose the mechanistic, economic and even psychological models then current. This social model installed the logic of human emotions side by side with the logic of costs or efficiency. After the Hawthorne studies it had to be granted that an informal structure of social relations did exist behind the formal organizational structure and that numerous phenomena could not be explained on any other grounds.[51]

From studies of the sort pioneered by the Mayo group sprang the emphasis on the worker as a group member which has dominated in organizational sociology since 1940.

In its impact on managerial thinking and practice, the work of Mayo and his colleagues resulted in increased emphasis on human problems (including personal problems) in labor management; increased emphasis on the design of work operations and task groups in a way that would take into account a need for sociability and the tendency to informal association of workers; increased emphasis on securing cooperation through acceptance and consent rather than through merely issuing orders; increased emphasis on two-way communication. It stated a need for the training of managers in the understanding of group processes, group relations and personality; and implied that there was a body of knowledge and a set of skills that could be applied in these fields.

As Dubin indicates in his encyclopedia article, much of this thinking resonated with the postwar democratic ethos and found substantial application, first in American and then in British and European industry.

NOTES

1. E. Mayo, "Revery and Industrial Fatigue," *Personnel Journal,* 3, no. 8 (December 1924): 273–281.
2. E. Mayo, *The Human Problems of an Industrial Civilization,* (Boston: Harvard Business School, Division of Research, 1933).
3. Mayo, The Human Problems, p. 38.
4. Mayo, *The Human Problems,* p. 45. In the same book Mayo reports with evident pleasure the independent but converging discovery and technique in England of what we have come to call non-directive interviewing, quoting from Industrial Fatigue Research Board No. 43, *A Study of Telegraphists' Cramp,* by M. Smith, M. Culpin, and E. Farmer. The authors reported that it had proved possible to get the point of view of a person with sufficient clearness to yield an insight onto the relation of the work he does to his general attitude to life. Also, "It often happened that when once started the subject would give a very detailed personal account of himself, in which case the investigator would not interfere with questions."
5. Mayo, *The Human Problems,* p. 45.
6. In a later discussion Mayo attributes the reduction in labor turnover primarily to the increased responsibility taken by the workers, which induced consultation, discussion, and teamwork, rather than to the rest pauses. See E. Mayo and G. F. F. Lombard, *Teamwork and Labour Turnover in the Aircraft Industry of Southern California* (Boston: Harvard Graduate School of Business Administration, 1944).

7. Mayo, *The Human Problems*, p. 52.

8. Mayo, *The Human Problems*, Ch. 3.

9. T. N. Whitehead, *The Industrial Worker* (Cambridge: Harvard University Press, 1938).

10. F. J. Roethlisberger and W. J. Dickson, *Management and the Worker* (Cambridge, Boston: Harvard University Press, 1939).

11. These are described by Roethlisberger and Dickson, *Management and the Worker*.

12. See discussion in E. A. Shils, "The Study of the Primary Group," in H. D. Lasswell and D. Lerner, eds., *The Policy Sciences—Recent Developments in Scope and Methods* (Palo Alto: Stanford University Press, 1951).

13. Mayo, *The Human Problems*, p. 164.

14. H. A. Landsberger, *Hawthorne Revisited. Management and the Worker, Its Critics and Developments in Human Relations in Industry* (New York: Cornell University Press, 1958).

15. J. B. Fox and J. F. Scott, *Absenteeism: Management's Problems* (Boston: Harvard Graduate School of Business Administration, 1943); and E. Mayo and G. F. F. Lombard, *Teamwork and Labour Turnover in the Aircraft Industry of Southern California* (Boston: Harvard Graduate School of Business Administration, 1944. Reprinted in a joint binding 1957).

16. Mayo and Lombard, *Teamwork and Labour Turnover*, p. 8.

17. Mayo and Lombard, *Teamwork and Labour Turnover*, p. 17. See also Mayo, *The Social Problems of Industrial Civilization*, (Boston: Harvard Graduate School of Business Administration, 1945).

18. Mayo and Lombard, *Teamwork and Labour Turnover*, p. 2.

19. Mayo and Lombard, *Teamwork and Labour Turnover*, p. 23.

20. Mayo and Lombard, *Teamwork and Labour Turnover*, p. 27.

21. Mayo and Lombard, *Teamwork and Labour Turnover*, p. 28.

22. Shils, "The Study of the Primary Group."

23. E. Durkheim, *The Division of Labor in Society*, tr. G. Simpson, (Glencoe: The Free Press, 1947).

24. Landsberger points out that the picture of the individual as socially isolated and disorganized is Mayo's, not that of Roethlisberger and Dickson as portrayed in *Management and the Worker*, where they point in fact to certain closely knit relations and to substantial variability in such closeness.

25. C. Kerr, "What Became of the Independent Spirit," *Fortune*, 48 (July 1953): 110–111.

26. J. H. Goldthorpe, D. Lockwood, F. Bechhofer and J. Platt, *The Affluent Worker: Industrial Attitudes and Behaviour*, (Cambridge, England: Cambridge University Press, 1968), p. 180.

27. H. Blumer, "Sociological Theory in Industrial Relations," *American Sociological Review*, 12 (1947): 271–278.

28. Mayo and Lombard, *Teamwork and Labour Turnover*.

29. Fox and Scott, *Absenteeism*, p. 28.

30. Landsberger says that this view is, again, that of Mayo, not of Roethlisberger and Dickson as expressed in *Management and the Worker*. Their emphasis, he says, is not on poor communication or insensitive supervisory behavior, but on constant technological change and on the disquieting effects of such change on occupational prestige groupings. See Landsberger, Chapter IV.

31. E. Mayo, *The Social Problems of an Industrial Civilization*, (Boston, Harvard University Graduate School of Business Administration, 1945), p. 75.

32. Several of these suggestions are contained in E. Mayo and G. F. F. Lombard, *Teamwork and Labour Turnover*.

33. This term appears to have been introduced by H. L. Sheppard in "The Treatment of Unionism in Managerial Sociology," *American Sociological Review*, 14 (1949), pp. 310–313.

34. This was no doubt influenced by the fact that trade unions were not in fact a prominent part of the Hawthorne industrial relations scene at the time of the Roethlisberger and Dickson studies.

35. My Cambridge colleague, Peter Duncan, points out the inconsistency between the argument that because of their in-plant concentration the Mayo's group research lacked the power to explain workers' behavior and the fear that their theories could be used by managements to manipulate workers.

36. See my later chapters on conflict.

37. D. Bell, "Adjusting Men to Machines," *Commentary*, 3 (1947): 79–88.

38. Mayo, *The Human Problems*, pp. 175–176.

39. Mayo, *The Human Problems*, p. 177.

40. T. N. Whitehead, *Leadership in a Free Society. A Study in Human Relations Based on an Analysis of Present-day Industrial Civilization*, (London: Oxford University Press, 1936), p. 254.

41. Whitehead, *Leadership in a Free Society*, p. 254.

42. Whitehead, *Leadership in a Free Society*, p. 169.

43. Whitehead, *Leadership in a Free Society*, p. 170.

44. R. Dubin, "Workers," *International Encyclopedia of the Social Sciences*, 16 (New York: Macmillan, 1968).

45. R. Dubin, "Industrial Workers' Worlds: A Study of the Central Life Interests of Industrial Workers," *Social Problems*, 3 (January 1965): 131–142.

46. Goldthorpe, et al, *The Affluent Worker*, pp. 144 and 145.

47. Goldthorpe, et al, *The Affluent Worker*, p. 179.

48. Dubin, "Workers," pp. 564–571.

49. See M. Argyle, G. Gardner, and F. Cioffi, "Supervisory Methods Related to Productivity, Absenteeism and Labour Turnover," *Human Relations*, 11, no. 1 (1958): 23–40.

50. G. C. Homans, "The Study of Groups," *International Encyclopedia of the Social Sciences*, 6 (New York: Macmillan, 1968).

51. O. Benoit Guilbot, "The Sociology of Work," *International Encyclopedia of the Social Sciences*, 7 (New York: Macmillan, 1968).

5 : Kurt Lewin, Field Theory, and Group Membership[1]

KURT LEWIN (1890–1947) was a German psychologist who lived and worked in that country until 1933, then left and settled in the United States where he worked for fifteen years.[2] While in Germany he was associated with the Berlin Gestalt group of psychologists, much of whose influence appears in his subsequent work. The Gestaltists held that direct experience was *organized* and that what one perceived was determined by the whole, of which the object on which one was focusing was part. One of their central ideas was that psychological phenomena should be conceived as existing in a "field," that is, "as part of a system of coexisting and mutually interdependent factors having certain properties as a system that are not deducible from knowledge of the isolated elements of the system." [3]

FIELD THEORY

Lewin applied and developed field theory into an area far wider than perception. He emphasized as causal elements in behavior social and psychological forces bearing on the person insofar as these were immediately operative on and in him at the time of that behavior. Key elements in the social field of the individual were the groups of which he was a member or to which he aspired. The groups to which an individual belonged were the ground for his perception, feelings, and actions.

Lewin conceived of behavior as a change in the state of a given field over a given period of time.[4] In trying to understand individual behavior, the field that he regarded as relevant was the "life space" of the individual, by which he meant the person together with his psychological environment *as this existed for him*. In the same way, the "life space" of a group was the group together with its environment *as it existed for the group*. This raises the question of what one means when one says something "exists" for a person or group or is real to them. Obviously, what the person consciously perceives in his environment is real for and to him. But, as Lewin pointed out, there are elements in the environment and in the mental functioning of persons of which they may be unaware or only partially aware but which also have demonstrable effects on them. These include unconscious mental states. Lewin therefore included such factors in the life space.

Lewin's conceptions of field and life space gave him a particular way of dealing with historical events. He asserted that the only determinants of behavior at a given time or over a given period were the properties of the field at that time. This was not to deny the impact of the past but to argue that it mattered to the explanation of current behavior only insofar as it exerted its effects currently, that is, left a residue. What should be taken into account in analyzing behavior was not the past, present, or future as this could be objectively identified or estimated but its effects or presence in the life space—what Lewin called the "psychological past," "psychological present," and "psychological future." As Lewin saw it, a person's views about his past may be incorrect, or his fears for the future might be unjustified—nevertheless they are real presences in his current life. Also, the psychological past and psychological future (past and future as envisaged) can form important elements in the present psychological field. (It is easy to see the correctness of this viewpoint when one thinks of individual career decisions. Clearly, whether a man decides to stay in his present job or to accept a transfer will depend largely on what he has made of his past career experience and what he estimates as likely to happen in the future, whether he is in fact right or wrong.)

Lewin insisted that the field which influenced a person should be described not in objective terms but in the way it existed for the person at the time his behavior was being studied. A teacher, he pointed out, would never succeed in giving proper guidance to a child if he did not understand the psychological world in which the child lived. To substitute for that world the world of the teacher or anyone else would not be objective but wrong. In other words, the state of a person and of his environment are not independent of each other, since the person reacts to the environment as he perceives and conceives it.[5]

Practically all studies of change in work groups and organizations have come to adopt this viewpoint—an important element which encourages or blocks people from changing is their own estimate of the consequences for them.

The meanings of what are objectively the same phenomena differ for different people, that is, manifest themselves differently in their life space. As Lewin said, while the passengers in a riverboat are enjoying the scenery, for the pilot the shape of the hills may mean that he should turn sharply, and waves in the middle of the river mean dangerous rocks.

Field theory emphasized that any piece of behavior was a result of a multitude of factors—indeed, the scientific task of the social scientist was largely seen as the identification of the presence, relative strength, and interdependence of the several factors operative at the time. Lewin argued that it was advantageous to start with a characterization of a situation as a whole rather than by picking out one or other isolated element whose importance could not be judged until the other main elements were found. After this first approximation, the various parts of the system could be examined more closely.

Lewin sought in one part of his work to explain behavior in situations that are "cognitively unstructured," that is, in which the person does not know what to do in order to gain his objectives (this might apply, for instance, if he is in a new employing organization). In such situations behavior is often exploratory, vacillating, contradictory, inefficient, unstable, and attended by conflict. Perception of the situation shifts rapidly and is readily influenced by minor cues and suggestions from others.[6] This form of analysis highlights the effects of lack of a "cognitive map." Apart from adolescents, Lewin and his colleagues applied these ideas to minority group members, the physically handicapped, and the nouveaux riches.

Lewin emphasized the reality of social and psychological variables and processes. He underlined the fact that groups have properties of their own that are different from the properties of their subgroups or their individual members; this is in principle no different from the fact that molecules have properties which are different from the properties of the atom or ions of which they are composed. There is no difference of reality between the properties.

EXPERIMENTAL METHODS
IN SOCIAL SCIENCE

Lewin has been the outstanding leader in the application of laboratory-style experimental methods to human study. Very many experiments of this type now contribute to our knowledge of the results of differing methods of supervising work forces, results of differing methods of decision-making, social influences on judgment, effects of interaction, and social isolation and levels of aspiration.

Unlike Mayo he originated styles of research, mainly in the laboratory but to some extent also in the field, embodying specific hypotheses and replicable results. "I am persuaded," he wrote, "that it is possible to undertake experiments in sociology which have as much right to be called scientific experiments as those in physics and chemistry." [7]

Lewin's argument about experimental methods in social science is important because it deals with the question of how far one can rely in a field like organization studies on laboratory experiments. Formidable obstacles have been seen in the way of scientific analysis of human behavior: much real-life interaction takes place in very large social units in such a dispersed manner and over such long periods of time that it is extremely difficult to study it comprehensively and systematically. As an example, Lewin pointed out that if one wanted to determine the meaning of a foreman's conversation with a worker, it might be necessary to study the foreman or his interaction with his men over weeks or months and also to observe meetings of workers, of management, and between workers and management. He knew that social anthropologists approach these matters through protracted observation, the use of selected informants and the use of questionnaires, but his view was that certain of the issues could also be approached experimentally. This followed from his field theory approach: he pointed out that the *pattern* of a total field was sometimes more important than its size and that it was possible to study fundamental social constellations experimentally after transposing them to a smaller size, in a way that would leave the essential structural characteristics unaltered. Experiments would be artificial if merely one or two factors were reproduced in the laboratory but not if the essential pattern were reproduced. We should be able to investigate the properties of large groups on relatively small-scale *models*. We do not need, he said, to study whole nations to understand how far our perceptions of others depend on our own culture. We can compare experimentally in the laboratory one form of group leadership with another or one style of persuasion with another. This can be done without losing sight of the fact that in real life contrasts and loyalties arising from outside the small face-to-face group might affect behavior.

Lewin also advocated the conduct of real experiments with existing "natural" social groups. This poses great problems because expense would rule out the conduct of formal experiments with populations of factory size or nation size. But, as he said, social scientists can enter into collaborative arrangements with business managers and administrators in which different styles of leadership or different structures could be formally evaluated and compared. He pointed out that group experimentation has the scientific advantage that it is a form of social management: to be successful it must take into account all the factors that are important for the case at hand. His famous dictum is that there is nothing so practical as a good theory. It is to Lewin and his colleagues that we owe the notion of action research, that is, the notion of the social scientist as an active colleague with administrators in planned social change, learning about the character of social situations by trying to change them.

CHANNEL THEORY

Lewin introduced the idea that communications and influences reached the field of psychological force on a person by traveling through channels that could be systematically identified. At points of these there were also identifiable roles and persons who facilitated or obstructed passage through these channels. These were "gatekeepers," a concept he first used in his food research on the role of the housewife. He pointed out that food comes to the table through various channels, including the shop, the pantry, the garden or the gift, and that it moves step by step through each channel, with varying speeds and numbers of steps between intermediate points. Some channels get blocked or moves through a channel get resisted while others get opened up; for example, eating in restaurants may increase and eating at home diminish under certain conditions. But food does not move through a channel by its own impetus; entrance and movement is effected by persons acting in effect as "gatekeepers." These might be housewives, husbands, maids, or shopkeepers. In studying food habits, therefore, it was necessary to understand in detail the main channels through which food arrived at the table and what pressures and what opposition there was from whom and for what reasons at various stages in the channel; in particular, what external and subjective forces bore on the gatekeepers. He thought the same ideas applicable to any organized institution. Social life in an organization could be conceptualized as flowing through channels: thus discrimination between staff members was linked with particular gates (for example, committees) and gatekeepers (managers) who determined who was hired, transferred, or promoted. Channel theories have the advantage that they include more than personal psychology and group influence. As Lewin and his colleagues showed, technological, economic, cultural, and psychological variables interact to affect the path and charasteristics of a social channel.

Channel theory has subsequently been effectively used by other investigators to study the flow of new information, ideas, and techniques to housewives,[8] to medical practitioners,[9] and to farmers.[10] The concept has usefully emerged of a particular category of gatekeepers who constitute opinion leaders, that is persons who are disproportionately influential among their acquaintances in determining attitudes to new commodities or ideas. It has usually to be empirically established in each case who the local opinion leaders are on a particular issue. Sofer reports a case in an industrial firm in which, on his advice, the senior management successfully released news of crucial changes in policy through selected staff who, although fairly junior in status, had long service and were well known to be persons to whom others referred back for clarification on new events.[11]

QUASI-STATIONARY EQUILIBRIUM

Lewin introduced the idea of a "quasi-stationary" level in social processes within groups, by which he meant that groups often contain constellations of forces that lead to self-regulating processes. At a physiological level, the body is kept in a relatively constant level over extended periods by certain regulatory processes. Similarly, a worker who does not feel well may compensate for this by deliberately greater effort. In the same way again, self-regulatory processes exist within groups—if a worker is absent others tend to make up for this deficit, or, if senior leaders leave, contributions like theirs may appear from other group members. Group processes and social habits such as speed and level of production were not static affairs but live processes. Like moving rivers, they kept a recognizable, characteristic form over time. In both cases the determining constellation of causal forces could be ascertained—there were definable causes of social consistencies akin to the river's sources of water and the contours of the river bed.

Unless quasi-stationary equilibrium existed it would, of course, be even more difficult than it is to study social behavior, because there would hardly be much point to sampling group behavior if it did not repeat itself or remain constant over periods.

At the same time it is, naturally, of great scientific interest to know what forces cause a particular form of self-regulation or quasi-stationary equilibrium—for instance, in the case of output control.

Along Lewin's line of reasoning, level of output (or of prejudice) would be analyzed as a quasi-stationary equilibrium. As he would see it, deviation by an individual would result in increased efforts by others to bring him into line or, failing that, to expel him.

LEVEL OF ASPIRATION

Lewin opened up a fruitful area of experimental research on level of aspiration, that is, the degree of difficulty of the goals toward which people strive. In his early work he emphasized that whether a person feels he has succeeded depends on the relation of his performance to his ambitions rather than on the objective accomplishment in itself. His ambitions, the standards he sets himself, and his evaluation of his achievements are affected by cultural setting: in Western cultures the characteristic first reaction to a level of aspiration situation is to choose a level above previous performance and under most conditions this relationship is maintained. Standards for performance derive from the person's self-image and from groups of which he is a member or serve as models. The person is affected in his expectations by the average of his past performances, by the trend of these (whether stable, upward, or downward) and, more than other single performances, by his latest performance.

Like much of Lewin's work, results that can be gained in this field (greatly developed since Lewin) can be widely applied, for instance in understanding relationships between motivation and occupational or organizational mobility; the standards that individuals and work groups set themselves; preparedness to take risks; and reactions to success and failure.

EXPERIMENTAL STUDIES
OF LEADERSHIP STYLE

Lewin left a legacy of studies by his group on topics such as leadership, group standards and values, and social atmosphere. Among other things the studies pointed to (1) what seems to be the greater efficacy of demo-cratic (participative) than other forms of management and (2) what seems to be the greater efficacy of decisions backed by group agreement and group support than individual edict. This work contrasted the conse-quences for behavior when the forces on people are imposed by others (*induced forces*) with situations in which the forces stem from their own needs (*own forces*). The main findings were that participation in goal setting is more likely to create own forces toward a goal while at the same time reducing the necessity for superiors to exert continuous pressure or influence. This has, of course, subsequently become the heart of the argu-ment put by many contemporary organizational theorists against close supervision.

The experimental studies of Lewin's group in these fields helped to pro-vide scientifically based arguments in favor of democracy as against the dictatorial government systems then emerging. This work further stimulated changes in styles of leadership in industrial and educational groups and training programs designed to help people identify their own characteristic group behavior and learn more effective methods of working with others.

Lewin has been called the "outstanding psychological exponent" of de-mocracy. "More clearly than anyone else has he shown us in concrete operational terms what it means to be a democratic leader and to create a democratic group structure."[12]

The classic studies on leadership style (conducted between 1938 and 1942) were by Lewin with members of his group or by his colleagues separately under his stimulus.[13]

In a first exploratory study, Lippitt matched two hobby groups of five eleven-year-olds and made them the object of an experiment on two con-trasting styles of leadership. One group was led in an authoritarian way, that is, the leader (1) took the initiative in starting new paths of action for his subordinates, (2) gave commands without explanation, (3) introduced changes without consultation, and (4) criticized people's work without adding proposals for alternative action. In the democratic group the leader (1) made all policies a matter for group discussion and decision, (2) sketched out the general steps to the group goal, (3) suggested alternatives from which a choice could be made, (4) let members choose work partners and divide up the work as they liked, and (5) tried to be objective and factual in praise and criticism.

The authoritarian type of leadership led to a higher degree of aggressive-ness of members toward each other; a greater diversion of attention and interest to objects and persons outside the group; a greater tendency to pick scapegoats as objects of hostility; a lower level of interest in the work being undertaken; less appreciation of the group's product; and a greater inclination to work individually and in isolation rather than together in a generally accepted division of labor.

Subsequently Lippitt and White studied the consequences for group behavior of democratic, authoritarian and laissez-faire types of leadership. In the latter new category there was complete freedom for individual or group decisions, with a minimum of leader participation; the leader (1) supplied materials and answered questions on request, taking no other part in work discussion; (2) did not participate in the work at all; and (3) made no attempt to appraise or regulate the course of events.

In the earlier study, each group continued as authoritarian or democratic throughout. In this series, the way of handling the four groups used was varied deliberately in the course of the study to determine whether a change in their management would bring about the predicted modification in group structure. At the end each group had experienced each type of leadership and each leader had had a turn at working each way. In this way the experimenters ruled out differences caused by the personality of members and of the leaders.

In assessing the results one must bear in mind the fact that the central aim of the groups was not productivity or high quality work. It was just as important for the boys to enjoy themselves under club conditions.

The results I mention are based on both experiments. The autocratically managed groups tended to create mutual hostility and aggression, with scapegoating and on some occasions submissive behavior and destruction of the boys' own property; and latent discontent expressed in dropping out and relief shown later after these groups ended. There was more dependence on the leader in these groups and less individuality was shown.

The laissez-faire groups were relatively disorganized (by the boys) and less satisfying than the democratic groups. Taken as a whole, the democratically run groups were the most efficient, that is, when one takes into account the achievement of both work and social goals. From the narrower work-goal point of view, the largest amount of work was done in autocracy and the least (and worst quality) in laissez-faire.

The key overall finding was the importance for group satisfaction and group output of the style of behavior adopted by the leader and the type of structure fostered on each occasion.

In a separate study following the same type of reasoning, Bavelas and Lewin describe "a rapid retraining of mediocre leaders into efficient democratic leaders." [14] The field involved was recreation and the trainees selected so that their age and substantial experience would present particularly difficult cases for retraining. Subjects were matched and divided into an experimental group and a control group, both of which were observed before and after the training of the experimental group. In the training sessions Bavelas and Lewin tried to make group leaders "more sensitive to the multitude of ways in which a leader can meet the various social situations." This was done through reciprocal observation by leaders of each other; through study of films comparing democratic, autocratic, and

laissez-faire leadership; and through the adoption of democratic methods
by the experimenters. The results showed in the experimental group a reduction of authoritarian control methods and an increase in "democratic
initiative-stimulating" methods; a shift toward more varied teaching methods which also relied more on independent efforts of students; and a
change to higher morale. Bavelas and Lewin add that

In spite of the new and added responsibilities inherent in democratic leadership,
the trainees felt keenly their own greater calm and poise, after they discovered
that group discipline no longer depended upon their constant vigilance.[14]

GROUP DECISION-MAKING

Lewin carried out a pioneer experiment in changing food habits with
six groups of women, the groups ranging in size from thirteen to seventeen
members.[15] The aim was to increase the use of beef hearts, sweetbreads,
and kidneys—foods to which most housewives and families feel an aversion.

In three of these groups, lectures were given which (1) stressed the
health properties of these foods, especially their vitamin and mineral value;
(2) linked the problems of nutrition with the war effort; (3) pointed to
the economy of the foods; and (4) informed those present of ways
of preparing these dishes in an attractive way. Duplicated recipes were
distributed. The women were then asked if they might be interested to
serve these meats.

In the other three groups, (1) a short introduction was given in which
the experimenter (again) linked the problems of nutrition, war effort, and
health, (2) a discussion was started (instead of making the main event a
lecture); this centered on the food provision problems of such housewives,
the general problems of change in family food habits, and the problems in
particular that would be entailed in a change to using sweetbreads, beef
hearts and kidneys, (3) only after interest had been voiced and toward
the end of the discussion did the experimenter offer the remedies, recipes,
and preparation techniques used in the previous work. The women were
then asked how many would be interested to serve these meats.

In both groups the experimenter ascertained before and after the experiment how many had served any of the foods in the past and how many
served them afterwards.

The follow-up showed that only 3 percent of the women who heard the
lectures served one of the meats never served before, while, after the
group decision meetings, 32 percent of the women who had attended and
had not previously used the meats served one of them.

Lewin concluded from this that discussion of a problem and a possible
course of action emerging from this leads to a much higher level of involvement than a lecture or set of instructions where one is a passive
listener. In understanding the way decisions are reached we need, he

argued, to consider not only personal motivation but also the social forces bearing on the person—in this case the interest of those around one and the tentative expression of opinion that the action might be worth taking.

In a later version of this experiment, Lewin compared effects of a request from an authority unconnected with a group with a decision taken by a small group.[16] The content of the request was to use whole wheat rather than white bread.

In eight groups (four matched pairs), appeal by impersonal request was less successful than a group decision. In the former, whether or not people did as requested continued to depend on their personal taste. On the other hand, a group goal accepted by the members was more likely to override personal taste. This showed the significant influence on motivation and conduct of a decision taken collectively by a group.

Work subsequent to that of Lewin has raised questions about what really causes the greater effectiveness in these cases of group-based decisions, which might come either from greater interest engendered or from public commitment to a decision. But Lewin's argument was that in these situations group membership and identification with colleagues with whom one had shared the decision-making process exerted forces that held a person in a position and helped to keep him from temptation to deviate.

Whatever the precise derivation of the forces involved, the Lewinian studies showed clearly that group-decision methods produce more change than the exertion of influence directly from outside.

RESEARCH IN INDUSTRY

The early work of Lewin and his colleagues in industry was particularly associated with a manufacturing plant owned by the Harwood Manufacturing Corporation in Virginia.[17] In this company, the employees were mainly local women. Their wages were higher than they had received elsewhere and they liked their jobs, but their turnover was high, their work pace was slow and their output low, about half as much as for workers in the same grade in northern plants. Conventional financial incentives for extra output were not successful and direct supervisory pressure resulted only in increased turnover. To help solve these problems, Lewin suggested that the firm stop putting pressure on individual employees, deal with them as group members, and show them that it was possible for them to reach without strain the production standards set by management. To meet this latter suggestion the firm brought in from another plant sixty highly skilled and experienced operatives who soon met the production standards. The original employees slowly began to improve their output; so far as can be judged this was because the previously unattainable goal now appeared practicable.

The company later employed one of Lewin's close associates, Alex

Bavelas, to conduct a research program on human factors in factory management. Building on the leadership style studies of Lippitt and White, and on Lewin's food-habits experiments, Bavelas studied the effect of giving a group of employees more control over their output and letting them take part in setting goals. He led a series of meetings at which personal work methods were compared, the difficulties of increasing production were discussed, and ideas were thrown up on ways of reducing these difficulties. Management agreed to make certain of the changes suggested, and the worker group decided to try to raise output to a level not previously attained. They did so and maintained the new level for five months, while no comparable increase took place elsewhere in the plant. Lewin's explanation for this was that a decision to change had to be made to link motivation with action—a decision seemed to have a "freezing effect" because it stimulated individuals to keep to their intention and because participation in or agreement with a decision constituted a commitment to a group. Bavelas then tested discussion on its own *versus* decision by holding discussion meetings about raising production, without decisions—only a small increase in output followed.

In another Harwood experiment Bavelas introduced increased self-management in the work situation. This was conducted with two groups of workers paid on a piecework basis but required to turn in a minimum quota. Members of one group were allowed to plan their own hourly or daily work level, so long as they maintained the quota: they raised their production .to an appreciably higher level and maintained this. Over the same period the production level of a control group remained unchanged. Lewin and Marrow commented particularly on the fact that the increase was brought about without external pressure and without increased tension.

Bavelas was succeeded by J. R. P. French, who continued the association with Lewin. A leadership training program was introduced which concentrated on problems of winning cooperation and involved self-examination of behavior, feedback to participants on their impact on others, and group problem solving. Instead of relying on lectures and discussions of theory, the staff involved supervisors actively through techniques in which they tested alternative ways of handling problem situations, and these were commented on by audiences of colleagues.[18]

One problem in the Harwood plant was the opposition of employees to the employment of women over thirty, despite the labor scarcity occasioned by the war. When objective evidence was offered that women over thirty could acquire the requisite skills, staff remained skeptical. French suggested that senior staff themselves conduct an inquiry into the relative efficiency of older workers already employed by the firm, leaving it to them to specify criteria of efficiency (including speed of learning, output, absenteeism, and labor turnover). The team making the enquiry discovered that the older women compared well with others, and in this way convinced themselves.

Their own active participation in collecting the evidence and considering its implications were evidently necessary to change their opinions.[19]

Another Harwood problem concerned difficulties of changing work methods in response to technical innovations or variations in demand and competition. Such changes always meant that some workers had to move from jobs where they were highly skilled to others where they had again to be put in the position of learners, with attendant loss of status, lowering of morale, and feelings of failure. Workers resisted such transfers, which were accompanied by resistance, hostility, and a falling-off in production. French and Coch (the personnel manager) approached the problem by experimenting with alternative ways of introducing change, each involving a different amount of collaboration by employees in working out the details of the new job arrangements.

The first variation involved no participation by employees in planning the changes in type of work they were expected to make, though an explanation was given to them. The second involved participation through representation of the workers in designing the changes to be made in the jobs. The third involved total participation by all members of the group in designing the changes. The experimental groups were roughly matched for efficiency and observed cohesiveness in the groups.

The no-participation group averaged lowest production after the change, hostility was expressed against the supervisor, there was a lack of co-operation with him, there was conflict with the methods engineer and deliberate restriction of production. The represented group learned the new methods faster and were more cooperative. The total participation group recovered fastest, and their output was as good as or better than that of the represented group.

Taken overall, the experimenters found that the rate of recovery was directly proportional to the amount of participation and the rates of turnover and aggression were inversely proportional to the amount of participation.[20]

The experiment was partially replicated in a Norwegian factory in 1956 where nine four-man groups were changed to producing new products with a new piece rate. Four control groups participated little in planning the changes but the others participated to an extent similar to the total participation in the first experiment.[21] (Apart from the geographical difference, larger numbers were involved and subjects were established male workers, not young women as in the Harwood case).

The experimental groups showed greater job satisfaction and more favorable attitudes to management. But an important (cultural) variable was found to be expectations—how much participation was thought legitimate. There were probably more persons in this study who thought that even the amount of participation they were given was less than they felt legitimate.

There was no difference in production, partly because of strong group standards restricting production.

GROUP DYNAMICS TRAINING

Lewin was one of the founders of the method for learning about processes in small groups widely known as "group dynamics training." The central event is a T (Training) Group in which members of small groups act as participant observers in learning about group structure, group processes, and the impact of group membership on individuals. Participants are helped by specialists in group processes to use their experience of interpersonal relations in carefully designed meetings or specially created communities as so-called laboratories for developing their insight into what happens when people meet to work together and into their own typical behavior in group situations. They are helped to examine their own assumptions, expectations, attitudes and goals, and to project themselves into the roles of others in order to gain a measure of objectivity and detachment in considering their own ways of relating to others. The assumption is that increased insight will lead to increased competence in leadership and in obtaining cooperation from others.

In the United Kingdom a closely related form of work takes place under the name of "group relations training." [22]

The initial contribution of Lewin and his colleagues in this field came in response to a request to him in 1946 from the Connecticut State Inter-Racial Commission to help train leaders and conduct research on ways of combating racial and religious prejudices.[23] Lewin organized a two-week conference with forty-one student-members which would try simultaneously to train its members, to measure changes that took place in them, and to analyze the change process. The idea was that the participants would in this way learn more effectively how to change community members.

Student members of the conference were first interviewed about what they hoped to gain from the conference experience; their hopes included acquiring insight into change processes and into their own attitudes and values.

At one point in the conference program, student-members asked if they might attend the meetings of the staff at which reports were made on processes in the member-groups, that is on their own behavior. It was apparently through the attendance of the students at these meetings that the staff discovered the role of direct feedback to people of information on the way they have been behaving, as observed and interpreted by an experienced and impartial outside person. Such sessions became the heart of the conference, with a regular dialogue now taking place between those whose behavior was being analyzed and those who were making the analysis. The behavioral data of the staff were being enriched and the student members increased their understanding of the meanings and ramifications of their own behavior.

Participants were interviewed six months after their return to work. About three quarters reported that they were using methods learned at the conference and about the same proportion spoke of increased sensitivity to the feelings of others.

An important consequence of this experience was the establishment in 1947 of the National Training Laboratories.[24] This organization has conducted and stimulated a substantial number of programs in group dynamics as well as influencing methods used in other areas of social science teaching and action research.

Lewin died in 1947 before the first N.T.L. Session.

Discussion

CONTRIBUTIONS TO UNDERSTANDING

Lewin's work has had a major impact on the way that social scientists have come to view behavior in organizations. His ideas have reduced the temptation to ascribe behavior purely to the motives or attitudes of individuals. He has taught social scientists to extend analysis and explanation to include a much wider range of influences, including the structure of group memberships and relationships in which persons are always embedded, and the value systems that govern modes of interaction. His field approach imposed on the social scientist the discipline of attempting to enumerate even if crudely the totality of forces bearing on a situation before trying to analyze a problem in detail or suggesting remedial action. Even if one emerges with an analysis particularly emphasizing one set of factors, a Lewinian approach is a reminder that one is isolating from a wider set of causes.

Lewin extended our notions of what constitutes reality. The ways in which a person sees the world around him are concrete for him and have to be treated as real by those who have dealings with him, even if they differ in their diagnosis of what the situation "is really like."

He helped to correct the atomistic view of individuals implicit in conceptions of communications as stemming from a central source to individual members of an organization, a community, or a wider society. Instead, he showed that there were communication and information paths that could be reliably identified, and along which were key persons who exerted disproportionate influence. Again in the field of communication and information, he established the importance of feedback to individuals and groups in helping them to assess their own efforts and the repercussions of their actions, and to redefine the standards to which they might realistically aspire.

He and his colleagues pioneered research indicating the connection between participating in a decision and being willing to carry it out in the spirit intended.

Lewin opened up new possibilities of obtaining social science data through experimental means, chiefly through his ingenuity in designing small-scale models of interaction that contained salient features of the larger systems about which he wished to generalize. He also showed the scientific pay-off possible in collaborative research between social scientists and administrators, making it possible to study real life situations and to test hypotheses about the effects of changes.

While the impact of Lewin's ideas was widespread he particularly influenced two major research institutes. These were the Institute of Social Research at the University of Michigan, to which his Research Center of Group Dynamics moved from the Massachusetts Institute of Technology, and the Tavistock Institute of Human Relations. Both Institutes have put considerable emphasis on field theory in explaining organizational phenomena. Both have been leaders in their respective countries in collaborative research designed on Lewinian lines simultaneously to produce scientific results and to benefit the operational systems within which the research is carried out.

CONFLICT AND CONFLICT RESOLUTION
Lewin acknowledged that

On whatever unit of group life we focus, whether we think of nations and international politics; of economic life, . . . of race or religious groups, . . . of the factory and the relations between top management and the worker, . . . we find a complicated network of . . . conflicting interests.[25]

It has, however, been pointed out by L. Coser that Lewin displayed contradictory attitudes on the subject.[26] When, in 1939, he wrote on the position of Jews in Europe, he was, as Coser says, quite "militant," writing that

More than words of self-defense are necessary to change social reality. Certainly Jews will have to try everything to ally themselves with any other force seriously fighting Fascism. . . . Only the efforts of the group itself will achieve the emancipation of the group.[27]

He saw aggressive behavior as appropriate for a minority group in a conflict situation. In the same paper he showed that he saw the "positive" effects of conflict when he commented that Jews living together in the Diaspora were kept together partly by the pressure of hostile majorities.

But, as Coser points out, seven years later Lewin discusses conflicts with a view to their avoidance or management rather than through expressing them or fighting them out, and he is by then writing that the research need for social practice can best be characterized as research for social management or social engineering.[28]

At this stage in his work Lewin was assuming that social conflicts are dysfunctional and disintegrating and that the social scientist must concern himself with their reduction.

Lewin's (later) approach to conflict is exemplified by the case study he provides and commends of Bavelas' intervention in "The Solution of a Chronic Conflict in Industry." [29] The case began with a confrontation between a mechanic and a supervisor about priorities in maintaining machines, about their respective competence, and about the allegedly hostile remarks that were being made by them about each other in discussions with operatives. Bavelas focussed on the contributions to the problem made by "objective" work difficulties stemming from the technology in use. He engaged the disputants in collaboration with him in fact-finding so that they became involved in diagnosis and thereby more prepared to identify themselves with a consequent solution. He redirected attention to the production task of the plant. He demonstrated that on some points disputants started in agreement.

Lewin points out that in this case the procedure of the psychologist was based on the hypothesis that the permanent conflict is at least partly the result of some fault in the organization of production [30] and that the production system has to be analyzed to lay open the source of the difficulty. He notes that the operatives were brought in to the fact finding and suggestions for new procedures were sought from them—in order to gain their later cooperation.[31] The facts were collected largely through group discussion, with the advantages that a richer and better balanced picture of the problem was built and the atmosphere of openness created increased readiness to cooperate. Bavelas had taken into account the importance for the disputants of their work environment in their life space. He had done much to lower the general level of emotionality at every step in the procedure. Bavelas had also taken into account the importance of the perceptions of the leading disputants. Fact finding was made the cornerstone of the change but the facts would have played no part in the solution unless participants had accepted them as correct. Lewin writes on this point that:

It is correct that a "sufficiently objective" picture of the production channels and problems should arise from the investigation. But it is equally essential to realize that the "subjective" view of the participants counts most.

This case contains evidence bearing on the criticisms commonly made of work in the Lewinian tradition that it neglects in-plant power variables; that it does not take into account the wider social environment of the plant; and that the attempted solutions of the problems posed are manipulation of people. Lewin makes one direct comment here on the power issue in that he describes Bavelas as sensitive to power relations in securing permission to approach subordinates (by going through supervisors). There is again just one reference to "environmental" factors when he refers to the importance to operators of fairness and underlines the importance of fairness in American culture. But these mentions are peripheral to the main thrust of his explanation of the case. In regard to the issue of manipulation, Lewin is himself rather defensive in his discussion. He asserts that Bavelas had not tried to trick anyone into an agreement and that his presentations were in line with the facts. At the same time, it is undeniable from Lewin's own description that Bavelas had deliberately tailored his presentations. In Lewin's words,

The reality is presented correctly, but those aspects are brought into the fore which are linked with the psychological situation of the person in question and are helpful in bringing about favourable permanent motivation. Rather than speaking of dividing authority, the psychologist points to the possibility of making decisions and of taking responsibility which is actually not the mechanic's job.

And shortly after, Lewin adds,

Wherever possible the individual is praised; his feeling of insecurity or anxiety is eased . . . ; everything is done to have the persons appear in a good light to each other without becoming unrealistic.

IMPACT ON ORGANIZATIONAL PRACTICE

Lewin's work has had important effects on practice. These have derived partly from the accounts of his experimental work; partly from the conceptions of organization and behavior implicit in his approach; and partly from the work of social science consultants in disseminating his ideas. The dissemination process has been accelerated by the popularity of group dynamics training, with its central notions of the importance of group membership, the social psychological processes that stem from involvement and the use of feedback.

Very large numbers of industrial managers, civil servants, and social service administrators have by now been exposed to management courses. In their social science content these courses typically underline the operational implications of findings by the Lewin school on democratic versus authoritarian style of decision-making and on the importance of participation in decision-making processes. They have been taught, among other things, that conservatism and "resistance to change" are institutional or group phenomena usually more amenable to change through approaches to groups of colleagues rather than to individuals.

There is a further Lewinian influence in the instruction now commonly given on the importance of perception, emotion, and social psychological processes in intergroup and interpersonal conflicts. "Practitioners" are now beginning to emerge within firms, who conceive their responsibility as defusing tense situations by refraining from taking sides while helping disputants to gain insight into their situations, to see the points of view of their opponents, and to realize how they are themselves perceived.

TECHNICAL LIMITATIONS IN RESEARCH

Some of the major studies done by Lewin and his colleagues do not stand up well to close examination today.

In the Food Habits experiments there were many obscurities. One cannot tell from the experiments exactly what it was that "worked" in enabling participants to persevere with attempts to change their behavior. Was it the experience of sitting in with persons facing similar problems? Was it the relationship with the experimenter? Or was it the process of working over problems and rehearsing the difficulties to be faced subsequently?

The leadership experiments similarly left many questions unanswered. How far were the results attributable to the expectations of members and the extent to which these were met? How far were they attributable to the meanings implicit in permission being given to research workers to attempt new methods of administration? How far had the whole Harwood culture been permeated by Lewinian ideas and what limits did this place upon their representativeness?

Despite Lewin's emphasis on group dynamics, one learns little from his work about what actually goes on within groups. He reports particular types of outcome after particular types of treatment; and we are not informed at all about the nature of the intervening processes. Paradoxically these constitute in his own work exactly the same "black box" approach as in behaviorist schools of psychology that deal in inputs and outputs, stimulus and response, rather than in the dynamics of process. This pioneer of the social psychological study of the group actually told us remarkably little about what goes on inside groups. This came later, partly from his successors and partly from social psychologists with a more clinical orientation.

It may seem over-critical to point to the limitations of the original research of Lewin and his colleagues in view of the new vistas of technique and substantive findings they opened up. At the same time this provides some antidote to the prevalent tendency to over-interpret the findings or to generalize too freely from them. These over-interpretations and over-generalizations are, no doubt, partly Lewin's own responsibility in that they are connected with his eagerness to establish the superiority of democratic rather than authoritarian methods of conducting social life. Much of this has been corrected by the sober qualifications made by colleagues and successors. But this work has caught public imagination in a way that other social research has not, with the result that it is the early conclusions from the classic Lewinian experiments that have become the currency of new generations of social science users.

N O T E S

1. For a brief authoritative statement on Lewin as a social psychologist, readers should see R. Lippitt's section on him in D. Sills, ed., *International Encyclopedia of the Social Sciences,* 9 (New York: Macmillan, 1968), and M. Deutsch's article on "Field Theory" in volume 5 of the same publication. I deal with Lewin here only as a direct contributor to the understanding of behavior in organizations.

2. At Cornell, in the School of Home Economics, at the Iowa Child Welfare Research Station (from 1935 to 1944) and at the Massachusetts Institute of T⸱ ⸱hnology, where he set up a Research Center for Group Dynamics. This center moved to the University of Michigan after his death.

3. M. Deutsch and R. M. Krauss, *Theories in Social Psychology,* (New York: Basic Books, 1965), pp. 15–16.

4. The sections here on field theory and changes in a field are based mainly on K. Lewin, *Field Theory in Social Science. Selected Papers,* D. Cartwright, ed., (London: Tavistock Publications, 1952).

5. Similar ideas as to the importance of studying persons' environments so far as possible from their own standpoints have a long and honorable history in sociology and social anthropology. Early in this century Emile Durkheim and his colleagues studied the ideas which primitive people held about themselves and the world around them, that is the ways in which they represented their environments to themselves. Different cultural groups have been shown by anthropologists to see the same physical and social events differently and to differ both in what they regard as evidence about these events and the interpretations they place on the evidence. It is necessary, though extremely difficult, for social scientists to collect and understand evidence of this sort. This is partly because it is so difficult to get outside one's own standpoints and partly because one cannot ask the other persons directly about their standpoints: these rest on bases that are unacknowledged and unanalyzed. See J. Beattie, *Other Cultures. Aims, Methods and Achievements in Social Anthropology,* (London: Cohen & West, 1964).

6. See Deutsch and Krauss, Ch. 3.

7. *Resolving Social Conflicts. Selected Papers on Group Dynamics,* G. W. Lewin, ed., (New York: Harper, 1948), p. 71.

8. E. Katz and P. Lazarsfeld, *Personal Influence: The Part Played by People in the Flow of Mass Communications,* (New York: The Free Press, 1964).

9. J. S. Coleman, E. Katz and H. Mendel, "The Diffusion of an Innovation Among Physicians," Sociometry, (1957): 253–270.

10. F. E. Emery and O. Oeser, *Information, Decision and Action: A Study of the Psychological Determinants of Changes in Farming Techniques,* with the assistance of J. Tully, (Melbourne: Melbourne University Press, 1956).

11. C. Sofer, *The Organization From Within,* (London: Tavistock Publications, 1961).

12. G. W. Allport, Foreword in K. Lewin, *Resolving Social Conflicts. Selected Papers on Group Dynamics,* G. W. Lewin, ed., (New York: Harper, 1948).

13. See K. Lewin, R. Lippitt and R. K. White, "Patterns of Aggressive Behavior in Experimentally Created 'Social Climates'," *Journal of Social Psychology,* 10 (1939): 271–299, and R. Lippitt and R. K. White "The Social Climate of Children's Groups," in R. G. Barker and J. Kounin, eds., *Child Behavior and Development,* (New York: McGraw-Hill, 1943), pp. 485–508. Accounts of this series of experiments are also

given in R. Lippitt and R. K. White, "Leader Behavior and Member Reaction in Three Social Climates," in D. Cartwright and A. Zander, *Group Dynamics,* 3rd edition, (London, 1968), and "An Experimental Study of Leadership and Group Life" in Maccoby et al, *Readings in Social Psychology,* (New York: Holt, Rinehart & Winston, 1938).

14. A. Bavelas and K. Lewin, "Training in Democratic Leadership," *Journal of Abnormal and Social Psychology,* 37, no. 1 (1942): 115–119.

15. Reported in 1947 in "Group Decision and Social Change," *Readings in Social Psychology,* T. M. Newcomb and E. L. Hartly, eds., (New York: Holt, Rinehart & Winston, 1947). The research was probably conducted in 1941–1942.

16. "Forces Behind Food Habits and Methods of Change," *National Research Council Bulletin,* no. 108 (1943).

17. This is described by A. J. Marrow, who was at the time an officer of the company, in his book *The Practical Theorist: the Life and Work of Kurt Lewin,* (New York: Basic Books). The Harwood studies took place between 1940 and 1947.

18. Marrow notes that French used many of the same techniques at the first session of the National Training Laboratories in Bethel, Maine, in 1947 pointing out that the in-plant program came first.

19. The whole study is described in J. R. P. French and A. J. Marrow, "Changing a Stereotype in Industry," *Journal of Social Issues,* 1 and 2 (1945).

20. L. Coch and J. R. P. French, "Overcoming Resistance to Change," *Human Relations* (1948): 512–532.

21. A full report of the Norwegian experiment is in J. R. P. French, J. Israel and Dagfin, "An Experiment on Participation in a Norwegian Factory: Interpersonal Dimensions of Decision-Making," *Human Relations,* 13, no. 1 (1960). A paper by Coch and French in E. Maccoby, T. M. Newcomb and E. L. Hartley, eds., *Readings in Social Psychology,* 3rd edition, (New York: Holt, Rinehart and Winston, 1958) refers to both the original Harwood and later Norwegian studies.

22. See discussion in Chapter 11 on the work of the Tavistock group during the war and subsequently, and also Chapter 19 on laboratory methods in intervention by social scientists in organizational change.

23. This account is based on Marrow, *The Practical Theorist,* and R. Lippitt, *Training in Community Relations,* (New York: Harper & Row, 1949).

24. Although a, or the, key figure in the intellectual foundation of the work of the National Training Laboratories, Lewin did not write as extensively directly on the internal dynamics of groups as on other subjects. His ideas on the subject can, of course, fairly easily be inferred from his other work, particularly that concerned with inducing changes in persons by using group forces. Two of his articles bearing directly on laboratory training are K. Lewin and P. Grabbe, "Conduct, Knowledge and Acceptance of New Values" (which appears in *Resolving Social Conflicts),* and K. Lewin, "Frontiers in Group Dynamics" (which is in *Field Theory in Social Science).* An account of laboratory training methods by three leading figures in the N. T. L. program is L. P. Bradford, J. R. Gibb and K. Benne, eds., *T-group Theory and Laboratory Method: Innovation in Re-education,* (New York: Wiley, 1964).

25. K. Lewin, "The Research Center for Group Dynamics," *Sociometry Monographs No. 17.* (New York: Beadon House, 1947), p. 7.

26. L. Coser, *The Functions of Social Conflict,* (London: Routledge and Kegan Paul, 1956), pp. 25 and 26.

27. "When Facing Danger," *Jewish Frontier,* (September 1939), reprinted in *Resolving Social Conflict,* p. 163.

28. K. Lewin, "Action Research and Minority Problems," *Journal of Social Issues,* 2 (1946), pp. 34–36.

29. This case was first published in *Proceedings of Second Brief Psychotherapy*

Council, (Chicago: Institute for Psychoanalysis, 1944). It is reprinted in *Resolving Social Conflicts,* pp. 125–141. The subsequent quotations are from this paper.

30. Thus conceptualising the problem in what we would today describe as socio-technical terms.

31. Lewin repeatedly emphasized the importance of the principle in inducing change that complete acceptance of previously rejected facts can be achieved best through the discovery of these facts by the group members themselves.

6 : Classic Experiments in Social Psychology I. Asch, Sherif, and Milgram on Group Membership and Conformity

THIS chapter describes and discusses certain outstanding experiments in social psychology which have particular relevance to the behavior of persons within small task groups and within more complex organizations made up of task groups. These experiments point to the profound influence which groups have on the judgments and behavior of their members and to forces which influence members to adhere to group values and standards, sometimes against their spontaneous inclinations.

While this chapter deals primarily with the topic of relations *within* small groups, the next deals mainly with relations *between* small groups.

My object in including an account of these experiments is to point up their relevance to the study of organization. As one reads these accounts, one immediately recognizes many of the group forces which Taylor, Mayo, Myers, and Lewin discussed in relation to organizations. The experimental studies demonstrate the effects of group forces more directly and dramatically; help us to assign weights to the amounts and directions of group forces exerted under specified circumstances; expose the process of influence to analysis over time; and provide indications of the circumstances under which persons tend to accept or reject attempts at influence.

At the same time, it is prudent to indicate some of the factors distinguishing experimental laboratory groups from real-life task groups in organizations.

The average age of organizational colleagues is higher than that of laboratory subjects (who are usually college students). Organizational colleagues usually know each other, or at least know of each other, while members of laboratory groups are strangers to each other. Organizational colleagues relate to each other in established roles and do not form these anew in each interaction. The association of organizational colleagues usually continues over years while that of laboratory groups typically lasts only a few hours or, at most, a few days. The tasks on which organizational groups are engaged are genuine tasks, not tasks contrived for the occasion or resembling games. The rewards and penalties associated with organizational membership matter more to members than those associated with laboratory group membership. Every work group in an organization is functionally related to other work groups and in many cases the membership of these work groups overlap. Hierarchical differences exist between associates in an organization. It is normally the ambition of persons at the middle and higher levels of organizational hierarchies to ascend the hierarchy.

After an account of certain of the classic experiments on group membership and conformity, I discuss their probable implications for organizational functioning.

GROUP INFLUENCE ON JUDGMENT
WHERE STIMULI ARE AMBIGUOUS

An impressive stream of experimental research in social psychology since the mid-1930s has illustrated the tendency of individuals to be influenced or controlled by the judgmental norms of groups of which they are members.[1]

The classic experiments in this field were conducted by M. Sherif and S. Asch. In their work we see the influence of the group upon an individual (his tendency to conform) even when no special moral rightness attaches to group judgments and even when the sanctions attaching to deviation are not obvious but are subtle and indirect. Their work illustrates the force of group standards on the individual, the way these acquire an element of "should," "rightness" or being "proper," and "required," even where there is no moral principle underlying the standards. (One is justified in extrapolating to the conclusion that if group standards affect the individual substantially even where there is no special moral principle or no special sanctions involved, the scope for their doing so is even greater where such moral principles and sanctions are involved.)

Sherif illustrated the effect of group norms upon individual judgment in a pioneer laboratory experiment.[2]

For his experiments Sherif selected as the object of judgment a particular perceptual phenomenon, the autokinetic effect. This refers to the fact that when one looks at a stationary pin point of light in a completely dark room, it seems to move after a few seconds, though the amount of movement that one thinks one sees varies between people.

In one part of the experiment Sherif started with individuals who were required to make their own judgments about the amount of movement that was apparently taking place. The judgments of each subject were found to concentrate around a central tendency and on successive days their level remained substantially constant. But there were consistent and substantial differences between the judgments of the different individual experimental subjects. Each established for himself a range over which movement appeared to be taking place and a norm (standard) of the amount of movement he perceived.

Then Sherif brought together in the same experimental situation two or three subjects whose respective levels of estimation were known and whose estimates differed from each other substantially. In the new situation each announced aloud how much movement he thought had taken place. Under these conditions the judgments of the individuals approached each other significantly. Each departed from his previously established judgments and converged toward a common level. (The same result was obtained when subjects had no prior individual experience.)

In a variation, Sherif first placed the subjects in the group situation together, then, after some experience of this, got each of them to work on his own again. In this case the initial agreement was closer than before, and in the individual sessions the subjects maintained the judgments they had established in the preceding group sessions. That is, individual judgments after group experience were more uniform than individual judgments before group experience, and a measure of stability was maintained even after the group members had been separated from one another.

The central finding from this work is, that having formed their individual judgments, people then modified them to a common level on learning the judgments of others in a group situation. At first Sherif was merely pointing to the fact that interaction with others and knowledge of their views led people whose initial judgments were widely divergent gradually to converge. A norm finally arose for his research cases because of this process of convergence. In his initial work, he meant by a norm merely the average modal judgment, that is, he used the term "norm" in the statistical sense of "standard." In his later work he suggested that there was an element of social constraint, that is, that what becomes the central "statistical" standard of a group, their usual, most frequent, most common standard of judgment or behavior, tends to become enforced by the group as the right way to think or behave.[3]

Quite apart from the issue of moral rightness, Sherif's experiments, like those of Asch reported below, illustrate vividly the Gestalt principle that perception of an item is influenced by its context. In this case, the perception of the amount of movement of the light is affected by the social context—the presence of others.

GROUP INFLUENCE ON JUDGMENT
WHERE STIMULI ARE UNAMBIGUOUS

In Sherif's work the stimulus about which the convergence occurred was ambiguous and there was no right or wrong answer on the amount of movement actually occurring. The next important question posed was by Asch: if the judgment that had to be made was less ambiguous, more definite and clearer would individuals still be affected by the known judgments of others so as to move toward them in those judgments?

To study this question, Asch gathered groups of seven to nine college students in a classroom and explained that they would be shown lines differing in length and that their task would be to match lines of equal length.[4] The experimenter would place on a board two sheets of cardboard. The one on the left contained a single line, the standard; the one on the right three lines of which one was equal to the standard line on the left. The task of the students was to select from the three lines the one equal in length to the standard line. Each subject had to call out in turn which line on the right was the same length as the one on the left.

In the first two trials the discriminations were simple and each individual monotonously called out the same judgment.

Suddenly this harmony was disturbed at the third trial. While all other subjects called one of the three lines equal to the standard line, one seated toward the end, claimed some other line to be the correct one. As the experiment proceeded this behavior was repeated several times, the same individual continuing to disagree with the group from time to time. After one or two disagreements, this deviant person would begin to look bewildered and worried at the contradictory judgment of the whole group, fidget, smile in an embarrassed way, speak to his neighbor, or stand up in an attempt to look more carefully at the card.

The reason for this behavior is that all but that one person were, unknown to him, cooperating with the experimenter by giving unanimously wrong judgments. They had been instructed which (wrong) line to choose; to act in a natural, confident way; to behave as if they were equally new to the experiment; to present a united front in defending their judgments if necessary; and to leave the naïve subject near the end of the seating.

Repeated for thirty-one critical subjects, the experimenter found that two-thirds of their responses were correct and independent of the majority trend but one-third were errors identical with those made deliberately by the majority.

By contrast, the errors obtained in a control group of subjects who reported their judgment privately in writing were 7.4 percent of the total.

Thus, while the preponderance of estimates by critical subjects were correct and independent, there occurred a pronounced movement toward the majority. Their erroneous pronouncements contaminated one-third of the estimates of the critical subjects. The group majority deeply affected the one person in the minority, even though he was usually objectively correct and their judgment went against the objective evidence of his senses. Convergence toward a common position took place even though the stimulus was not ambiguous.

Asch experimented further with the size of the discrepancy between the judgment of the majority and that of the individual, making the majority judgment differ more glaringly. Increasing the objective discrepancies did not abolish or decrease the majority effect. He experimented with the provision of one or more extra people who answered correctly. Providing the critical subject with at least one partner strikingly diminished the number of his wrong answers.

Asch discusses the dynamics of the individual's behavior, why the person in the minority of one behaves as he does. He makes the point that considerable variability existed in response among the minority persons, some of whom remained much more steadfast than others. This finding has been borne out in many studies of personality in relation to persuasibility and attitude change—even where convergence and conformity are observed, substantial differences exist between individuals in the extent to which they alter their views when confronted with those of other persons.

CONSENSUAL VALIDITY

The Sherif and Asch studies illustrate in a dramatic way that one's judgment can be affected by others. This seems to be the case not only in judgments of physical facts but also in judgments of what is right and wrong.

We tend to lean in our judgments on "consensual validity," that is we regard our judgments and opinions as correct if others think the same, the convergence or conformity apparently replacing objective measurement or research where this is impossible or inconvenient.

GROUP INFLUENCE ON BEHAVIOR

The Sherif and Asch experiments dealt with judgments. Subsequent experimental studies have shown that similar convergence and conformity effects occur with other forms of behavior. Contributors to a fund to buy a gift for a departing secretary have been shown to subscribe sums similar in amount to those listed before them. Subjects who were given a list with subscriptions averaging 25 cents contributed an average of 28.5 cents, and those presented with a list averaging 75 cents contributed an average of 63.5 cents.[5]

Willingness to sign a petition asking for new administrative action has been shown to be affected by whether another person has already signed the petition in the presence of the subject. Where another person had just signed, 89 percent of those asked signed the petition; with no such person present, 58 percent signed. When another person present had just refused to sign, only 29 percent of subjects signed the petition.[6]

In a similar study, students were asked under different conditions to agree to take part in a psychological experiment. When asked in the presence of a person who had just agreed, 67 percent of subjects also agreed; when asked with no one else present, 41 percent agreed; when asked in the presence of someone who had just refused to take part, only 38 percent agreed to do so.[7]

A striking experiment on the effects of group pressure on behavior was reported by Milgram in 1964.[8] He relates his work directly to that of Asch. He pointed out that there is an important distinction between conforming in one's judgment and in one's behavior. A person may, he says, pay lip service to the norms of a group but then be quite unwilling to carry out the kinds of behavior the group norms imply. Or, more than this, he may accept at verbal level a group standard or belief and yet be unable to translate this into action. The main point of Milgram's 1964 experiment was therefore to see if persons would perform under group pressure acts that they would not have performed in the absence of social influence. The studies we have described immediately above do, of course, give us some indications that behavior is significantly affected by the presence or absence of others and by the way others are seen to behave. These areas of behavior are not really crucial to the person. The Milgram experiment goes much further. Here subjects are required to act in a way that seems physically harmful to others, that is, quite contrary to those normally required of them, and which can be assumed to be contrary to their internal beliefs and standards.

Milgram's group pressure experiment had followed a previous set in which he had studied obedience by instructing a "naïve" subject to administer an electric shock to a victim.[9] We need first to describe these. Each subject is invited to take part in what appears to be a learning experiment ostensibly set up to study the effects of punishment on memory. As the experiment proceeds, the subject (in the role of teacher) is instructed to administer apparently increasingly more intense shocks, going from a low voltage to "Danger: Severe Shock," to a learner if he does not make correct responses to a test. The victim (in fact a confederate of the experimenter) deliberately fails to give correct answers and responds to the shocks as if he is feeling first discomfort, then moderate, then severe pain, to the point where he ceases to respond at all, presumably because he is beyond response. In the first series, each of forty subjects went beyond the expected break-off point of very strong shock, and twenty-six obeyed the instructions of the experimenter to the end, going on until they were administering the most potent shock.

In the group pressure variation, Milgram posed the question of whether a group would induce an individual to give more severe shocks than he would otherwise be inclined to give. Milgram's experiments to test this involved eighty men, aged twenty to fifty, equally distributed for age and occupational level between experimental and control conditions. In this variation, the experimental group consists of three "teachers" testing and then "punishing" a "learner-victim." Two of the three teachers, as well as the learner, are confederates of the experimenter and only the third teacher is a real experimental subject. The procedure is the same as before, except that a group process now enters the decision as to how much shock to administer when the learner responds incorrectly. The two confederates are required to suggest an increasing shock to be given each time, then the third has also to suggest a level and then has actually to give the shock (as he believes), the arrangement being that the shock to be given is the lowest of the three suggested. Exactly as before, the learner-victim makes errors, and complains of discomfort and pain when the apparent shock level rises. In a control group the naïve subject is also instructed to administer a shock each time the learner errs, but he is told that he is free to select any shock level.

In these group pressure experiments the presence of the confederates significantly increased the level of shock suggested by the experimental subject and administered by him. The average level to which the experimental subjects went was significantly higher than those in the control groups. Only two control subjects administered shocks beyond the tenth voltage while twenty-seven experimental subjects went beyond this point.

Personal Variations in Susceptibility to Influence

Social psychological studies have shown that propensity to be influenced by others (or to maintain relative independence) is a stable individual characteristic showing up repeatedly in different situations. In one such study, Ferguson ascertained the responses of a sample to religious, humanitarian, and nationalist issues, then told respondents the answers given by a fictional majority. When the attitude test was repeated, those persons who changed their attitudes on one of the issues in the direction of the reported majority also changed on the others.[10]

One of the main personality attributes closely related to propensity to conform appears to be dependency on others. Children tend to conform more than adults, and women more than men, and, among male adults, there is also some evidence that those who rate high on dependency in personality tests conform more than others.

Most of the studies we have described involve making responses in the presence of others. This condition has been varied in experiments where respondents are asked to make their judgments privately, that is, are told that these will not be communicated to other members of the group. Some tendency to conform continues to be found but less than in the public situations.[11]

A further finding in such experiments has been that subjects feel tense, uneasy, and under stress when confronted with a consensus among others which runs contrary to their own impressions. Stress declines when the individual agrees with the group. These findings are derived partly from subjective reports of respondents and partly from physiological measures.[12]

Group Norms and Personal Identity

A recent discussion of group formation by M. and C. W. Sherif [13] makes several points important to understanding the relationship between group membership, group norms and the influence of these upon the person. They draw particularly on studies, including their own, in which new groups were formed and studied while they developed norms. They point out that a group norm does not necessarily refer to an average of individual behavior, but indicates rather what is expected as proper, moral, or ideal. Usually some latitude is provided and individual members may vary somewhat in the extent to which they adhere to the norms. In other words, a person may vary a fair amount before facing risks of being criticized or expelled.

Since the acceptance of group norms is an important aspect of group membership, and membership is a factor in self-concept, members tend to experience guilt or shame if they violate the norms. This is one reason why in stable groups the great bulk of conforming behavior occurs without direct social pressure or threat of sanctions.

An important factor in determining how far the attitudes and behavior of a person are influenced by a particular group is the importance of that particular group in his life. His personal identity becomes tied to the main groups of which he is or has been a member and this exerts a stabilizing force on his adherence to the key group norms.

Deviation from Group Norms

A number of factors apart from personality determine how far persons allow themselves to be influenced or resist being influenced.

A paper by Festinger in 1950 [14] and a book by Festinger, Schachter and Back [15] summarized some of the main propositions which could by then be stated with some confidence. These emerged out of a program of experiment and field studies. Festinger begins with the fact that where one can test the validity of one's opinions against physical realities dependence on others for validation tends to be low. But where the issue is a matter of belief the dependence on "social belief" (the opinions of others) is high. An opinion, a belief, an attitude, is, he says, correct, valid, and proper to the extent that it is anchored in a group of people with similar beliefs, opinions, and attitudes. People tend to move into such groups, and out of groups which do not agree with them. If there is a discrepancy in opinion, attitude, or belief within a group, forces to communicate arise, particularly if agreement is thought necessary for some goal shared by group members and particularly if individual members are dependent on this particular group for reaching that goal.

Festinger quotes an experiment by Schachter at this point which showed that when a deviate maintained an extremely divergent point of view five times as many communications were addressed to him as to others in increasing attempts to get him to conform. Those group members who did not want the deviant to remain in the group tended to stop communicating with him toward the end of the discussion. (This is the well-known phenomenon of "sending someone to Coventry" when he does not subscribe to norms of attitude or behavior which colleagues consider important to their common interests.) The group has power over the opinions and attitudes of a member to the extent that he wishes to remain in the group, that is, to the extent that membership of the group is attractive to him. But, if the person's opinion is supported within some other group of which he is also a member, he will be more resistant to attempted influence. In other words, the nonconformist is likely to have competing loyalties and outside affiliations.

In a discussion of status and conformity, E. P. Hollander examines the paradox that leaders both conform to group norms and yet may act to alter them by influence. He suggests a highly plausible explanation in essentially social process terms as follows:

Early in interaction, conformity to group expectancies serves to maintain or increase status, particularly as it is seen to be combined with manifest contributions to the group; at a later phase, however, the status thus generated permits greater latitude for idiosyncratic behavior. Thus, if an individual conforms to expectancies early in his exposure to the group and if he shows characteristics of competence, he accrues credits. For evident deviations from expectancies, or poor performance, he loses credits. If he exhausts his credit balance completely, pressures are applied to remove him from the group, or, at the very least, he is no longer perceived to be a member. At the other pole, if he continues to amass credits he attains a threshold permitting deviations from common expectancies, but with constraints imposed by newly differentiated expectancies.[16]

This conclusion appears to have been anticipated by E. C. Hughes, writing in 1946.

It is characteristic of social groups to demand of the newcomer a strict conformity which will show that he accepts the authority of the group; then, as the individual approaches the center of the group and becomes an established member, they allow him a little more leeway.[17]

Persons of low status in groups are also especially apt to deviate from group norms. As Homans says, the group loses some leverage on the behavior of such persons. If a person has low status and interaction with him has been reduced

the next time he has a choice whether or not he will do something they want, he is the less apt to do it the less they have to take away from him in the way of esteem and interaction. He has nothing to lose by nonconformity . . . if the risks of innovation are there to be taken, upper status people are better able to take them than others, for they have less than the others to gain by doing the same old thing and less to lose by trying something different.[19]

Discussion

There are two important themes in the study of organizations to which these experiments and discussions relate directly. These are, first, the pressures that appear to be exerted on members of organizations (particularly on staff in administrative grades) to subscribe to leading organizational values and, second, the pressures exerted by work groups on their members.

FORCES TOWARD CONFORMITY
WITH CENTRAL ORGANIZATIONAL VALUES

As the young person moves toward a particular type of occupational and organizational fate, he comes to accept it as inevitable, proper or appropriate for him, to develop appropriate values and attitudes, and to shed those that would be discordant.

The person enters the organization predisposed to accept its influence, to be pervaded by its values, and to identify his fate with it.

The individual learns the behavior appropriate to his position through interaction with others who hold normative beliefs about what his behavior should be, and who reward or punish him for correct and incorrect actions.

The new member, whose work identity is not yet stabilized, is anxious to demonstrate his competence, his fitness for membership, his potential contribution, and his preparedness to learn and collaborate. He tends to respond readily to influences upon him, more particularly to those emanating from immediate colleagues and seniors who show a readiness to guide, instruct, and help him, to induct him into the procedures, and to offer him colleagueship—provided, of course, that he will share their ideology.

Long-service members need to maintain their self-esteem and tend to adopt some part of the organization's work and implicit purposes as their own.

The new entrant is first an object of appraisals and training and later also an appraiser and trainer with part of his function now being to impart organizational values and encourage identification with them. In so doing, he tends further to accept these as his own.

The work roles available have embedded in them a contribution to some centrally defined organizational objective. Either occupants of those roles accept those objectives as their own or go through motions consistent with the attainment of those objectives, a process which tends in itself to turn into the commitment which they may have originally intended only to simulate.

Insofar as progress is accessible, the hierarchical system of status, authority, power, esteem, and material rewards functions as an incentive system to adopt or conform to central organizational values.

There is a set of clear-cut images for the individual of what he can become and of what rewards can be associated with this.

The experience of managing others tends to align one with the organization. One tends to adopt the viewpoints of one's employer once one has to start choosing persons to help or succeed one in the functions for which one feels responsible.

In the case of the man whose work becomes predominantly managerial, a substantial component of his expertise becomes his knowledge of the organization and his familiarity with its culture, problems, and personnel. He becomes a specialist in the politics of his employing organization. This makes the possibility of alternative organizational memberships less salient in his life.

Past investments in a career within the organization will have involved sacrifices in terms of organizational values. Continued subscription to organizational values helps to provide a rationale for past investments.

Because work organizations are synthetic, deliberately created, special purpose associations, involving massive investments, their managements try to screen out from the start those persons who do not appear to have appropriate motives and values for effective organizational membership; to recruit only those who are prepared to adjust themselves to organizational values; and, so far as potential administrators are concerned, to select those who are especially cooperative and malleable. Entry into the organization, and early contacts and experiences tend to be carefully designed so as to impinge on the newcomer in ways that will elicit his interest and enthusiasm and begin to bind him to the organization. Substantial efforts continue, through training courses, conferences, counselling and assessment procedures, and the informal diffusion of managerial iedologies to support and reinforce commitment to the organization.

LIMITING AND OPPOSING FACTORS

Certain factors in work organizations will mitigate pressures to conformity.

The organization is not a total institution. The organization member is under its direct influence only part of the day. He has a life apart from the organization, and personal needs and pressures other than those associated with the organization. He has reference groups and membership groups other than those involved in the job. Indeed, part of the contribution of the executive or technical specialist may stem from his external affiliations and identifications, since these help to give him independence of mind and judgment.

There are prevalent at any given time within a large organization several leading values which are equally respectable and acceptable as guiding philosophies for individuals and groups but which, in fact, contradict each other—growth versus consolidation, technical excellence versus mass marketing, concern for shareholders versus concern for customers. These provide scope for legitimate deviations, in the sense that adherence to some of these values excludes others.

The hierarchical form of organization of the industrial firm frees some persons of high status (whose tasks are, in any case, largely innovative) as well as persons of limited mobility from pressure to conform in their behavior and values.

Many organizations, and certainly all industrial organizations, are pervaded by a felt need to maintain or increase their economic strength by innovation. Unusual behavior and ideas tend, therefore, not to be rejected out of hand, but to be scrutinized in case they are of potential value.

Much of the behavior of the organizational member and many of the decisions he executes are prescribed for him by his seniors rather than being a spontaneous group product. They are not the result of a process with which the person necessarily feels identified, so that he may not feel closely bound by them.

It is within the terms of an organizational contract for a member to maintain a predominantly instrumental relationship with his employing organization, that is, to confine himself to fulfilling his role obligations without adopting the values of his employers.

Organizations consist of overlapping primary groups constituted on the basis of geographic proximity, task similarity, and complementary or linked occupational fate. For the individual organizational member his work life consists of operating membership of at least one and, more likely, several of these. Since the dominant values of each group differ somewhat from each other and from central managerial values, there is always some scope for choice by the individual and for support in his choices.

NOTES

1. R. B. Zajonc, in the entry under "Conformity," *The International Encyclo-paedia of the Social Sciences,* 3, (New York: Macmillan, 1968) has defined a social norm as a uniformity of behavior among the members of a given group that is not the result of physiological or biological uniformity among them. His entry discusses the Sherif and Asch experiments described below and their implications for theories of conformity.

2. Originally reported in *Archives of Psychology,* no. 187 (1935), also in *The Psychology of Social Norms* (New York: Octagon, 1936, reprinted 1966).

3. On this point see entry on Norm by W. L. Kolb in Gould and Kolb, eds., *A Dictionary of the Social Sciences* (London: Tavistock, 1964), who quote from Sherif's subsequent discussion of the implications of his experiments in M. Sherif and C. W. Sherif, *An Outline of Social Psychology* (New York: Harper, 1948).

4. Reported in S. E. Asch, *Social Psychology* (New Jersey: Prentice-Hall, 1952), Chapter 16.

5. R. R. Blake, M. Rosenbaum, and R. Duryea, "Gift-Giving as a Function of Group Standards," *Human Relations,* 8 (1955): 61–73.

6. R. R. Blake, J. S. Mouton, and J. D. Hain, "Social Forces in Petition-Signing," *Southwestern Social Science Quarterly,* 36 (1956): 385–390.

7. M. E. Rosenbaum, "The Effect of Stimulus and Background Factors on the Volunteering Response," *Journal of Abnormal Psychology,* 53 (1956): 118–121.

8. S. Milgram, "Group Pressure and Action against a Person," *Journal of Abnormal and Social Psychology,* 69, no. 2 (1964): 137–143.

9. See report in S. Milgram, "Behavioural Study of Obedience," *Journal of Abnormal and Social Psychology,* 67, no. 4 (1963): 371–378.

10. L. W. Ferguson, "An Analysis of the Generality of Suggestibility to Group Opinion," *Character and Personality,* 12 (1944): 237–243. Quoted in Zajonc, "Conformity."

11. M. Deutsch and H. B. Gerard, "A Study of Normative and Informational Social Influences Upon Individual Judgment," Journal of Abnormal and Social Psychology, 51 (1955): 629–636; and J. W. Thibault and L. H. Strickland, "Psychological Set and Social Conformity," *Journal of Personality,* 25 (1956): 115–129.

12. The subjective reports come from Asch's studies and the physiological from K. W. Back et. al., "An Interpretation of Experimental Conformity Through Physiological Measures," *Behavioural Science,* 8 (1963): 34–40; and E. D. Lawson and R. Stagner, "Group Pressure, Attitude Change and Autonomic Involvement," *Journal of Social Psychology,* 45 (1957): 299–312.

13. *International Encyclopaedia of Social Sciences,* 6 (New York: Macmillan, 1968).

14. L. Festinger, "Informal Social Communication," *Psychological Review,* 57 (1950): 271–282.

15. L. Festinger, S. Schachter and K. Back, *Social Pressures in Informal Groups* (New York: Harper and Row, 1950).

16. E. P. Hollander, "Conformity, Status and Idiosyncrasy Credit," *Psychological Review,* 65, no. 2 (1958).

17. E. C. Hughes, "The Knitting of Racial Groups in Industry," *American Sociological Review,* 11 (1946): 517.

18. G. C. Homans, *Social Behaviour, Its Elementary Forms* (London: Routledge and Kegan Paul, 1961).

7 : Classic Experiments in Social Psychology II. Sherif on Intergroup Conflict

IN this chapter we turn to experiments on relations between groups, particularly to studies of the conditions under which groups cooperate and conflict with each other.

In this case we have the advantage of a brilliant series of investigations by Sherif, in which we leave the laboratory for the field experiment. Sherif, perhaps more than any other social psychologist except Lewin, has been ingenious in designing field studies which retain some of the main virtues of laboratory experiments, including matching of samples, close observation, comparison of before-and-after situations, and, to a certain extent, measurement of behavior.

At the same time one has to keep in mind again the youthfulness of his subjects, the fact that they were not indefinitely committed to each other as colleagues, and the fact that they interacted largely in designed tasks in which games were prominent. Nevertheless, any student of organizational life will immediately notice how Sherif's researches accord with his own experience. In particular, students of intergroup conflict will find that Sherif is reporting, reproducing at will, and manipulating exactly the same processes as occur between real-life groups.

Again, group norms form a leading theme in this chapter, because of their intimate link with the topic of conflict. In elucidating that link, Sherif has considerably enlarged our understanding of adherence to norms.

Inducing Conflict

In 1949 Sherif conducted a field experiment designed to test two major hypotheses. These were: (1) When individuals having no established relationships are brought together to interact in group activities with common goals, they will produce a group structure with hierarchical statuses and roles within it. (2) If two ingroups thus formed are brought into functional relationship under conditions of competition and group frustration, attitudes and appropriate hostile actions in relation to the outgroup and its members will arise and will be standardized and shared in varying degrees by group members.[1] As Sherif and his colleagues remarked in 1961, testing of these hypotheses is less concerned with the discovery of new facts than with intensive study through laboratory methods of the particular factors involved in the rise of group structure, group codes, and group norms and in ingroup and outgroup delineations.

To test the hypotheses set out above, twenty-four boys of about 12 years of age from similar lower middle-class backgrounds were brought to an isolated camp site for eighteen days. The boys did not know each other beforehand. No visitors were permitted.

For the first three days all twenty-four boys were housed in one large bunkhouse. They associated freely and all activities were camp-wide, that is, potentially including all boys. They formed their own budding friendship patterns and developed their own leaders or potential leaders. Two groups of twelve were then formed, with friendship subgroups split as far as possible and with the two groups equated for physical size and strength, ability in games and intelligence. The boys were told they had been divided to make it easier to carry out their preferred activities. They were given different colors and divided on a group basis to go to different bunkhouses. For a period of five days the two groups lived, worked and played separately. They had separate tables for eating, they went on separate hikes, they swam at different times or places. Their activities were designed to have a common goal which was appealing to everyone and which made it necessary for everyone to participate and cooperate. By the end of this stage each group had developed an identifiable group structure, including a leader and other defined statuses. Each had certain songs as their own; characteristic views on subjects of common concern; characteristic norms about what to do and how to do it; and sanctions for deviation from these norms. Friendship preferences moved from the previous budding relationships toward ingroup preferences. Each group developed strong ingroup loyalty, solidarity, and group identification. Although there was no consistent hostility or enmity toward the other group and very little functional contact between the groups, each began to refer to the other group in a clear-cut differentiated way—what we do and they do, our pond and theirs. Mentions were made of territorial boundaries and raids. Talk about the other group began to be derogatory and the groups expressed a desire to compete with each other in sports.

Former friendship choices (from Stage 1) were no longer operative. Former friends ignored each other.

In a third stage, which lasted a further five days, the groups were brought together into relationships that were competitive or frustrating to each other. This enhanced ingroup solidarity, increased democratic interaction within the groups, and heightened ingroup friendships. At first, relations between the groups were amiable and the teams cheered each other in the competitive events which took place between teams organized for athletics, soccer, tug-of-war and cleaning of bunkhouses. But, having started as "two, four, six, eight, who do we appreciate" it soon developed into "two, four, six, eight, who do we appreciHATE." Intergroup rivalry rapidly increased; the group on top were accused by the others of dirty tactics and cheating. Each group told the staff the other group were responsible for name-calling and friction.

Situations were also arranged in which it seemed that one group interfered with or frustrated the other. A party was organized with half the food on display crushed and broken, and one group was allowed first access. They took the better food. The second group accused them of being pigs and hogging things. The groups began swearing at each other, brandishing knives and scuffling. Next day, one group dirtied the other group's breakfast table and derogatory posters were hung up. At lunch the groups lined up and began to throw table knives and saucers at each other.

At this stage the staff stopped the fight and discontinued this phase of the experiment. They spent the rest of their time trying to reduce hostility as much as possible by proceeding to camp-wide activities, intervening in quarrels, and so on so that the boys could return home in reasonable shape. One important event was a competitive game with another camp.

Separate experiments in the program directed by Sherif in the 1950s brought out the effects of group structure and of status membership on judgments of the performance of group members. These studies followed the lead provided by the sociologist W. F. Whyte, who had noted that in a street-corner clique in which he was a participant-observer, level of performance in bowling was brought, over time, into line with relative status in the clique.[2] The first of the 1950 studies of performance and status was by Harvey.[3] Harvey found that the higher the status of a member, the greater his tendency and that of other group members to overestimate his future performance. In a more elaborate and larger-scale experiment conducted in 1953,[4] Sherif and his colleagues formed groups of boys along the lines of their 1949 study. Each group was taken separately to a hall where every boy took a turn at throwing a ball at a target twenty-five times and judgments of his performance were made by all members. (In this case the experimenters were dealing with judgments of performance after the actual behavior.) The investigators found that the performance of members of high status was overestimated by other group members, while that of members of low status tended to be underestimated. The extent of over- or under-estimation was positively related to the status rankings.

Conflict and Cooperation

In a further experiment, conducted this time at Robbers Cave State Park, Sherif and his colleagues followed the same general plan but made the central issue the reduction of intergroup hostility.[5] They brought together twenty-two boys all aged about eleven, and of similar education, religious and social class background. None of the boys knew each other before. The boys were kept in two separate groups of eleven during the first phase of the experiment, and each group lived and played together for a week. A status structure developed within each group. Attitudes became stabilized toward group members, especially toward those who were prominent. Norms became standardized in both groups in relation to experiences and behavior which became important to them; for example, toughness and cursing were acceptable in one group but not the other. Deviation from norms led to criticism or being ignored. Each group classified certain places and facilities as "ours". The object of the next phase was to bring the groups together under conditions that would be perceived as competitive and reciprocally frustrating. The process was in part spontaneous, as each group, once they knew of each other, became anxious to play competitive games against each other. They were told that there would be a tournament of contests, and were shown attractive trophies and prizes to go to the winners. During this phase each group used self-justifying and self-glorifying words in relation to themselves and invective and derogatory terms in relation to each other. These competed at first with the wide social norm of good sportsmanship toward opponents. This gave way after two days to increased name-calling, derogation, and avoidance of each other. When one group burnt the flag of the other, plans were made by the flag-owners to reciprocate by fighting, and staff subsequently had to stop the fisticuffs that developed. Later, destructive raids were made and the staff had again to intervene to avoid possible injury. "The end result of the series of competitive contests and reciprocally frustrating encounters was that neither group wanted to have anything whatsoever to do with the other under any circumstances." [6] Negative attitudes had crystallized toward the outgroups, and social distance had developed between group members. The hypothesis that the process of competition and frustration would produce an increase in solidarity within each group was confirmed, except that within the defeated group there was at first an increase in internal friction and an expression of wishes to leave the group. Where this happened, heightened solidarity was then achieved through united cooperative action by the ingroup against the outgroup.[7] Both the winning group and the other continued to glorify themselves. At the end of the second phase the groups were asked to make ratings of their own group and the other. Members of both groups tended to rate the outgroup unfavorably (expressing negative stereotypes) and themselves favorably. The experimenters then returned to the question of the effect of group membership on judgment of performance, giving each member of both groups a task that could be measured and evaluated; the performance of ingroup members was judged significantly higher than that of members of the outgroup. The investigators concluded that "the relationship between groups has consequences not only for the formation of values or social norms within the group, but for the perception and judgments of individual members as well." [8]

A third phase of the experiment began with a series of planned contacts between the groups, lasting fifteen minutes to an hour. These conflicts involved such activities as going to a film together or having meals together. The key variation then introduced was to bring the groups together under conditions involving superordinate goals, the attainment of which was compelling but which could not be achieved by the efforts of one group alone. The hypothesis was that under such circumstances the groups would tend to cooperate toward the common goal. The experimenters put the boys into problem situations all dependent for their solution on communication, planning, and joint action by both groups. In one case both groups were warned several hours in advance that there was trouble in the water-supply system. The experimenters turned off a valve at the water tank and stuffed the open faucet on the tank with pieces of sacking. Several hours after the first warning, the pipes leading to the camp were drained through use. Both groups were summoned to a central place, where the camp administration declared its inability to cope with the water situation within a reasonable time. They said the defect might be leakage somewhere along the pipeline, at the reservoir pump, or in the supply tank, also that in the past vandals had been known to tamper with the supply system. Therefore, to solve the problem several parts of the system had to be attended to and about twenty or twenty-five people were needed to discover the difficulty that day.

Both groups volunteered to tackle the situation, though the details were made up from one group or the other.

When it was discovered that the faucet was stuffed with sacking, the groups pooled their implements for removing it, took turns at the work, accepted suggestions from each other, and rejoiced together when it was over.

This did not eliminate friction. An hour later at supper there was again an exchange of invective on group lines.

A second problem situation dealt with the hire of one of two films everybody wanted very much to see. The groups were called together and told that the camp administration could put up half the money (they knew that one group could not provide all of the rest) for one of the films. The groups cooperated in suggesting how to divide the balance, jointly made computations of per capita contributions, agreed how much each person should contribute, and decided together which film they should see.

Despite these cooperative efforts, seating at the film more or less followed group lines.

In a third problem situation all the boys were taken to an overnight camp some distance from food. When they arrived they went swimming Near lunch time they returned to a laid table with no food on it, to which they all rushed. A staff member announced that he was going to get food nearby, in a truck.

The truck simply would not start. Someone suggested that if twenty boys pulled the truck (on the tug-of-war rope) it would start. After several attempts by the whole group it did, to a chant of "heave-ho" used by one of the groups in previous tug-of-wars.

While the truck was away the question arose of whether the groups should take turns to prepare the food when it came or do so jointly. One group, with some internal dissension, decided to prepare theirs separately.

In fact when the food arrived, all the boys simply started preparing the food together—this was without fresh discussion and in spite of the decision by the one group.

The truck pull had to be repeated that afternoon. This time both groups knew what to do and carried out the plan with the same success. But on this occasion the two lines of rope were not pulled separately by the two groups. The groups intermingled on both ropes. Henceforth, group lines were blurred on such cooperative occasions.

In the closing hours of the experiment, the two groups decided on their own initiative to put on a joint program entertaining each other with skits and songs at a campfire. Also, each requested that they leave the site together in one bus.

In their summary observations on this phase, the experimenters conclude that, as hypothesized, when groups in a state of friction are brought into contact under conditions embodying superordinate goals, the attainment of which is compelling but which cannot be achieved by the efforts of one group alone, they cooperate toward the common goal. They add that the cooperation has a cumulative effect on the reduction of existing tensions. The experimenters checked friendship choices at the end of the third phase and found that there was a substantial shift now in the proportion of persons chosen from the outgroup. (The comparison was with a test made at the end of the first phase.) There was a similar shift in a favorable direction of characteristics attributed to the outgroup.

In their discussion of the findings, Sherif and his colleagues give central importance to what they call "the nature of functional relations between the groups," whether, for instance, the groups are in what we would today call win-lose situations, whether one has (legitimate) claims on the other in the way of managing or controlling them or using their possessions, or whether they have complementary goals. At the same time, they say that even though this is the limiting condition, other factors must be considered as well in accounting for intergroup behavior, such as norms for behavior toward the other group and stereotypes of the ingroup and outgroup. These other determining factors include, they say, the kind of leadership prevailing within each group, the degree of solidarity, the prevailing ingroup norms, appraisals by each group of their relative strengths and resources, and critical experiences in the life histories of the individual members.

Intergroup behaviour at a given time can be explained only in terms of the entire frame of reference in which all these factors function interdependently.[9]

Discussion

GROUP NORMS IN
INTERGROUP CONTEXTS

One of the most striking features of the Sherif research is the speed with which persons who are in geographic proximity with each other and taking part in joint activities develop and stabilize a culture of their own, including characteristic norms about what to do and how to do it and sanctions for deviation from these norms. These norms extend even to the extent of the production of shared distorted judgments of members of different rank.

When told of potential competition with another group, each group begins to standardize ideas that stress their own competence and the inferior standards and motivations of others. Symbols are developed by both groups and each attacks or derogates the symbols of the other. After the competition members of the successful group adhere more closely to each other. The solidarity of the defeated group is at first much reduced, then regained through hostility and resistance to the winners—highlighting the role of projection of hostile feelings toward external groups in maintaining ingroup solidarity. Much more clearly now than in the studies of single groups described in the previous chapter, it emerges that group norms, conformity, and reactions to deviation depend significantly on the place of a group within a larger enclosing structure and on its relations with other groups.

It is also notable that, once a group establishes its own identity and boundaries and crystallizes its own norms and attitudes, these persist into subsequent phases of interaction despite the accumulation of new experiences and evidence that challenge previous ideologies.

The resultant situation has been well summed up by the Sherifs.

The evidence indicates that when relations between groups are generally those of harmony and cooperation, the evaluative core of stereotypes attributed by one group to the other is generally favourable. Since few groups which have existed for a long period of time have managed to maintain completely harmonious relations at all times, some attributed traits, even in a generally favourable stereotype, will be negative or uncomplimentary. However, even such unfavourable traits are affected in some degree by the favourable evaluative core. Likewise, when relations between groups rather consistently involve conflicting aims and interests, a generally unfavourable evaluative core results; even traits which might be favourable in other contexts are affected by this negative evaluation.[10]

ADULT GROUPS IN COMPETITION

The Sherif experiments described were conducted with adolescent boys who did not know each other well beforehand or were brought face-to-face for the first time in competitive situations where one group's gain represented the other group's loss.

Shepard has reported on a series of group experiments with adults in management laboratories which also involve intergroup competition and analyzes their behavior both during and after the competitive events.[11] His results reinforce and elaborate those of Sherif and bring them closer to an organizational context.

He describes in an essay the common outcomes of such encounters, starting from two face-to-face groups of about twelve members who already have some experience of working together.[12] The two groups are given the same task and each elects a representative to present its solution to a judge. Each group, he remarks, begins with its own internal loyalties and unresolved tensions, and these are easily projected outward in the form of competitiveness. Once they start the task which is to be judged competitively, members move toward a more rigid and hierarchical set of relationships than they had before. When the spokesmen for each group first confront each other (in the presence of their constituents), each group rates its own spokesman higher, with the other just below him. As the encounter proceeds, the rating of one's own spokesman stays high but that of the other spokesman falls. If the encounter is protracted, each side begins to downgrade even its own spokesman. Expectations of him are unrealistic. As far as ratings of the quality of the groups' performances are concerned, each group typically rates its own high and that of the other as medium.

Shepard remarks that "individuals may be good losers, but groups almost never are."[13] After the judge has given his decision, the winners often upgrade the other group's solution slightly, though keeping it below their own. But the losers are less charitable. They never feel that justice has been done and they think the judge was wrong. They do not concede that both solutions may have been good or that the decision was difficult to make. When an item is common in the solutions of the groups, the losers do not perceive it to exist in the others. Shepard concludes from these reactions to losing that conflict sharpens belief in the uniqueness of one's own group and reduces the sense of common features or interests.

Winners become euphoric and smug. Losers first deny the reality of losing and argue that their solution really was better. Then, even if told there will not be another contest, they make hypothetical plans for winning next time. Finally, the group tends to split and scapegoating starts, with one member claiming that if his suggestions had been accepted by his colleagues their side would have won. While this may seem a destructive process, Shepard points out that at least the losers realize that they have internal problems and must work on them and this may lead them to change their internal structure. The winners, by contrast, are in Shepard's words, "trapped in the rigid structure which won for them." [14]

A second type of "conflict trap" is suggested to exist subsequently for the relationship between the groups. It now becomes difficult, Shepard says, to establish any relationship between the two groups other than that of winner or loser. "There is a complete lack of empathy between them." [15] After the experiment has been carried out, it takes, he says, many hours of intensive work with both groups to get them into creative problem solving.

COOPERATION AND CONFLICT
IN COMPLEX ORGANIZATIONS

The experiments which we have been discussing have generally focused on either conditions of conflict or of cooperation. In real-life organizations, particularly in relations between work groups, both conditions usually apply simultaneously. On the one hand, there are common organizational ends such as making a profit, remaining competitive, manufacturing a product, providing a service, and meeting a deadline, in which all groups are collaborating. On the other hand, there are standing conflicts and oppositions of interest on such matters as division of the income arising from collaboration, allocation of resources, distribution of prestige and power, and recognition of contribution.

Success and failure in the struggles that occur over such issues often affect personal and departmental fates over years and sometimes over occupational lifetimes. For this reason, the struggles are acute and persistent—though limited in their intensity by what is generally conceived as the overriding interest of all parties in keeping the organization going.

Apart from the question of shared interest between the parties, all bureaucratic organizations contain in their administrative systems apparatus for controlling, mitigating, and, if necessary, suppressing intergroup conflict, an element absent from the research we have been discussing. This is treated in some detail in the second half of this book.

NOTES

1. This account is based on M. Sherif and C. W. Sherif, *Groups in Harmony and Tension* (New York: Harper, 1953); on M. Sherif and C. W. Sherif, *An Outline of Social Psychology* (New York: Harper, 1956, revised edition); and further discussion by M. Sherif, O. J. Harvey, B. J. White, W. T. Hood, and C. W. Sherif, *Intergroup*

Conflict and Cooperation. The Robbers Cave Experiment (Oklahoma: Institute of Group Relations, 1961).

2. W. F. Whyte, *Street Corner Society,* (Chicago, University Press, 1943), Ch. 1.

3. O. J. Harvey, "An Experimental Approach to the Study of Status Relations in Informal Groups." *American Sociological Review,* 18, no. 4 (1953): 357–367.

4. Reported in M. Sherif, B. J. White, and O. J. Harvey, "Status in Experimentally Produced Groups," *American Journal of Sociology,* 60, (1955): 370–379.

5. The account here is based on Sherif, Harvey, White, Hood, and Sherif, *Intergroup Conflict,* and M. Sherif and C. W. Sherif, *An Outline of Social Psychology* (New York: Harper, 1956, revised edition).

6. Sherif et al, *Intergroup Conflict,* p. 111.

7. Sherif et al, *Intergroup Conflict,* p. 114.

8. Sherif et al, *Intergroup Conflict,* p. 147.

9. Sherif et al, *Intergroup Conflict,* p. 199.

10. M. Sherif and C. W. Sherif, *Groups in Harmony and Tension* (New York: Octagon, 1953).

11. The experiments are described in "An Action Programme for Organization Improvement," *Foundation for Research on Human Behaviour* (1960).

12. H. A. Shepard, "Responses to Situations of Competition and Conflict," in R. L. Kahn and E. Boulding, eds., *Power and Conflict in Organizations* (London: Tavistock Publications, 1964).

13. Shepard, "Responses to Situations of Competition and Conflict," p. 131.

14. Shepard, "Responses to Situations of Competition and Conflict," p. 133.

15. Shepard, "Responses to Situations of Competition and Conflict," p. 133.

8 : The Search for Principles of Management

THERE is a considerable body of literature bearing on organization and management customarily referred to as classical theory or principles of management. This literature is based mainly on the reflections of managers, teachers of business and public administration, and industrial consultants. The literature embodies personal experience, thinking, and judgment rather than formal empirical research. The writers drew on practical experience and on observation to define what they considered the salient features of efficient organization and to describe the way they thought organizations should be run. Their work was in part a response to a felt need among managers for guides to action that they could understand and master.

Taylor's management techniques and examples had related mainly to lower levels of management. He provided many of the ideas for the framework later adopted by the administrative management theorists discussed in this chapter. But their scope was wider. They took a top level management view rather than a shop-floor view of administration.

I describe the approach of some of the leading contributors to these management theories, taking the account up to the 1940s. Since that time there has been more of an amalgamation between the content and style of the classical approach and empirical research-centered formal social science.

Babbage

An early English attempt to discuss and express principles in industrial management was the work of Charles Babbage, the Cambridge mathematician. In his book published in 1832,[1] he said that the bases of advantages gained through the division of labor had not yet been understood with sufficient precision. He stated these in what he called principles in the manner briefly summarized below.

A smaller part of a total process needed to be learned by the apprentice, less time need be wasted by his master in teaching and him in learning.

Less material is wasted. Time is saved in switching from one physical or mental task to another. Tools do not have to be changed as frequently to suit a fresh user. Higher standards of work are reached and it is easier to acquire high standards. A workman constantly occupied in one process is more likely to perceive better tools for doing the job and this is often the best step toward the development of a machine.

Babbage felt that a major advantage of division of labor was the freedom this gave the employer to secure workers appropriate for different tasks.

He indicated that the division of labor could be applied with equal success to mental operations, using the same economy of time. He refers to the remarkable speed with which French scientists responded to a request from their Government to produce a series of mathematical tables to facilitate the extension of their recently adopted decimal system. The tables could be rapidly prepared by splitting off parts of the work that would consist of simple numerical calculations and allotting these to persons with little arithmetical background. Babbage foresaw that those people who did this work would be superseded by "calculating engines" and went on to explain how it was possible, because of the mathematical properties underlying tables of numbers following a law, to perform arithmetical calculations by machinery and how such a machine might work.[2]

In these extracts it appears that Babbage is searching for principles in the sense of explaining why it pays to run a factory in a particular way. He is perhaps implying that manufacturers not already dividing work up in this way should do so, though he is not offering guidance on how exactly labor should be divided, or up to what limits, or on what sort of task. He is probably using the term "principle" as a proposition explaining a commonly observed phenomenon by treating it as an effect of causes he claims to identify.

Elsewhere in the same book he proceeds to at least one direct recommendation in the area of personnel management.

It would be of great importance, if, in every large establishment, the modes of paying the different persons employed could be so arranged, that each should derive advantage from the success of the whole, and that the profits of the individuals should advance as the factory itself produced profit, without the necessity of making any change in the wages agreed upon.[3]

FAYOL [4]

The first explicit and broad framework appeared in a book by Henri Fayol, printed in French in 1916 under the title *Administration Industrielle et Générale*.[5] Fayol was trained as an engineer and became a highly successful industrialist.

Urwick says of Fayol:

In the first quarter century of the scientific study of business management his is the only European figure worthy of a place beside that of F.W. Taylor . . .

Fayol showed beyond question, what Taylor himself appreciated, but what many of his imitators have failed to emphasise, that better management is not merely a question of improving the output of labour and the planning of subordinate units of organization, it is above all a matter of closer study and more administrative training for the men at the top. Seldom in history can two men working in an identical field have differed so sharply in methods or in the details of their careers and yet have produced work which was so essentially complementary.[6]

Fayol reviews "some of the principles of management which I have had most frequently to apply," adding later, "it seems at the moment especially useful to endow management theory with a dozen or so well-established principles, on which it is appropriate to concentrate general discussion."

He refers to fourteen principles, as follows:

1. Division of work
2. Authority
3. Discipline
4. Unity of command
5. Unity of direction
6. Subordination of individual interests to the general interest
7. Remuneration
8. Centralization
9. Scalar chain (line of authority)
10. Order
11. Equity
12. Stability of tenure
13. Initiative
14. Esprit de corps

These are, of course, labels rather than principles, but it is possible to extract from his commentary under each label an opinion, generalization or recommendation. His principles then run somewhat as follows:

Division of work permits of reduction in the number of objects to which attention and effort must be directed and has been recognised as the best means of making use of individuals and of groups of people . . . In the make up of a good head personal authority is the indispensable complement of official authority . . . Application of sanction to acts of authority forms part of the conditions essential for good management. First the degree of responsibility must be established and then the weight of the sanction . . . discipline is absolutely essential for the smooth running of business . . . agreements must be set side by side with command. It is important that they be clear and, as far as is possible, afford satisfaction to both sides . . . the best means of establishing and maintaining [discipline] are—1. good superiors at all levels, 2. agreements as clear and fair as possible, sanctions (penalties) judiciously applied . . . For any action whatsoever, an employee should receive orders from one superior only. Such is the rule of unity of command . . . This rule seems fundamental to me and I have given it the rank of principle . . . Men cannot bear dual command . . . [the] principle [of Unity and Direction] is expressed as: one head and one plan for a group of activities having the same objective . . . A body with two heads is in the social as in the animal sphere a monster . . . in a business the interest of one employee or group of employees should not prevail over that of the concern . . . means of effecting [reconciliation of interests] are 1. firmness and good example on the part of superiors, 2. agreements as fair as possible, 3. constant supervision . . . [Remuneration] should be fair and, as far as is possible, afford satisfaction both to personnel and firm (employee and employer). . . . The question of centralization or decentralization, is a simple question of proportion, it is a matter of finding the optimum degree for the particular concern . . . The objective to pursue is the optimum utilization of all faculties of the personnel . . . the degree of centralization or decentralization . . . is a problem to be solved according to circumstances, to the best satisfaction of the interests involved. . . . The scalar chain is the chain of superiors ranging from the ultimate authority to the lowest ranks . . . So long as [two persons under different superiors] remain in agreement, and so long as their actions are approved by their immediate superiors, direct contact may be maintained, but from the instant that agreement ceases or there is no approval from the superiors direct contact comes to an end, and the scaler chain is straightway resumed . . . It is an error to depart needlessly from the line of authority, but it is an even greater one to keep to it when detriment to the business ensues. . . . The formula is . . . in the case of material things "A place for everything and everything in its place." The formula is the same for human order "A place for everyone and everyone in his place" . . . the head of the business should strive to instil sense of equity throughout all levels of the scalar chain. . . . The initiative of all . . . represents a great source of strength for business . . . it is essential to encourage and develop this capacity to the full. . . . Harmony, union among the personnel of a concern, is great strength in that concern. Effort, then, should be made to establish it.

It is obscure to what exactly Fayol meant to refer by the term "principle." At some points he appears to mean the fourteen labels or headings under which he placed his comments (which are, of course, neither principles nor recommendations) and thereby to imply that his comments and recommendations under these are merely his personal opinion. At other points it seems that the reader is expected to regard the recommendation usually found under a label as "the principle." Fayol appears to weaken his whole case that there are principles to be propounded by qualifying his presentation as follows:

For preference I shall adopt the term principles while dissociating it from any suggestion of rigidity, for there is nothing rigid or absolute in management affairs, it is all a question of proportion. Seldom do we have to apply the same principle twice in identical conditions; allowance must be made for different changing circumstances, for men just as different and changing and for many other variable elements.[7]

He adds later that "this list has no precise limits." [8]

Some of his "principles" are descriptive, or prescriptive and exhortative.

Several are moral precepts about administrative behavior. Other of his statements are too abstract for application in a concrete situation. What they are clearly not, from the viewpoint of contemporary social science, are descriptions of how organizations work or recommendations that would in fact be useful to another administrator. This is hardly a criticism of Fayol's work, as he should be judged in context and by the standards of his time. In that perspective it must be appreciated that he was a pioneer in advancing the notion that it was useful and possible for potential and practicing managers to learn from each other, that experience in running organizations could be reflected on, analyzed and described in a systematic way, and that it would be profitable to generalize from that experience.

Lee

A remarkable contribution was made in 1921 by John Lee, a prolific writer on economic matters. Some of his thinking was in the mainstream of the search for principles of management, in the Taylor/Fayol tradition. But he also made what are in retrospect profound comments on the limits of that tradition and anticipated in his views on industrial functioning much of what has become the dominant doctrine of the 1960s.[9]

He begins by pursuing the topic of industrial democracy. He refers soon to the importance for management of recognizing the existence of a "group mind" and working with that entity. What he appears to mean is partly a matter of group cohesiveness among workers, partly the potential for greater cooperativeness among all employed in a particular firm, and partly the thoughts and feelings of workers. He favored greater participation by workers in the control of industry, as well as management by professionally competent men willing to consider themselves representatives of the total staff. Democratization of the universities might help, he thought, to produce men and possibly women as business leaders: these could be drawn from all social classes and would be respected for their technical expertise in administration.

He soon sounds a note which sociologists will recognize as distinctly Durkheimian in its emphasis, though Lee does not include Durkheim among the many sources on which he draws.[10] He suggests that

Organization . . . raises the whole tone of the individual. It calls on each to contribute his best, and when it has done so it is an "organism" healthier and saner than any one of the individuals who are portion of it.

We have . . . to discover in what form this spirit of cooperation can best be developed . . . Management may be of two kinds. It may divide up into sections each like the other . . . or it may divide up into sections each having differences . . . The former method is the territorial method of division. The latter method is the functional. With the functional method of dividing responsibilities there will be much more cohesion of the whole than with the merely territorial method, for the simple reason that functions cannot be separated sharply and the very overlapping becomes a factor in cohesion.[11]

This is extremely close in its meaning to Durkheim's contention that complex division of labor requires close interdependence between the groups of persons involved and realization of their need for each other.

At a later point Lee compares the functional (task specialization) method with the alternative of giving managers responsibility for whole operations, to the detriment of the latter approach.

The disadvantage lies in respect of cohesion. There is no co-ordination, no compulsion towards discussion, no correlation of differing points of view. The functional system in its essence is a system based on points of view. It realizes that no one mind has all points of view. It aims at specialized knowledge in the psychological sense that there is not only a knowledge of fact, but a knowledge of fact in perspective.[12]

Lee goes on to warn directors of organized effort that recent influence is not likely to have as much weight as commonly supposed. "In the sum of instincts which make up the group mind the dead have had far more influence than the living." [13] Translating this into a modern idiom, one would say that he is reminding readers of the force of our collective social inheritance.

A set of recommendations follows on the work of the chief executive—emphasizing the desirability of delegation by him and a flow of information toward him, centered on a separate "functional officer." His next recommendation must have been revolutionary for the time, judging from the diffident preamble, but it is logical enough, given the premise of the functionalist argument:

Is there any reason why the functional method should not apply equally to the human relationship? It might, therefore, be the best way to leave the human relationship to the staff management, supervising it a little distantly as all other functions are supervised.[14]

In other words, he sees specialization in personnel matters as one of the many positive features of the functional method. In Lee's view, the staff manager would play a crucial role in correlating the views of persons specializing as a result of the functional division of labor and would help foster the "group mind."

Lee makes pioneering references to the significance of unconscious factors in relations between superiors and subordinates. He quotes extensively from Jung on emotions in children deriving from their experiences with their parents, then continues as follows:

The resistance to supervisorial influence is often due to some brooding jealousy within the supervising ranks, some repressed hidden trouble . . .[15]

He appeals to management to understand the constructive aspects of un-conscious motivation and perception and to try to harness these in the collective interest.

He now tries to join his thinking with that of the scientific management movement.

I want . . . not merely to discover the best way in which work should be done, but the best way in which we can make good workers, which is a more inclusive aim. Scientific Management is too external, too merely mechanical, to achieve this higher aim.[16]

He criticizes scientific management for its narrowness, though he agrees with the general outlook. His criticisms relate largely to the concentration on junior levels and his feeling that the "human side" had not really been fully appreciated and that the judgment and creative possibilities of work-men had been excluded. A truly scientific management theory would, he suggests, build upon and modify traditional behavior rather than attempt brand-new methods violently opposed to methods of the past. He then makes the important point that:

Scientific Management . . . does not set out to ask the worker to co-operate in discussing the new methods . . . If it is to the interest of the worker that newer methods should be introduced it would also be to the interest of the worker that he should take part in the consideration of those methods. It is just at this point that Scientific Management has failed to carry the workers as a body.[17]

In the quotation above one sees an adumbration of what has become the participative point of view in decision-making. Shortly afterwards, Lee says firmly that

in short, as regards both the methods and the rewards of Scientific Management, I would act with the workers as a collective body.[18]

Lee anticipates (and in some respects goes beyond) appraisal pro-cedures which began to take systematic shape in industry about twenty years after his book. He emphasizes the important use that can be made of praise in the typical large organization where it is difficult for the individual to see the impact of his actions. He then adds penetratingly:

The chiefest value lies in the fact that it gives an added importance to silence . . . There is a silence which is more than eloquent. When the worker knows that praise or appreciation will follow really good work he will be able to interpret the full meaning of silence.[19]

Lee also edited a massive and ambitious compendium which appeared in 1928 under the title of *Dictionary of Industrial Administration*.[20] Con-tributors included Cyril Burt, Professor of Education, London University; E. Farmer, Investigator to the Industrial Fatigue Board; R. G. Hawtrey of the Treasury; H. Northcott, Labor Manager of Rowntrees; T. H. Pear, Professor of Psychology, Manchester University; C. H. Renold, Managing Director of Renolds; O. Sheldon, a Rowntrees Manager; L. Urwick, also then at Rowntrees; and a variety of other academics, civil servants, consultants, and industrial managers. Among the subjects included were psychological tests of aptitude and intelligence, time and movement studies, personal factors in accidents, monetary aspects of trade cycles, repetitive work, principles of direction and control, university education for industry, and physical aspects of factory work.

Sheldon

Oliver Sheldon was an executive at the Rowntree chocolate concern in England. His *Philosophy of Management* was first published in 1924 and reprinted in 1965.[21] The new edition also reprints the foreword by B. Seebohm Rowntree, a leading Quaker industrialist well known both for his encouragement of progressive management and for his own original social survey on poverty in York, the site of the Rowntree business. Rowntree recommended the book to readers partly because

Mr. Sheldon's book is a valuable contribution to the development of a better managerial practice. . . . No one who reads it can fail to grasp the principles which underlie good management. And the author recognizes that business has a soul.[22]

The book did indeed emphasize as the essentials of a sound management approach three major elements. One was the intellectual discipline of industrial history and economics. Another was what the author refers to sometimes as the science of management and sometimes as the technique of management. This included inter alia for Sheldon,

the theory and practice of Organization; of Commercial and Industrial Law; of Banking, Finance and Insurance; of Costing, Research and Statistics, of Standards and their application; of Planning Systems; of Factory Lay-out and Location; of Sales Promotion and Advertising; of Office Routine; of Traffic Management; of Applied Psychology; of Personnel Management.[23]

Sheldon was unusual in stressing as a third component "the philosophy upon which our practice of management is founded"[24] and in asserting that "ethics is as essential to management as economics."[25] By this he meant, for one thing, that it was important to understand the place of industry in the social structure, the relation of wealth and material objects to human well-being and to what one might call ultimate values. But, more than this, he suggested that management needed a codified philosophy based on an ethic of service to the community, and himself provided the elements of such a scheme. Sheldon realized that the proper or best way to manage could not rest altogether on technical premises or rules but always involved in some respect a value judgment on the part of the manager. He suggested that the methods of industry should be subjected to a double valuation, ethical as well as economic.[26] And again,

A scientific analysis of the various features of management is useless, if the fundamental fact be overlooked that management is not solely the scientific employment of a machine which shall produce in rigid ratio to the care exercised in its construction, but rather the art of combining human and material factors into a single harmonious enterprise.[27]

Sheldon is, however, probably best known among students of management for his detailed model of an organizations for a hypothetical factory (complete with pull-out chart), designed around operational functions and coordinated by committees. This design appears as a chapter in his book. In concluding his discussion he states:

There is no complete ideal, but the following may be regarded as necessary principles:—

a. The main division of the functions of the business should be based upon a scientific analysis of the work to be accomplished.

b. Like functions should be grouped together and clearly defined, especially "border-line" duties.

c. Positions should be determined by a proper interlocking of work and faculty, job and man.

d. Co-ordination should be the sole concern of the chief executive, such co-ordination being continued lower down the organization.

e. The leadership of the workers should be single, direct and intimate.

f. The executive management should be supplemented, firstly, by a committee organization to provide co-ordination, facilities for advice and investigation and the training of subordinates; secondly by such expert Staff organization as circumstances require.

g. Positions should be determined irrespective of individuals, and so graded as to allow of a methodical progression from one to another.

h. The whole form of organization should be charted, published to all concerned and kept up to date.[28]

But he tempers his recommendation with the reflections that once an organization has existed for some time it cannot be changed hastily but that it is better to await the right moment. As he implies, when we speak of organizing we often mean reorganizing, which brings its own special problems.

It is often better temporarily to tolerate the unscientific than to create a ferment of human feeling. For industry is primarily human. It must not become the playground of scientist and engineer.[29]

Mooney and Reiley

A major attempt to provide a conceptual framework of management principles, on similar lines to Fayol's, was made in the United States by Mooney and Reiley, two General Motors executives, in 1931. This became very popular. They introduce their work as follows:

The entire book is based on the thesis that there are fundamental principles of organizations, structural in character, which may be identified in every form of human association, and that the orderly correlation of the principles furnishes the key to their more efficient application in all fields of collective human effort.

The purpose of this book is to expose the *principles of organization,* as they reveal themselves in various forms of human group movement, and to help industry to protect its own growth through a greater knowledge and a more conscious use of these principles in the pursuit of all industrial objectives.

That efficient organization must, above all, have its formalism, and that this formalism must be based on principles, is the essential thesis of this book.

We have attempted to discover, identify and correlate these principles. . . . This examination has covered the principal movements of history that have been inspired by political, military or religious purposes. We believe that, through this research, we have found the principles that we sought.[30]

Thirty-nine chapters follow, of which five discuss social organization in ancient societies and the middle ages, five discuss religious organization and four military organization. The rest discuss various aspects of contemporary industrial organization. These discussions appear to be meant to supply the reader with the raw material from which the authors worked in extracting their principles or to exemplify their importance in practice, though they do not in fact do so systematically. Indeed such a task would stagger the imagination of the social scientist of today. On the other hand, if the principles are viewed as concepts, as useful tools in describing and analyzing administrative forms and more or less universal administrative problems, one can see how the authors may have derived some of them from their study of historical and comparative material or could use them on it. They do from time to time illustrate their use of a concept in their theoretical chapters from the historical material.

The key chapters that entered into the mental equipment and vocabulary of the new administrative theorists were entitled "What Is Meant by Organization and its Principles"; "The Co-ordinative Principles of Organization"; "The Scalar Principle of Organization"; "The Functional Principle of Organization"; and "The Staff Phase of Functionalism."

The chapter on "The Co-ordinative Principle" calls this the first principle of organization and the one which contains all the others. "The others are simply the principles through which coordination operates, and thus becomes effective." [31] At this point the reader begins to search for a principle in the sense of a proposition attempting to state a relationship between two sets of variables but none in fact follows. What follows is a set of statements to the effect that coordination requires the existence of authority and that this comes before the exercise of leadership. Authority, the authors say, is a right because it inheres legitimately in the structure of the organization. A discussion follows on the importance of community of interest and mutuality of interest. The writers commend the cultivation of a sense of human mutuality to "our more enlightened industrial leaders." [32]

In the next chapter, "The Scalar Principle," the authors state that there must be a process through which coordinating authority operates from the top throughout the organized body. This, they say, is a tangible reality, observable in every organization. They call it the Scalar Process, agreeing that it is sometimes called the hierarchical form in organization, namely the gradation of duties according to authority and corresponding responsibility.

In the chapter "The Functional Principle of Organization," Mooney and Reiley define "functionalism" as "the differentiation or distinction between kinds of duties." [33] The end and aim of formal coordination, they say, is simply the correlation of functions. They say that in every organization there must be some function that decides objectives and procedures (the determinative function); another that acts on this (the applicative); and another that construes the decisions (interpretative). They say that all jobs involve one of these three things. The organizer should know that these "functional principles" are universal in organization and must identify them in every job and make them the basis of his correlation. This, the authors go on to say, is what Taylor did in his system of functional foremanship, which is based on distinguishing between planning and performing. At this point the link of their work with scientific management shows itself clearly: they are apparently trying to do for administrative systems what Taylor did for production systems, that is identify their separable components with the intent of helping them to become recombined in a way more conducive to efficiency.

By the "staff function in organization," Mooney and Reiley mean "the service of *advice* and *counsel,* as distinguished from the function of authority or command." They refer to the military distinction between "line and staff," describing the "line" as synonymous with the "scalar chain" and stating that "every staff function must adhere to some line duty in a dependent relationship." [34] They add that the universality of the staff function in organization entitles it to rank as a principle. They emphasize the precedence of line jobs. Presumably they are suggesting here the importance in practical operations of unity of command, attached exclusively to line executives. They appear to be making a recommendation, or, if they are describing something, they are describing a notional division of labor rather than real-life situations. They must surely have known from their own experience that people in line jobs are not the only persons who determine what is done. (It is, of course, one of the main problems with work of this type that it is extremely difficult to sort out from each other conceptualization, analysis, description, and recommendation.)

In a contribution to the Gulick and Urwick collection of 1937,[35] Mooney's essential thesis appears to be that the way established organizations are structured does not appear to be due to chance, that the central features of their structures can be identified and assembled in a systematic way, and can be kept in mind or deliberately or more firmly implemented in the name of industrial efficiency. Where organizational troubles are found, he says, such as an organization being shot through with politics, this is almost certainly due not to (substandard) personnel but to the inattention on the part of administration to the necessities of formal organization, and the application of its principles. (This argument is, of course, confusing because he appears to be arguing first that certain features of organization are universal and essential, then to say that troubles occur when they are absent. Presumably he meant that successful organizations have these features and others lack them or do not carry them through fully enough.)

In a 1947 book[36] Mooney repeats his view of coordination as "the first principle of organization." He goes on to say

Co-ordination . . . is the orderly arrangement of group effort, to provide unity of action in the pursuit of a common purpose.
When we call *co-ordination* the first principle, we mean this term expresses the principles of organization *in toto;* nothing less. This does not mean that there are no subordinate principles; it simply means that all the others are contained in this one of co-ordination. The others are simply the principles through which co-ordination appears and thus becomes effective.[37]

The first paragraph appears to define or describe a concept rather than to be a principle in the sense of a proposition that summarizes the way people either behave or should behave. Perhaps coordination could be more helpfully described as a component of organization. I hesitate to say of "successful" organization because one can imagine cases in which an organization is functioning successfully even though, or perhaps because, its various activities are not closely coordinated.

Mary Parker Follet [38]

Mary Parker Follet was a distinguished American student of government and politics who extended her interests to business administration. Her main writings were published between 1920 and 1941. She was able in her work to draw on her background of political theory, her studies of government, experience in Boston in the fields of vocational guidance, placement, and wage determination. It is also evident that she read widely and with understanding in philosophy, sociology, psychology, and biology. She did not carry out empirical studies of business and industry but was well-informed and constantly drawn into consultations.

An example of the sophistication of her approach is provided in "Constructive Conflict",[39] the first paper in a 1941 collection, but originally published in 1926. She intended this as an illustration of the contribution contemporary psychology was making to business administration. She took as her problem the most fruitful way of dealing with conflict and asked readers to think of conflict as neither good nor bad but as the appearance of difference of opinions or interests. Instead of condemning conflict, she said, we should set it to work for us. There were, she said, three main ways of dealing with conflict: domination, compromise, and integration. Domination was the victory of one side over the other, was easiest in the short run, but brought problems later. In compromise both sides have to give up a little, so usually start by asking too much, so that one cannot know what each really thinks he should have. This ignorance was a barrier to dealing with conflict fruitfully. A third possibility was beginning, she said, now to be realized, integration or reaching a solution in which desires of both sides find a place without a sacrifice by either. She provides an example of integration by describing a technical invention devised to meet the expressed need of two groups of workmen to undertake their tasks simultaneously. The idea was to find a creative solution rather than put disputants into a situation in which they merely vindicated their prior judgments. She pointed out that "conflict as the moment of the appearing and focusing of difference may be a sign of health, prophecy of progress."[40] If one does not fight over something, the people concerned might not work out an improved method of dealing with the problem. This, she said, was setting friction to work, making it do something. The first step toward dealing with a conflict in a constructive way was to bring it into the open. Social conflict should be revealed in the same way as the personal conflicts of the patient cooperating with a psychiatrist. The desires of different sides should be brought into view and compared; when oriented toward each other they might acquire different values. There was nothing discreditable in having personal motives but the question to consider was what weight to give them. As parties brought motives and evidence under examination realignment of interests (and groupings) might take place and these might change the conflict. We arrived at confrontations prepared to fight and full of preconceived notions of what the others were like: this helped to create an unfavorable situation to which one would again have to respond. One's behavior helped to *develop* the situation to which one was responding.

This was an unusual approach to take to conflict, both in the sense that Mary Parker Follet sought to study conflict objectively as a social process and in the sense that she suggested that it was a process with certain positive functions. A similar, though much more embracing, approach had been set out by Simmel in the first decade of the century, and he too had suggested positive functions.[41] But his work did not appear significantly to affect the mainstream of social science (let alone management theory) until its popularization and refinement by Coser in 1954.[42] It is likely, therefore, that Mary Parker Follet had arrived independently at her point of view, in this respect remaining in advance of many social scientists for two or three decades.

Mary Parker Follet is well known to students of management for her discussion on the giving of orders (which appears in the same book) which left as its legacy the phrase "law of the situation." She begins the discussion by saying that we give orders every day, that if we could understand the principles underlying this we could "take a conscious attitude toward our experience." (Her insistence on the importance of insight and self-monitoring comes through at several points in her work. She felt that a conscious attitude could lead to more deliberate decision on which way to act and then to an experimental approach of trying new behavior and watching the result.) She pointed to problems in being either authoritarian or avoiding giving orders and proposed her own solution:

My solution is to depersonalise the giving of orders, to unite all concerned in a study of the situation, to discover the law of the situation and obey that. . . . This is what does take place, what has to take place, when there is a question between two men in positions of equal authority. . . This is ideally what should take place between foremen and rank and file, between any head and his subordinates . . . both should agree to take their orders from the situation.

We have here, I think, one of the largest contributions of scientific management; it tends to depersonalize orders. From one point of view, one might call the essence of scientific management the attempt to find the law of the situation. With scientific management the managers are as much under orders as the worker, for both obey the law of the situation. Our job is not to get people to obey orders but to devise methods by which we can best *discover* the order integral to a particular situation.[43]

At this distance it strikes me as extremely odd that this precept should issue from the same writer who had emphasized the importance of facing conflict and differences of view and interest. It denies the importance in superior-subordinate situations of the perceptual and emotional difficulties certain to attend relationships in which parties have differing status, power, and rights. It is also highly reminiscent of Taylor's optimistic hope that his methods would end wage disputes as pay would be "scientifically" determined and come out of the arena of conflict.

In a closing chapter of the same book, which was written toward the end of her life, she stated what she called "Four fundamental principles of organizations." These were

1. Co-ordination by direct control of the responsible people concerned.
2. Co-ordination in the early stages.
3. Co-ordination as the reciprocal relating of all the factors in a situation.
4. Co-ordination as a continuing process.[44]

By the first principle she meant to emphasize that control should be effected by cross-relations between heads of departments rather than up and down the line through the chief executive. By the second she meant that managers should consult each other before they had made up their minds. By the third she means that influence should be allowed and recognized to be mutual, also that facts should be seen in their contexts; situations should be assessed not by adding the component facts together but by seeing them in their relationship with each other.[45]

By her final principle she meant that there should be standing arrangements for coordination, so that review processes should continue through planning to operation back to new planning and so on. At this point Mary Follet achieves a remarkable formulation which shows her at the height of her intellectual power.

Unless we look on control as a continuing activity, we shall not get out of the fallacy that we can solve problems. The belief that we can is a drag upon our thinking. What we need is some process for meeting problems. When we think we have *solved* a problem, well, by the very process of solving, new elements or forces come into the situation and you have a new problem on your hands to be solved. When this happens, men are often discouraged. I wonder why: it is our strength and our hope. We don't want any system that holds us enmeshed within itself.[46]

Gulick and Urwick

Gulick and Urwick's writings were mainly in the 1930s and 1940s. Gulick was an American specialist in public administration and Urwick a British industrial executive who had experience of the Army and international organizations and later became one of the best known industrial consultants in the United Kingdom. Like Taylor, Gulick and Urwick believed that there are principles of management, that management is a matter of technique. This was explicitly put by Urwick in 1933, as follows:

These principles can be studied as a technical question, irrespective of the purpose of the enterprise, the personnel composing it, or any constitutional, political or social theory underlying its creation. They are concerned with the method of sub-dividing and allocating to individuals all the various activities, duties and responsibilities essential to the purpose contemplated, the correlation of these activities and the continuous control of the work of individuals so as to secure the most economical and most effective realization of the purpose.[47]

In a paper written in 1934 and also reprinted in the 1937 volume, Urwick criticizes Fayol for not being adamant enough about the general validity and range of application of his principles.[48]

Gulick and Urwick were concerned with the utility of bringing together in a single area a large amount of different types of work, to make possible the most effective divisions of work and specialization; to make the maximum use of labor saving machinery and mass production.

They were concerned with partitioning and centralizing services as soon as scale permitted this (for example, typing pools, engineering and staff departments, that is, various forms of process rather than purpose specialization).

They aimed at homogeneity of task (process) within each department, so that the management had only a limited number of skills and processes to combine in the most economic ways. Each department would ideally be self-contained so far as its special process was concerned.

They thought it desirable to bring collections of tasks under single directors who would have total responsibility and all immediate control and authority. Not only would there be specializations of skills within the department, there would also be specialists in coordination at the head of departments and relating departments with each other.

Gulick comprehensively developed for the higher levels of organization the ideas Taylor had put forward on specialization within organizations, under the name of functionalization.[49] The basic idea was to combine units of work that could be identified as homogeneous and to separate the heterogeneous.

Gulick considered the division of work to be the foundation of organization and the reason for organization. However, such division was limited, he said, by the necessity to avoid subdividing beyond the full time of one man, by local custom and technological constraints,[50] and by the difficulty of tearing apart intricately related activities. The more work was subdivided the greater the need for supervision and coordination.

Gulick said that the executive can personally direct only a few persons and must rely on them in turn to direct others, the same arrangement being repeated until the last man in the organization is reached. Rigid adherence to the principle of unity of command was of great importance: a man could not serve two masters. Even Taylor had gone wrong in setting up separate foremen to give orders to workmen on different matters. The efficiency of a work group was directly related, Gulick said, to the homogeneity of the work they were doing. Their work must be homogeneous and a unit based on specialization should not be given technical direction by a layman.

Gulick suggests four bases for grouping work units: (1) the purpose to be served (2) the process to be used (3) the clientele to be served or material to be handled (4) the place where the activities will proceed. Each of these bases, he said, has its own advantages and disadvantages. Departmentalization by purpose orients a group to a common goal, focuses their activity, elicits loyalties, and makes possible accountability by the criterion of whether the purpose is achieved. But it is hard in practice to avoid overlap and conflict, the system breeds over-centralization, the department falls behind in its use of up to date specialists and specialist expertise, and it becomes independent and hard to control. Departmentalization by process encourages the use of up-to-date technical skill by bringing together a large amount of technical work, encourages labor-saving devices, and collects under the same supervision common technical skills, thus stimulating professional cooperation, standards, and pride. But grouping by process emphasizes the way things are done rather than the aim of the work and develops segmented approaches directed by narrow specialists and, therefore, requiring increased coordination from the top. Departmentalization by clientele reduces the number of departments or persons a client must be brought into contact with or a product must pass through and reduces traffic problems but minimizes advantages of specialization by function, requires duplication of facilities, and can too easily be dominated by client groups. Departmentalization by place increases coordination of services and control within given physical boundaries, can improve adaptability to local needs, decentralization by geographical area, and facilitates delegation to subordinates with best knowledge of local conditions. But it increases difficulty of maintaining consistent overall policies, increases the cost of supervision, and creates difficulties where tasks do not coincide closely with specific physical boundaries.

Gulick goes on to say that there is apparently no one most effective system of organization. Each member of the enterprise is working for some major purpose, uses some process, deals with some persons, and works or serves at one place. While the primary basis of division was of great significance, choice had to depend on the results desired at a given time and place; on the developmental stage of an organization or department; on the technology used; and on the number of men at work and their geographical distribution.

Urwick made an attempt in 1944 in a short book to relate logically in a common scheme the contributions to date of the main writers on administration.[51] He emphasized the convergence in the field. He again described the "art and science" of administering groups as a *technical* skill, resting on science and consisting of principles and methods, a body of professional knowledge. Later on in the same book he becomes more cautious and describes the technique of administration as "emerging" and a "true science of administration" as (only) "ultimately possible." The student, he says, in his concluding statement, can do no more than suggest an arrangement of ideas and principles which may help others to make their own synthesis out of their own experience.

Urwick stated in this book that organizing was a draftsman's job, a designing process. The organizer could and should try to draw up an optimum distribution of duties and responsibilities as if he was starting off with a clean sheet, then make "small-adjustments of the job to the man" to allow for what the people employed were actually like. This would help to ensure that anyone appointed to a senior job would have a clear idea of how his role fitted in, the attached responsibilities and the standards expected. If jobs were clearly put together along lines of functional specialization, it would be easier to train people for succession to jobs rather than to do what their predecessors did because of their particular personalities or experience. Unless the organizer had principles to quote, personnel would play politics in promotion matters. The structure should be planned for the continuation of activities into the future (the principle of continuity). Urwick now begins to discuss principles which should guide the administrator in determining necessary activities and grouping them so that they could be allotted to individuals. He relies largely on Mooney and Reiley and Fayol. What follows is a mixture of statements of what I have earlier referred to as elements or concepts (such as coordination, unity of command, delegation, authority) and precepts (such as "make decisions which are clear, distinct and precise.") "see that the plan of operations is strictly carried out," "impose penalties for mistakes and blunders." Several of the precepts are drawn from Taylor, whose work on shop floors is thought by Urwick to have much wider application. These include the propositions that authority and responsibility should correspond and that every person in an organization should be confined so far as possible to one leading function. Urwick describes infraction of this principle (using the term now in the precept sense) as "immemorial folly," and describes specialization as "the way of progress in human organization." He adds some of his own preceptive observations, such as those on leadership: "The leader must be sensitive to the rights of all"; leaders must "play fair with each other"; "a chief should never allow a subordinate to be criticized by others outside the chief's area of responsibility." Urwick underlines the importance of delegation and the associated Taylor notion of "the exception principle" that once powers are delegated only unusual occurrences need be brought to the attention of seniors. He repeats Fayol's admonition to define duties clearly and warns that the consequence of vagueness is poor morale and "politics."

Urwick is the first of the writers we have mentioned who explicitly tries to provide guidance on methods. He deals first with ways in which executive functions should be differentiated. The boundaries between groups of activities assigned to individuals should, he said, be correctly determined and clearly indicated, otherwise overlapping, duplication, and confusion would be inevitable and it would be impossible to match authority and responsibility.[52] Urwick distinguishes between three methods of determining the limits or boundaries in functional differentiation. Under the unitary method the limits are determined with reference to persons, things, or areas. Under the serial method a product passes through a range of departments, each carrying out some process connected with it. Under the subjectival method actitives are bounded with reference to a particular subject or an aspect of management. Urwick saw a drift in all forms of undertaking to the subjectival because of the increasing degree of "specialized authority," that is, areas of management in which highly specialized professional knowledge was required. He regarded this as sound and in line with the "principle of specialization." The manager should not be a jack-of-all trades or he would be a master of none. But this method increased difficulties of coordination, partly because the limits were abstract, in the realm of ideas, because the same words meant different things to different people and because many subordinates would have to obey two masters—one in charge of their sub-jectival speciality and one in charge of the unit in which they happened to be working. Urwick thought the difficulties over this were exaggerated but makes no more acknowledgement than this to the unity of command ideas which he had earlier quoted with approval. Urwick goes on to divide activities into (hierarchical) levels such as criticism and review, liaison, supervision, and operations. He thinks that methods for assigning executive grades had not yet been worked out but suggests questions to be asked in making an analysis: these relate to degree of supervision by the superior and the executive's responsibility for results. At this point Urwick denies that a successful organization is built by applying one of the principles or methods enumerated in this chapter to the exclusion of others.

The art of organization consists in determining the correct method to apply at each point and to each aspect of an undertaking, and so to build up a struc-ture in which the method or methods used at each point and the degree to which they are used result in the balance which is most effective for the purpose of the undertaking.[53]

This appears to be a negation of almost everything that has gone before and to constitute advice to the administrator to do what he feels best in the light of his circumstances and the task of the organization. He goes on neverthe-less to advocate clear definition of objectives aimed to secure "uniformity of doctrine"; the inclusion of identical elements in the training of executives in the same concern; the use and publication of organization charts, manuals, and bulletins; and limitation of the use of committees. These recommenda-tions are sometimes stark assertions and sometimes supported by quotations from the conclusions of others based on their own practical experience.

Urwick greatly popularized the "span of control principle." Graicunas had originally formulated the span of control proposition in 1933 [54] as fol-lows. If a superior divides his work into two or three parts and delegates them "freely and properly" to two subordinates, he will not have enough to do, but if he has six or more subordinates and gives them direct access to him he will be too busy, and delay and confusion will result. The prob-lem was likely to be exacerbated by superiors anxious to extend their power and by subordinates eager to draw themselves to the attention of their seniors. A principle, said Graicunas, should be added to the practical ex-perience of those interested in organization. This rested firstly on "the span of attention": "in the vast majority of cases the span of attention is limited to six digits. The same holds good of other intellectual activities." Secondly, the burden of responsibility depended not on the number of direct one-to-one relationships between superiors and subordinates but also on his relationships with them as subgroups and as a group and also on their cross-relationships with each other:

the group and cross relationships increase more rapidly than the number of subordinates assigned, because each fresh individual adds as many more cross and direct group relationships as there are persons already in the group. Irrespective of the manner of counting, the number of relationships increases in exponential proportion . . . in cases other than routine work, the rapid increase of cross and direct relationships is the governing factor which actually limits the number of persons which can be effectually and efficiently supervised by one person. Hence the number of lateral divisions in each descending level of responsibility should be restricted to a maximum of five and, most probably, only four.[55]

Graicunas argued that the evolution of modern business was towards increasing specialization and that this enforced organization by function with a correspondingly greater need for coordination, thereby creating a wider and wider range of group and cross-relationships. This would make the principle he had described of greater importance in all forms of organization.

Discussion

INTERNAL CONTRADICTIONS AND AMBIGUITIES
The main principles or, as I should prefer to call them, precepts of management, of the sort we have been describing have come under heavy fire during the past two decades.

The particular principles have been attacked as erroneous or misleading, particularly by H. A. Simon, who asserted in 1949 that the currently accepted "principles of administration" were "little more than ambiguous and mutually contradictory proverbs." [56] He suggested that in practice there had been a consistent retreat from the notion of principles.

If we study the chain of publications extending from Mooney and Reiley through Gulick, the President's Committee controversy, to Schuyler Wallace and Benson, we see a steady shift of emphasis from the 'principles of administration' themselves to a study of the *conditions* under which competing principles are respectively applicable.[57]

I would not regard such a shift in emphasis as damning, since it seems to me to be standard practice in social science to build generalizations on a basis of successive approximations to reality. This appears to involve continuous elaboration of the generalizations and further differentiation of the circumstances in which they apply.

Simon is, however, extremely damaging in his criticisms of the particular principles that have been put forward. He takes, as one example, the two interrelated principles of hierarchy and unity of command. According to these, authority and responsibility should flow in a clear, unbroken line from the highest executive to the lowest operative, and no members of an organization should receive orders from more than one superior.

Unity of command, Simon says, is usually taken to mean that any one individual in an administrative organization will accept the authority of only one other person in the organization. This does not provide any reason why an individual cannot accept certain decisional premises from one superior and other, non-conflicting, premises from another—for example, the authority of a line superior in determining the program of his unit and of the financial department as to what records he should keep. Or why he should not accept orders from one foreman as to the speed of his lathe and another as to its proper maintenance.

There are methods other than unity of command, adds Simon, that are in common use to prevent or resolve conflicts. These include the practice of the individual receiving orders from several superiors but obeying only one in case of a conflict; dividing the specific areas over which each superior has exclusive authority; or (as in the army) being subject to the authority of all individuals of a given rank; obeying the last but bringing the conflict to the attention of the person issuing the order.

Discussing Gulick's ideas for grouping work units by purpose, process clientele, or place, Simon points out that purpose, process, clientele, and place are competing bases of organization, and at any given point of division the advantages of three must be sacrificed to secure the advantages of the fourth.[62] If, for instance, the major departments of a city government are organized according to purpose, persons in the same relevant specialities (say in law, medicine, or statistics) will be distributed between the departments and the advantages of organization by process will thereby be partly lost. Similarly, the principle of specialization according to purpose would lead to a different result from specialization according to clientele, and a choice has, in fact, to be made between these. A health department can argue persuasively that it should include the health of schoolchildren under its aegis because this must be coordinated with the overall community health program (specialization by purpose). But the school board can argue equally plausibly that it should control health care and nutrition with its responsibility for education and wholesome leisure (specialization by clientele).

Simon adds that the key terms are ambiguous. The same activity may be described as purpose or process according to the view of the person describing it. For a secretary, the typing of a letter may be a purpose (objective or end of activity) but for her boss it is a process (means toward an end). A health department conceived as a unit to care for the health of a community is a purpose organization, but it can also be conceived to be a unit making use of medical knowledge to carry out its work, that is, as a process organization. There is no such thing, Simon suggests, as a single purpose organization (which is implied in Gulick's paper). He suggests that there is only a distinction of degree between a "purpose" and a "process." A "process" is an activity whose immediate purpose is at a low level in the hierarchy of means and ends (as in the typing example above), while a "purpose" is a collection of activities oriented towards a higher level in the means-end hierarchy. From the point of view of the manager from whom the letter originates, his purpose may be to persuade a committee member to attend a meeting, but for his own superior this may be merely instrumental to his own purpose of getting the committee to take a particular decision. Simon adds that "clientele" and "place" are not in fact strictly separable from "purpose" but part of it and usually assumed by it.

Simon points out that even where problems of proper usage can be solved, "the principles of administration give no guide as to which of these four competing bases of specialization is applicable in any particular situation." It is difficult, he says, to find logical or empirical grounds for giving precedence to one over the other.

Adding a gloss to this critique, March and Simon point out in their book of 1961 [58] that costs of coordination must be balanced against the potential gains of specialization. They point out that as the size of an organization increases, the marginal advantages occurring from specialization may become smaller, while coordination costs become larger. This means that the balance of advantage shifts to purpose organizations as size increases. This has, in fact, been abundantly demonstrated by Chandler, in his account of trends in the organization of large American firms.[59] He shows that as they have grown to operate on a larger scale in more distant geographical areas, both in their home country and abroad, they have tended to decentralize as much as possible of the whole operation to locally organized units.

In regard to the span of control principle, Simon pointed out that a contradictory proposition can be stated which can be supported by arguments of equal plausibility: namely that administrative efficiency is enhanced by keeping at a minimum the number of organization levels through which a matter must pass before it is acted on. If these levels are not kept to a minimum, inefficiency, red tape, and waste can ensue because of the intervention of extra supervisory levels between administrators and operative employees.

A restricted span of control inevitably produces excessive red tape, for each contact between organization members must be carried upward until a common superior is found. If the organization is at all large, this will involve carrying all

matters upward through several levels of officials for decision, and then downwards again in the form of orders and institutions—a cumbersome and time-
consuming process.[60]

Both the increase and the decrease in span of control have, Simon points
out, some undesirable consequences. While proponents of a restricted span
of control have suggested three, five, or even eleven as suitable numbers of
subordinates, they have not been able to answer the crucial question of why
the particular number selected should be correct. (This is a question, one
might add, that is unanswerable without some reference to task and technology.)

An important criticism of the supposed advantages of the restricted span
of control notion has been made by J. C. Worthy of the Sears Roebuck
concern in the U.S.A. He bases his comments partly on experience and
research in his own company and partly on his observations elsewhere. The
essence of his criticism is that the close supervision associated with a restricted span of control inhibits independence, confidence, self-reliance
and mutual reliance among subordinates. On the other hand, where an
executive has to manage less closely and without as much help from direct
formal authority, he has to win cooperation in a manner more satisfying
in the long run. Worthy writes as follows:

A number of highly successful organizations have not only paid little heed but
have gone directly counter to one of the favourite tenets of modern management
theory, the so-called "span of control" . . . On the contrary, these organizations
often deliberately give each key executive so many subordinates that it is impossible for him to exercise too close supervision over their activities. . . .

The individual executive is thrown largely on his own to sink or swim on his
own ability and capacity. He cannot rely to more than a limited extent on those
above him, and these superiors, by the same token, cannot too severely restrict,
through detailed supervision and control their subordinates' growth and development.

Not all individuals can function effectively in this type of set up . . . Those
who are able to adapt to this type of organization, however, are likely to be not
only better executives but also the type of people who can build and maintain
team-work and co-operation and a high level of employee morale . . . because
these results are a natural by-product of their ways of operating and a reflection
of their own personalities.

On the other hand, in organizations characterised by many levels of supervision and elaborate systems of controls, the individual not only has little
opportunity to develop the capacities of self-reliance and initiative but the
system frequently weeds out those who do. Furthermore, those who survive in
this type of organization are often likely, by virtue of the very qualities which
enabled them to survive, to have personalities and ways of operating which do
not make for greatest skill in building employee team-work and co-operation. . . .

In the more simple types of organization structures, where management has
been effectively decentralized, an executive accomplishes results and moves to

higher levels of responsibility chiefly to the extent that he is able to secure the willing, enthusiastic support of his colleagues and subordinates; he does not have the "tools" (with which a more centralized system would to some extent provide him) to accomplish the result in any other manner. The outcome is not only a higher level of accomplishment but, at the same time, a more satisfying type of supervision and a higher level of employee morale.[61]

PRINCIPLES AND VALUES

During the course of our exposition of the ideas of those classical and neoclassical writers who have sought to formulate principles of industrial management, we have noted certain reservations and limitations. As has been seen, the term "principle" has been used in a variety of ways to mean concept, element, hypothesis, proposition, linking variables, and precept. The value-based "principle" has been common: this means that the recommendation can be relevant to the reader's problem only if he shares the value premises of the person making it. In regard to several of the principles, in the sense of statements of particular linkage between particular variables (such as the "span of control principles"), it may seem at first that no question of values other than efficiency arises. All that is asserted is that managers find difficulty in supervising more than five or six subordinates and if a senior management wishes to avoid such difficulty they should arrange otherwise. But operating in accordance with this principle is likely to precipitate the problems of having a tall, multilevel organizational structure. The administrator is left to make a choice between these two alternatives which can be based only on value-rooted preferences or on intuition. There appears to be no principle which tells one which is better. The factors of personal preference and judgment now become salient and there is no basis for a management theorist to recommend to an administrator which he should choose— other than his own value premises. The juxtaposition of the two alternatives highlights the fact that there is no one *desideratum* on which one can base a choice, not even efficiency: administrators do not in fact try to maximize efficiency and are usually prepared to sacrifice some efficiency for the sake of peace and quiet or to avoid upsetting colleagues and subordinates. Perhaps the most than can be supplied to administrators in the way of principles is a set of research results which will show, for instance, what happened when a limited span of control was given precedence over its alternatives and vice versa. Such research would have to specify several other conditions, including task, technology, size of the organization, and dominant environmental values (say for authoritarianism and democracy). The administrator could then compare the situations studied with his own and make his own inferences. The principles of management adduced up to the 1930s and even into the 1940s were not, of course, empirically based along such lines and could not provide such guidance: they were based on the personal experience of managers and consultants, on their reflections, and on the convergence of their views. It was not until the late 1930s that an empirical sociology of the organization began to be built.

We should not dismiss contributions of these theorists and theories because of the limitations of the "principles." The writers had wide experience of various types of organization, they were wise in the ways of management and, as intelligent outsiders, they could often help men engaged in practical management by pointing out to them the probable consequences of acting in one way rather than another. They provided statements which, even if regarded as no more than hypotheses, provided starting points for systematic research. Some reliance on prior experience, estimate, and approximation based on propositions stated as highly abstract generalizations is likely to continue indefinitely. Even our contemporary volume of social research cannot keep up with the range of situations presented in the real world. A leap will always have to be made by even the most knowledgeable administrators and advisers from accumulated theory to practical decision.

CONCEPTIONS OF ORGANIZATION
AND BEHAVIOR

We have discussed the limitations of the principles of management put forward by the management theorists. It is also helpful to ask whether their aims and concepts of organization and their assumptions about organizational aims and human nature were valid. These are interconnected issues.

They write as if the aims of the organization are fixed or known in advance and the administrative task is merely one of then dividing up the work to be done. It might seem in a commercial organization as if the aim is fixed, because businessmen are thought to want to maximize profit. But the notion of maximization lacks precision. In practice, it is hardly an aim at all. Few business leaderships try to maximize profit to the extent that they alienate competitors, customers, and staff. They aim, as has repeatedly been shown, rather for levels of profit that are felt to be sufficient or adequate, or at growth and a larger share of the market, or at a level of diversification that will bring them security. Similarly, few if any public service administrators aim to maximize efficiency to the extent of damaging the budgetary opportunities of other agencies or to the extent of providing a maximum of satisfaction to their consumers. Even if they did attempt the latter they would have to choose between satisfying a few very highly or a larger number to a lesser degree.

In fact, it is unlikely that there be one constant overriding aim in any organization. There are always several competing aims and the standing issue is what should be the relative weight given each, what compromise should be reached between them. This varies over time with shifts in the internal distribution of power within the organization and with changes in the opportunities offered within the environment. Even if the relative weight of the aims were fairly constant over a period, it is likely that as personnel resources and opportunities change so would strategies for achieving the central aims. The inconstant nature of organizational aims and strategies highlights the fact that these are not givens but are problematic facets of organizational functioning—aims and strategies have continually to be formed, adapted, revised, and renewed. And they often follow largely on structure, particularly on the internal balance of power, rather than the other way round.

These considerations imply that the administrative problem is much more complex than distributing the total task to be done in a way that maximizes the division of labor and facilitates coordination. It is largely a matter of brokerage and of handling political problems. Indeed it is evident today to students of organizations that the division of labor in existence at any given time is apt to generate particular policies, that is, structure can be cause as well as effect of policy. And a major preoccupation of senior management is precisely what steps to take to ensure that appropriate policies are generated.

It is an oversimplification to view any organization as one bounded unit acting in a unitary way towards a shared aim. It is more useful to accept the fact that organizations are made up of diverse categories and groups of persons pursuing multiple objectives. While the management theorists have emphasized the importance of every constituent group striving toward shared, collective goals it is unlikely that diverse groups will share the goals of senior management with equal intensity.

Lastly, the prescriptive theories tend to concentrate on the formal anatomy of the work organization, giving relatively little attention to the communal, interactional and motivational aspects or regarding these as irrelevant disturbances. This is not to say that they recommend unkind or inhuman behavior, only that the social consequences of bringing together subgroups of people into an enterprise are not well understood. Little room is left for such phenomena as breakdowns of communication, the operation of power as a variable, negative reactions to close supervision, overidentification with task associated with specialization, and the development of subobjectives distinct from, and sometimes opposed to, those of senior management. Employees tend to be viewed as inert or passive means to the aims of their seniors rather than as sources of quasi-independent action.

NOTES

1. C. Babbage, *On the Economy of Machinery and Manufacture,* (London: Charles Knight, 1832).
2. Babbage, *On the Economy,* p. 176. He noted that the same principle had oc-

curred to an earlier Italian writer, Gioja, and expressed in *Nuovo Prospetto delle Scienze Economiche,* (Milan, 1815). Babbage is famous in Britain as a pioneer of the ideas that have led to the construction of computers. He designed on mathematical principles a "calculating engine" or "difference engine" intended to yield perfect accuracy in extended calculations.

3. Babbage, *On the Economy,* p. 177.

4. 1841–1925.

5. References in this chapter are to a translation of this book by C. Storrs, published under the title *General and Industrial Management,* (London, Pitman, 1949).

6. L. Urwick, "The Function of Administration with Special Reference to the Work of Henri Foyol," in L. Gulick and L. Urwick, eds., *Papers on the Science of Administration.* (New York: Columbia University Press, 1937), p. 129.

7. Fayol, *General and Industrial Management,* p. 19.

8. Fayol, *General and Industrial Management,* p. 41.

9. I draw here on his *Management. A Study of Industrial Organization,* (London: Pitman, 1921).

10. He does, however, quote liberally from MacDougall, inter alia, to the integrating effect of more insight into the mutual dependence of large occupational groups.

11. Lee, *Management,* pp. 16–18.

12. Lee, *Management,* pp. 31 and 32.

13. Lee, *Management,* p. 27.

14. Lee, *Management,* pp. 37 and 38.

15. Lee, *Management,* p. 49.

16. Lee, *Management,* p. 56.

17. Lee, *Management,* p. 68.

18. Lee, *Management,* p. 72.

19. Lee, *Management,* pp. 84 and 85.

20. J. Lee, *Pitman's Dictionary of Industrial Administration. A Comprehensive Encyclopedia of the Organization, Administration and Management of Modern Industry,* (London: Pitman, 1928).

21. O. Sheldon, *The Philosophy of Management,* (London: Pitman, 1924). Reprinted with an introduction by A. W. Rathe (London: Pitman, 1965).

22. Foreword to second edition, p. xii.

23. Sheldon, *The Philosophy,* p. 262.

24. Sheldon, *The Philosophy,* p. 261.

25. Sheldon, *The Philosophy,* p. 261.

26. Sheldon, *The Philosophy,* p. 78.

27. Sheldon, *The Philosophy,* p. 72.

28. Sheldon, *The Philosophy,* p. 143.

29. Sheldon, *The Philosophy,* p. 131.

30. J. D. Mooney and A. C. Reiley, *Onward Industry!,* (New York: Harper, 1931).

31. Mooney and Reiley, *Onward,* p. 19.

32. Mooney and Reiley, *Onward,* p. 24.

33. Mooney and Reiley, *Onward,* p. 45.

34. Mooney and Reiley, *Onward,* p. 61.

35. Gulick and Urwick, Papers.

36. J. Mooney, *Principles of Organization,* (New York: Harper, 1947).

37. Mooney, *Principles,* p. 5.

38. 1868–1933.

39. H. C. Metcalf and L. Urwick, eds., *Dynamic Administration. The Collected Papers of M. P. Follett,* (London: Management Publications Trust, 1941). This is a posthumous collection spanning the period 1925–1932.

40. Metcalf and Urwick, *Dynamic Administration,* p. 34.

41. "Conflict," translated by Kurk H. Wolf, in G. Simmel, *Conflict and The Web of Group-Affiliations,* (London: Macmillan). The original version of the essay "Conflict," in German, appeared in 1908 as part of a book by Simmel. The 1955 publication is posthumous.

42. L. Coser, *The Social Functions of Conflict,* (New York: The Free Press, 1954).

43. Metcalfe and Urwick, eds., *Dynamic Administration,* pp. 58 and 59.

44. Metcalfe and Urwick, eds., *Dynamic Administration,* p. 297.

45. In a separate paper, also given originally in 1932 and published in the Gulick and Urwick 1937 collections as "The Process of Control" she refers to correspondence in progressive business thinking (presumably her own) with recent developments in science and philosophy. The convergence was on the idea that the essential nature of a unity is discovered not alone by a study of its separate elements but also by observing how these elements interact. Just as the behavior of wild mice was governed by an environmental complex, rather than by various components of that complex one by one, so the ablest business man sees the solution of his problem as depending on the interacting of elements in an environmental complex. (She makes no mention of the distinction expressed here between a generalized description of behavior in one situation and what the most adaptive behavior is in another. "This seems to me," she adds, "of the utmost importance for industry or for any other joint endeavour. This seems to me as important a principle for the social sciences as Einstein's theory of relativity for the natural sciences," p. 163.

These passages appear to anticipate or parallel the classical statements of what is known in psychology as Gestalt theory by W. Kohler in 1929, *Gestalt Psychology,* (New York: Liveright) and by K. Koffka in 1935, *Principles of Gestalt Psychology,* (New York: Harcourt Brace). An essential aspect of Gestalt theory is that psychological phenomena should be conceived as occurring as part of a system which has features not deducible from knowledge of its individual components and which has properties of its own.

46. Metcalfe and Urwick, eds., *Dynamic Administration,* p. 304.

47. L. Urwick, "Organization as a Technical Problem," written in 1933, reprinted in Gulick and Urwick, eds., *Papers.*

48. Urwick, "The Functions of Administration."

49. L. Gulick, "Notes on the Theory of Organization, With Special Reference to Government in the U.S.," in Gulick and Urwick, eds., *Papers.*

50. This is one of the few occasions on which these writers on management mention the technological variables.

51. L. Urwick, *The Elements of Administration,* (London: Pitman, 1944).

52. It is common among the classical and neo-classical writers to emphasize the importance of clarity of role definition. As more recent studies of behavior have pointed out, a certain amount of ambiguity can also have advantages in human institutions, for instance the advantage of giving more efficient colleagues the right to make good the deficiencies of the less efficient. See discussion by W. E. Moore and M. W. Tumin, "Some Social Functions of Ignorance," *American Sociological Review,* 14 (December 1949).

53. Urwick, *The Elements,* p. 68.

54. V. A. Graicunas, "Relationship in Organization," (*Bulletin of the International Management Institute,* 1933). Reprinted in Gulick and Urwick, *Papers.*

55. Gulick and Urwick, *Papers,* p. 185.

56. H. A. Simon, *Administrative Behaviour, A Study of Decision-Making Processes in Administrative Organization,* (New York: Macmillan, 1948), p. 240.

57. Simon, *Administrative Behaviour,* p. 240.

58. J. G. March and H. A. Simon, *Organizations,* (New York: Wiley, 1961).

59. A. D. Chandler, Jr., "Strategy and Structure," chapters in *The History of the*

Industrial Enterprise, (Cambridge, Massachusetts: M.I.T. Press Research Monographs, 1962).

60. Simon, *Administrative Behaviour,* p. 26.

61. J. C. Worthy, "Organizational Structure and Employee Morale," *American Sociological Review,* 15, no. 2 (April 1950).

9 : Decision Making

IN his celebrated book of 1948 [1] Herbert Simon declared that "a theory of administration should be concerned with the processes of decision as well as the processes of action." [2] The notion existed, he said, that decision-making is confined to the formulation of overall policy. But

On the contrary, the process of decision does not come to an end when the general purpose of an organization has been determined. The task of "deciding" pervades the entire administrative organization quite as much as does the task of "doing"—indeed, it is integrally tied up with the latter.[3] *

He points out that decision is a matter of compromise: the alternative that is finally selected never permits complete or perfect achievement of objectives, but is the best solution available under the circumstances.

Rationality in Decision-Making

While Simon gave particular attention to rationality in decision-making, he emphasized that he was not implying that human beings are always or generally rational, pointing out that this "misconception . . . has been decisively refuted by modern developments in psychology and sociology." [4] He pointed out that the concept of rationality in administration posed multiple problems, including the issue

in terms of what objectives, whose values, shall rationality be judged. Is behaviour of an individual in an organization rational when it serves his personal objectives, or when it serves the organizational objectives? [5]

He suggested that this difficulty be met by using the term "rational" in conjunction with appropriate adverbs. Thus, a decision would be "objectively" rational if it maximized given values in a given situation, "subjectively" rational if it maximized attainment relative to the actual knowledge of the subject, "organizationally" rational if it were oriented to the organization's

* Reprinted with permission of The Macmillan Company. *Administrative Behavior: A Study of Decision-Making Processes in Administrative Organization,* Herbert A. Simon. © 1947 Herbert A. Simon. Revised edition © 1957 by Herbert A. Simon.

goals, "personally" rational if oriented to the individual's goals.[6] Actual behavior would, in fact, fall short of "objective" rationality because of incomplete knowledge, because of the necessity to use imagination about the future, and because only a few out of all possible forms of behavior ever come to mind. The pattern of human choice was often more nearly a stimulus-response pattern than a choice among alternatives.

Decision-Making
and Compromise

When choices took place in a group situation—as was common—the consequences of a course of action became dependent not only upon the individual's selection of a particular alternative, but upon the selections of the other members of a group as well. Modifications of organizational (shared) objectives usually represented compromises between several groups of potential participants in order to secure their joint cooperation.

When the individual decided on a particular course of action, some of the premises upon which this action was based might have been imposed on him by the exercise of the organization's authority over him, some might be the result of his training, others of his desire for efficiency, still others of his organizational loyalty. The line of demarcation between the suggestion of a superior and a command was not clear: both would usually be liberally mixed together and the reaction of the subordinate would be mediated by conviction.

Simon pointed out that administration is group activity and that one correlate of this is that information and advice flow in all directions through the organization. An apparently simple way to allocate the functions of decision-making would be to assign to each member of the organization those decisions for which he possesses the relevant information. But the basic difficulty in this is that not all the information relevant to a particular decision is possessed by a single individual. Two basic pulls apply in determining the degree of centralization in decision-making. The need for responsibility, expertise, and coordination pull toward the center. But pulls come in the opposite direction because much information relevant to decisions originates at operating level, and because separation of decision from action increases costs in time and manpower. Information is not automatically transmitted but comes through persons who are aware of its consequences for them, and who (deliberately or unwittingly) modify, elaborate, or withhold it. Generally the organization structure will include the specification of a formal system of communication, but this will be supplemented by a rich network of informal communication based on the social relationships that develop in the organization.

Values in
Decision-Making

Simon holds that values enter substantially into administrative decision-making, affecting the objectives chosen, the degree to which the objectives are to be attained, and the proper distribution between persons and groups of costs and benefits. He describes a decision as efficient when it dictates that choice of alternatives which produces the largest result for a given application of resources. This formulation is, he says, analogous to the concept in economic theory of maximization of utility. He does not assert that the criterion of efficiency does dominate administrators and decisions "but rather that if they were rational it would." [7] But, he adds, "There is no assertion that such rationality is a common characteristic of actual behavior." [8] It is theoretically possible to relate resources to results in a systematic and optimal way, but in fact momentous decisions are normally made without doing so because of lack of knowledge and the magnitude of the task.

The ablest administrators are the first to admit that their decisions are, in general, the sheerest guesswork; that any confidence they evidence is the protective shield with which the practical man armors himself and his subordinates from his doubts. [9]

Composite Decisions

We are reminded by Simon that decisions are not made by organizations but by human beings behaving as members of organizations and that personal or departmental values enter the decision process alongside organizational values. He emphasizes that identification with work group or function are so pervasive that "one cannot participate for fifteen minutes in administrative affairs without meeting examples of them." [10]

Using a term "composite decision" suggested to him by C. I. Barnard, Simon underlines the point that

almost no decision made in an organization is the task of a single individual. Even though the final responsibility for taking a particular action rests with some definite person, we shall always find, in studying the manner in which this decision was reached, that its various components can be traced through the formal and informal channels of communication to many individuals who have participated in forming its premises. When all of these components have been identified it may appear that the contribution of the individual who made the decision was a minor one indeed. [11]

Limits of Rationality

In *Models of Man,* Simon carried further his analysis of limits of rationality.[12] *

Traditional economic theory postulates an "economic man" who, in the course of being "economic" is also "rational." This man is assumed to have knowledge of the relevant aspects of his environment which, if not absolutely complete, is at least impressively clear and voluminous. He is assumed also to have a well-organized and stable system of preferences, and a skill in computation that enables him to calculate, for the alternative courses of action that are available to him, which of these will permit him to reach the highest attainable point on his preference scale.

Recent developments in economics, and particularly in the theory of the business firm, have raised great doubts as to whether this schematized model of economic man provides a suitable foundation on which to erect a theory—whether it be a theory of how firms *do* behave, or of how they "should" rationally behave. It is not the purpose of this paper to discuss these doubts, or to determine whether they are justified. Rather, I shall assume that the concept of "economic man" (and, I might add, of his brother "administrative man") is in need of fairly drastic revision, and shall put forth some suggestions as to the direction the revision might take.

Broadly stated, the task is to replace the global rationality of economic man with a kind of rational behaviour that is compatible with the access to information and the computational capacities that are actually possessed by organisms, including man, in the kinds of environments in which such organisms exist.[13]

He made the important point there that

the state of information may as well be regarded as a characteristic of the decision-maker as a characteristic of his environment . . . what we call "the environment" may lie, in part, within the skin of the biological organism. That is, some of the constraints that must be taken as givens in an optimization problem may be physiological and psychological limitations of the organism (biologically defined) itself.[14]

He indicates internal and external constraints define rationality for a person.

Because of the psychological limits of the organism (particularly with respect to computational and predictive ability), actual human rationality-striving can at best be an extremely crude and simplified approximation to the kind of global rationality that is implied, for example, by game-theoretical models.[15]

It is interesting to note that Simon makes no mention here of the role of colleagues, external advisers, and so on in reducing the restrictions following from these characteristics of the individual human being. He is apparently more concerned to underline that persons tend to make choices within a range of alternatives more limited than the whole range objectively available to them.

* Reprinted by permission of the author.

He goes on to say that, in most global models of rational choice, all alternatives are evaluated before a choice is made but, in actual human decision-making, alternatives are often examined sequentially. This has the important consequence that

When alternatives are examined sequentially, we may regard the first satisfactory alternative that is evaluated as such as the one actually selected.[16]

Level of aspiration, he points out, may be an important factor in choice between alternatives and this depends upon "previous aspiration levels and previous levels of attainment." [17]

"Satisficing"

In this book Simon introduces the concept of "satisficing" which has become universally adopted in the context of decision-making. In discussing ways of simplifying the choice problem so as to bring it within the powers of human computation, he says,

The key to the simplification of the choice process . . . is the replacement of the goal of *maximising* with the goal of *satisficing*, of finding a course of action that is "good enough." [18]

It appears probably that, however adaptive the behaviour of organisms in learning and choice situations, this adaptiveness falls far short of the ideal of "maximising" postulated in economic theory. Evidently, organisms adapt well enough to "satisfice"; they do not, in general "optimize." [19]

Since the organism, like those of the real world, has neither the senses nor the wits to discover an "optimal path"—even assuming the concept of optimal to be clearly defined—we are concerned only with finding a choice mechanism that will lead it to pursue a "satisfactory" path, a path that will permit satisfaction at some specified level of all its needs.[20]

In his introduction to a second edition of *Administrative Behavior*, published in 1958, which is otherwise unchanged, Simon rejects unambiguously as unreal the assumption that men in organizations can be regarded as maximizing. What they really do, he says, is to look for a situation which is satisfactory or good enough.

Under the general heading of "The Limits of Rationality," he argues that

The central concern of administrative theory is with the boundary between the rational and non-rational aspects of human social behaviour. Administrative theory is peculiarly the theory of intended and bounded rationality—of the behaviour of human beings who satisfice because they have not the wits to maximise.[21]

Simon remarks that, since his earlier book, he wants to propose two crucial amendments to change the economic man into the man of limited rationality.

1. While economic man maximises-selects the best alternative from among all those available to him; his cousin, whom we shall call administrative man, satisfices—looks for a course of action that is satisfactory or "good enough." Examples of satisficing criteria that are familiar enough to business men, if unfamiliar to most economists, are "share of the market," "adequate profit," "fair prices."

2. Economic man deals with the "real world" in all its complexity. Administrative man recognises that the world he perceives is a dramatically simplified model of the buzzing, blooming confusion that constitutes the real world . . . He makes his choices using a simple picture of the factors that he regards as most relevant and crucial.

What is the significance of these two characteristics of administrative man? First, because he satisfices rather than maximises, administrative man can make his choices without first examining all possible behaviour alternatives and without ascertaining that these are in fact all the alternatives. Second, because he treats the world as rather "empty" and ignores the "interrelatedness of all things" (so stupefying to thought and action), administrative man is able to make his decisions with relatively simple rules of thumb that do not make impossible demands upon his capacity for thought.[22]

Simon appears to see as the central factor limiting rationality the inability of human minds to grasp more than a proportion of all knowable facts and possible consequences of action. But he is aware at the same time —though he does not elaborate on this—of the distorting effects of emotions on cognitive processes. He appears to feel that his point about the limitations imposed by imperfect knowledge and predictive capacity is sufficient to destroy the notion of the rational maximizer. He also appears to give less emphasis than social psychologists to the part played by emotion in organizational affairs, because he is concerned to assert that

human behavior in organizations is, if not wholly rational, at least in good part *intendedly* so. Much behaviour in organizations is, or seems to be, task oriented —and sometimes efficacious in attaining its goals . . . it is precisely in the realm where human behaviour is *intendedly* rational, but only *limitedly* so, that there is room for a genuine theory of organization and administration.[23]

In a later work [24] Simon connects more explicitly his assertion of the importance of the satisficing principle with psychological studies of the formation and changes of aspiration levels. These studies show, inter alia, that when performance falls short of level of aspiration, search behavior (particularly search for new alternatives of action) is induced. At the same time, the level of aspiration is adjusted downward until goals reach levels that are practically attainable. He cites empirical evidence that business goals are in fact set in satisficing terms. One series of studies shows that businessmen often set prices by applying a standard mark-up to costs. Another series showed that the rate of interest was not an important factor in investment decisions. A study attempting to test the satisficing model more directly found evidence that firms whose share of market was steady or increasing strove less vigorously to increase sales than firms with a declining share of market.

In a joint work published in 1961, Simon and his colleagues state the proposition that

Most human decision-making, whether individual or organizational, is concerned with the discovery and selection of satisfactory alternatives; only in exceptional cases is it concerned with the discovery and selection of optimal alternatives. To optimize requires processes several orders of magnitude more complex than those required to satisfice. An example is the difference between searching a haystack to find the *sharpest* needle in it and searching the haystack to find a needle sharp enough to sew with.[25]

Simon reverted also, in his 1958 introduction, to the composite quality of administrative decisions.

Discussions of administrative centralization and decentralization often bog down on the question: "Who *really* makes the decisions?" Such a question is meaningless—a complex decision is like a great river, drawing from its many tributaries the innumerable component premises of which it is constituted. Many individuals and organization units contribute to every large decision.[26]

C. I. Barnard:
Decision-Making
and the Executive

In 1958 C. I. Barnard published an elaboration of a series of lectures on executives and organizations he had given in Boston in 1937 and which had already had some currency among social scientists and managers.[27] In his discussion of decision-making he distinguishes firmly decisions relating to organizational ends from those relating to personal ends, asserting that "organizational" ends and acts must usually be explicitly formulated and coordinated and impose a requirement of logicality. This could perhaps have been more appropriately expressed as a relative matter, but one can see that what Barnard is driving at is that, since organizations are systems of collaborative effort around defined purposes or missions, a demand arises from participants for a rationale for decisions and actions which can be widely justified in terms of the relating of means to ends.

It is the deliberate adoption of means to ends which is the essence of formal organization. This is not only required in order to make cooperation superior to the biological powers and senses of individuals, but it is possibly the chief superiority of cooperative to individual action in most of the important cases of enduring organizations.[28]

Barnard is not implying that unconscious, "automatic" or nonlogical action is absent or unimportant in organizations. The contrary is the case. But he is asserting that logically-based or logically-attempted means-ends decisions and executive behavior are the very essence of organizational life and, like Simon therefore, that if we want to understand organizations the study of organizational decision-making is an essential requirement.

Continuing his discussion of the distinction between organizational and personal decisions, he suggests that "a sort of dual personality" is required of individuals contributing to organizational action, the private personality and the organization personality. In his organizational capacity, the individual may well take decisions other than those he would take were the assets his own; he is compelled to take account of whether the decision is properly his, with whom he must share it and who apart from himself will have to execute it. The aptness of the decision depends, further, on knowledge of facts and organizational purpose and is therefore bound up with organizational communication. Central or general organization decisions are best made at centers of the communication system, so that such decisions must be assigned to those located at the central positions.

In other words, Barnard sees a strain toward logic in organizational systems and a tendency for executive decisions to be located at intersections of communication systems to which information can flow.

Barnard then suggests rather surprisingly that the making of decisions is burdensome and that people tend to avert or avoid decisions if they can. He applies this particularly to the executive in an organization who must, he points out, ward off all but the decisions necessary to his role if he is to retain his capacities: his difficulties in doing so are in part a consequence of the tendency of others to burden him with their own decisions. (It is a pity that Barnard did not follow up the issue of conflicts around decision areas, in view of his difference from the assumption most people would make that executives like power and enjoy making decisions even if this trespasses on the rights of others.) Barnard classifies occasions for decisions by an executive into those that arise from the requirements of a superior authority, those referred to him from below, and (the most important tests of capacity) those where he must determine for himself whether something must be done or corrected.

The most important obligation is to raise and decide those issues which no one else is in a position to raise effectively.[29]

From the point of view of the relative importance of specific decisions, those of executives, says Barnard, properly call for first attention. But, as he says, from the point of view of aggregate importance, it is the position of nonexecutive participants in an organization which should enlist major interest.

It is easily evident merely from the inspection of the action of the nonexecutive participants in organization that coordination of action requires repeated organization decisions "on the spot" where the effective action of organization takes place. It is here that the final and most concrete objectives of purposes are found, with the maximum of definiteness. There is no further stage of organization action. The final selection of means takes place at this point.[30]

Barnard is saying that the executive's work consists largely of facilitation of effective decisions by others, clarifying and presenting issues and choices. But, toward the upper end of the decision pyramid, choices are between ends; at the lower, choices are, so to speak, "technological," between means.

Barnard then perceptively discusses the diffuseness of decisions and of their effects. As he says, the evidence bearing on the effects of a decision is often indirect or difficult to collect—effects must be inferred from consequences of which the decision is probably only one cause.

One important decision is to not decide. In a striking formulation, Barnard says,

the fine art of executive decision consists in not deciding questions that are not now pertinent, in not deciding prematurely, in not making decisions that cannot be made effective, and in not making decisions that others should make.[31]

In another novel statement, Barnard suggests that we consider existing purposes, that is, the results of previous decisions, as part of the decision-making environment. He is, of course, perfectly correct. Prior decisions structure the situation for decisions and the observed fate of earlier decisions enter into the feasibility of new decisions. To take an obvious example, if previous attempts at decentralization have failed, colleagues will not react sympathetically to a fresh suggestion to decentralize. The rest of the environment for decisions consists of physical objects and of men and institutionalized behavior: these have to be split into those items material and immaterial to the decision, that discrimination being in itself part of the budding new purpose.

Barnard concludes from this reasoning that within complex organizations there is a technique of decision, "an organizational process of thinking," that may not be analogous to that of an individual. In organizations, "decision is in its important aspects a social process, and the process of decision in individuals . . . is a psychological process socially conditioned." [32]

Barnard consistently emphasizes that organizations are cooperative systems, formed because certain ends cannot be achieved by individual action. As a consequence, decisions in organizations are, for him, non-personal— that is, acts related not to individual ends but made with coordinative action in mind. Another result is that the efforts of the individual in an organization result from decisions that are in part *necessarily* made by others acting non-personally.

Lindblom: Incremental Change
through Successive
Limited Comparisons

The issue of rationality in decision-making was again taken up insightfully by C. E. Lindblom in 1959.[33] He begins by contrasting two possible approaches to policy-making. In one approach the administrator would try to list all related values in order of importance, rate all possible policy outcomes as more or less efficient in attaining a maximum of these values, systematically compare all these alternatives, then make the choice that would, in fact, maximize his values.

Alternatively, the policy-maker might set as his principal objective one relatively simple goal, disregarding most other values as beyond his present interest, and without ranking the few values that he regards as immediately relevant. He would outline the relatively few policy alternatives that occur to him, and compare them, leaning heavily in doing so on past experiences with similar steps to predict what might happen if the same steps were repeated. He would combine into one a choice among values and a choice among instruments for reaching values. This would not, as in the first method, approximate a more mechanical process of choosing the means that best satisfied goals that were previously clarified and ranked. The policy-maker would expect to achieve his goals only partially.

Lindblom points out that the second process is much commoner and is in fact inevitable. The former assumes intellectual capacities and sources of information that men do not in fact possess and would make unrealistic demands on time and money in complex problems. At the same time, attempts to analyze the process of rational policy formation continue to imply the first approach and not the second.

The common tendency to describe policy formulation even for complex problems as though it followed the first approach has been strengthened by the attention given to, and successes enjoyed by, operations research, statistical decision theory and systems analysis. The hallmarks of these procedures, typical of the first approach, are clarity of objective, explicitness of evaluation, a high degree of comprehensiveness of overview, and, wherever possible, quantification of values for mathematical analysis. But these advanced procedures remain largely the appropriate techniques of relatively small-scale problem-solving where the total number of variables to be considered is small and value problems restricted.[34]

The rest of the paper is an attempt to clarify and formalize the second method, which he describes as the method of "successive limited comparisons" or the "branch" method. Under the "branch" method, one builds out from the current situation, step by step and by small degrees. Under the "root" (or rational-comprehensive method) one starts every time from fundamentals.

Describing the method of "successive limited comparisons", Lindblom says that it is often extremely difficult or impossible to clarify or rank values in advance of alternative policies. There is too much disagreement on central objectives or subobjectives, values are in conflict with each other, there may not have been enough prior discussion to alert people to the values involved, and it is hard to weigh intensity of feeling against numbers of persons having a particular attitude. Values are unlikely to be shared and reconcilable. Typically the administrator chooses among policies in which these values are combined in different ways. He cannot first clarify his values and then choose among policies. The administrator focuses his attention on marginal or incremental values, choosing between one policy that gives him more of one desideratum and another that gives him less of that desideratum but more of another. In the method of successively limited comparisons simplification is achieved by (1) limiting policy comparisons and choices to those policies that differ in relatively small degree from those at present in effect, and (2) ignoring some of the possible consequences, even if they may be important, leaving other parties to watch their own interests. Under this method

Policy is not made once and for all, it is made and re-made endlessly. Policy making is a process of successive approximation to some desired objective in which what is desired itself continues to change under reconsideration.[35]

Using past experience, the administrator moves by small steps, none of which are expected to bring a final resolution of his problem, while he avoids big jumps that would go beyond current knowledge or be irretrievable. It is possible in this way to test his predictions as he goes or to remedy errors.

Lindblom asserts with helpful candor that the incremental, limited comparison approach is superior to the root approach precisely because we so often lack adequate theories to apply to problem areas, that comparative analysis is sometimes a systematic alternative to theory. Instead of having to understand all the consequences of each aspect of each policy, the policymaker needs know only the consequences of each of those aspects of the policies in which they differ from each other, mobilizing past experience in the service of this objective.

Dror: Combining Rational and Extra-Rational Models

In a paper published five years later, Y. Dror criticized Lindblom's justification of policy and decision-making through incremental changes closely based on past experience.[36] He agrees that Lindblom's formulation is closer to reality than the models of decision-making accepted in the "management sciences." But he feels that Lindblom's influence might reinforce these ways of making decisions, which are suitable only under certain limited conditions.

As Dror puts it, the method Lindblom describes maximizes security in making changes. But, Dror argues, incremental change by successive limited comparison is only adequate if the results of present policies are reasonably satisfactory, if there is continuity in the nature of the problem, and if there is continuity in the available means for dealing with it. If the first condition does not obtain, it is worth taking risks with new policies. If the problem is a new one incremental change is impossible. Finally, changes in knowledge and technique may suggest quite new ways of dealing with problems and outdate the former means and their users.

Dror points out that all three conditions are often absent in contemporary society, characterized as it is by rapid changes in level of aspiration, drastic redefinitions of issues, and dissatisfaction with available means of action.

Dror suggests that it might be possible to combine the "muddling through" and rational comprehensive models into what he calls a "normative optimum model." This would require efforts to increase rationality content through more explication of goals, extensive search for new alternatives, and specification of expectations. At the same time, we should recognize the part played by "extra-rational" processes in three ways. First we should concede that we lack resources and capacity for complete rationality. Second, we should allow a place for intuitive judgment and holistic impressions. Third, we should employ in decision-making and problem solving the new techniques of case discussion, brainstorming, and group dynamics sessions.

Lindblom replied in the same issue of the journal.[37] He agreed with Dror that muddling through was not in all circumstances a defensible strategy for decision-making. He pointed out, however, that, so far as public decisions go, the three conditions put by Dror are in fact met in stable political democracies, for examples in the fields of policy making on taxation, reform of the judiciary, anti-trust operations, zoning and traffic control.[38]

Lindblom was skeptical about whether his model would reinforce inertia and reluctance to innovate. Logically speaking, he says, one can make changes as rapidly through a series of incremental steps as through more drastic and less frequent alterations. At the same time, this is probably easier for decision makers, as incremental changes are not fraught with great risks of error or political conflict.

Pfiffner: Administrative Rationality

In "Administrative Rationality," J. M. Pfiffner bases a description of the typical decision-making process on an analysis of 332 actual administrative decisions.[39] As he says, this study confirms Simon's concept of the administrator as satisficer and Lindblom's argument that real decision-making differs from the notional rational-comprehensive approach. In fact, Pfiffner's formulation goes further.

The orthodox concepts of rationality conform to those usually attributed to economic man, the scientific method, and engineering man. Rational decision-making is thought of as the gathering of all pertinent facts, canvassing the alternatives for action, and selecting the one which will produce maximum results through a thought process which physiology associates with the cerebrum . . . our principal thesis [is] that administrative rationality differs from orthodox concepts of rationality because it does take into account an additional spectrum of facts. These are the facts relative to emotions, politics, power, group dynamics, personality and mental health.[40]

Pfiffner makes the point that policy is not made only from above but is the resultant of many forces, including the attempts of lower echelons to preserve or gain autonomy. While the senior ranks try to maintain control, they characteristically run into opposition and become involved in negotiation, compromise, and truce. One result is that policy is as much a result of agreement as command.

He enriches the picture of the use of information in decision-making. The information available is normally derived from others, incomplete, difficult to verify because of time limitations, and often so complex as to be susceptible to more than one interpretation. It is screened through a mesh of conflicting considerations, knowledge, and experience. Information does not flow in an orderly way up the hierarchy but flows in multiple directions along overlapping and elusive channels.

Pfiffner introduces the part played by personal values in decision-making. He concludes that among the "standards of validity" that a decision has to meet, there may have to be included (1) some degree of conformance with the personal interests and values of the decision maker, (2) conformance with the values of superiors, (3) acceptability to those who would be affected by the decision and those who will have to implement it, (4) face validity in the sense that it looks reasonable in its context, (5) a built-in justification which will furnish excuses and justifications in case the results are not as hoped.

This raises the question of how personal and organizational interests are reconciled. How does it happen that personal interests do not simply override the organizational? Pfiffner's answer is as follows:

People bring to administrative decision-making their own personal value systems which they inject into the substance of decision-making while clothing their decisions with the formal logic of "the good of the organization" . . . But this does not lead to chaos because there is a large element of commonality in personal value systems as related to organizational goals . . . the cybernetics model . . . postulates an organization based upon the animal prototype with a single brain and memory. Our research indicates, contrarily, that the organizations dealt with in our cases were pluralistic, their members having multiple loyalties and expectations. Instead of being unitary and monocratic they were, rather, federations of co-operation, co-existing organic units working together for common ends.[41]

It is not entirely clear from the above whether Pfiffner means that the ends are common between or only within the federated subgroups that make up organizations. One assumes the latter. As he says, personal values enter decision-making, but the outlook of managerial employees comes over time to acquire organizational or at least suborganizational components. So much is this the case that managers may take strong personal standpoints on organizational matters which genuinely fuse personal and occupational or organizational identities. As studies of my own point out, some managers even have difficulty in conceptualizing their own interests, aptitudes and inclinations as entities separate from the roles their seniors allot them to perform.[42] So, in interpreting what Pfiffner means by "personal" values or goals entering administrative decisions, I think we must not assume that "personal" should be taken to refer only or mainly to extra-organizational, private considerations. The processes of identification with departmental and organizational interests and the building of personal identity from organizational interests would weigh heavily against this—quite apart from the internal ethical system of the administrator himself and pressures emanating from his colleagues.

Pfiffner raises the question of whether administrative decision-making is rational. As he says, from one point of view it is more rational than the classical model because it considers social and psychological data virtually ignored there. To say that administrative decision-making is less rational because it includes these non-rational data is to imply that the politician is less rational than the engineer. The administrative decision maker tries to please as many people as possible, including himself, thus adding a strong political tinge to the decision process. He imitates or refers to what others are doing; he stays in line with tradition (which excuses him if something goes wrong); he conducts experimental or pilot programs; he takes the advice of superiors and consults others implicated; he accepts that there may be more than one reasonably satisfactory solution to a given problem; he takes commonsense shortcuts; he guesses how people are likely to react to his decisions and he modifies and presents these in a way that is meant to reduce resistance.

The human considerations that the administrator takes into account are identical with the subject matter of the sociologist student of organizations.

The effective administrator takes into consideration a set of data which roughly corresponds to the data that social scientists are interested in. To be sure, it is not refined in the way that experimental social scientists would like to refine it nor is it analyzed or described in the way that the cultural social scientists would do it, but the fact remains that he is taking into account the probable human reactions to his decisions and actions.[43]

Bales: Committee Decisions

R. F. Bales points out that most decisions are made in conference and normally require a series of further conferences for their implementation.[44] It is important therefore that such face-to-face meetings be successful in the minimal sense of avoiding breakdown and in the more positive sense of exchanging information, getting a better understanding of a situation, and posing problems. Bales suggests on the basis of his studies, that something like a fifty-fifty balance is necessary between questions and answers and that, without enough time for questioning and reaction, members may carry away tensions that will eventually operate to vitiate what was only a superficially successful decision. Members of a committee do not seem to feel strongly bound by a decision unless they have taken part in making it: while one may agree with the questions and answers of others, there is probably, says Bales, no adequate substitute for some actual verbal participation. He reports that there are about twice as many positive reactions in most meetings as there are negative reactions. Lack of disagreement is a danger signal: it indicates lack of involvement or a feeling that members do not feel free to express their opinions. It is also unrealistic, Bales says, to expect few disagreements—"as in an ordinary discussion there is always a certain percentage of opinions and suggestions so unrealistic, exaggerated, or unsuitable that not to disagree means not to solve the problem."

It appears from Bales's paper that suggestions are an outcome of a successful meeting, not a way of obtaining that success. In making a suggestion, a man expresses his feelings and prejudices and confronts others with a choice between rejecting his assumptions and the implications of what he proposes or constraining themselves by accepting. According to Bales, most successful groups first assemble information, then make inferences from this and try to form common opinions, and, only after such groundwork of accepted facts, common inferences, and sentiments, get to more specific suggestions. He suggests that this order follows not from wisdom but from a sort of natural selection; for example, suggestions made early tend to wither for lack of support or because everyone does not share the data on which the suggestion is based.

Discussion

Simon brought to central consideration the decision-making aspects of administrative behavior. In a recent article he reminds us that his concern follows logically from the work of Max Weber, who emphasized that one of the main factors that differentiates contemporary work organizations from other institutions is the rationalization of their operations.[45] As Simon says, because organizations are goal-oriented, administrative behavior is largely concerned with finding effective patterns of activity directed toward the goals and with influencing subordinates to develop these patterns.

Barnard is in the same tradition. He argues that cooperation between people in the achievement of ends that they cannot achieve alone is the essence of organizations. Decisions about how this is done impose a discipline of explicit formulation and at least attempted rationality. Decisions, he says, tend to be made on a basis relating to "organizational purpose" rather than to individual motives or aspirations. Although he brings out the special responsibility of executives to take decisions it is clear from his work that he realizes that organizational decisions are usually cooperatively made and bear on the way people should cooperate.

It is implicit in both Simon's and Barnard's work that decision making pervades the organization. While each major policy decision lays down the general approach to a problem that a management want to be followed, this generates a large number of subdecisions for each level of personnel as to how the policy is to be interpreted or implemented in particular classes of case and situation. In addition, the necessity arises at every level for making decisions for which no guidance or insufficient guidance is available. Both deliberate and spontaneous, adaptive decisions taken over years may effectively determine subsequent policy formation or circumscribe the number of policy choices subsequently available. This line of reasoning was followed later by Cyert and March [46] who pointed out that in an established organization, scope for decision making is constrained by prior decisions, explicit or implicit, expressed in earlier investments, previously approved budgets, moral commitments to individuals and departments, contracts of employment and so on. This means that every decision need not be made anew and that the decision maker's range of choice in new decisions is narrowed. To put this in Barnard's terms, past decisions are an important part of the environment of new decisions.

Lindblom asserts that it is characteristic of administrators to manipulate standing arrangements marginally, to alter the weights allotted to standing commitments rather than to reconsider from scratch. He argues that this is the most sensible or economical mode of procedure for a body facing standing problems. His argument appears to have special force under conditions of relative stability when the electorate of an administrator is not undergoing drastic change and when the tasks to be performed on the environment remain much the same from year to year. An additional advantage is that marginal incremental changes allow experimentation without major commitment before irreversible moves are made in a new direction. Dror responds that this approach limits human choice too closely. It provides an environment for organizational participants and for those affected by the decisions which limit the application of increased human ingenuity and of fresh knowledge, particularly where new problems are being encountered.

This sounds like a conservative-radical argument which is less a matter of rational adjudication or for empirical research than of philosophical preference. From our point of view it is useful to note that most established organizations in fact tend to follow the pattern described by Lindblom, though intermittent attempts are common in the history of most large organizations to obtain objective advice on the choices theoretically open to them. This is often done by commissioning external consultants, who are less bound in their analyses by the institutionalized practices and standing commitments of their clients.

Despite his emphasis on decision-making, Simon makes it clear that he is not implying that managers spend all their time making decisions.

Only a small fraction of the time of administrators is spent in actually choosing among courses of action once they have been presented for selection. A larger fraction is spent . . . searching for situations and problems that call for attention and filtering and interpreting incoming information about the changing environment that might signal such situations and problems. An even larger fraction is spent in designing action alternatives, that is, sharpening the formulation of problems to which attention has been drawn by intelligence activities, specifying possible courses of action, and elaborating and evaluating them. Approval of an action, the final act of choice, takes place in administration only within this larger context of intelligence and design activities.[47]

Simon argued that a theory of administration should be concerned with *processes* of decision. His own work does not in fact concern itself with description and analysis of social process, though he is closely familiar with the results of such processes and is justified in generalizing about these. Bales' account of decision-making in committees helps to supply this dynamic aspect, dealing with actual interaction, within bodies constituted to take decisions. His work is based on laboratory simulations, not on field studies of real-life groups of administrators, but successfully highlights sequences of behavior that affect the quality of decisions and the likelihood that participants will carry these out in the spirit that they were formulated. A subsequent formulation by I. L. Janis elaborates the picture by showing the importance of what he calls 'groupthink,' that is, the tendency of members of decision-making groups to become committed after a quite early stage in proceedings to a line of reasoning which then becomes virtually impossible to question or challenge without the application of severe, if usually informal, social sanctions.[48] Both Bales and Janis deal with committee-type decisions rather than those that involve several departments of an organization or move through several hierarchical levels: an account and analysis of such a decision is contained in Chapter 15 of this book. Simon disposed of the myth that people maximise utilities, pointing out that all decisions are imperfect and matters of compromise; that personal, departmental, and organizational identifications and aims compete with each other; that values, tradition, emotion, and prejudice blur "objectivity"; that choice is circumscribed by limits on the capacities and aspirations of the choosers and by the impracticality of isolating single problems for attention in the face of multiple preoccupations. His contributions have been conceptual and theoretical rather than empirical and descriptive. But his approach fits closely with what we know from studies of what people actually do. The realism he imparts is not derived from knowledge of the associational needs of organizational participants or their tendency to attribute values to what they do. Rather, he sees bounded rationality as adaptive behavior by decision makers in environments whose complexity is grossly disproportionate to human knowledge and computational powers. Satisficing is a central means used by decision makers for matching the choice process to their information-collecting and information-processing limitations.

This formulation poses the question of the kinds of decision likely to be made in circumstances where rationality and information are imperfect and incomplete—which, since Simon, we must now accept as the typical situation. One lead on this comes from J. A. Robinson, who states that where information is scanty, evaluative criteria for choice are likely to become more important than empirical or factual criteria.[49] Robinson adds that the type of decision made will be likely to depend on the situation the decision makers are in. They will be involved in one way where conditions are relatively stable and in another in situations that appear threatening to their goal, require a relatively short response time, and are unanticipated. It is also clear that the elements of uncertainty in decisions provide opportunity for persuasion and power politics within the organization, so that the adoption of particular solutions to problems may be mainly due to the persuasiveness or the power of their proponents.

Important variables in decision-making derive from the structure of the organization in which the decisions are made. These variables affect ways of reaching decisions and the nature and quality of decisions. In the long run the decision-making process has certain circular properties since the structure of the organization is itself a product of a long chain of decisions, explicit and implicit.

The importance of organizational structure to decision-making becomes apparent as soon as one begins to list structural differences between any one organization and another. These include the extent to which the organization is centralized or decentralized in its operations; the number and relative power of levels in the hierarchy of authority; the extent to which labor is divided and departmental and personal roles specialized; the extent to which procedures are programmed or improvised. There are equally important, though more subtle regularities in organizational behavior which closely affect decisions and which we may also class as structural properties though of a less formalized nature. Among these are the patterns of recruitment to the levels of the organization at which decisions are made; the communication paths through the organization (some planned, others unplanned); the extent of participation in the decision-making process; and the receptiveness of decision-makers to feedback from those on whom their decisions impinge.

NOTES

1. H. A. Simon, *Administrative Behaviour: A Study of Decision-Making Processes in Administrative Organization,* (New York: Macmillan, 1948).

2. Simon, *Administrative Behaviour,* p. 1.

3. Simon, *Administrative Behaviour,* p. 1.

4. Simon, *Administrative Behaviour,* pp. 61 and 62.

5. Simon, *Administrative Behaviour,* p. 76.

6. Simon, *Administrative Behaviour,* pp. 76 and 77.

7. Simon, *Administrative Behaviour,* p. 182.

8. Simon, *Administrative Behaviour,* p. 182.

9. Simon, *Administrative Behaviour,* p. 182.

10. Simon, *Administrative Behaviour,* p. 206.

11. Simon, *Administrative Behaviour,* p. 221.

12. H. A. Simon, *Models of Man, Social and Rational,* (New York: Wiley, 1957).

13. Simon, *Models of Man,* p. 241.

14. Simon, *Models of Man,* pp. 242 and 243.

15. Simon, *Models of Man,* p. 244.

16. Simon, *Models of Man,* p. 252.

17. Simon, *Models of Man,* p. 255.

18. Simon, *Models of Man,* pp. 204–205.

19. Simon, *Models of Man,* p. 261.

20. Simon, *Models of Man,* p. 271.

21. Simon, *Administrative Behaviour,* introduction to second edition, p. xxiv.

22. Simon, *Administrative Behaviour,* introduction to second edition, pp. xxv and xxvi.

23. Simon, *Administrative Behaviour,* introduction to second edition, pp. xxiii and xxiv.

24. H. A. Simon, "Theories of Decision-Making in Economics and Behavioural Science," *The American Economic Review,* 49 (June 1959).

25. J. G. March and H. A. Simon, with the collaboration of H. Guetzkow, *Organizations,* (New York: Wiley, 1961), pp. 140 and 141.

26. Simon, *Administrative Behaviour,* introduction to second edition, p. xii.

27. C. I. Barnard, *The Functions of the Executive,* (Cambridge, Massachusetts: Harvard University Press, 1958).

28. Barnard, *The Functions,* p. 186.

29. Barnard, *The Functions,* p. 191.

30. Barnard, *The Functions,* p. 192.

31. Barnard, *The Functions,* p. 194.

32. Barnard, *The Functions,* pp. 198 and 199.

33. C. E. Lindblom, "The Science of Muddling Through," *Public Administration Review,* 19 (Spring 1959).

34. Lindblom, "The Science," p. 80.

35. Lindblom, "The Science," p. 86.

36. Y. Dror, "Muddling Through—Science or Inertia," *Public Administration Review,* 24, no. 3 (September 1964).

37. C. E. Lindblom, "Contexts for Change and Strategy: A Reply," *Public Administration Review,* 24, no. 3 (September 1964).

38. Lindblom included in this list national security, foreign aid, and agricultural price supports. In these cases it appears to me that he is wrong and Dror right in view of the speed of change today in the technological, political, and economic factors bearing on national affairs in these areas.

39. J. M. Pfiffner, "Administrative Rationality," *Public Administration Review,* 20 (Summer 1960).

40. Pfiffner, "Administrative Rationality," p. 126.

41. Pfiffner, "Administrative Rationality," p. 128.

42. C. Sofer, Men in Mid-Career (Cambridge, England: Cambridge University Press, 1970).

43. Pfiffner, "Administrative Rationality," p. 131.

44. R. S. Bales, "In Conference," *Harvard Business Review,* 32 (1954).

45. H. A. Simon, "Administrative Behaviour," *International Encyclopaedia of the Social Sciences,* 1 (New York: Macmillan, 1968).

46. R. M. Cyert and J. G. March, *A Behavioral Theory of the Firm* (Englewood Cliffs, New Jersey: Prentice Hall, 1963).

47. Simon, "Administrative Behaviour," p. 77.

48. I. L. Janis, *Victims of Groupthink: A Psychological Study of Foreign-policy Decisions and Fiascos,* to be published.

49. J. A. Robinson, "Decision-making. Political Aspects," *International Encyclopaedia of the Social Sciences,* 4 (New York: Macmillan, 1968).

PART III

Applied Social Sciences in Wartime

10 : The U.S. Army Studies and Their Legacy

WE have mentioned earlier the part played by psychologists in Britain and the United States in the 1914–1918 war and the stimulation given by the wartime experience to "industrial psychology." This process was repeated during the 1939–1945 war. It was, however, different in several important respects. One was the prominence, especially in Britain, of participation by psychoanalytically oriented psychiatrists. A second difference was that of scale, especially in the United States, where social science participation was at a level unprecedented in history, either during war or peace. Both sets of experiences were significant for advances in regard to the uses to which social sciences can be put—though the latter possibilities have perhaps been only partially exploited.

Far-reaching studies were made in the American army during the 1939–1945 war by the research branch of the United States War Department's Information and Education Division. The senior professional member of the research group was Samuel Stouffer. At the end of the war the original material was re-analyzed under the auspices of the United States Social Science Research Council, and four volumes were published.[1]

Research as an Instrument of Administration

One aspect of this program was the important part played by social research in national military policy. This illustrated some of the potentialities of social sciences for management. The research workers demonstrated a new capacity to ascertain before decisions are made the opinions of the people who will be affected, thereby enabling policy makers to base policies on knowledge rather than intuitions and impressions. They demonstrated at the same time that they could measure changes in attitudes over time so that one could in some important respects check after the event whether a decision —for instance the decision to mix black and white troops in the same units— had succeeded. The army had assumed it was better to keep white and colored soldiers apart, as relations would worsen with contact. A formal study showed the opposite: where there had been contact there was less prejudice and discrimination. This led to a reversal of policy.

One of the first studies was made the day after Pearl Harbor on a representative cross section of 1,500 enlisted men in one infantry division in training. This was full of knowledgeable criticisms of the training methods and the leadership of the army which had not yet adapted to the requirements of modern warfare. As one result, plans were revised for the new Officers' Candidate Schools.[2] The army, it was now realized, could replace guesswork about morale problems with evidence. Detailed analyses showed that one set of problems stemmed from the fact that Officers' Candidate Schools created considerable anxiety in candidates, also that many who started as enlisted men lost, once they were officers, the habit of seeing the enlisted man's point of view. The research workers were able both to collect facts and to establish reasons for the situations they described.

Several of the studies were used in personnel administration. A test was developed with the medical side of the army which was used for psychiatric screening in all induction stations during the war. Further tests were designed for placement that took into account not only aptitudes (already done to some extent in the First World War in the light of what was then known in psychology) but also interests and motivation. This permitted significantly more individual choice and satisfaction. As Stouffer remarks,

In World War I psychologists first measured *aptitudes* on a large scale. . . . By World War II psychology was ready with improved techniques of measurement and classification to aid in the selection of airplane pilots, navigators and bombardiers, and to assign soldiers generally on a basis that took account of their abilities . . . In World War II the Research Branch found that aptitudes and attitudes were like the two blades of a pair of scissors. Men who got a chance to volunteer for their specific assignments were much better satisfied than those who never got a chance to choose.[3]

One of the most valuable studies was carried out in connection with the establishment of demobilization priorities. The President and the War Department decided that the order of demobilization should be determined in terms of what the soldiers themselves wanted. Representative samples of soldiers all over the world were asked about this, and the key variables that emerged as those they thought should be taken into account were length of service, overseas duty, combat duty, and parenthood. The weightings were also largely derived from these studies, and a system was then adopted in close correspondence with the wishes of a maximum of soldiers. The establishment of an objective system of this type was accepted favorably, even by those whose own priority for return did not emerge as high. The usefulness of the social scientific approach is underlined by the fact that these reactions to the scheme were systematically checked on a representative worldwide sample of soldiers.[4]

The research workers state that

there can be little doubt that the point system for determining priorities for demobilization, with the emphasis on how it was derived from the men's own opinions, and the early initiation of operation of the system, blunted what could easily have been rather explosive attitudes of resentment and feelings of injustice among soldiers.[5] *

The research workers point out that the army had a choice between demobilizing whole units or individuals.

There can be little doubt that the Army took a considerable gamble with destiny in adopting a system of demobilization of individuals rather than of units. If men were robots the arguments advanced by Army Ground Forces for discharge by units—in order to keep veteran combat organizations intact—would have had great plausibility.[6]

The choice taken appears to be a triumph for what Pfiffner later described as "administrative rationality" in organizational decision making.[7]

Apart from these major studies, attitude surveys were used as standard practice to collect systematic information rapidly and economically on such matters as factors determining the amount of care men took to avoid physical illness, preferences between various types of housing, clothing, and recreation, and problems of social relations with foreign allies and with former enemy populations in occupied territories.

PREDICTION AND EXPERIMENT

The studies showed that they could go beyond description to prediction. The research unit did a precombat study of all the enlisted men in 108 rifle companies in four divisions just before the Normandy invasion. After two months of fighting, it was established that on the average the companies with the lowest morale indices before combat had 60 percent more non-battle casualties in Normandy than the companies with the highest.

The research branch conducted small-scale controlled experiments that were used as a basis for policy choices. They used them, for example, in helping the army to decide whether to continue traditional physical training methods (exercises, hikes, etc.) or new methods. Two samples of new recruits matched for physical proficiency were selected. Each sample was given differing treatment. After six weeks they were retested. The research workers found greater proficiency in those using the new methods and preference for them. As a consequence the old program was scrapped and the new adopted.

Experiments were conducted on propaganda, presenting two-sided arguments as against one-sided study. The result was that two-sided propaganda worked better with better-educated soldiers, one-sided with others.

* From *The American Soldier: Combat and Its Aftermath*, vol. II of *Studies in Social Psychology in World War II*, by Samuel A. Stauffer, et al. © 1949 by Princeton University Press. Reprinted by permission of Princeton University Press.

Long-Range
Theoretical Importance

Apart from their practical usefulness, several of the wartime studies and postwar analyses had long-range theoretical importance for the study of organizations and occupations.

The problems of an army are, of course, not the same as those of peacetime organizations. But they do replicate many of the endemic problems associated with collaboration and conflict between individuals, groups and departments collectively engaged on an overall task; the problems associated with the formation, operation, and disbanding of work groups; and the universal processes associated with achievement, recognition and morale among colleagues of different status and educational standard.

The rest of this chapter is concerned with those parts of the research that made new contributions in these fields or were particularly developed by the research workers and other social scientists in the decade following the war.

INTERMEDIATE ROLES

IN LARGE ORGANIZATIONS [8]

Stouffer and his colleagues contributed to our understanding of the strains felt by persons in intermediate roles in hierarchically organized situations. Officers felt that a noncommissioned officer should not let the men in his squad forget his rank even when he was off duty; privates felt this very much less. Officers felt that a noncommissioned officer should teach his men to obey rules and regulations without questioning them; a much lower percentage of privates thought this. Officers thought the noncommissioned officer should not help the men to get fatigue duties done; far fewer privates thought this. From this research the generalization emerges that in hierarchical organizations the intermediate leaders are subject to different demands and expectations from above and below (usually for productivity from above and for human consideration from below), and this leads to actual or potential conflict in their behavior. The military studies further showed—and this has been borne out elsewhere—that the intermediate leader usually bends towards the subordinates, because he is more dependent on them for the gratifications of everyday association.

Merton and Kitt point out that one of the contributions of *The American Soldier* is to make possible systematic analysis of the attitudes or evaluations of "like-statused" individuals within diverse social structures. These structures may differ in degree rather than in kind and show, for instance, the consequences of being of an intermediate status, whatever that status is intermediate between.

EFFECTS OF ROLE
AND STATUS ON ATTITUDES

Stouffer and his colleagues demonstrated the manner in which people see the world as they wish to, and the way in which, in accordance with this, one tends to exaggerate the contribution of one's own group to a collective enterprise. Of a large sample of American soldiers 78 percent said the United States was doing more than its share in the war. Only 22 percent said the same of Russia, and only 5 percent said this of England. On exactly the same lines, both Negroes and white soldiers claimed that members of their own "race" were doing more in the war than the other.

The wartime studies showed that differences in role and status lead to mistaken judgments by groups of each other. Officers showed a general tendency to overestimate the morale of soldiers and to underrate the strength of their dissatisfactions. Misperceptions of this sort were not linked only to rank. In a mixed unit in the United States, which contained some men who had been on overseas service and some who had not, 78 percent of non-returnees were quite satisfied with the returnees' lot and believed that all or most of the men appreciated the position of the returnee. But only 35 percent of the returnees were in fact satisfied with the amount of appreciation they got.

CERTAINTY AND STRESS

The studies brought out the importance of certainty in the endurance of stressful roles. Although the air force had especially dangerous duties, their morale was higher than in any other part of the army. One of the reasons was found to be that members had a stipulated tour of combat duty, that is, after completing a stated number of missions they knew they would be able to return home for a period. In contrast, especially during the early part of the war, infantry men could not look forward to some definite respite of this type. The importance of certainty again became evident when the men returned to the United States: their main preoccupation was to learn what the army was going to do with them. This practice combined with others (including careful selection and close medical attention) to produce a situation in which morale was highest in the most dangerous section of the armed forces. As Lazarsfeld says, this is a tribute to careful social engineering.[9]

EDUCATION AND OUTLOOK

There were several significant findings on the relationship between education and attitudes. Relatively uneducated men found it difficult to appraise situations realistically, were fearful of not grasping what they were supposed to do, were reluctant to criticize, hesitated to use channels of redress formally open to them, and were defeatist in regard to their own prospects for promotion. Lazarsfeld remarks that these findings contribute material for a general "portrait of the underdog." [10]

THE INDIVIDUAL, THE PRIMARY GROUP,
AND THE LARGER SOCIAL STRUCTURE

One of the army researchers' most enduring contributions was to the understanding of the relations between the individual, the primary group of which he is a member, and the larger employing organization. This was not, of course, the central objective of their work, but an incidental outcome of administrative practical needs. The research workers brought out potential generalizations as they went and in their subsequent re-analysis of the material, and others have continued the task, using the wartime studies as a goldmine of research on primary groups. Rich and voluminous though this material is, one should remember that it consists of studies of attitudes, not of group processes—though the latter can be inferred from the former, especially where panel designs were used. The wartime studies

portrayed the American soldier as typically without deep personal commitment to a war which he nevertheless accepted as unavoidable . . . in general he gave little concern to the conflicting values underlying the military struggle, and when asked for his conception of the reasons for American participation he could rarely give a consistent account. Although he showed a strong but tacit patriotism, this usually did not lead him in his thinking to subordinate his personal interests to the furtherance of ideal aims and values.[11]

In their responses to survey questions, officers and enlisted men alike attached little importance to idealistic motives—patriotism and concern about war aims.[12] They were also highly critical of the army, in the sense that they felt resentful about those deprivations and thwartings of personal goals which did not appear to be necessary to the attainment of the collective goal of winning the war.[13] The studies showed, however, the key role played by primary group relations in maintaining morale and efficiency.

The group in its informal character, with its close interpersonal ties, served two principal functions in combat motivation: it *set and enforced group standards* of behaviour, and it *supported and sustained the individual* in stresses he would otherwise not have been able to withstand. These are related functions: the group enforced its standards principally by offering or withholding recognition, respect and approval, which were among the supports it had to offer, while the subjective reward of following an internalized group code enhanced an individual's resources for dealing with the situation.[14]

The authors of Volume 2 comment repeatedly on the distinction:

Pride in outfit and other aspects of intragroup bonds could be maintained at a high level without any corresponding tendency for the men to acquiesce with enthusiasm to the demands that the Army made on them.[15]

The pride that the combat man felt in his outfit gave him a certain amount of support in his combat role. There were other ways in which group membership afforded him resources of power and security. The recognition, respect and approval received by a member in good standing both reinforced the approved patterns of behaviour and gave the individual the security of belonging. On a very practical level, the soldier could count on being looked out for by his buddies if he were in a tough situation.[16]

Making a direct comparison in his later paper, Stouffer says:

Compared with the feeling that one must not lose face in the eyes of one's fellows or let them down, patriotism, hatred of the enemy and other stereotyped explanations of what keeps a person going in combat seem to have been negligible factors.[17]

These findings on the importance of his primary group to the individual soldier should not be misinterpreted to mean that the corporate fighting goals of the army and the patriotism and loyalty in the names of which the army made demands on him did not matter. There were, first, several reasons why soldiers tended to play down these larger considerations. It was considered pompous to talk about them. If asked about the most important factor affecting his behavior, the soldier was inclined to talk about what was immediate and obvious to him. Informal interpersonal relations are bound to be emphasized when the respondent has in mind combat-type situations in which one has to rely on spontaneous and willing help from colleagues. The background factors appeared to have mattered deeply in the sense that they provided, in Shils' words,

a set of generalised moral predispositions or *sense of obligation* . . . the soldier who thought first of getting the job done must, in some way, have accepted the legitimacy of the "job" and felt some degree of obligation to carry it out. The general setting of their goal was given by their identification with the United States and this made for an acceptance of specific commands from their officers. But even the 39 percent who mentioned "ending the task" as a motivating consideration might have been lax and reluctant had they not been subject to the pressure of their colleagues who, more or less hiding the same belief, added the autonomous weight of their approval and affection for those who conformed and disapproval for those who were deviant.[18] *

Acceptance of the legitimacy of the war was an important precondition for the formation of primary groups which had the more positive and immediate function of strengthening the soldier's will to exert himself under dangerous conditions. In most cases, moral considerations of duty and legitimacy moved in the same direction as formal military sanctions and primary group sanctions and appear to have reinforced each other.

Loyalty to one's buddies and more generally to one's outfit was a stringent and prevalent code.

Loyalty to one's buddies was founded on the fact of vital mutual dependence and supported by the cluster of sentiments grouped under the term "pride in outfit" . . . Combat veterans in both Pacific and Mediterranean theatres agreed in rating highly the supporting value of this motive in keeping them fighting when the going was tough. Asked about five possible sources of support in combat, the proportion who replied that thinking "that you couldn't let the other men down" helped them a lot, constituted a majority of the Infantry veterans in each theatre and was second only to the proportion who said they were helped a lot by prayer.[19]

Students of organizations reading these results will naturally wonder whether the distinction was not exaggerated between indifference or ambivalence toward higher authorities and positive feelings towards one's immediate fellows. The conclusion of the research workers was, however, that this split in outlook was firmly maintained:

Since the soldier's outfit was the vehicle that conveyed him into danger and kept him there, one might expect feelings of antagonism toward it to have developed. But most of the men seemed to view the outfit in the personal terms of the men and leaders who had been in it, who could not be blamed for keeping them in combat, and managed to divert their hostility to the war, the Army, or higher headquarters, who kept them in combat, or to more fortunate persons to the rear. There was probably little ambivalence in expressions of pride in the smaller combat unit.[20]

It would have been valuable to know the precise differences in feelings about the successively larger groupings of which the men were members. Unfortunately there are not systematic data about this.

There are no data from combat troops as to the relative degree of pride the men felt in the successively larger groupings of which they were members. Such unit symbols as the shoulder patch, however, fostered identification and pride on a broader basis than the unit of immediate contact. Among ground and service troops, members of a given combat division shared the same shoulder patch. Rarely were there distinctive regimental insignia. Forward troops not assigned to a division—mostly service troops, except for some artillery and armoured units—would wear the shoulder patch of the corps or army to which their unit was attached. For members of divisions, identification with the division undoubtedly eclipsed their identifications with these larger groupings, which were sometimes unstable as divisions were transferred from one corps or army to another.[21]

In a discussion of the relation of primary groups to larger social units, Shils concludes from the wartime studies of Stouffer and his colleagues that the army obtained its inner cohesion

not simply by a series of commands controlling the behaviour of soldiers disciplined to respect the symbols of formal authority but rather through a system of overlapping primary groups.[22]

His own research with Dicks of the German army during the war came to conclusions that converged on those of Stouffer and his team.

This study, made on the basis of a great number of interviews with German soldiers, showed that the main motivation of the German soldier derived from his loyalty to an authoritarian primary group, the protective leader of which was the noncommissioned officer and, to a lesser extent, the junior officer. The larger structure of the army was significant as a system of supply which enabled the junior officers and noncommissioned officers to maintain their protective and nutritive roles, and as a source of strategic and tactical directives which did not place too much strain on the protective role of the officer as the leading figure of the primary group. Direct identifications and loyalties to higher authorities played little part in this structure; and the system broke down only when primary groups could not be formed because of initial incorporation difficulties (e.g. linguistic and other barriers) and when the primary group leader could no longer fulfill his protection functions.[23]

LEADERSHIP

In assessing the relative importance of more immediate leadership against higher leadership, Stouffer and his colleagues concluded that

Unless the larger command was personalised by a highly popular individual commander, on the one hand, or unless things were going very badly, on the other, men did not give much concern to what went on above. Their confidence in their own immediate leadership was probably a more important factor in combat motivation.[24]

As Shils later puts it, effectiveness in the execution of authoritative commands depends inter alia on the quality of relations with authority. Soldiers who said their officers took a personal interest in their men and were willing to go through what they asked their men to go through felt more ready for combat than those who felt hostile to their officers.[25] The research workers say themselves

The officer who commanded the personal respect and loyalty of his men could mobilize the full support of a willing fellowship. He therefore had at his disposal the resources of both the formal coercive system and the system of informal group controls. If, however, the officer had alienated his men and had to rely primarily on coercion, the informal sanctions of the group might cease to bear primarily on the combat mission.[26]

When describing the characteristics of the best combat officers they had known, the men mainly mentioned helpfulness to others and taking a personal interest in their problems. The next most frequently mentioned quality was leadership by personal example.[27]

Shils suggests that confidence in the officers might sometimes be derived from the soldier's needs rather than the actual characteristics of the officer. This suggestion is prompted by reports that the attitudes of officers were in fact more repressive and less tolerant towards their men than the non-commissioned officers. Shils comments that this seems to accord with the general proposition that, where a person is confronted with two levels of authority, affection and trust tend to go to the higher level while negative feelings are expressed towards the nearer level which is more obviously the agent of deprivations even if these emanate from further up.[28] This is, of course, what psychoanalytic theories refer to as the phenomenon of "splitting."

Attitudes to officers varied between geographical areas, evidently partly because, outside combat, primary group relations between officers and men were hampered by the exclusion of the men from special facilities for officers. Attitudes to officers were less positive under these conditions, both because differences in degree of deprivation were underlined and because there was less for the officer to do in looking after his men or in leadership against an enemy.

Shils again expresses useful cautionary remarks against overinterpreting the importance of the immediate commanding officer in isolation from his organizational context. While it is true that the men personalized these matters, the officer could not assume and maintain his role without the support of the whole institution.

It would be extremely shortsighted to neglect the great importance of the higher levels of the military hierarchy in setting goals, in organizing the provision of facilities and in providing many of the conditions which effectively accrue to the credit of the immediate company officer. The protection of the men and the sense which they have of it, is not just a result of the officer's personal qualities. . . . It is made possible by the weapons which other parts of the organization provide, by food and clothing provided by other parts of the organization and by the larger tactical and strategic dispositions which are the context of the operations of the company.[29]

PRIMARY GROUP SUPPORT FOR DEVIATION

The controls of the primary group could operate either in favor of, or in opposition, to the larger organization. There were clear-cut codes about "goldbricking" (dodging work, lying down on the job). When the group felt that a task was necessary or knew they would all be punished if it was not done, the individual goldbricker became an object of scorn. But if the group as a whole felt they were justified in slacking, they opposed the man who did not slack. The relation between primary group bonds and reactions to orders from above is brought out in the following quotation: *

[The] concern of the enlisted man to win the respect of his fellows implies, of course, that in any situation in which there is a conflict between the officers and the group, his identification will tend to be with the group, not the officers. From this it also follows that if the group as a whole supports an order, he will be in

---

* From *The American Soldier: Adjustment During Army Life,* vol. I of *Studies in Social Psychology in World War II* by Samuel A. Stauffer *et al.* © 1949 by Princeton University Press. Reprinted by permission of Princeton University Press.

an untenable position in not obeying. If the group as a whole does not support an order, he will be in a weak position if he is conspicuous in obedience.[30]

The army studies repeat and elaborate the findings of the Mayo team on restriction of output.

It can be one of the most effective forms of aggression against the Army— particularly against a disliked order or a disliked leader—which can be indulged in by soldiers. "Goldbricking" when practiced by consensus as a group enterprise can be a game, even conducive to high spirits in a group. But the attitude of the group toward one of its members who is a chronic "goldbricker" is something else again. For he doesn't carry his share of the load and accordingly tends to become an object of scorn.[31]

When informal groups are strong and the dominant view is opposed or indifferent to the goals and methods of senior management they can effectively oppose these.

JOINING AND LEAVING ESTABLISHED GROUPS

Several of the studies throw light on reactions to the process of joining or leaving an established primary work group. At one phase of the war, men without combat experience were used as replacements of casualties in units all of whose existing members had had combat experience. The replacement men become proud of their new unit membership but developed feelings of inferiority about their abilities because they were among men who had taken part in a difficult action in which they had not themselves taken part. At the same time they appeared to feel uneasy because they were among men who knew the ropes and shared intimate relationships.

The responses were compared of veterans with high and low proportions of replacements. Those with smaller proportions were

somewhat more likely to say that there was "very good" teamwork and cooperation . . . 26 percent versus 18 percent respectively . . . the replacements in the companies in which they were in a smaller minority were also slightly more likely than replacements in the other group of companies to say teamwork was very good (39 percent versus 32 percent). And in both groups of companies, replacements gave a considerably more favourable rating than veterans. The most plausible interpretation would seem to be that the assimilation of large numbers of replacements into a company actually did impair to some extent its smoothness of functioning, and that this was recognised by both veterans and replacements.[32]

Shils suggests on this and other evidence that the larger the proportion of newcomers the greater the resistance of the established primary group to their assimilation.[33]

Where men had become integrated into a primary work group and then had to leave it they showed marked anxiety. Soldiers who returned to the United States after service overseas exhibited nervous symptoms, were dissatisfied with their jobs, and did not feel they belonged in their new contexts. They preferred to serve if possible with and under others who had returned in a similar way. They tried, says Lazarsfeld, to re-enact the life in the primary groups they had left behind.[34]

RELATIVE DEPRIVATION

One of the main intellectual legacies of the Research Branch work lay in their use of the concept of "relative deprivation," illustrated in the quotations below on social mobility in the army.

Those soldiers who had advanced slowly relatively to other soldiers of equal longevity in the Army were the most critical of the Army's promotion opportunities. *But relative rate of advancement can be based on different standards by different classes of the Army population.* For example, a grade school man who became a corporal after a year of service would have had a more rapid rate of promotion compared with most of his friends at the same educational level than would a college man who rose to the same rank in a year. Hence we would expect, at a given rank and a given longevity, that the better educated would be more likely than others to complain of the slowness of promotion. The facts bear . . . this out . . .

A similar phenomenon appeared to operate between different branches of the service . . . among privates and noncoms in each educational group, . . . the Air Corps men tended to take a dimmer view of promotion opportunities for men of ability in the Army than did the Military Police.

Without reference to the theory that such opinions by soldiers represent a relationship between their expectations and their achievements relative to others *in the same boat with them,* such a finding would be paradoxical indeed. For chances of promotion in the Military Police were about the worst in any branch of the Army.[35]

The notion that one's deprivation was always viewed relative to that of others was used to explain many of the otherwise paradoxical findings of the surveys. To quote another instance, almost everyone expected that Northern Negroes stationed in Southern camps would be more dissatisfied than Southern Negroes stationed in Northern camps. In fact their morale was found, says Stouffer, to be as good or better.

It finally appeared . . . that relatively to civilian Negroes in the South the Negro soldier apparently perceived himself to be well treated. But when a Southern Negro at a Northern camp compared himself with civilian Negroes making big money in the war industries he apparently felt himself not so fortunate.[36]

As Stouffer remarks in the same paper, since one's deprivations are always viewed relative to others, the research problem is to find out who the others are.[37] And, one may add, why one group is selected for use in the judgment rather than another. As Merton and Kitt later pointed out in their well-known essay on reference groups, woven around the use of relative deprivation in the American soldier, the "others" in terms of whom soldiers judged their fate were by no means always obvious. Sometimes they were actual associates, sometimes they were in some pertinent respect of the same status or in the same social category; and sometimes they were in some pertinent respect of different status or in a different social category.[38]

The term "reference group"[39] was not used in *The American Soldier,* although, as Merton and Kitt say, many of the studies bear upon the theory of reference group behavior and "relative deprivation" is a closely related concept. It was essentially a reference group concept, used as an interpretative intervening variable to explain why persons with particular status attributes took the attitudes they did towards their experiences. Stouffer and his colleagues had repeatedly brought out the fact that one's evaluation of one's objective situation depends on whom one compares oneself with.

Merton and Kitt underline the importance of the question of under what conditions one takes one's associates as a frame of reference for self-evaluation and attitude formation and under what conditions non-membership groups provide the significant frame of reference. While it is well known that the groups to which one belongs shape one's behavior, we often orient ourselves to groups other than our own in shaping our behavior and expectations. Social scientists need to search out the processes by which both happen; to determine which category of groups has the greater pull and why; and when non-membership groups are chosen to identify why one has been chosen over another.

The general hypothesis is suggested by Merton and Kitt that

some similarity in status attributes between the individual and the reference group must be perceived or imagined in order for the comparison to occur at all. Once this minimal similarity obtains, other similarities and differences pertinent to the situation will provide the context for shaping evaluations.[40]

They make the important point that reference groups tend to be shared, to be held in common by enough people in a social category to be characteristic of them. These frames of reference are common because they are patterned by social structure.

Again, recasting *American Soldier* data into their own theoretical framework Merton and Kitt make a helpful contribution to theories of social mobility in organizational and other contexts.

They quote the finding that a panel study of three groups of enlisted men found that those men who expressed attitudes in line with the established military mores subsequently received promotions in proportions significantly higher than the others. So far as the army leadership went they were conformist, but in their membership groups they were non-conformists. What are the consequences, Merton and Kitt ask, of positive orientation to a group other than one's own? They suggest that those men who, through anticipatory socialization take on the values of the non-membership group to which they aspire, find readier acceptance by that group while defecting from the mores of their membership group. To the degree that the individual identifies himself with another group he alienates himself from his own group. Judging, they say, from the data in the American Soldier and from other studies of group defection,

there is a continuous and cumulative interplay between a deterioration of *social relations* within the membership group and positive *attitudes* towards the norms of a non-membership group . . . If the possibility [of affiliation with the group] is negligible or absent, then the alienated individual becomes socially rootless. But if the social system realistically allows for such change in group affiliations then the individual estranged from the one group has all the more motivation to belong to the other.[41]

At the organizational level, suggest the same authors, positive orientation toward the official mores would appear to support the legitimacy of the structure and help to keep the structure of authority intact.

N O T E S

1. These were: (1) *The American Soldier: Adjustment during Army Life;* (2) *The American Soldier: Combat and its Aftermath;* (3) *Experiments on Mass Communication;* (4) *Measurement and Prediction,* (Princeton, New Jersey: Princeton University Press, 1949). In this chapter I refer only to Volumes 1 and 2. The authors of Volume 1 were S. A. Stouffer, E. A. Suchman, L. C. de Vinney, S. A. Star, and R. M. Williams, Jr. The authors of Volume 2 were S. A. Stouffer, A. A. Lumsdaine, M. H. Lumsdaine, R. M. Williams, Jr., M. Brewster Smith, I. L. Janis, S. A. Star, and L. S. Cottrell, Jr. Two valuable short commentaries have appeared on the findings and on leads they provide for peacetime social research. These are S. A. Stouffer, "A Study of Attitudes," *Scientific American* (May 1949): 3–7, and P. F. Lazarsfeld, "The American Soldier—An Expository Review," *Public Opinion Quarterly,* 13 (Fall 1949): 377–404.

2. Stouffer, "A Study of Attitudes," p. 1.

3. Stouffer, "A Study of Attitudes," pp. 4 and 5.

4. Stouffer et al, *The American Soldier,* 2, p. 531.

5. Stouffer et al, *The American Soldier,* 2, p. 595.

6. Stouffer et al, *The American Soldier,* 2, p. 548.

7. J. M. Pfiffner, "Administrative Rationality," *Public Administration Review,* 20 (Summer 1960). See discussion in Ch. 9.

8. This topic is also discussed in chapter 15 on Leadership in *Bureaucratic Organizations.*

9. Lazarsfeld, "The American Soldier."

10. See the earlier data on this point summarized in G. Knupfer, "Portrait of the Underdog," Public Opinion Quarterly, 2, no. 1 (1947). Lazarsfeld says of the Stouffer studies that "the new data corroborate many of the earlier findings but they are probably richer than all previously available information combined." Lazarsfeld, "The American Soldier."

11. Stouffer et al, *The American Soldier*, 2, p. 149.

12. Stouffer et al, *The American Soldier*, 2, p. 111.

13. Stouffer et al, *The American Soldier*, 1, p. 431.

14. Stouffer et al, *The American Soldier*, 2, pp. 130–131. For a full discussion of the relations between the man and the immediate group of which he was a member see Chapter 3, "Combat Motivation Among Ground Troops."

15. Stouffer et al, *The American Soldier*, 2, p. 140.

16. Stouffer et al, *The American Soldier*, 2, pp. 142 and 143.

17. Stouffer, "A Study of Attitudes," p. 6.

18. E. A. Shils, "Primary Groups in the American Army," in R. K. Merton and P. F. Lazarsfeld, eds., *Continuities in Social Research: Studies in the Scope and Method of the American Soldier* (New York: The Free Press, 1950), p. 22.

19. Stouffer et al, *The American Soldier*, 2, p. 136.

20. Stouffer et al, *The American Soldier*, 2, p. 139.

21. Stouffer et al, *The American Soldier*, 2, p. 139.

22. E. A. Shils, "The Study of the Primary Group; in H. D. Laswell and D. Lerner, eds., *The Policy Sciences—Recent Developments in Scope and Methods,* (Palo Alto: Stanford University Press, 1951), p. 64.

23. Shils, "The Study of the Primary Group," p. 64. Reports of this work appear in H. V. Dicks, *Psychological Foundations of the Wehrmacht,* (London: War Office, Directorate of Army Psychiatry, 1944), and E. A. Shils and M. Janowitz, "Cohesion and Disintegration of the Wehrmacht in World War II," *Public Opinion Quarterly,* 12 (1948).

24. Stouffer et al, *The American Soldier*, 2, p. 145.

25. Shils, "Primary Groups in the American Army."

26. Stouffer et al, *The American Soldier*, 2, p. 118.

27. Stouffer et al, *The American Soldier*, 2, p. 134.

28. Shils, "Primary Groups in the American Army."

29. Shils, "Primary Groups in the American Army," p. 34.

30. Stouffer et al, *The American Soldier*, 1, p. 418.

31. Stouffer et al, *The American Soldier*, 1, p. 420.

32. Stouffer et al, *The American Soldier*, 2, p. 258.

33. Shils, "Primary Groups in the American Army."

34. The problems of the U.S. returning soldiers are of course closely paralleled by those of the U.K. former prisoners of war described in the preceding Chapter on the U.K. wartime work.

35. Stouffer et al, *The American Soldier*, 1, pp. 250 and 251.

36. Stouffer, "A Study of Attitudes," p. 5.

37. Stouffer, "A Study of Attitudes."

38. R. K. Merton and A. S. Kitt, "Contributions to the Theory of Reference Group Behaviour," in Merton and Lazarsfeld, eds., *Continuities in Social Research.*

39. This term was first introduced by H. H. Hyman in "The Psychology of Status," *Archives of Psychology,* no. 269 (1942). The ideas associated with the use of the concepts of "relative deprivation" and of "reference groups" received great impetus from the synthesis contained in the Merton and Kitt article. See discussion by H. H. Hyman under "Reference Groups" in *International Encyclopaedia of the Social Sciences,* 13, p. 354.

40. Merton and Kitt, "Contributions to the Theory," p. 61.

41. Merton and Kitt, "Contributions to the Theory," pp. 93 and 94.

11 : The Tavistock Group
in England

MUCH of the British wartime work of 1939–1945 was carried out in collaboration with military administrators by a group of colleagues who had either worked at the Tavistock Clinic, a voluntary out-patient center for psychotherapy, or subsequently joined the clinic and its postwar sister institution, the Tavistock Institute of Human Relations.

The very composition of the Tavistock Group (psychiatrists, psychologists, anthropologists) showed the way things were moving in the understanding of men at work. Emphasis was placed on psycho-social variables in individuals and groups, on the importance of the small group in which the individual was a face-to-face member, on the capacity of groups to solve their own problems, on the need for primary groups to be closely integrated in larger structures, and on the need to understand roles as well as people. The psychiatrists were brought face-to-face in their new army roles with the complex realities of large organizations confronting specific, problematic operational tasks. Psychiatric perspectives usually concern internal personal dynamics, the inner subjective world of a person in treatment. The new perspectives had to be concerned with assessing and predicting how people would behave in particular roles and relationships, in particular group situations and particular social structures. Even where the aim of the work was therapy or rehabilitation, under wartime conditions the key question was less that of ameliorating personal suffering than restoring the person to operating efficiency in his unit as rapidly and economically as possible.

There were three main strands in the Tavistock wartime work which I will discuss here. One was in the area of group selection of officers. Here emphasis moved from attempts to identify the personality attributes of prospective leaders to the simulation of problematic situations requiring leadership and to the observation of personal behavior in those situations. Secondly, the group developed new forms of therapy which revolved around the workings of groups and organizations and systematically drew the attention of patients to the link between their personal behavior and unsatisfactory social environments. Thirdly, in civil resettlement work they constructed and manipulated specially designed transitional communities as bridges between wartime experience and civil life.

Group Selection

THE WAR OFFICE

SELECTION BOARDS

In peacetime the process of selecting administrative personnel for government service, professions, or private enterprise is a long one, involving school, university, subsequent careers, examinations of all kinds, the exercise of personal choice, interviews, etc. This is impossible for selecting officers in an expanding army under conditions of manpower shortage. Time is vital and there are few obvious pointers to ability for military leadership in the history of candidates. Public opinion demands, moreover, that selectors should not stick to one social type or class.

Up to 1942 officer selection in the British army was based on nomination by a commanding officer and then a very short interview before a command board of three senior officers. The technique, says Morris, was that of the simple interview. Upon the candidate's answers to questions and such traits of character or deportment as were visible during the 20 minutes or so he was before the Board, was based the assessment of his suitability.[1]

Morris expands the reasons for the abandonment of the old procedure as follows. The failure rate had risen to alarming proportions. This had a bad effect on morale in the ranks and as a consequence too few applications for commissions were received. The shortage of applications was probably aggravated by a widespread belief in the ranks that there was a class bias in selection. Psychiatric breakdowns of the selected men were too frequent.

The officers had hitherto come mainly from one sector of British society. This was the same sector as the selectors and their judgments were probably quite shrewd. But a new situation had now arisen in which there was an urgent need to increase the size of the officer corps. Selection had, moreover, now to take account of the scope of the officer's job in a modern war involving a conscripted citizen army. A high margin of error had ceased to be tolerable. It was inevitable, Morris says, that the flow of candidates should begin to approximate to a complete cross section of the population and not surprising that, faced with candidates of unfamiliar behavior and background, the traditional methods should be found inadequate.

The new method of officer selection by War Office selection boards was adopted in the British Army during the period 1942–1945 and carried out under the adjutant-general by the director of selection of personnel, assisted by the director of army psychiatry.

A WOSB team consisted of a president, military testing officer, psychiatrist, and psychologist. They accepted or rejected candidates for officer training and forecast the probable future standard (six months after commissioning) of accepted candidates.

The selection procedure lasted three days. Candidates were organized into groups of seven to nine on arrival. The program consisted of:

1. Written work. This consisted first of intelligence tests, yielding a rating to each candidate in relation to a sample of the army as a whole and showing whether he was, say, in the top 1 percent to 10 percent. Secondly, there were "personality pointers," that is, questionnaires and other written work (such as stories the candidate was required to write about indistinctly portrayed scenes) which enable the psychologist to make inferences about the personality of the candidate and to alert the selection team to what to watch or take up with him in interview. Thirdly, there were mathematical papers for technical candidates.

2. Military tests. One type of test consisted of individual situations where a candidate was briefed on a military or non-military situation and asked what action he would take. The test situations allowed for a variety of solutions. A second type of test concerned "man-management" situations where a candidate had to deal in interview with a personnel problem. A third type consisted of individual obstacle situations where the candidate was required to make the best score he could in overcoming physical obstacles or dealing with tasks. A fourth type consisted of command group situations where candidates were placed in turn in charge of the candidate group and faced with some problem or task that had to be planned, organized, and executed by the group. Fifthly, there were leaderless situations in which the group was faced with a task or situation without any leader having been appointed by the testing officer. Sometimes these were group discussions where members chose and discussed a topic. Sometimes they were group tasks, for example, improvising with limited materials found on the spot a method of escaping as a group over a wire entanglement including electrified wires and alarms.

3. So far as the candidate was concerned the procedure ended with one or two interviews. Where required, for instance for engineering candidates, there was a technical interview by a selection officer who also had at hand the technical occupational record of candidate, his qualifications, and the mathematics paper done in the written work period. Every candidate had an "officer quality" interview of twenty to thirty minutes with the president, who could use his commanding officer's report and his questionnaire responses. The president could, if he wished, at this stage take up with the man his past achievements (with special reference to activities involving leadership), his hobbies and games, his conceptions of an officer's responsibilities and role, his knowledge of current affairs, and his reasons for wishing to become an officer.

Some candidates also had a psychiatric interview, as a result of which the psychiatrist might advocate rejection but might equally well be able to reassure selectors, where this point had arisen, that there were not psychiatric grounds for turning a man down.

The procedure concluded with a board conference at which observations and opinions of all officers who had had dealings with the candidate during the procedure were pooled. After each discussion a final decision was made by the president, together with a grading on potential. Successful candidates were then guided to a particular arm of the service thought to be fitted to their capabilities.

This approach to officer selection embodied a number of features to which it is worth drawing attention.

First, it is clear that the selectors were attacking the selection problem in terms of social psychology. They were implicitly rejecting the approach widespread at the time and still prevalent in many quarters today that assumes ability to lead to be tied to attributes of the individual personality. Personality characteristics are in fact difficult to locate and test precisely and it is difficult for an outside observer to decide how to weigh one characteristic against another and what the net effect of their interaction will be in behavior. The WOSB approach was to view leadership as a form of participation in a social situation involving some technical and physical problems at the same time as interpersonal relations and membership of a larger organization. Whether someone succeeds or fails as a leader was felt to depend largely on the requirements of the particular situation in which he was placed and on who else was involved. As J. R. Rees, one of the leading figures of the period, has said:

Leadership is not a single quality possessed by some and not by others but is a way of describing the effectiveness of an individual in a specific role within a specific group united for a particular purpose.[2]

On this line of reasoning, many different sorts of people can be expected to play leadership roles—if they are correctly placed. Following those lines, it is interesting to note that, to provide criteria for selection, an independent analysis was made of roles filled by officers in modern warfare.[3]

Second, the designers of WOSBs did not rely particularly on the previous occupational history of the man; on whether, for instance, he had taken work responsibility for others in a job before joining the army. This was apparently partly because they would not have regarded leadership as a specific, identifiable entity irrespective of the context in which it was exercised: on this view leadership in another field would not be accepted as sufficiently predictive of leadership capacity within the army. But the WOSB designers were in any case confronted with a situation in which many candidates had had little occupational experience before joining the army so there would not be a great deal of accumulated experience to make an informed judgment.

Thirdly candidates could do badly in some parts of the procedure and then well in others. There was no suggestion that there is a personal quality of leadership running through all situations and relationships.

An important aspect of the thinking behind the new selection technique is brought out by the description of W. R. Bion, one of its originators and a seminal figure in much of the wartime work.

The essence of the technique . . . was to provide a framework in which selecting officers . . . could observe a man's capacity for maintaining personal relationships in a situation of strain that tempted him to disregard the interests of his fellows for the sake of his own . . . The problem was to make capital of this emotional field in order to test the quality of the man's relationships with his fellows.

This was done by a method so simple and so obvious, when it has been propounded, that its revolutionary nature can easily be lost sight of. . . . The man found he was not entered in a free-for-all competition with other candidates. Instead he found himself the member of a group and apparently, all the tests were tests not of himself but of the group . . . it was the duty of the observing officers to watch how any given man was reconciling his personal ambitions, hopes, and fears with the requirements exacted by the group for its success.[4]

Rees has underlined the wider social significance of the approach to officer selection through group methods,

Bion's "leaderless group" principle marked a notable advance in psychological methods of investigating interpersonal relations. The basic idea underlying the method is that when a group of candidates are presented with a problem that they have to solve as a group, i.e. no leader is appointed by the testing officer nor is any help given, then a situation arises that reproduces the fundamental conflict between the individual and society . . . the individual is motivated by a desire to do well for himself personally, but by placing him in a situation where he can only operate through the medium of others, his spontaneous attitudes toward cooperation are revealed.[5]

The question naturally arises of how effective the WOSBs were in comparison with other selection procedures, especially those they superseded.

This is an extremely difficult question to answer because of such factors as the training period that intervened after selection, the complications involved in the comparison with the older methods, variability in the judgments of superior officers and difficulties in comparing the work situations of officers.

During the training stage reports were, however, obtained for a period during which the new WOSBs and the old procedure boards operated simultaneously.[6]

PERCENTAGE RATED

	Above Average	Average	Below Average	Total Number
WOSB	35	40	25	721
Old Procedure	22	41	37	491

A statistically significant difference was shown in favor of the WOSB method.

There was also some positive evidence on the success of gradings by WOSBs in relation to performance by the selected officers during their period of subsequent service. A small statistically positive relationship was found between WOSB gradings and the opinions of the commanding officers under whom the new officers actually served.

As in many field experiments, it is misleading to base a judgement of success or failure on relatively narrow technical considerations such as the statistical evidence quoted. Evaluating the success of the WOSBs involves recognition of the situation to which they were a response, that is, the need to raise army morale in regard to applications for commissions and the need to provide the army as rapidly as possible with enough officers "satisfactory in quality" for operationally definable military situations. Garforth claimed that the new method represented a marked advance on any previous attempt to devise practical, logical and sound methods of rapid selection of executive personnel.[7] Rapidity was indeed one of the features of the procedure. The period over which the selection decision was made was extremely short, a matter of a few days. But the program compensated for shortness of time by the substitution of trained, multiple, concentrated, and organized observations. The intelligence tests and psychological procedures revealed certain fundamental capacities, while technical ability and practical performance, involving an element of stress, were displayed in situations that simulated actual army contexts. To be sure, the judgment by one human being (or even a group of human beings) of the personality and potential of another can never be completely scientific or objective. But as the WOSBs showed, it is possible to determine systematically the field of evidence on which that judgment should be made and to secure a range of contributory opinions that can be systematically put together.

SELECTION FOR MANAGEMENT

WOSBs left an important legacy in the forms taken by selection for management traineeships after the war. When the war ended one of the Tavistock group, Ronald Hargreaves, joined the Unilever industrial concern as chief medical officer. On his recommendation, the new Tavistock Institute, formed to apply and develop in civil life some of the approaches devised during the war, was invited to collaborate with the Unilever personnel department in improving selection procedures. One major outcome of the long collaboration that then ensued was the institution of the Unilever Company's management development scheme, whose selection phase I describe in some detail below because of the prevalence of similar procedures in England and the United States.

Selection began with a "screening" process based on correspondence or brief exploratory interviews, leading to the production of short-lists of eight or nine candidates seen together at Unilever in a group procedure lasting one and a half to two days. For a time I was associated with the scheme as one of the Tavistock advisers at that group procedure. A typical procedure ran as follows: First, candidates were met by a Unilever personnel administrator and a Tavistock adviser and told in what events they would be asked to participate. The administrator would then leave and the Tavistock adviser would give candidates two intelligence tests (usually one verbal and one non-verbal) together with a projective task, which was an abbreviated version of the "Object Relations Test" developed at the Tavistock Clinic.[8] This requires the person to write accounts of events in a series of vague, open pictures, mainly involving shadowy pictures of persons. Of the written materials, the adviser passed on to the company only the overall scores of the young men on the intelligence tests: the rest of the information was treated as confidential to him. At the end of the first afternoon candidates were given written details of a simple business task to study in preparation for the next day: it was explained to them that no previous business knowledge was needed for this task and that there were no right or wrong answers. The procedure resumed next morning with a session at which candidates met four selectors (senior Unilever managers) and a board chairman, usually the head of the personnel division or his deputy. Each selector and candidate was asked to introduce himself briefly in two or three minutes, saying something about his past career and present activities. No instruction was given as to the order in which candidates should speak. Immediately after this, candidates were asked to form a group on their own (with selectors and advisers on the outside of their circle), to choose any topic they liked and, as soon as they had reached agreement on a topic, to proceed to discuss it. After this, candidates and selectors separated for a break, during which selectors exchanged their early impressions and learned the intelligence test ratings. The chairman would point up convergences and disagreements on each candidate so that the points raised would be checked during the rest of the day. The entire group then reassembled and candidates were again asked to carry out a task on their own, this time the business problem handed them the day before. This ended the morning. Selectors and advisers again compared notes over lunch and discussed their remaining doubts and uncertainties. After lunch the adviser would interview each candidate on his own and the candidate would then go on to a final interview with two selectors. The procedure ended with a full board conference of chairman, selectors, and advisers, at which each candidate was discussed and a decision taken as to whether or not to offer him a traineeship.

Such procedures enable selectors systematically to compare each candidate with seven or eight contemporaries. Their observations of candidates take place over several hours; they do not have to rely on a fleeting impression. The procedure acknowledges the fact that there is no one way of leading a group; one person may be more active than another in initiating a discussion, or summarizing what has been said, but it may be that another is more influential in encouraging quieter people to contribute or reconciling differences between antagonists. From the employer's point of view both may be equally eligible for careers involving positions of formal leadership, though they will lead in different ways and their styles may be appropriate to different situations. The procedure also accepts as an operating principle the fact that a candidate's abilities are uneven: he may do badly in some events and well in others.

Having seen each candidate in action in the group events selectors are put in a position to discuss with him in subsequent personal interviews a situation which both know. Selectors can check the candidate's view of the situation and perception of the part he has played against his own. Selectors operate as a group in assessing candidates and this overcomes some of the problems of blind spots in a one-to-one interviewing situation.

Many of the features mentioned above are deliberately designed into group selection procedures. There are, however, as in most social arrangements, several unanticipated consequences of such procedures. One such consequence is that the selection procedure becomes an informal training procedure for those managers who act as selectors, especially those who are fairly regularly called upon. Their appreciation of the complexities of the human personality is likely to be enriched through participating with colleagues and social-science trained advisers in repeated assessment discussions. They have the opportunity to discover their own persisting biases in judging the capacities of other persons. They learn about the problems of their personnel department in recruiting, selecting, and placing new members of the concern. They increase their range of knowledge about the type of work done in the concern outside their own departments. They learn more about the standards of performance expected by their colleagues.

All this is not to say that group selection schemes are without their problems. The group tasks successfully simulate real management situations in that they involve objective problems as well as interpersonal relations in which candidates must both cooperate and conflict while under the scrutiny of seniors. But they constitute committee-type situations which represent only partially the situations and processes of the type in which the new manager will find himself during the early phases of his career. On the other hand, it could be argued that they contain in concentrated form many of the major social psychological elements of real managerial life.

There is a separate set of problems connected with relations between members of the selecting group. They are colleagues with continuing relationships with each other and the selection event becomes incorporated within the structure of those relationships. It is perfectly possible that decisions about candidates become a part of organizational politics in the sense that, for reasons that have nothing to do with the procedure, some selectors will want to please or frustrate others, or, having disagreed once, may be reluctant to do so again soon afterwards. My own observations incline me to the belief that selectors working as a group tend to be conservative in a way that favors the candidate to whom no one takes exception rather than the unusual person who is not acceptable to everyone. Hesitation on the part of selectors may combine with the personnel department's expectation of difficulty in placing an unusual man so as to prejudice his chance of appointment and so bringing new thinking.

Apart from operational problems, selection procedures which incorporate intelligence tests and projective psychological materials pose ethical issues. Several commentators have suggested that use of these tests constitutes invasion of privacy, conveying to prospective employers information that most people would regard as nobody else's concern. It could be argued that the candidate has chosen to apply to an employer whom he knows is using these techniques and is thereby accepting them. This argument is less true for projective procedures than intelligence tests, since the candidate would need to be a professional psychologist to understand what it is that he is conveying. He is a party to an arrangement that he does not understand. On the other side, it can be argued that executive work draws on so many aspects of the personality that prospective employers are entitled to learn more about candidates for managerial traineeships than is available through traditional methods. In the Tavistock procedures the ethical problem has to some extent been reduced by two practices. Firstly, the adviser does not report to the selection board what he finds in the projective materials, but uses them to inform himself on the personality of the candidate. Secondly, he accepts professional responsibility for communicating to the candidate what he has learned, tries to be helpful in the way he conveys it, and discusses the implications. This might involve a discussion which is more like a vocational counseling session than a selection interview. At the same time, problems must persist in that the adviser is the paid agent of the employing organization, not a personal adviser to the candidate, and has been put into position to use his knowledge of him in some ways which he might not approve—for instance, in discouraging the employer from appointing him. These are partly ethical problems of applied social science. But they are also problems of the roles and rights of large organizations and individuals in our present type of society.

SOCIAL-PSYCHOLOGICAL JOB DESCRIPTIONS

Quite apart from selection procedures, a noteworthy innovation of the Tavistock group has been the development of a new type of job description, usually in connection with selection for senior managerial posts. In assessing the WOSBs, B. S. Morris has remarked that, despite the steps taken in this direction, not enough attention had been paid to environmental variations in officers' roles, particularly to variations in social structure, stress, and relationships. This was more, he said, than demanding better job analyses of the type already done in the army and in industry: it meant carrying out job analyses of a kind radically different from those that had been attempted. The innovation in the subsequent Tavistock work was to build up job descriptions which were accounts of real life situations a new job-holder would enter (rather than only lists of duties), together with references to the main pressures he would experience from colleagues. Many such descriptions have been built up by Tavistock staff members. One, for instance, was prepared by A. K. Rice during the course of his well-known series of studies in India; [9] it gave a picture of the problems likely to be encountered by a professional entering a large established business dominated by one family. The same approach was used by Sofer in one case, again in a family business, where the operational problem was identical [10] and in studying the roles of teachers of management studies.[11] Such sociological job descriptions help to inform prospective applicants candidly of the perils and opportunities that go with the post and, if they wish, to withdraw their applications if this discourages them. At the same time, preparation of the job description with the employing group can serve to elucidate for them the nature of their own situation, the expectations they have of a newcomer, and the nature of the strains to which they may be exposing him.

THERAPEUTIC COMMUNITIES

The work described in this section initiated major changes in the treatment of neuroses through "administrative" methods and opened up new possibilities for therapy and education through participant-observation.

To start with the work of W. R. Bion, this involved for the first time deliberate manipulation of a human community to bring into prominence organizational processes and to make the study of those processes the central task of organizational participants. This pioneer effort is described by Bion in a joint paper with J. Rickman.[12]

In the first part of that paper Bion describes his work when he was put in charge of the training wing of a military psychiatric hospital involving about one hundred men. He says that he was unable to settle down to work because he was continually besieged by patients and staff with what were presented to him as administrative problems. In effect he reconceptualized these as neurotic problems of persons writ large in organizational terms.

He takes us over his reasoning as follows. His task was to produce self-respecting men socially adjusted to the community and therefore willing to accept its responsibilities, whether in peace or war. It was their problems in this area that had brought the men into the hospital. Bion asked himself what common danger they faced here and what could unite them. The common danger, he decided, was the existence of neurosis that endangered his own work with the men and the successful working of the institution in its rehabilitative aspects. The need, he concluded, was to display neurosis conspicuously as a problem of the organization and to encourage members to work collectively to overcome it. But how was the group to be persuaded to tackle neurotic disability as a communal problem? He decided that the organization of the training wing should be designed to throw into prominence the way in which neurotic behavior added to the difficulties of the community, destroying happiness and efficiency. The main aim of the training wing, he decided, would have to become the education and training of the community in the problems of interpersonal relationships (and in their link with neurotic symptoms and personal responsibility).

He conducted a six-week experiment in which the men were told the following regulations would in future apply: There would be one hour's physical training daily. Each man would be required to be a member of one or more groups--for handicrafts, map reading, etc., or he could form a fresh group. A man feeling unable to attend should go to the rest room. A parade would be held daily for the general business of the training wing. Unknown to the patients this parade was to provide them with an opportunity to step outside their own framework and look on its workings with the detachment of spectators—to act as a sort of therapeutic seminar.

The groups formed and some extra ones were devised for timetabling and other activities. Nevertheless, although there were so many groups and so much freedom for any person to follow his inclinations, very little happened at first. The men were not using the training facilities available to them, though they had complained before that very little was available to them in the army. Bion pointed this out as a problem for them to deal with together rather than for him alone and the training wing quickly became self-critical. During the initial period of inactivity the ward had been allowed to become dirty. This was treated again as a problem of the total community not of the doctor on his own. The members of the wing asked permission to organize an orderly group whose task it was to keep the wards clean throughout the day. The ward now began to be more presentable.

Within a month of the inception of the scheme, substantial changes had taken place. Whereas at first it was difficult to employ the men, now it was hard to find time for them to do the things they wanted to do. Groups were operating outside parade hours. Absence without leave was rare. The wing had what Bion describes as an unmistakeable *esprit de corps* and smartness. The meetings became increasingly concerned with the expression, on the part of the men, of their ability to make contact with reality and to regulate their relationships efficiently with others, and with their tasks.

As a member of the wartime group put it subsequently, such an approach to therapy

is an attempt to use a hospital . . . as a community with the immediate aim of full participation of all its members in its daily life and the eventual aim of the resocialization of the neurotic individual . . . The daily life of the [hospital] community must be related to real tasks, truly relevant to the needs and aspirations of the small society of the hospital, and the larger society in which it is set . . . full opportunity must be available for identifying and analyzing the interpersonal barriers which stand in the way of participating in a full community life.[13]

In the second part of the Bion-Rickman paper Rickman reports on a pioneer application of group therapy for patients in the hospital division of the same institution. Each patient first gave a psychiatrist a personal history, then went to a group discussion every morning; later in the day he could, if he wished, see the psychiatrist for a private discussion. Such discussions centered on the man's difficulty in putting the welfare of the group first during his membership of the group.

Topics in the groups included the handling of newcomers to the institution and to the discussion group; factors making for discontent in the ward; and personal needs versus the needs of the group or ward as a whole. Rickman reports a readiness and an eagerness to discuss the social implications of personality problems.

He developed a conception of "the good group spirit," which had been his aim, as involving: a common purpose; common recognition by members of the group of its boundaries and of their position and function in relation to that of larger units of groups; a capacity to absorb and lose members; freedom from internal subgroupings with rigid exclusive boundaries; recognition of individual contributions to the group; and capacity to face discontent within the group and the means to cope with it.

Rickman says his experiment pointed to a need for further examination of the structure of groups and of the interplay of forces within groups. Psychology and psychopathology had, in his view, focused too much on the individual, often to the exclusion of the social field of which he was part. Useful work could be done in the study of the interplay of individual and social psychology viewed as equally important interacting elements.

Another member of the wartime group has emphasized the advance for psychiatry constituted in the approach adumbrated by Rickman and Bion.

Until comparatively recently the tendency was for psychotherapy to be regarded as something which mainly concerned the sick individual. And in the treatment of the individual the manifestations of his neurosis were looked upon essentially as problems besetting him alone . . . on the whole, psychotherapists in the past focused their attention on the individual patient with but little consideration for the social field of which he is part . . . The tendency today is no

longer to look upon the sick patient as an entity in himself . . . The concept that
has enriched psychopathology is that man is *primarily* a social being, and not
primarily self-sufficient and only secondarily in need of others in order to satisfy
his instinctual needs . . . In [a] sense individual psychology *is* fundamentally
social psychology, the psychology of interpersonal relationships, and the key
problem in psychopathology has become that of the particular kind of related-
ness of the individual toward society, to others and to himself. In short, the
viewpoint has gradually become crystallized that what our neurotic patients are
suffering from essentially, is a disturbance in their interpersonal relationships.[14]

At that time the ethical issues involved in wartime medicine were not
prominently raised. It has taken an unpopular war to bring dramatically
into question incompatibilities between war as a "killing art" and medicine
as a "healing art." As *Time* put it in a brief but eloquent discussion on
recent requests by physicians in the U.S. for redrafting or for excusal from
military service:

Whether to patch the wounded soldier so that he may live to kill again or be
killed presents an ethical dilemma to some doctors . . . For the psychiatrist in
uniform, the problem can be even more distressing. Within the spirit of his profession, how can he morally justify his military duty, which is to "adjust" to the
brutalities of combat a mind that has rejected those very brutalities?[15]

As well as advancing psychiatric theory, the pioneering experiments of
Bion and Rickman indicate the extra illumination that can be provided by
the addition of a psychodynamic approach to the sociological study of
organizations and groups. Rickman and Bion showed that what are from
one point of view purely administrative or managerial problems, are
simultaneously personal and interpersonal problems expressed in organizational terms. The structure and operation of a group situation are full of
meanings for participants, of which they may be only partially cognizant.
Insight into the world of underlying and supplementary meanings may well
be necessary for the effective administrator or for the sociologist seeking
to explain behavior that does not meet the usual "rational" criteria.

CIVIL RESETTLEMENT UNITS [16]

The Civil Resettlement Units were designed to deal with problems
surrounding the repatriation of former prisoners-of-war. The former
prisoner was prone to self-deprecation for not sharing all the dangers and
excitement of fighting. Both the expatriate and his family had, while apart,
made relations and developed values and interests that helped them adapt
to the separation. The families sometimes felt that they had had as much
hardship as the man. To those at home the repatriate might seem strange
or difficult when he returned after an absence of what might have been
years. To him they were visible through the eyes of a well-informed

stranger. Many of the reunited husbands and wives had difficulties with each other, contributed to by personal changes during the separation and ignorance of what had happened to each other. Many of the repatriates felt that they restarted civil life at a disadvantage and that they were handicapped by lack of skill at home and work. Repatriates appeared often to feel bereft of the support of their military group or misunderstood except by people who had been through a similar experience.

The central notion was to develop a program within regional residential units which would enable these to act as transitional communities through which the men might hope to pass with profit. The units were to be run so far as possible on a basis of participation and self-government rather than impersonal military authority. This meant selecting staff who could tolerate such a system.

The scheme was built with the help of already repatriated men, that is, with persons representative of the ultimate consumers of the service, and the first description of the scheme sent to soldiers was based on 200 sample interviews with repatriates.

The men who attended did so as volunteers. They could leave when they wished, though they were paid and accommodated by the army for the period of their stay. After the scheme had been in operation some time repatriates were allowed to attend for a period as civilians, at Ministry of Labor rates for government training.

So far as possible, men were sent to units near where they hoped to live and work. This would enable the staff, too, to familiarize themselves with local conditions, which would be important since they were to help reintroduce the returned soldier to civilian life. Apart from their dealings with the soldiers, the staff would have to help local people learn about and get used to the problems of the repatriates and cooperate in showing them various lines of work.

Wilson describes the civil resettlement operation functioning in Britain by 1945, through twenty regional CRUs, each taking about 250 repatriated prisoners of war for periods varying from a few days to three months.

The senior staff at each unit consisted of an administrative group of five, nine case workers, four syndicate officers (each acting as "parent" to sixty men), and five specialist officers. The latter were a vocational officer, a woman social worker, a technical officer, a Ministry of Labor liaison officer, and a doctor. Work groups consisted of fifteen men.

Vocational counselors and staff from the Ministry of Labor helped the men evaluate the work plans they had formed and to think out and observe what would in practice be involved. The technical officers gave men workshop experience in the unit. The women social workers helped with matrimonial problems. Having women on the staff helped the men to get used to a mixed community.

Length of stay averaged five weeks. This was divided into three main phases. In the reception phase the men were encouraged to choose dormitory places on the basis of acquaintanceships struck up in the first hours. They were taken on tours of the unit. They formed themselves into groups of fifteen that would be related to one syndicate officer for the whole period. They had an introductory group discussion with their syndicate officer and each man had a short personal interview with him. These events were designed to help the man directly but also to help him justify not going straight home to family (the first visit home, for the weekend, was after three days). The man was encouraged to explore his plans with his family at each home visit and work them over again at the unit when he returned.

During the second, orientation, phase the men explored surrounding industrial opportunities. They were able to test out how far their plans were daydreams, how far there were real employment opportunities. Repeated discussions took place with the vocational counselors, who helped them plan visits to prospective work sites. During a final, planning, stage the men devised detailed personal plans, and engaged in job rehearsals, sometimes as amateurs trying out an activity without the burden of responsibility. This helped them to build confidence and to deal with embarrassments on meeting noncombatant civilian workers.

The workshops helped the men to learn domestic skills that would enable them to be useful as returned men-about-the-house, and to make objects they could take home to their wives. At the same time they could test out with workshop colleagues how much they liked this sort of environment.

A psychiatrist led group discussions with syndicate groups on personal and vocational aspects of their return to civilian life. Psychiatrists also saw men on request. Both group attendance and individual interviews were voluntary.

Wilson points to the need to help the men deal with their anxieties about returning to civilian life without the support of army discipline and the need to wean them away from dependence on the army. He describes the CRUs as transition communities in which there were gradual but increasing opportunities for acceptance of responsibility and for the display of initiative. He underlines the symbolic importance for participants, serving soldiers and the civilian public of the CRUs as institutions especially designed to help the returning men with their resettlement problems.

An elaborate follow-up study was made. This is reported by Adam Curle.[17] A major part of this consisted of a field study in which, in one area, socially comparable samples of fifty repatriated prisoners of war who had been through CRUs were compared with a hundred who had not. These were further compared with forty families from the same area who were taken to represent the civilian norms at the same socio-economic level.

The following represents part of the results.

Distribution of Degree of Settlement [18] Between CRU and Non-CRU Samples

	Percentage		
	More Settled	Less Settled	Sample Size
CRU Sample	74	26	50
non-CRU Sample	36	64	100

It appears that the CRUs were helpful in the resettlement process, though the evidence is limited by the post hoc character of the data and the fact that respondents likely to profit from the CRUs might have been more likely to join them.

Some Residues
and Later Developments

Soon after the end of the war W. R. Bion conducted a series of interpretative group meetings with members of the Tavistock Clinic and Institute and certain close associates. These gave rise to a theoretical formulation of social processes occurring within small groups, including dependence behavior, fight, flight, pairing between members, election of the "sickest" as temporary leaders, and the emergence of "hidden agendas." He saw these unconscious processes as conflicting with the manifest tasks which the group might be meeting to tackle. He regarded these processes as products of group behavior, connected with, but not the same as, the dynamics of the individual personality.[19]

Bion's theories had a considerable influence upon those members of the Tavistock who continued to work with groups and with external group practitioners and research workers. They have been proclaimed by some observers as among the most important insights ever attained into the operation of small groups. Their import has, however, probably been reduced by the idiosyncratic, semiprivate character of Bion's language; by the closeness of his work to psychoanalysis (which is not universally acceptable to social scientists); and by the elusive character of group processes themselves, which reduce their popularity as a field for systematic study.

GROUP RELATIONS TRAINING

During the last decade Bion's work on groups has had a revival in England because of the development by the Tavistock group of laboratory methods of training in group relations. These methods were in some respects similar to those already in use under the auspices of the National Training Laboratory in the United States and its allied institutions. At these centers research findings concerning behavior in small groups have been applied in the training of executives, social workers, and other persons in positions of responsibility, under the general label of "group dynamics." Emphasis is on the exploration of personal experience and behavior in a small group while the group is in being. Accompanying this is a program of role-playing (dramatization of typical social situations followed by analysis of what happened), demonstrations, and opportunities to study new social skills. The first formal Tavistock program of this type was conducted in 1957 in collaboration with a team from the University of Leicester.[20] This took the form of a residential conference lasting a fortnight. As in the case of the American version, a small study group (known in the United States as a T group) was at the heart of the proceedings of a residential conference, epitomizing in its aims that of the conference as a whole. J. D. Sutherland describes the aims of the study group as follows:

All those who have to work with groups know that apart from the psychological forces helping groups to obtain their ends, others interfere with the productivity of the group in relation to its main task. Past theories about work have tried to explain achievement in terms of forces which arise almost entirely within the individual. This is not based on a clear understanding of the psychology of work . . .

Because there is a general tendency to avoid the explicit recognition of these forces and especially the interfering ones, it requires a special social situation to confront them so that their nature and intensity can be experienced, and especially in such a way that this experience can be used constructively by the individuals concerned and not lead to increased tendencies to avoid them. The special social situation which experience shows most useful for this purpose consists in having a group meet without an "external" task to be done, but with the specific task of examining the kinds of feelings and attitudes that arise spontaneously, these feelings and attitudes being those which each individual brings to any group situation, or which develop within it independently of whatever the external task may be. Along with the group, there is present a Consultant experienced in the social and psychological forces which generally appear in such situations, whose task it is to comment on what is happening with a view to giving the group greater awareness of this. Although he does not occupy the conventional role of leader, i.e. one who regulates and controls the efforts of the group, there is rapidly established a strong link and meaningful interaction between the group and himself. At times quite intense feelings can be evoked in the group and the Consultant, judging his contributions according to the phase of group life and the needs of those present, preserves his objective role of suggesting to the group what forces seem to be giving rise to these manifestations.[21]

In his study group at the Leicester conference the member was given no task other than that of learning about group relations by experiencing and analyzing the processes occurring in the group. Membership was made up of people from different occupations. Parallel arrangements were made for "application groups"; these consisted of people with similar or complementary work problems and were designed to enable participants to test any new understanding they gained in connection with the types of problem they normally encountered in their own work. Again, a consultant worked with the group but this time his task was to help elucidate the objective problem presented, not to comment on events within the group. While the study groups were conceptually closely linked with the work of Bion (as was the overall idea of studying the structure of one's own community as a training exercise) the application group relied to a substantial extent on case conference procedures developed at the Tavistock Clinic for the psychological training of medical practitioners, probation officers, social workers, and marriage counselors. There was in addition a lecture series concentrating on the teaching of social science concepts and theories bearing on relations between individuals, groups, and organizations.

Subsequent residential training conferences have followed much the same pattern, except for two innovations. One has been the introduction of an intergroup exercise designed to illuminate problems encountered between work groups, and the other has consisted of interpretative sessions attended by the whole conference membership.[22]

Training events of this sort have become firmly established in England and the United States and are attended by industrial executives, social scientists, teachers, prison governors, ministers of the church, and many others who feel that their work will be advanced through understanding of group processes. They remain contentious in some circles. This appears to be partly because of the novelty of procedures which confront the person with reactions to his behavior in group contexts; partly because of popular wariness of activities apparently close to the conceptual apparatus of psychoanalysis and the methods of group therapy; partly because of the stress contingent on self-discovery. While the focus is on group and intergroup processes and not on the individual personality, it is inevitable that persons coming to this sort of activity for the first time will learn new things about themselves and that they will feel ambivalent about both the prospect and experience. Again, as with the use of projective materials in selection procedures, ethical problems arise. In this case one set of ethical problems is posed by the strain that can be imposed on some persons in interpretative group situations for the sake of new learning experiences. Another set of problems arises from the fact that some persons may attend partly against their will or despite severe reservations, either because they are more or less instructed to do so by their seniors or because they feel their refusal to go (or stay once they arrive) will be interpreted as a desire to conceal something. Furthermore, while it may well be held to be socially desirable that persons in positions of social responsibility (like prison governors, for instance) should undertake such training even if it is painful, it has to be borne in mind that insight is indivisible. A training program that succeeds in altering the characteristic relationship patterns of a senior administrator is virtually certain to have its impact too on his family relationships. A problem common to these events and the selection and appraisal procedures is, of course, that effectiveness in executive tasks involves a large proportion of the personality rather than merely a set of skills or techniques. From the point of view of an employer, persons are resources to be deployed for organizational ends, and group relations training comes to be viewed by those who sponsor participants and pay their fees as a means for increasing their effectiveness. New techniques in increasing understanding of social processes pose in crisp form the issue of where along the line of management development attempts to influence personal functioning cease to be legitimate.

The substantial training program in group relations by the Tavistock group has not been accompanied by a comparable research effort. This is largely due to the form of financing these activities, that is, almost entirely from fees for conference attendance, but partly due to the great difficulty and expense that is involved in systematic study of what are in effect community social processes.

GROUP PROCESSES
AND SOCIAL STRUCTURE

Notable research constitutions have, however, been made in a conceptually related field—the relations of group processes to social structure—by E. Jaques and I. E. P. Menzies, who are both psychoanalysts and have both been prominent members of the Tavistock Group.[23] In the *Changing Culture,* Jaques argued that difficulties he observed between groups of managers and workers, particularly in the early stages of his work with them, served largely expressive functions. The difficulties were, for instance, means through which workers could continue to regard and treat management as persons opposed to their interests, could demonstrate lack of confidence in management and could use the present to inject feelings related to past problems. Jaques implies that in some cases the persons concerned preferred problems to solutions and wanted attempts at solutions to fail, though they may not have realized either of these things. In other cases leaders appear to have searched for problems rather than tolerate feelings of isolation brought about by inactivity. He suggests that crises may in a sense be welcome because some persons can then dominate without guilt while others can allow themselves to feel dependent. Where managers held multiple roles these could in effect be manipulated to enable the persons concerned to get into subjectively comfortable positions. Criticism by one group of another might serve the function of avoiding intragroup tensions. Scapegoating management could fall within this category. One of the most important ideas in the book is that the groups of persons involved were often in a form of unwitting collaboration with each other to use their relationships to express feelings and attitudes not strictly related to the work situation.

Jaques noted that some palpably inaccurate perceptions of roles and role relations were tenaciously adhered to in the face of evidence that contradicted these. He concluded that certain role confusions were strongly, though unconsciously, motivated and that

role confusion is an unconsciously motivated defense to which individuals have recourse in order to avoid the anxiety produced by disjunctions between their personalities and the demands of the roles they carry.[24]

In a later work Jaques introduced the concept of "social systems as defense against anxiety." He makes it clear that he does not wish to suggest that social relations serve only those functions. He writes that

individuals may be thought of as externalizing those impulses and internal objects that would otherwise give rise to psychotic anxiety, and pooling them in the life of the social institutions in which they associate . . . And the reason for the intractability to change of many social stresses and group tensions may be more clearly appreciated if seen as the "resistances" of groups of people unconsciously clinging to the institutions that they have, because changes in social relations threaten to disturb existing social defenses against psychotic anxiety.[25]

Menzies has shown, in a study of a hospital, that institutions can develop which act as defense mechanisms against tasks in a work system that arouse anxiety.[26] As examples of such defensive institutions she points to a division of labor which spreads the nurse thinly over a large number of patients, so that she undertakes only one task for them rather than becoming personally related to them; to a depersonalization and categorization of patients that denies the significance of the individual; to detachment and denial of feelings; to ritual elements in task performance; and to the reduction of responsibility through checks and counterchecks and obscurities in definition. An important aspect of such socially structured defense mechanisms, says Menzies, is an attempt by individuals to externalize and give substance in objective reality to their characteristic psychic defence mechanisms. Her paper raises the distinct possibility that what attracts persons and gives meaning to certain forms of work is the opportunity to match unconscious personal needs with aspects of the defensive ideologies and institutions of the work system.

Both the Jaques and Menzies studies cast light on meanings found in the person-organization relationship and in colleague relations by indicating the existence of links between latent aspects of both personality and organizational functioning. They expand our understanding at the same time of the psychological functions performed by persisting features of organizational life and some of the reasons why such structural features are often so intractable to change.

NOTES

1. Descriptions of the backgrounds of these Boards and their design and operation are supplied in F. I. De La P. Garforth, "War Office Selection Boards (O.C.T.U.)," *Occupational Psychology,* 19 (April 1945): 97–108. Reprinted from the *Royal Engineers Journal* (December 1944); and B. S. Morris, "Officer Selection in the British Army, 1942–1945," *Occupational Psychology* (October 1949).

2. J. R. Rees, *The Shaping of Psychiatry by War* (London: Chapman Hall, 1955), p. 70.

3. B. S. Morris, "Officer Selection in the British Army, 1942–1945."

4. W. R. Bion, "The Leaderless Group Project," *Bulletin of the Menninger Clinic* 10 (May 1946): 77.

5. Rees, *The Shaping of Psychiatry by War,* p. 69.

6. Morris, "Officer Selection in the British Army, 1942–1945."

7. Garforth, "War Office Selection Boards."

8. For an account of this technique see H. Phillipson, *The Object Relations Test,* (London: Tavistock, 1955).

9. Rice's best known work in this series is reported in *Productive and Social Organization: The Ahmedabad Experiment,* (London: Tavistock, 1958).

10. C. Sofer, *The Organization from Within* (London: Tavistock, 1961), and C. Sofer and J. Hutton, *New Ways in Management Training,* (London: Tavistock, 1958).

11. Sofer and Hutton, *New Ways in Management Training.*

12. W. R. Bion and J. Rickman, "Intra-Group Tensions in Therapy: Their Study as the Task of the Group," *The Lancet* 245 (November 27, 1943): 678–681.

13. T. F. Main, "The Hospital as a Therapeutic Institution," *Bulletin of the Menninger Clinic,* 10, no. 3 (May 1946): 67.

14. J. Kelnar, "Treatment of Inter-personal Relations in Groups," *Journal of Social Issues,* 3, no. 2 (Spring 1947): 29 and 30.

15. *Time,* 27 July 1970, p. 52.

16. A detailed account of the work appears in A. T. M. Wilson, "The Serviceman Comes Home," *Pilot Papers* I (London: Pilot Press), on which this section is partly based.

17. Reported in A. Curle, "Transitional Communities and Social Re-Connection," *Human Relations,* 1, nos. 1 and 2 (1947).

18. The index of degree of settlement included fifteen criteria, having to do with attitudes toward and relations with wife, children, neighbors, workmates, and impersonal authorities.

19. Bion's conceptualization of group processes was first published in a series of papers in *Human Relations,* 1, nos. 3 and 4 (1948); 2, nos. 1 and 4 (1949); 3, no. 4 (1950); 4, no. 3 (1951). See also his subsequent book, *Experiences in Group and Other Papers* (New York, Basic Books, 1961).

20. A report is contained in E. L. Trist and C. Sofer, *Exploration in Group Relations* (Leicester: Leicester University Press, 1959).

21. J. D. Sutherland, "The Study Group Method of Training," appendix of Trist and Sofer, *Exploration in Group Relations,* pp. 56 and 57.

22. For an account of the Tavistock group relations conference subsequent to 1959 see A. K. Rice, *Learning for Leadership* (London: Tavistock, 1965).

23. Jaques was the leader of the well-known Glacier Metal Company project reported in *The Changing Culture of a Factory* (London: Tavistock, 1951), and then

left the Tavistock Institute. Miss Menzies is a current staff member and has been at the Institute for most of its postwar history.

24. Jaques, *The Changing Culture of a Factory*, p. 300.

25. E. Jaques, "Social Systems as Defence against Persecutory and Depressive Anxiety," in M. Klein et al, *New Directions in Psychoanalysis* (London: Tavistock, 1955), p. 479, in which he makes more explicit the ideas adumbrated in "The Changing Culture of a Factory."

26. I. E. P. Menzies, "A Case-Study in the Functioning of Social Systems as a Defence against Anxiety: A Report of a Study of the Nursing Services of a General Hospital," *Human Relations*, 13, no. 2 (May 1960).

PART IV

Generalizations

12 : Propositions on Organizational Behavior

Organizations as
Subsystems of Larger
Social Collectivities

ORGANIZATIONS are products of their societies, subsystems of larger systems. They act as agencies delegated to carry out specific tasks for the wider population, or they carry out, on the initiative of certain of their own members, functions that are tolerated and for which a demand exists. In either case the concept of an organization is inseparable from that of a market or body of consumers.

Every organization is suffused with the dominant values of its environment. But at the same time members impinge actively on their external environments and can appreciably affect social structure and culture.

Efforts are characteristically made by those leading organizations to protect investments and reduce uncertainty in the conditions under which they operate. This is attempted by such means as securing a measure of control over supplies and suppliers, by differentiating themselves from competitors, and by binding employees to themselves through combinations of material and symbolic inducements.

Members of a work organization are simultaneously members of many other groupings to which they have competing or complementary allegiances. Their power position within the organization depends largely on their relations with such groupings (which may indeed exist primarily to increase their organizational bargaining powers). Apart from the question of power, all members of any organization are influenced in their behavior and outlook by external groupings and by the standards or valuations that these groupings exhibit or that are attributed to them.

Technology and Task
as Determinants
of Internal Structure,
Style of Behavior,
and Personnel Composition

The structure of work organizations and the behavior of their members is substantially influenced by the nature of their tasks and by the character of the technology they operate, in the sense both of physical equipment and of systems of work. Task and technology are far from absolute determinants but do provide constraints on what can be done. Some combinations of task and technology foster solidary small-group interaction and isolation from external authority. Others foster personal independence. Still others require continuous consultation up and down the line of authority.

The shape of the administrative hierarchy (number of levels and power associated with each level) and style of management will be affected by task and technology, as will the type of technical and administrative expertise (and the mix between them) associated with the key leadership roles.

Technology, task, and style of management will have effects on the sort of employees at all levels which the organization attracts and retains.

The Organization
as a Role-System

Organizations are associations of persons, each of whom is allocated a specific role in a work system and division of labor in which work is divided into subtasks, distributed between roles, and subsequently combined into some form of output.

Each role has a rank relative to each other, and a specified area of jurisdiction and carries with it a specified amount of authority over persons and resources.

At least the broad outline of duties associated with each role is prescribed or commonly accepted or understood by the role occupant and other members of the organization. But each role has a discretionary content since it is impossible to provide for all contingencies that may arise.

The discretionary scope of roles is particularly important at the senior levels of the organization where tasks are relatively diffuse and possible lines of approach are more open to uncertainty and debate.

The person's occupancy of his role is conditional on his continued technical competence and willingness to perform the associated duties and to collaborate with colleagues and seniors. There is normally an appreciable range in the standards, or level of performance, at which occupancy of the role can continue to be maintained. The precise standard attempted will depend not only on the capacity of the role occupant but also on his appreciation of the equity of the bargain he has been able to make with his employer in regard to the exchange of his services for rewards; on the comparisons he makes with the alternative bargains available to persons like himself; on the influences exerted on him by colleagues; on their joint definition of their situation; on their relationship with management and colleagues; and on their assessment of their relative power position.

All organizational roles involve collaboration and coordination with others, although such collaboration varies in its visibility and in its meanings to the role occupant. In view of the complex division of labor characteristic of contemporary organizations, roles designed to ensure coordination are of special importance. The success or failure of the division of labor pivots on them.

Success in coordinating work involves attributes, skills, and temperamental capacities somewhat different from determinants of technical competence. These are, however, impossible to specify independently of the work system, of the characteristics of other persons involved, and of the history of past association. Leadership cannot be divorced from "followership" and leadership functions are normally widely shared by colleagues playing reciprocal or complementary roles.

Leadership and the coordination of work involve leaders in cross-pressures between competing needs, persons, and groups. Persons with managerial responsibilities are normally subject to role overload: it is impossible for them to carry out conscientiously their obligations to every person and group with whom their responsibilities involve them. Quasi-resolutions of the attendant conflicts and reduction of personal stress typically ensues through such means as personal ranking of priorities; implicit bargaining (which may permanently or temporarily reduce mutual obligations); rotation of priorities through time; and through the establishment of filters so that only the most urgent demands penetrate.

Particular work roles have attendant sets of attitudes in the sense that these tend to be acquired by most persons taking up those roles. The attitudes can be predicted with a fair measure of accuracy from the position of the role in the organizational division of labor and in the administrative hierarchy. Attitudes are particularly firmly anchored when similar roles are held by persons in close contact with each other.

The Organization as
a System
of Subgroups

As well as being a hierarchically organized structure of roles and persons, the organization is a network of overlapping primary groups variously linked on basis of geographic proximity, task similarity or complementarity, shared occupational fate, and so on. The person will have multiple membership of such subgroups and in the course of developing and maintaining such memberships will come particularly to value some of them.

Particularly important in determining behavior is the subgroup whose members together constitute the governing system of the organization. They are the main single source of policy, decisions, control, and sanctions, the main initiators of new work systems and changes in the division of labor, the main designers of new organizational roles and definers of the status and duties of the occupants of these roles.

Their internal powers are limited by the extent to which their interests, wishes and expectations coincide with other members of the organization; by the extent to which they control resources valued by those other members; by influence exerted from other directions; and by the countervailing power of other groupings, especially when these groups receive external support.

The effective power possessed by the governing system as a unit and by its individual members will depend not only on their formal status but also on their personal qualities and interpersonal bonds. Managers of the same formal rank will differ widely in their operating authority and their authority will, in many cases, spill over the boundaries of their official areas.

Colleague relations in subgroups play a key role in mediating between the individual and the larger organization. Such sub-groups are important channels of communication. Even where they are not used by senior management to transmit instructions and information, important announcements and news are referred back to the group by the individual member for translation, for interpretation, and for assessments of their potential significance for his colleagues and himself. These translations, interpretations, and assessments help to determine how far managerial action is supported and how far it is opposed.

Alongside the cooperation between persons and groups that forms the raison d'etre of their cooperation there proceeds constant struggles for power, for autonomy, for prestige, and for increased shares of the economic benefits produced by collaboration. These struggles are never entirely resolved.

The potentially damaging effects of conflict are normally limited by the fact that the perceived advantages of continued cooperation outweigh the perceived advantages of pursuing the conflict to a point where cooperation ceases. They are further limited in their intensity and effect by the fact that allegiances differ around particular disputes, so that the cost of pursuing one set of values can be loss of allies in pursuing another.

Organizational conflict entails reduction of collaboration; damage to defeated opponents diversion of energy from work to war; reduction of effectiveness in competition; unrealistic beliefs about opponents; self-doubt; and potential overspill to areas of interaction not directly involved in the conflict.

At the same time conflict allows subgroups to pursue their legitimate interests and to exert the power potentially available to them; avoids the involvement of management of the organization in the interests of only one subgroup of members; allows external social values to suffuse the organization; reinforces group bonds and boundaries; clarifies interests; corrects imbalances in reciprocities; and stimulates structural and procedural resolutions that might otherwise not be attempted.

The Organization as
a Human Community
and Value System

While the members of an organization are recruited to fill work roles they interact in practice as many-faceted persons. They are more than personnel resources for the formal administrative system. They manifest their own needs, some of which sustain and some of which undermine that system. They develop institutions supplementary to those of the administrative and work systems that perform functions for them other than the provision of income.

Individual personality and associations of persons adapt, transform, or break through the boundaries of "rational" organizations and procedure.

The living human association is a mixture of and compromise between, designed and spontaneous behavior, blending economic and technical aims and procedures with personal desires and group interests.

The existing structure and ways of behavior become infused with values beyond technical requirements. This is partly because of the stability and predictability they provide and partly because they have emerged as means for maintaining integrity and fulfilling personal aspirations. A proportion of members become committed to the enterprise, and delegate care of themselves and the satisfaction of their ambitions to the care of the enterprise. They subscribe to the image of the organization, assign it a character and build something of this image and character into their personal identities.

These processes of commitment aid communications and order, provide the organization with forces toward self-maintenance, provide meaning for participants and motivate their contributions. The same identifications may also weaken the purely technical resourcefulness of the organization by limiting the freedom of the management to make new deployments of its resources. Identification with the organization, as it has been and now is, constitutes resistance to change to what it might become.

Strains Toward Rationality

There is a persisting strain in all work organizations toward the maintenance or increase in rationality or efficiency with which resources are related to ends. This pressure derives from sources external to the organization (such as government, investors, shareholders, and competitors) and from the subgroup empowered to direct the activities of the organization.

At the administrative level this strain towards efficiency manifests itself within contemporary organizations in bureaucratic principles that emphasize the distribution of power, authority, and prestige on the basis of expertise and technical competence; the stipulation of general rules for the conduct of business; the specification of areas of jurisdiction and responsibility for each work role; the grading of roles in a hierarchy of authority; the separation of organizational from personal resources and considerations; objectivity and impersonality in dealings with employees and customers; accountability in the use of resources; and carefully maintained written records.

At operational levels, the same strain toward efficiency is manifest in the efforts of the governing subgroup to rationalize the flow of work and the ways in which it is carried out. Pressure is exerted to keep output up and costs down and to avoid waste and idleness of physical and human resources. The techniques of production engineering, operational research, statistical decision theory, and systems analysis are employed in attempts to ensure that production problems are analyzed from first principles and that theoretically possible combinations of resources and methods are explored in relation to the most desired outcomes. Efforts are made to devise systems of work that will encourage employees to identify their economic and personal interests with those of their employers; to link contributions with payments; to match aptitudes with position in the division of labor; to develop individual specialization; to find faster and cheaper ways of getting tasks done and relating them to each other; and to specify and control the work behavior of employees.

In the personnel sphere, employees are treated so far as possible as organizational resources. Systematic efforts are made, in particular, to rationalize and objectify the recruitment and selection of potential managerial personnel. The more promising recruits are routed through the organization in a way that accelerates their acquisition of experience, prepares them to replace those above them, and increases the span of time over which they can be deployed at higher levels. The promotion system is used as an incentive system and as a sanctioning system, to reinforce ambition in employees and to provide or withhold advancement on the basis of a combination of current performance and promise for the future. Performance and promise are regularly appraised in the hope that increased self-knowledge will encourage the employee to try to change in ways that will accord with the needs and standards of his seniors.

Constraints on Rationality

The strain toward economic rationality is limited, tempered, and countered in a number of ways.

No organization pursues only economic ends. No organization can deviate substantially for long from the dominating values (including those outside the economic sphere) of the society that contains it. Most organizations have to keep their staff in the face of competitors whose attractions may lie in spheres other than or additional to the economic inducements they can afford to offer.

Whatever a management wants in the way of rationality as conceived from its standpoint, what it actually gets is determined by bargaining with groups of persons who also possess economic power and who pursue at least partly independently defined objectives and interests.

At the highest policy levels, alternatives compete with each other and the selection of any one carries opportunity costs in terms of the forfeiture of others; all decisions are matters of compromise between gains and losses; knowledge is incomplete; the future and the behavior of other significant bodies is impossible to predict precisely; and a high degree of uncertainty has to be tolerated. The full range of policy alternatives does not necessarily come to mind. The range of possible policies is constrained by historical considerations embodied in an "organizational memory" precluding the higher management from pursuing certain actions that, by purely objective standards, are clearly within the range of possibility. Historical constraints include past achievements or failures in relation to levels of aspiration. Decisions are not made by organizations but by persons and groups who are members of organization.

Organizations are, in effect, lead by groups rather than by single individuals, and what is decided is influenced by interplay between individuals (often between groups as well). This interplay is affected by cross-pressures experienced by senior administrators as they weigh against each other the different values of colleagues to whom they owe loyalties and consideration as well as by their own personal judgments of the desirable.

Instrumental aspects of leadership have always to be balanced against the institutional, that is the need of staff to derive meaning from their cooperation and to associate under conditions of reciprocal trust and consideration. A theoretically advantageous stance in relation to the external world has to be balanced against the capacity and willingness of organizational members to maintain that stance.

The very process of bureaucratization generates forms of professionalism and specialization that result in conservatism, timidity, rigidity, and dependence on seniors and may divert attention from the need for adaptability in the face of changing circumstances. Juniors lean on the rules to protect their rights, and seniors may easily become trapped in a cage of prescription.

Behavior emerges that may or may not be in line with that wanted by the management. This behavior may be adaptive in the sense that it improves on that formally prescribed in securing organizational ends, or that it meets convivial and associational needs of employees.

With growth in the use of scientists and professionals, bureaucratic structures and prescriptions are challenged and modified by staff whose training, dispositions, and affiliations incline them to discipline that is derived from outside the organization, internalized, or rooted in peer groups of colleagues. As such persons gain power they widen the range of objectives pursued at the more senior levels.

In the operational processes the strain toward rationality is tempered by combinations of persons to protect their own standards and needs, to generate and maintain their own norms and to provide countervailing power against that exercised by management and by colleague groups. Pure rationality in the sense of efficiency is tempered by the need of managers at all levels to balance amicable everyday face-to-face relations with subordinates against hypothetical targets.

In the sphere of career management, the strain toward rationality is tempered by the necessity to maintain morale; by the necessity to honor commitments to persons whose continued cooperation is valued or whose treatment provides visible symbols of the integrity of management; by the need to take risks in hiring and promoting staff and to experiment with novel forms of training and reward; by imperfections in knowledge; and by the formation of personal bonds and alliances between particular seniors and subordinates. It is tempered by the need to protect disappointed employees from disgrace or disappointment that can result in hostility or withdrawal of cooperation.

Socio-dynamic Aspects
of Interaction

Interaction between and within the work groups in the organization will be infused with emotions. Some facets of this emotional system will be widely known, others will be unevenly perceived and understood, and some will be invisible to most of the participating persons. Part of the emotional system will contribute to the maintenance needs of the human association constituted by the organization, serving to maintain morale at times of stress and to give meaning to the work and to continued cooperation. Other parts of the emotional system will unite subgroups of the large system while constituting barriers between them, their colleagues, and the senior management.

An important element within the emotional system will be loyalty to close colleagues with whom a shared viewpoint has developed.

All work groups in the organization will attribute to certain others inefficiency, reluctance to cooperate for the common good, and hostility to themselves. Such attributions will have some elements of reality but will also constitute projective systems with defensive functions, serving to protect each work group against feelings of insecurity about its own performance and against strains generated in the course of internal interaction.

No work group will keep consistently to its task. Each will alternate instead between manifest tasks and what would appear from outside to be emotional interferences with the real work. However described by the members, the sources of this interference will be largely in their own interaction, including the hopes and disappointments of members concerning each other.

Social Process
as Capital
and Constraint

An important part of the working capital of the organization is the previous history of association and collaboration of its members.

At the same time the organization is constrained by its history and by the culture its members have built in regard to the opportunities it can take; the problems it can avoid; the methods it can use in taking opportunities and solving problems; and the personnel it can deploy in these efforts.

The relevant factors include contracts; past budgetary decisions; standing relations with external bodies and internal subgroups; technical expertise that has been developed (and excluded) in accordance with past contingencies; recruitment and training policies and career commitments that must be honored; the institutionalized division of labor between existing employees (particularly between members of the governing system); the desire to get the benefit of past financial and emotional investments: the expectations that participants have developed of each other.

A local system of norms, values, ideas, and theories will have developed about the functions of the organization; its place in the division of labor; and its rank order in the fields in which it operates.

Each phase in the history of the organization leaves residues that persist, helping to determine what will happen next. In some cases these residues facilitate the success of new operations, in others they handicap them. In either case, no organization faces new situations with a blank sheet and what seems theoretically possible to an external observer in the relation of existing resources to management ends may in practice be quite out of the question.

Meanings of
Work Roles [1]

The behavior of members of an organization is significantly affected by the psychological functions of work roles for them and by the meanings that have developed around their occupational investments and their participation in the particular organization.

Work roles provide economic returns that are means to ends distinct from the work itself. Work provides the person with opportunities to relate himself to society, to contribute to society, and to maintain a view of himself as a productive member of society through an output of goods or services. (The converse of this is widely recognized in the phenomenon of alienation.) Having a work role enables a man to maintain status and self-respect. Work roles enrich opportunities for interaction with others. They contribute to personal identity, largely by providing opportunities for identification with particular persons, skills, or contributions to society. Work roles structure the passage of time by scheduling, timetabling, requiring one's regular presence at particular places and times. Work helps to ward off depressing or distressing thoughts and feelings. Work provides scope for personal achievement, that is, meeting and surpassing objectives widely recognized as valuable or praiseworthy. Work provides opportunities for assuring oneself of one's capacity to deal effectively with one's environment and developing that capacity. At the level of unconscious personal dynamics, work keeps one in touch with reality, provides one with a sense of mastery and freedom and serves as a sublimation for sexual and aggressive impulses.

Orientation to work (and to colleagues and employers) varies at different levels of the organizational hierarchy. At the lower levels involvement in the organization and identification with management aims is uncommon; where involvement is strong this is predominantly with immediate colleagues with whom the person is in close interaction. At middle and senior level a higher proportion of employees are found who see themselves as exchanging loyal service for security and progressively increasing income. Involvement will tend to be positive where moral expectations of the employer are faithfully met or ambivalent where it is felt that these are not being sufficiently honored. At these higher levels, a proportion of employees are highly involved with both their work group and the enterprise conceived as a whole, work is a central life interest and important in satisfying expressive and affective needs, work and non-work are intimately related, and work implies a whole way of life.

A substantial issue in the outlook of persons in middle-level and senior roles is their experience of advancement. Their past history with the organization and the current posts they hold are carefully evaluated against career advancement norms in the organization from the point of view of how fast they have moved, might have moved, or are still likely to move. Advancement is valued because it is thought to confer higher status in the external society; compensates for dissatisfactions in employment; reinforces self-esteem; brings increased power and influence in an immediate social circle; provides evidence of personal effectiveness; and confirms for the person that he has been building his specialization in the right direction, has made an appropriate investment in a particular occupation and organization, and has succeeded in conveying to his seniors the importance of his activities to the central operations of the organization.

Because of the factors just described, individual members of organizations and groups and categories who regard their interests as identical evaluate every major development within the organization in terms of its possible implications for their own careers and work relationships, resist developments that appear to threaten them, and try to influence organizational affairs so that these are conducted in a way that they conceive to be consistent with their own needs.

Ideology and Indoctrination in Organizational Life

A number of characteristic ideologies co-exist within the organization.

The ideology adhered to and promulgated at the level of senior management tends to emphasize the social value of the product or service that the organization provides; its distinctive qualities relative to that of competitors; the importance of satisfactions available from working in the organization as a member of a team with common ends; the link between the success of the organization and the economic opportunities open to employees; and concern at upper levels for the welfare of individual employees.

Active efforts are made by senior management to expose recruits to the management mode of thinking and approach to affairs. These efforts continue to be made at intervals through most of the employee's career, usually through courses systematically designed to impart skills together with information and viewpoints desirable from the point of view of management. Continuity is maintained through organizationally produced literature, announcements, exhortation and, often, in performance appraisal interviews. Particular attention is given to potentially promotable persons, to convince them that promotion is a proper objective for them and to encourage them to acquire the values as well as the skills that will be necessary in the next section of the organization they will enter.

The acceptance by employees of at least part of the managerial ideology serves to reinforce their feeling that they have made a correct occupational and organizational choice and have invested themselves appropriately as far as the work side of their lives is concerned.

Ideologies develop within each subgroup of persons carrying out similar functions to emphasize the particular value of what they do and their special place in the organization and the occupational world. They tend to adopt similar values and loyalties, to refer their behavior to each other and to subscribe to common theories that purport to explain their functions and their relations with outside persons. They employ a private language that highlights matters of concern to them and expresses the terms on which they relate to each other. This follows from sharing a common situation and common problems; every established group arrives at a definition of its situation, its problems and possibilities, and develops a degree of consensus as to the most appropriate way of behaving. As the individual member of the work group gains in local expertise, he protects and enhances its value for him by adopting the local ideology, which ranks his current activity high in comparison with the activities of other workers and explains to real and imagined audiences why it is so important.

These ideologies typically include some anti-organizational sentiments and theories that express skepticism about the motivation, integrity, and efficiency of the senior management. These ideas are particularly helpful to members of the organization whose career fates do not match up to their expectations, as they provide ready-made explanations, other than their own deficiencies, of why they have not been as successful as they wish.

The various ideologies current within the organization expose members to a range of ideas which they use to help make sense of their situations and to provide a rationale for their actions. To a large extent the ideologies are competitive with each other and mutually inconsistent. These ideas are selectively acquired and shed in accordance with organizational fate, especially in the case of mobile staff. But they are not lightly acquired or discarded since they express in symbolic terms crucial aspects of personal identity, group loyalty, cross-pressures, and resolutions of personal conflict.

Scope for Individual Judgment and Action

Despite environmental and technological constraints, the hierarchical distribution of power, the prescriptive aspects of roles, the pressures of group membership, and the weight of historical process, there is scope for personal judgment and action.

Social institutions are customary modes of behavior, not immutable laws. Dominant social values change perceptibly from generation to generation. No technology absolutely determines its associated social system. However clearly and firmly the formal distribution of power, influence travels in all directions. No organization can maintain unpopular procedures indefinitely: these will be redefined, reshaped or sabotaged at the operational level, and new procedures will be improvised. All roles have discretionary components; human beings would otherwise hardly be necessary to fill them. Persons with particularly high or low status in their groups are less bound than others by their norms. Individuals can transfer their central affiliations from one group to another. Persons at all levels are susceptible to argument and persuasion.

Conflicts within society and within the organization bring about altered balances of power, making it possible for groups and individuals to initiate policies and execute decisions that were unthinkable or impossible before.

These considerations apply even to quite stable organizations. But such stability is today uncommon. International agreement and government economic decisions can expand and contract markets. Technology and work systems can change quite suddenly, creating new occupations, techniques and work roles and outdating others. Organizations are subject to fission and absorption by larger organizations, substantially changing structure and personnel. Social research findings are indicating advantages of new forms of organization and these are being incorporated in the same way as new physical technologies. New and expanded educational institutions are producing generations of young men expressly equipped with the latest techniques and knowledge so that they can act as agents of innovation in existing work organizations.

All these circumstances provide scope for judgment and action either by individuals on their own or in concert with like-minded colleagues. And it appears to be a distinct component of contemporary man that he is in a state of tension that is discharged in action to master his physical and human environments, to demonstrate and test his capacities, and to express his definitions of the desirable.

NOTE

1. For a review of work on this topic, see C. Sofer, *Men in Mid-Career: A Study of British Managers and Technical Specialists,* Studies in Sociology, No. 4, (Cambridge, England: Cambridge University Press, 1970).

PART V

Bureaucracies as Working Communities

13 : Emergent Behavior.
Adapting and Creating Structure

WEBER saw the reason for the advance of bureaucracy over other ways of getting large tasks done as sheer technical superiority. As he explained it, that superiority lay in rationality in terms of competence and specialization; precision in operation (everyone knowing exactly what his duties were); speed, since everyone know what was to be done by whom and how to refer a problem from one part of the organization to another; reduction of friction between people, since each officeholder knew what was required of him and where the boundary lay between his responsibilities and those of others; steadiness, since the same sorts of decisions were given whenever the circumstances were the same; reliability, since business was conducted according to known or calculable rules and subordination of juniors to seniors in a strict and known way, so that one could get decisions at a particular level binding on all those below.

On the personnel side of organization, benefits were derived from labor being divided between people in an orderly way; persons being trained to become experts in their particular fields; persons gaining a habitual and virtuoso-like mastery of their subjects.

Subsequent writers have added to the list of advantages of bureaucratic forms of administration.

Laski underlined the fact that the work is professionalized; nepotism is guarded against: and the conditions of work operate in favor of economic morality and against corruption.[1]

W. E. Moore has added the expressive notion that bureaucracies have the virtue of securing cooperation between large numbers of persons without those persons necessarily feeling cooperative.[2] No matter what they feel about each other, or about their tasks, sheer discharge of their stated functions ensures that the total machine is working.

Gouldner pointed out that the existence of a predetermined set of rules such as exists in a bureaucratic enterprise has several important advantages.[3] Such rules act as substitutes for orders, since they comprise an explicit body of standing obligations. They narrow workers' areas of discretion. They remove some of the personal friction associated with strict surveillance while one works. They alleviate the problem of repeatedly choosing specific individuals for unpleasant aspects of jobs since those aspects become a routine part of certain jobs. They remove alibis for not acting as management wishes. The public character of the rules allows deviation to be detected by large numbers of people and makes punishments legitimate, since correct behavior and penalties for deviation are known in advance. Victimization is less likely to be alleged or suspected. The rules specify a minimum level of acceptable performance. They permit individuals to work without emotional commitment, if they so wish.

Gouldner also pointed out that the existence of the bureaucratic rules provides the supervisor with a crutch for his authority. This is true not only in the sense that he can exercise his power in the names of the rules, but also, paradoxically, that he can choose opportunistically where and when not to do so, knowing that "strategic leniency" on selected occasions gives him reciprocal informal rights over the person to whom he is lenient.[4]

Blauner points out that bureaucratic rules entail equality before the law of the organization.

Modern bureaucratic organisation is based on universalistic standards of justice and fair treatment and its system of rules has enhanced the normative integration of industry.[5] *

Disadvantages and Problems

Laski describes these as follows. In public bureaucracies, concentration of power in the hands of government officials can jeopardize the liberties of individual citizens. Large organizations become the preserve of oligarchies of specialists. It is hard to control the expert, with his special knowledge and data. Having to be open to constant justification of their actions, members of a bureaucracy forbear risks and experiment and conservative habits are built. Because of openness to criticism by the public, the members are anxious to secure a reputation for accuracy and insist on rehearsing every possible criticism: this leads to timidity.[6]

Merton considers that bureaucratic organization, as defined by Weber, is likely to have among its consequences red tape, formalism, and rigid rules.[7] He suggests that behavior becomes stereotyped in ways that are not necessarily appropriate to the specific set of circumstances currently confronting the administrator; that bureaucratization carries with it a risk of inappropriate response being made to changed (environmental) conditions; that there

* From *Alienation and Freedom* by R. Blauner (Chicago: University of Chicago Press, 1964). ©
1964 by The University of Chicago. Reprinted by permission of University of Chicago Press.

is a tendency in bureaucracies for goals to become displaced on to procedures and rituals.

The system, he says, can easily breed overconformity, timidity, and conservatism and what he calls "technicism," namely a tendency to retreat to the mechanics of one's job without adequate regard to whether these are suited to the problem in front of one. Discipline can become overemphasized, with great importance placed on people doing as they are told, whether or not they have been told to do the right thing. Specialization in a few activities involves deskilling, incapacitation in others. Specialists tend to become narrow-minded and blinkered, developing ways of not seeing circumstances that do not fit easily with their preprogrammed behavior. They are tempted to be arrogant and domineering. Lastly, he says, a defensive *esprit de corps* can develop among colleagues, who combine to protect persons and procedures rather than concentrating on problem-solving.

In a paper on the relations of individuals with employing organizations structured on bureaucratic lines, Argyris suggests that these relations are likely to be characterized by conflict and frustration.[8] He suggests that personal development in our type of society involves movement from passivity to activity, dependence to independence, subordination to equality or superiority, the shallow expression of a few abilities to deeper expression of many. He contrasts such trends, culminating in adult needs, with organizational arrangements that favor dependence in employees, subordination to and passive dependence on leaders.

A novel note in the consideration of bureaucracies has been struck by Michel Crozier.[9] Unlike Argyris he calls attention to the freedoms provided by the rules of bureaucracies for the so-called subordinate strata, including freedom to act independently of the needs or requirements of the organization and to ignore certain requests made by superiors.

He points out that people in these strata are well protected from criticism and insecurity by the narrow specification of their responsibilities and by institutional due-process laws regulating the conditions under which they can be penalized, dismissed, etc. Juniors are in a good position to lean on the rules and can completely discharge their obligations by adhering to such instructions as are issued to them. (This is by contrast to their seniors, who are much more exposed and vulnerable to criticism.) This can make for inflexibilities and rigidities in the system.

Crozier sees leaders of bureaucracies as captives of the system, in the cage of prescription, largely confined to judicial, arbitrational functions. He sees the organization and its leaders as relieved from life sentences only by the occasional need for technological reorganizations. The astute leader seizes (perhaps manufactures) occasions to remold as many of the administrative rules as he can. But it seems to Crozier that nothing less than a crisis is necessary before a bureaucratized system can alter radically.

Emergent Behavior
in Large Organizations

Weber's analysis of bureaucracy was, as we have said earlier, in ideal-type terms. He knew that the behavior of members of an organization does not precisely follow blueprints.[10] And he did not precede or follow his analysis with empirical field studies to examine exactly what does happen in practice.

A multitude of subsequent empirical studies of large organizations has, however, been conducted. These have shown that in the course of actual operations important new elements arise in the structure, emergent factors that influence the way subsequent operations are performed. Sometimes these matter just as much as the formal, bureaucratic elements. These new elements have sometimes been called "the informal structure" or "informal organizations" that are said to exist side-by-side with the formal.

This was, of course, a central point in the pioneering studies of the Mayo group, which particularly emphasized the negative consequences for management aims of informal organization at shop floor level.

In a technically sophisticated study Blau not only identified emergent behavior but penetratingly worked out its functions within the organization.[11] His work on this is based on an empirical study of a government employment agency. It is assumed, as he says, that government officials will approach the public in a spirit of formalistic impersonality—in Tacitus's words *sine ira et studio quorum causas procul habent* (without anger or partisanship because they have no personal interest in their particular cases). This is intended to assure equitable treatment of clients and rational, rather than emotionally dominated, operations. But this was not realized in actual practice in the agency he studied. Blau examined inter alia the dealings of staff with white collar workers as against others and with Negro and white applicants. He found that prevailing class and racial prejudices found expression in the organizational setting despite a multiplicity of rules and rulings emphasizing the fact that occupational qualifications alone must determine decisions. Staff were more eager to help white-collar clients and a white reception clerk was shown to act less favorably to black clients than white.

Blau also showed, however, that informal competitive relations between colleagues seeking to maintain their numbers of placements operated to reduce such discrimination. This indicates that so-called informal behavior or informal organization, can have consequences favorable to the official aims of the senior management.

The same point, on the latent positive function of informal organization, especially primary group relations, is made by E. Gross.[12] He shows that occupational specialists in two large organizations were able, by fraternizing over lunch, at coffee breaks, and after hours, to overcome problems of mutually hostile subcultures and indifference to other specialists. Here they were able to compare their specialist tasks and get to know more about the relation of their work to each other and to the overall task of the organization. Similarly, Gross showed that in the operation of the authority system of these organizations informal meeting and conversation overcame the defects of the formal communications system. In these conversations staff could raise problems obliquely or hint at problems without committing themselves irretrievably to formal statements that could have awkward consequences.

These studies by Blau and Gross help to balance the characterization of informal and spontaneous behavior in work communities as necessarily detrimental to the stated purposes of the senior management of the organization. We think now rather of formal organizations as consisting of networks of subgroups containing members who adapt their role and behavior in ways that may or may not fit in closely with what is asked of them, or which may reflect compromises between what they are asked to do and what they want to do.

A Case Study
in Bureaucratization

I summarize below a case in which a company rapidly took with my help several steps toward greater bureaucratization.[13] The case illustrates the positive functions of bureaucratic procedures, counterweighing the predominantly negative emphasis in a research literature that tends to emphasize the disadvantages of inflexibility, loss of autonomy, and so on.

The company approached the Tavistock Institute with a problem that was presented as one of selecting a chief accountant and secretary. The total personnel in the company numbered 500 and turnover was about a million pounds a year. Early inquiries elicited the facts that the company already had a man (Mr. Davis) in a post somewhat similar to this and that he was the brother-in-law of the Sales Manager, E. Adams, and a relative also of every other member of the board. All members of the board were descendants of the original founder of the firm or had married descendants. This was despite the fact that the firm was a public company. About 40 percent of the shares were held within the family, though a much smaller proportion was held within the board itself.

This was a family firm in more ways than one. In many cases several members of families unrelated to the board worked in the company. Partly owing to long-established family tradition of this type, and partly because of technical specialization, staff turnover was very low. Twenty percent of the employees had been in the company more than twenty-five years.

The members of the board whom I first met said they had offered the new post to Davis but he had turned it down because it did not carry membership of the board. He was now considering emigrating to Australia and would like the senior post in their affiliated concern there, which was then vacant. It then turned out that the question of Davis's board membership was an issue of long standing. He had been recruited to the company by his father-in-law, then vice-chairman of the company, with the prospect of qualifying as an accountant and becoming secretary within seven years. He had done this. According to Davis, his father-in-law had given him to understand that he would eventually go on to the board. The present directors did not feel bound by this. They felt that even if the offer had been made, their former vice-chairman had not been empowered to make it. Davis added, in conversation with me on my first visit to the company, that a board vacancy had now arisen but that instead of him his young brother-in-law, G. Adams (younger brother of the sales director), was to be appointed. This was grossly unfair. The young man lacked his professional qualifications and he (Davis) was "as related to the family as anyone now on the board." Davis produced a kinship chart for my inspection to substantiate this: I was astonished that such a document was on the premises.

I was also interested to find at lunch, which was in the boardroom, that those who normally ate there together were the board members, Davis, and G. Adams; that is, all the family members. Meanwhile, other managers equal in rank to Davis and Adams ate elsewhere.

When I next met the board I suggested that we defer the selection matter but clarify the needs of the business, the needs of the family, and the appropriate relationship between the two.

At these discussions, members of the board confirmed that their policy had been to recruit potential executives and board members from the family; no one other than a family member had ever been on the board. To elect such a person would mean breaking a long company tradition. The younger board members wondered whether the time had not now come to make such a change. The wish of the family to retain their financial and emotional interest had to be balanced against the need to run the company effectively under increasingly competitive conditions. Economic viability mattered to the board members, their wives, and other relatives as shareholders. While the younger board members were the first to convey that they might be prepared for the change, their doubts about maintaining the existing system turned out to be shared by their seniors. These doubts were reinforced when discussion turned to the quality of the company's managers at the level below the board. It became clear to all of us that inadequacies at this level were probably a consequence of reserving the most senior posts and directorships for family members. This realization posed in crisp form the board's dilemma about the post they wanted to fill. They could hardly expect to recruit a man of the quality they wanted if they had to tell him that he had no chance of promotion and that family members would always receive preference for places on the board. We also discussed the discomfort of young family members who came into the company and rose rapidly within it. They could not know how far they owed their positions to their family connections and how far to their own abilities.

After about six weeks of discussions around these issues, the board approved a new personnel policy. This included a statement that future directors would be appointed mainly from senior managers in the business and that non-family members would be eligible for board membership. From time to time appointments would in future be made of management trainees, that is, young men of above average education, intelligence, and promise, who could be given a training that would accelerate their rate of learning and maximize the period over which they might effectively discharge managerial responsibilities. Such traineeships would be open to non-family members, and all applicants would compete for the traineeships on an equal basis.

In keeping with the new policy, the board agreed to conduct group selection procedures, with impartial assistance from personnel specialists from outside the company, for both the new English post and the position in Australia in which Davis was interested.

Several months later the board took further steps that consolidated and extended its degree of bureaucratization. A management committee was formed which included all departmental heads, leaving only major policy decisions to the board. All members of this new committee now lunched in the boardroom. Systematic assessment procedures were instituted to determine the promotability and training needs of managerial staff at lower levels.

Increasing and Decreasing
Bureaucratic Modes
of Operation

In the case just described one can attribute the bureaucratization of the firm to the strains precipitated by family tension when family and firm were insufficiently segregated and to the need to remain profitable in the face of increasing competition. In helping the board move in this direction I was bringing them into line with standard contemporary arrangements in Western societies for rationalizing the personnel side of their operations.

Other factors likely to increase the degree or spread of bureaucratization in an organization would certainly include increase in size. This brings an expanded need for formal standing rules, categorization of persons and

fferentiation of levels of authority, clarification and specification of
onsibilities, recording of decisions, accountability, and so on. An
in the use of bureaucratic methods can also be expected to follow
takeover of one firm by another or from the appointment of new
.....s from outside a department or firm. In either case, the new leadership would not have available the established informal channels and relationships that existed for their predecessors.

Katz and Eisenstadt point out that there are recognizable circumstances
in which the degree of bureaucratization of an organization is reduced.[14]
Reduction in size and loss of a monopoly are examples. A reduction in degree of bureaucratization also appears to follow where tasks are dangerous
or unusual and the persons involved are closely dependent on each other;
when a work group is isolated from social contacts outside the organization;
and when the most senior members of the organization are absent and
unable to scrutinize closely what is done. Katz and Eisenstadt cite here the
behavior of soldiers in combat as described by Stouffer et al; [15] of a naval
unit on a small unpopulated Pacific island as described by Page; [16] of night-
shift workers as described by Lipset et al; [17] and of miners described by
Gouldner.[18]

They describe a case, in the same paper, in which we can see forces
toward and against bureaucratization competing with each other. These
involve efforts in Israel to cope with new immigrants, many non-Western
in origin and unacquainted with the institutions, demands, and opportunities of a Western-type state. To deal with the immigrants, some of
the organizations concerned have had to grow, stricter chains of command have been established, and problems have had to be routed through
authorized channels. Nevertheless, in actual contacts between official and
client there has been "debureaucratization." The chief examples cited are
those in which officials become teachers in addition to or at the cost of
their other functions—nurses at baby clinics teaching immigrant mothers
how to take advantage of the services available to them, managers of food-
supplying organizations showing housewives in their homes how to cook
new foods, bus drivers teaching people how to queue at a stop.

The authors suggest that one part of the explanation for this behavior
is that the official cannot perform his role unless his clients know how to
perform theirs, and that another part is the ambition of some officials in
the new state to exercise social leadership.

It appears from their data and discussion that debureaucratization stems
partly from the professionalization that is required at the operational level
in the handling of immigrant problems. It is also clear from this paper
that influence against bureaucratization derives from external social influences, such as the smallness of the country; the shared economic and
military struggle; and the prevalent pioneering, egalitarian, and mutual-aid
ideologies.

As we are repeatedly seeing, it is impossible to understand organizational behavior without close regard to the wider setting in which the organization is embedded.

The Bureaucratized
Organization as
a Work Environment [19]

The bureaucratized organization constitutes a distinctive form of work environment.

Since formal authority emanates from the top and coordination of effort into a master plan is a central consideration, group and individual autonomy are not fostered. Tasks are assigned on the basis of overall organizational efficiency rather than on the basis of the preferences of particular occupational groups.

Creativity and innovation tend to be prerogatives of seniors.

For the sake of ease in handling large numbers of persons and cases, procedures are standardized as far as possible. This affects the way the person is required to treat objects and other persons, and the way in which he is himself treated.

The expertise of the individual or occupational group constitutes a resource to be used rather than something to be valued in its own right.

Rewards are associated with identification with and contribution to the purposes of the organization (in effect the senior management) and with position in the administrative hierarchy of the organization. The higher rewards are conditional on accepting responsibility for supervising the work of others and persuading them to concentrate on the goals of senior management.

Mastery of the routines and social system of the organization is valued. The persons who make the most progress tend to be specialists in the technical and political processes of their particular organization rather than practitioners of skills easily transferable to alternative employers. This binds them to the organization.

Since the organization is oriented to purposes which may be distinct from the work interests of the individuals who compose it, there tends to be an emphasis on extrinsic rewards of money and fringe benefits rather than on the personally fulfilling nature of the work. Opportunities for promotion and opportunities to occupy positions carrying higher salary, prestige, and responsibility tend to be emphasized rather than the content of the work.

Size and growth of the organization are valued in themselves so that more comes to mean better.

The issues are often too large, the outcomes too important and expensive, for individuals or even small groups of close colleagues to have their own way. When plans are formed, details get circulated and more and more people suggest changes, alter emphases, amend or add objectives. Often the initiators of a program do not feel they have effective control of events: they contribute rather to a social process which no one actively controls.

As a consequence of the complex division of labor, the individual manager or technical specialist does not often feel that he makes things happen and that what does happen is attributable to his intervention. The contemporary executive often works in an environment in which he cannot be sure of the connections between his behavior and its consequences, and in which the assessment by others of such connections is also a matter of estimate and subjective evaluation.

Technical Specialists
in Bureaucracies

With the increasing importance of science, technology, and ideas in contemporary life, many organizations (especially industrial organizations) have become large-scale employers of scientists, engineers, and other technical specialists and professionals. From the wide social point of view this has the valuable function of fusing scientific disciplines with bureaucratic organizational techniques, enabling large numbers of scientists and professionals to be marshaled for massive projects.

But special problems attend the employment of such persons and, in particular, their relations with seniors and with administrative colleagues.

It is a common bone of contention between industrial organizations and universities that science graduates (and even engineering graduates) are imbued during their training with the values of pure rather than applied science and are indifferent or resistant to considerations of practicality and profitability during their early years in industry. Scientists and professionals are said by their superiors and lay colleagues to be dismissive of routines; to resist authority; to pay insufficient attention to productivity, profitability, and similar organizational needs; to waste the organization's time (for example, by pursuing matters of only theoretical or aesthetic importance); to concentrate unduly on their own research interests; to want to share their findings with colleagues wherever they are placed rather than treat them as private and confidential assets of their employing organization. Scientists and professionals consider it important to maintain boundaries between themselves and laymen: within bureaucratized organizations these boundaries are lowered or penetrated.[20]

Endemic problems are likely to arise out of the fact that in formal organization devoted to the coordination of activities necessary for the realization of a specialized goal, senior executives are anxious to maintain adequate controls over those employees responsible for carrying out these subsidiary activities. From the point of view of the senior management these activities and the persons who carry them out are means to an end, not ends in themselves. Scientists and professionals in industrial and government organizations have to live with the fact that they and their work will be appraised by persons who may not be their professional peers but have the power to shape their occupational fates by virtue of being their superiors in office. They have to cope with control procedures over time, money, and the choice of work task which these organizations impose on all who work in them. The main route to promotion will probably lie through the ranks of executives, but this is likely to involve reducing one's "technical" work and placing one's scientific or professional status at risk.

Common difficulties of professionals in organizations, and between them and their colleagues, have been highlighted in a vivid distinction made by Gouldner between "cosmopolitans" and "locals." [21] This differentiates the interests of persons whose major orientation and commitment is toward their discipline and to colleagues wherever they are located from those whose more abiding interests and personal loyalty reside with their employing organization.

These distinctions are, naturally, oversimplified and commonly put in rather extreme form to make a point. While accepting that important conflicts do exist, it is as well to remember that most people do not lie at one or other extreme. Among scientists, the "local" who is indifferent to science and technology outside his company may be almost as rare as the "cosmopolitan" who regards his contributions to his company as accidental by-products and no more.

It is inevitable that there be a certain amount of strain when professional roles confront organizational necessities. But a variety of accommodative mechanisms arise or are developed to reduce the strain and to forestall or settle some of the incipient or actual conflicts.

One is the obvious one of creating for such people specialized roles in partially segregated substructures of the organization, for instance, specialized departments for basic research or research and development. This maintains boundaries between the specialist and his colleagues and helps to create a more favorable culture for the fostering of his work and values. Organizations, after all, are rarely monolithic entities with a unitary and uniform culture but consist of multiple interlocking and overlapping substructures and subcultures. At the same time, of course, differentiation has its costs in creating conditions for isolation and intergroup conflict.

It is possible to provide some internal variation in administrative arrangements within departments employing scientists and professionals, for instance by developing project teams whose leadership can be shifted with the needs of the particular task in hand, and by allowing for a measure of colleague control. [22] This can be combined with the provision of special types of leadership by a professional from the same field as other employees, whose task is to combine technical leadership and support with superordinate control and also to mediate between his technical colleagues and executives in other departments.

Organizations that employ professionals can usually create opportunities for them to achieve professional rewards while still serving the primary needs defined by the senior management, including attendances at conferences and publication of selected papers and cooperation with external scientists acting as advisers. Some major employers of scientists and professionals have set up dual career channels, one for line executives and one for scientists and professionals, permitting the latter to improve their prestige, income, and facilities without giving up their specialities.

A certain amount of self-selection must reduce the likelihood of problems. Bello [23] suggests that the most gifted and creative young scientists probably gravitate to the universities or towards employment with those corporations allowing most latitude to talented research workers. Quite apart from the question of relative ability, many of the most talented young graduates are more attracted by applied than theoretical work.

Then, even from a professional point of view, many industrial research laboratories have resources of equipment, manpower, and supporting services which the scientist would not find available to him in a university or research establishment. As Marcson points out in his previously quoted book, the employing organization and the recruited scientist change each other. The aims of pure knowledge need substantial colleague support, marked ability, and the capacity to persevere through periods of frustration and disappointment. Against this are placed the pressure of applied projects and the opportunity to please seniors with applied interests. The new researcher may discover the assigned research is as challenging and fascinating as anything he and his university teachers had thought up as a project for him. He may discover the pleasures of solving problems in the sense of working out how to render theoretical ideas commercially feasible and then seeing them applied in the way he and his colleagues have devised.

Even in the most enthusiastic and tenacious research worker adaptation and compromise are likely to ensue.

Perhaps the most important accommodation that takes place is a real overall modification of bureaucratic forms of administration to cater for the diverse needs of the variety of categories of specialists (including large numbers of professionals) nowadays required in large enterprises. Burns and Stalker have shown in a notable study how firms in a technologically demanding industry have suffered in comparison with their competitors where they have persisted with an authoritarian type of structure that has not provided a favorable context for innovation.[24] Pressure towards more flexible, more participative, more employee-centered methods of operation has also come independently from a stream of social research studies converging on the conclusion that a less closely regulated approach is more consistent with contemporary demands for democracy, better adapted to change, and leads to higher productivity.

A Case Study
of Technical Specialists

I have examined in a detailed interview study of forty technical specialists how far the problems described above are reported by them and how these appear to be posed or resolved so far as they are concerned. I had the advantage in this study of being able to compare the position of such specialists with others of the same age and approximate career and salary level. The technical specialists were employed in a chemicals firm which I call Novoplast and the contrast group of executives at a motor manufacturing firm which I call Autoline.[25]

In describing disliked aspects of their jobs, distinctly more of the Novoplast men complained about not having enough responsibility. This was particularly the case among those Novoplast respondents who were in research and investigation. The men criticized the routines and controls to which they were subject. They did not say that they should be free spirits and were prevented from this by unsympathetic administrators; rather, that if they were given wider scope they would be more effective in the exercise of their talents and that this arrangement would pay off better for the firm.

The Novoplast men played down the importance of their superiors as persons directly in charge of them. They portrayed them as persons in the background who were hardly necessary, though they might sometimes be called on for help in a technical or administrative matter.

There was far less of a problem for the technical specialists around the issues of practicality, profitability, and work of theoretical importance than the literature would suggest. The orientation of the Novoplast men was similar to that of engineers—the physical sciences profession par excellence, which defines its mission as the economical combination of knowledge and resources for practical ends. The Novoplast men turned out, somewhat unexpectedly, to be as interested as those at Autoline in being practical in relation to managerial goals. They shared the interest of administrative personnel in being members of a successful organization. This was not all they were interested in. But the men at Novoplast appeared to accept their role as the use of their training in concert with the resources supplied by their employing organization toward ends that they shared with their seniors.

Some of the Novoplast men spoke of the constraints they experienced on content of work, place, and time, but said these aspects were compensated for or outweighed by other considerations. These included the opportunity to see a project right through to the test of marketing feasibility, the access to massive technical resources, and the opportunity for personal effectiveness and achievement. For several of them, the intellectual challenge of a problem was added to rather than detracted from by the inclusion of an economic dimension.

The Novoplast men mentioned the conflicts they experienced between the demands of short-term usefulness and long-range personal and scientific interests. But they seemed to be managing such conflicts successfully. This was partly by compromising between opposing external demands and personal interests and partly by applying a "meta-prescription," or rule governing what are experienced as the competing demands of groups to which one refers one behavior.[26] The meta-prescription applying for most of the technical specialists in my sample was weighted in favor of the organizational role that the men had accepted.

As far as the local-cosmopolitan issue was concerned, the Novoplast men, like those at Autoline, were primarily oriented toward their own organization rather than toward external colleagues or scientific associations or establishments. This was not because they had become indifferent to their technical work. On the contrary. But they judged what they did only partly against what they would consider the values of the "scientific community" (in the sense of those who see their main concern as the advancement of knowledge through research and publication and see their social functions as discharged by those facts). They also judged their work against the values of persons doing the same kinds of applied work as themselves, especially in the same company. They remained keenly interested in technical work but saw meeting organizational needs as an important part of their work or, at the least, as an accepted part of their bargain with their employers.

There appeared to be several reasons why the aims and interests of the Novoplast men converged with those of their senior management.

For certain types of process, product, knowledge, and equipment, Novoplast is one of the world's leading institutions. Employees who have already invested themselves in the firm's expertise are probably in the best place if they wish to continue to pursue the same line. There can be few comparable assemblages of equipment and knowledgeable colleagues. The Novoplast men are members of their own, on-the-job, technical community.

There is some scope for identification and association with the external scientific community. The firm has a close and intimate association with universities and is a well-known supporter and provider of fellowships.

The men can see themselves as contributing to science and to society through scientific and technological progress by supplying new products based on their research and development.

The trained person at Novoplast who has proved his capability is given substantial capital resources, subordinate staff, and technical help to achieve departmental or sectional objectives. He can bring these people and resources together, mobilize them around a problem, and make an impact on his environment.

Several of the Novoplast men had either arrived at the firm with, or had acquired, executive leanings alongside their interests in science.

One prominent subgroup consisted of men who liked to regularize their work and have the discipline of the organization determine their work habits. About a third of the respondents said that while they were interested in their work and received definite gratifications from it, they wanted to control the part it played in their lives and structure its role. There were just about as many of these men as those who experienced the job as a dominant factor in their lives and as a primary source of satisfaction.

An important part appears to be played in the organizationally centered attitudes of the Novoplast men by the structure of opportunity of the firm. After a few years the possibilities of promotion look greater in operational rather than research fields. Even promotion in research often involves successful contact with senior colleagues outside research who have found one helpful and cooperative. The employee cannot antagonize a high proportion of those who make recommendations bearing on his promotability. It is inevitable that the man will be judged largely in terms of the objectives (both organizational and personal) of his senior managers and the contributions he makes to these.

Finally, a considerable acculturation or secondary socialization effect appears to act on the men. The virtues of usefulness, practicality, growth, and commercial success are constantly expressed in the company's operations—among other places in newsletters, training courses, and personnel appraisal schemes. I found, for instance, that in the appraisal interview schedule used by the firm no items referred to the employee's contributions to science or his participation in professicnal activities outside the company though many referred to his competence in the company's immediate affairs.

The Applied Scientist
as a Bureaucratic Phenomenon

The general implications of the Novoplast study include the importance of the emergence of a new and important occupational category.

Several of the Novoplast technical specialists would not have been able to have pure science careers in a university or research institute. At Novoplast they were having productive science-based careers in a scientific and intellectual environment which was satisfying to them and where they were useful both to their employers and the wider community.

Many others in the firm, who would be highly acceptable in academic work, felt that they had arrived at a viable compromise between freedom and constraint, reflective work and practicality. They found it an acceptable personal fate to be well-paid members of a large technical institution which supplied them with material resources and assistance that would not be available on a comparable scale elsewhere.

A career in a large industrial organization provides opportunities for business participation without the risk of losing one's own personal resources. Men with a training in science appear to enjoy this experience just as others do.

The men we have been describing constitute a new occupation or profession which is developing in response to the character of science-based industry in the present century. They are certain to become an increasingly prominent social and occupational category as work becomes more and more knowledge-based.

Within a bureaucratic organization there is inevitably some feeling among those who employ and manage scientists that they should be induced to identify themselves as much as possible with their employing organization, think of themselves as primarily instruments of that organization, and relegate their scientific identification to a secondary position. There are, on the other hand, substantial though longer-term disadvantages in having controlled or captured scientists. The captured scientist risks becoming divorced from his colleagues employed elsewhere and from his subject and, because of this, may eventually become less useful to his employer (or to society). If a policy of organizational secrecy prevails and the employed scientist cannot share his ideas with others, they will not share theirs with him. If the organization gains a reputation for restricting the freedom of its scientific staff, its capacity to recruit competent scientific staff will be impaired.

For some science-based organizations these issues may not arise in acute form. Many of the technical specialists will be or will become organization men in much the same way as engineers who join industrial organizations. Others appear to bridge the industrial and pure science worlds without strain.

The problem remains, however, from the organizational point of view, of keeping a sufficient proportion of men adequately connected with external science and scientists, and, from a community point of view, of maintaining in industrial organizations some scientists who are closely identified with the wider society and scientific advancement in general. These become crucial problems as we entrust our economic welfare and our continuing security to large industrial organizations capable of massive impact on their physical and human environments.

N O T E S

1. H. Laski, "Bureaucracy," *Encyclopaedia of the Social Sciences,* E. R. A. Seligman, ed., 3 (London: Macmillan, 1931).

2. W. E. Moore, *The Conduct of the Corporation,* (New York: Random, 1962).

3. A. W. Gouldner, *Patterns of Industrial Bureaucracy,* (New York: The Free Press, 1954), Chapter 9.

4. The phrase "strategic leniency" is Gouldner's. *Patterns.*

5. R. Blauner, *Alienation and Freedom, The Factory Worker and His Industry,* (Chicago: University of Chicago Press, 1964), pp. 181 and 182.

6. Laski, "Bureaucracy."

7. Merton, R. K., "Bureaucratic Structure and Personality," in his *Social Theory and Social Structure,* revised edition (New York: The Free Press, 1957).

8. C. Argyris, "The Individual and Organization: Some Problems of Mutual Adjustment," *Administrative Science Quarterly,* 2 (June 1957): 1–24.

9. Crozier, M., *The Bureaucratic Phenomenon. An Examination of Bureaucracy in Modern Organisations and its Cultural Setting in France,* (Chicago: University of Chicago Press, 1964).

10. As he wrote after distinguishing his three types of legitimate authority, "The fact that none of these three ideal types . . . is usually found in historical cases in pure form is naturally not a valid objection to attempting their conceptual formulation in the sharpest possible form."

11. P. M. Blau, *The Dynamics of Bureaucracy. A Study of Interpersonal Relations in Two Government Agencies,* revised edition (Chicago and London: University of Chicago Press, 1955).

12. "Some Functional Consequences of Primary Controls in Formal Work Organization," *American Sociology Review,* 18, no. 4 (August 1953): 368–373.

13. "An Industrial Setting. The Davidson Company," in *The Organization From Within,* (London: Tavistock, 1961), Chapter 1. The description in the present Chapter is greatly abridged.

14. E. Katz and S. N. Eisenstadt, "Some Sociological Observations on the Response of Israeli Organizations to New Immigrants," *Administrative Science Quarterly,* 5 (June 1960): 113–133.

15. S. A. Stouffer, et al, *The American Soldier,* (Princeton, New Jersey: Princeton University Press, 1949).

16. C. H. Page, "Bureaucracy's Other Face," *Social Forces,* 25 (1946).

17. S. M. Lipset, M. A. Trow and J. S. Coleman, *Union Democracy,* (Glencoe, Illinois: The Free Press, 1956).

18. Gouldner, *Patterns.*

19. See discussion in C. Sofer, *Men in Mid-Career,* (New York: Cambridge University Press, 1970), pp. 73–75.

20. Such problems are reported, for instance, in S. Marcson, *The Scientist in American Industry,* (New York: Harper, 1960); G. C. Homans, *The Human Group,* (London: Routledge and Kegan Paul, 1951); W. Kornhauser, *Scientists in Industry,* (Berkeley: University of California, 1962).

21. A. W. Gouldner, "Cosmopolitans and Locals: Toward an Analysis of Latent Social Roles," *Administrative Science Quarterly,* 2 (December 1957–March 1958): 446–450, 465–467.

22. See discussion in A. K. Rice and E. J. Miller, *Systems of Organization: the Control of Task and Sentient Boundaries,* (London: Tavistock, 1967).

23. Quoted in J. J. Beer and W. D. Lewis, "Aspects of the Professionalization of Science," *Daedalus,* 92, no. 4 (Fall 1963).

24. T. Burns and G. M. Stalker, *The Management of Innovation,* (London: Tavistock, 1961).

25. Reported in Sofer, *Men in Mid-Career.*

26. This term is from O. G. Brim, in O. G. Brim and S. Wheeler, *Socialization after Childhood: Two Essays,* (New York: Wiley, 1966).

14 : Decision Making in a Bureaucracy

A Case Study in
Organizational Decision-Making

I proceed now to describe, stage by stage, the behavior of a group of colleagues at work in forming a set of related decisions. The case illustrates the point of Simon, Lindblom, and Pfiffner that organizational decisions include much beside what we normally understand as purpose, rationality, and objectivity. It shows that organizations are constrained by their history and existing culture from optimising solutions to new problems. Multiple personal and group inputs are made into new decisions, and the emergent may be a decision that nobody particularly wants, recognizes as his own, or is committed to.

My opportunity to collect the data arose in the course of an assignment I undertook while on the staff of the Tavistock Institute of Human Relations. My role was as an adviser to the company described.

THE ALPHA COMPANY

Alpha is a large-scale vertically integrated concern controlling a whole series of activities from research, development, and manufacturing through wholesale and retail marketing. It has wholly or partly owned subsidiaries in many countries in the Western world.

Alpha maintains a headquarters office which is divided into a number of functional departments broken down into smaller divisions or branches.

The headquarters departments are, broadly speaking, of two types. First there are operational departments that are responsible for the direction of the operating companies. Direction is, however, a matter of degree. While final responsibility for the success of the subsidiary companies formally rests with these headquarters departments, the extent to which they can or would wish actually to control the companies depends in each case on the extent of their ownership in the company, its distance from London, and its record of success. And, as in all large decentralized concerns, much depends on reciprocal influence and respect and on the judgment of the man on the spot. He probably receives as much advice as formal instruction and contributes to the formation of long-range policies for his company as well as running it on a day-to-day basis. A second set of headquarters departments, the service departments, have the primary function of providing technical aid to companies. In a sense their work overlaps in style and content with that of the headquarters operating departments, since, as indicated above; the latter are also in effect largely advisory. The overlap is also considerable by virtue of the fact that the service side includes the department of finance and accounts, which monitors the commercial progress of the associates and subsidiaries and is therefore often likely to be the first to detect and initiate action on unwelcome events as these are expressed in accounts and returns.

Of the operational departments the one that concerns us most is the marketing department, headed by a general manager responsible to a marketing director who is a member of the board of the concern. The marketing department sells the company's products directly to large customers and indirectly through Alpha's associated marketing companies.

The marketing department contains an advertising and sales promotion branch which initiated the conference described below. This branch deals with institutional advertising, helps individual national marketing companies, and tries to ensure high standards in the execution of common policy.

Other branches and sections of the marketing department help customers in usage problems, maintain technical contact with suppliers, and undertake market research and strategic studies designed to increase Alpha's market knowledge and marketing efficiency.

Most of the actual selling is carried out by the individual companies in each country or area. These companies are most frequently wholly owned by the parent concern, though sometimes they are jointly owned with other firms or with local companies in which the concern holds a proportion of shares. Competition comes from the other international companies and also from independent local companies.

Each marketing company is staffed mainly by nationals of the country where it operates, though it is usual to have at least one or two senior executives who are British. Attempts are made to give senior or promising executives and technical specialists spells of experience with the London head office.

Formal contact is maintained with the various London policy-making, executive, service, advisory, and technical departments through conferences between the chairman of the parent company and heads of national companies; through courses organized by the personnel department; through conferences in London dealing with special problems; through visits of local personnel to London colleagues (and the reverse); and by a flow of letters and telephone conversations.

Considerable expenditure is incurred to advertise the name of the company in each country, to differentiate the qualities of its products from those of other producers or marketers, and to encourage consumers to use retail outlets selling the company's products. A national company will usually handle its national "prestige" advertising as well as brand advertising and take full responsibility for this. But it may be asked on occasion to collaborate in international campaigns that are initiated at the center, in which case it is likely to receive special financial and technical support.

DESIGNING AN INTERNATIONAL CONFERENCE

In May 1962 the manager of the central advertising branch of Alpha told me that he proposed to arrange a conference during the second half of September and had just received authorization for this. Participants (who would be members of Alpha's marketing associates) would be invited from Europe and possibly further afield. He asked me to help design and conduct the conference and I agreed to do this.

He told me that one aim of the conference would be to give participants information on company policy. The conference would possibly help to take a policy decision. This was connected with a new product the company had ready for marketing. At that time the product and the campaign that would accompany its launching, whenever this might be, were referred to by the code name of Intro. It had not yet finally been decided whether to launch the product and, if so, on what date and in what countries. (I had some prior knowledge of the product as the Tavistock had been asked to collect certain data bearing on its marketing.) Many members of the organization, including most of the staff of the central advertising branch, had heard of the product but not as a short-term practical marketing proposition.

At the same time the conference was intended to raise standards and develop skills in the field of advertising. This was its main purpose as the advertising manager conceived it at the time.

The advertising manager saw the conference as part of a continuing program of work with the marketing associates rather than as an event on its own. It would be necessary, he said, to follow up suggestions made at the conference and to provide technical support for subsequent innovations. Among other things, his Department had to ensure that the advertising techniques and claims of Alpha's associated companies in neighboring countries were, if not identical, at least consistent with each other and with the policy of the center.

The advertising manager (and his immediate colleagues) wanted to conduct the conference in a way that respected the responsibilities of the associate companies for their own marketing activities and advertising policy. He felt that his branch should aim only to provide knowledge, technical expertise, and advice. The head office had in the past said the same, but representatives of the associate companies had been convinced that they had received instructions rather than advice. The central advertising manager had himself been advertising manager of one of the associates, so knew how they felt.

As plans stood when the conference was first mentioned to me, the conference would last between one and two weeks and those advertising managers especially interested in innovation would be invited. We had a first tentative discussion of events that might contribute to the conference objective concerned with standards and skills. We thought that it might be useful to try to provide members with a conception of the overall marketing process that would show the place of advertising and advertising techniques. We thought that one useful training device might be to build up a job description of the role of advertising manager in a marketing associate; another might be to spend some sessions deducing overall marketing strategies from the advertising of various companies. We thought that it might be useful to bring in some technical contributions from outside Alpha, for example, a talk by a senior advertising man who dealt mainly with products different from theirs or a talk by a consumer research specialist on techniques of investigation. We had several further discussions at which we were joined by a senior assistant in the central advertising branch. We continued to concentrate on the training aspect.

During the course of discussions in June or July it was decided within Alpha headquarters that certain sales managers as well as advertising managers would be invited. Their presence was meant to demonstrate the necessity to conceive of advertising within wider marketing contexts. It was thought that this would strengthen the partnership between the advertising and sales sides of the associate companies and increase the likelihood that the conference experience would remain alive in them through the subsequent support they could give each other.

We began to develop the idea of a project that might usefully be conducted at the conference. After two days of lectures and discussions the seminar (as we were calling it for a time) could be divided into small groups (syndicates), each of which could be given a sales-cum-advertising problem to resolve, that is, the marketing of Intro which would sooner or later take place. Each group would be headed by a sales manager.[1]

We were still, at this point, treating the new product mainly as a vehicle for training conference participants in technical considerations pertinent to *any* product launching operation. We thought that exemplary use of the new product would lend special interest to the conference as something that would, at some undetermined future date, probably happen.

By July, however, the objectives of the conference seemed to have changed somewhat. My notes show that we now expressed these to ourselves as: to set advertising aims within a wider marketing context, to facilitate communication between the thinking at headquarters and at associate companies, to provide opportunities for the associated companies to learn from each other, and to prepare for the Intro campaign—whenever this might be.

By September we had again changed the plans. The main factor affecting us was that the decision to launch the new product had now been firmed up, that is, the intention had become definite to launch the product in the near future.

We now made provision in the conference design for an earlier input by headquarters staff of policy material on Intro. The role of the syndicates (which would be drawn from five countries) would now be to comment on the proposed British campaign and to compare it with their own plans.[2]

The conference design was mainly the responsibility of the central advertising branch and myself. But the ramifications of the Intro exercise and the fact that the conference was meant to have a formal training component necessitated discussions with other interested departments and branches. Several issues came up for discussion with these departments.

Perhaps the most fundamental issue was the amount of freedom delegates would have in regard to the total marketing plan to be presented to them. Were they free to overturn that plan or were they meant to comment only on its implementation, to respond only within the framework set by headquarters? This basic issue cannot be said to have been resolved before the conference and must have contributed to some of the uncertainty that occasionally developed about conference objectives and delegates tasks.

THE CONFERENCE

The conference was held over a ten-day period in November under the title of "Advertising Managers' Meeting." Delegates from associates were drawn from sixteen countries. There were altogether twenty-nine of them, including in each case the national advertising manager and in several cases one or two people responsible for sales. In line with the changing conference objectives, these were now people from the main marketing areas rather than, as originally contemplated, those most interested in experiment. It had been arranged that the sales managers would attend for the first three days. The central advertising manager acted as chairman or as a link figure between sessions chaired by colleagues senior to himself in his own department. He had four members of his branch with him, together with secretarial assistants. At most sessions, at least one (sometimes two or three) representatives were present from neighboring branches within the market services division (sales promotion, market research, technical publications, and standards); from other divisions within the marketing department (sales development, international services, regional marketing); and from departments outside the marketing department (information, staff and research center). In addition, several working sessions were attended by up to four members of an advertising company servicing the central advertising branch in international matters. I attended most of the sessions.

Our total number was therefore rarely below about fifty and sometimes up around seventy, many more than had been envisaged in the original planning and about twice as many as I had myself expected. I was astonished when I arrived on the opening day at the crammed conference room. I was also struck by the stringent security arrangements made to ensure that no unauthorized persons entered.

The conference seemed to have taken on a self-propelled momentum. As far as I could understand, its growth in size and importance came from an increasing realization within the company of the opportunity it provided to help in launching the new product (which the central advertising branch and I had not regarded as central in the early planning) and from the fact that so many headquarters branches were in one way or another involved in the conception, launching, costing, and monitoring of Intro.

Concern with the new product increasingly displaced training as the central theme of the conference. Insofar as training remained important, practical consideration of the handling of the new product became the vehicle through which it was handled.

Since it is impossible to report the conference in its full detail (for reasons of confidentiality and sheer length) I am selecting for report what I consider to be the key events.

The head of the market services division welcomed the delegates. He referred to the competitive character of the industry, the increased interest of higher management in justifying and assessing the effectiveness of advertising expenditure, the importance of solidly based and effective market research, and the necessity to use the most modern and firmly tested research techniques. He referred particularly to the sales managers and described them as "our masters in this field," underlining in this way the function of advertising and market research as services to sales.

This was followed with an explanation by the central advertising manager of the nature of the conference program. He referred especially to the fact that the objectives of the Intro part of the meeting were to be reached by a two-fold process. Delegates (he said) would receive information from the experts who had invented the product and from specialists in the marketing department and would have opportunities to discuss this with them. Second, delegates would discuss the problems of marketing Intro and would help form a checklist of problems to be dealt with. He said that, although the meeting was intended primarily for advertising managers, the presence of sales managers had been requested since advertising made sense only within the context of the wider marketing plan. The sales managers would chair four small syndicates grouped by countries according to similarities of problems, language, or experience. These syndicates would discuss the information or ideas presented to them in plenary sessions with a view to implementation in their particular areas, calling on the resources or knowledge of head office staff where required. It was considered that argument and counter-argument, the formation and modification of realistic plans and cross-fertilization of ideas, would be best engendered in such informal working groups. They would each report back to the plenary sessions on their findings and hear the conclusions of other syndicates. This would finally result in the formulation of a checklist of problems and a definition of objectives. (Looking back, this appears to me partly a post hoc rationalization. We had decided on syndicates mainly for their effectiveness in training, not in making or evaluating decisions.)

A talk by an external speaker on launching new products was given at this point. This was followed by a statement by the general manager, marketing department, on the thinking behind the new product. He ended, "We aim at a spring launch and the purpose of this meeting is to discuss how to do this. I am certain of success, which will depend to a large extent on the effectiveness of the presentation—which I am sure you will achieve." This was followed by the series of talks (with questions from delegates) on trends in the industry, attributes of Intro, and on marketing policy.

One of the headquarters speakers announced that Alpha had ahead the tightest launching time schedule that could be imagined and Intro had passed the point of no return. This was highly significant in view of the question that had been raised in the planning stage about how free the delegates were to overturn the overall plan. The name chosen for the new product was announced. The day concluded with the first meeting of the syndicates.

The syndicates reported next morning. Many critical comments were made. A number of problems were raised concerning likely marketing difficulties.

Two of the syndicates questioned the name announced for the product and made alternative suggestions. When the first syndicate did this, two discrepant responses came from the platform. A member of the market services department pointed out that the associate companies had been consulted before the decision had been taken, implying that a new name could not now be considered. The head of the market services division (in the chair) said, however, "We could perhaps consider a reconsideration of the name."

It was patently obscure to the delegates (and perhaps to the headquarters staff as well) how flexible the plans still were and to what extent delegates were expected to be merely passive recipients of headquarters decisions. This came up later again on the same issue of the name.

This was one reason why, it seemed, the syndicates were by no means always satisfied with the answers they received. At the same time some of the problems were of the sort to which no one at the head office could as yet provide a satisfactory solution. They could only make encouraging or supportive remarks.

It also became apparent at this point that communication difficulties were appearing between speakers and delegates. One element in this was that to many delegates English, the medium of the conference, was a foreign language. A second was the anxiety of speakers that they would be unable to answer questions correctly, would be caught unprepared or on the wrong foot in front of delegates, colleagues, and their own senior management. In some cases this led to a speaker restructuring questions put to him so that he could give a "sensible" reply, even when the reply was irrelevant to the issue posed.

The next day began with syndicate consideration of the presentations of the previous day on ways and means of communication. When the plenary session convened, the chairman (now changed to the manager of the promotional group) opened the session with an attempt to clarify what he referred to as the three main aims of the meeting. He said that the original aim has been "a quiet talk between the advertising manager and his advertising people" but that it had been decided to add other aims. He said that as matters now stood the first aim was for delegates to discuss the presentations made by people who had been studying the problems of Intro and to be given a very clear and thorough briefing on these. He added that at the same time as the specialists were briefing the delegates, London was briefing itself. A second aim was to evolve from the discussions a checklist of the problems that were likely to arise in the promotion and launching of this new product. The third aim was to collect, before the advertising managers departed, details of supporting material which Alpha London could provide. He added, "We would like to know your requirements so far as we can define them before you leave." (Changes in stated aim were taking place over time. Also, the platform and chair were being shared by headquarters executives who took varying views of the proceedings and what they were, or should be, about.)

The discussion that followed was, in the view of platform and delegates, a most productive interchange. As well as asking questions, syndicates made several suggestions that others described as useful in their own operations or that headquarters staff offered to investigate and follow up. There was less defensiveness or dodging of each other and much that could be recognized as real work on difficult problems. There was little in the atmosphere to suggest that the headquarters men on the platform were telling the rest what was what, or felt that they necessarily knew better on every subject, or pretended to have anticipated every probable problem. A notable contribution came from the training department representative. He suggested that salesmen might be taught to cooperate with the retailer, to face his problems with him, and to report back to his company on the dealer's problems. "Representative training," he said, "should provide ample opportunity to talk as well as to listen—as has been done here."

At the same time there were some problems. There were occasional resumptions of defensiveness among headquarters speakers, for example, somewhat mechanical and superficial replies were given to questions about relations with dealers. I had the impression, too, that one source of difficulty was the fact that delegates were often receiving their replies from specialists who were their juniors in the business. They were not enjoying this.

It was obscure to me at several points to what extent the head office staff were giving orders or making suggestions. There was some uncertainty too among delegates on the extent to which London had prepared a cut-and-dried campaign for them or they were free to pursue their own policies.

At this stage (early afternoon of third day) the central advertising manager referred himself to some of the outstanding questions (spoken and unspoken) on the minds of delegates. He pointed out that it was rare to hold a conference of this type before a launch date, and that it was a useful opportunity. Specialists and headquarters people like himself, he told delegates, were trying to answer questions, help with information and ideas, rather than defend a project. He and the chairman (again the market services manager) said that there were areas (including some thrown up by the conference) in which headquarters felt that it lacked a final answer and which they would proceed to study in greater detail.

The manager of one of the marketing branches then precipitated an incident that displayed the differences between headquarters colleagues on the way in which they should relate themselves to the operating companies and the extent to which headquarters should dominate. He began by elaborating the same theme as the previous speaker, denoting areas where there was some indicated action that could be taken by marketing associates. Referring back to the suggestion for a change of name of the new product, he said that it was impossible to change the name at this late stage. This astonished several of us in view of the undertaking earlier given by the market services manager to reconsider this. I then remembered that the speaker had been absent when the suggestion had first been mooted and the market services manager had responded. At this point the latter intervened from the chair flatly to contradict his headquarters colleague and to say that they had already undertaken to do what they could.

On the following Monday delegates heard presentations of research bearing on the Alpha company image and of the current thinking of the information department.

The next day, the next to last, of the conference, was entirely devoted to descriptions of the research techniques used in the development and testing of advertisements.

The conference concluded next morning. During a long opening session of two hours delegates continued with the description of their own recent activities.

ISSUE OF SUPPORTING MATERIALS
AND INFORMATION

During the whole of the conference all proceedings in plenary session were recorded by stenographers and also on tape.

Minutes were issued to the delegates before they left, enabling them to return to their companies with all the key documentation available on Intro.

On the initiative of central advertising branch there was a subsequent flow of materials and information between companies. This included draft advertisements and campaign details during and after the launch.

Three months after the advertising conference the advertising branch sent to each associate company participating in the launch two sets of documents. One was a paper dealing with the advertising approach to the new product, carrying a stage further the analysis of the problem begun at the conference. A set of draft editorial type advertisements accompanied this paper, together with a script for an advertising film.

The extent to which these materials were to be treated as directives or recommendations which the marketing associates were free to accept or reject is suggested by the advertising manager's opening statement in his covering letter that "the [enclosed] advertisements are for use, all or in part, as you consider best."

The letter referred back to the name of the product. "With regard to the product name," it said, "it will be recalled that certain associates at our meeting expressed a preference for an alternative name. This has been discussed here, but it has been ruled that the first proposal must stand."

Participants might have felt reassured by the fact that their suggestions had received the further consideration that had been promised. But a statement on the reasons leading to confirmation of the original decision would presumably have contributed further to their sense that their own opinions and work on this had mattered. So far as I have been able to discover, a formal re-evaluation of the proposal for the name had not in fact taken place at the head office. There had been further discussion among those responsible for the conference and their closest headquarters colleagues who together confirmed their view that the proposed name was the best link with the past product that it might eventually replace. Apart from this, there was the practical point that delay in launching would be caused by changing the name.

While the head office did not act on this part of the conference proceedings, they were significantly influenced by what had been emphasized about the problems likely to be encountered by associates in their relations with retailers. This became the focus of subsequent research, experiment, and policy.

REGIONAL MEETINGS AND EXCHANGES

As previously mentioned, the central advertising manager had envisaged that local, regional meetings with companies might be held after the main conference. These would be working meetings to consider detailed local planning and coordination between neighboring countries.

At the conference it was announced that the new product would be launched in April. This imparted a note of urgency to the regional meetings.

Three meetings were held in February, in various countries. (I did not attend these and my informants were the central advertising manager and his colleagues.) Each regional meeting was a one-day affair with the general aim of examining actions for which plans had been prepared. Headquarters had presented a general marketing strategy rather than detailed plans for each country and a fairly wide range of advertising claims and approaches between which associates could choose. This made it possible that inconsistencies and conflicts in advertising claims and arguments would occur unless subsequent consultation took place, particularly between countries with a common language. Differences were ironed out under the chairmanship of the central advertising manager.

Meanwhile other technical meetings were being held with marketing associates by other branches of Alpha headquarters office concerned with marketing, particularly with companies which had not had representatives at the international conference.

TRACKING RESEARCH

The product was launched simultaneously in nine countries. This provided an opportunity for the conduct of a research project which would assess each campaign as a whole and permit comparisons between one country and another. This research focused on the success or otherwise of the communications the companies were trying to make to the general public about the existence and characteristics of the new product. The material collected in this investigation would be used for a second international conference at which lessons might be learned from what had happened.

SECOND INTERNATIONAL ADVERTISING CONFERENCE [3]

In May 1963 the central advertising manager again involved me in conference planning. He told me that he planned a second conference in November. He wanted the central theme to be an assessment of the Intro exercise but wanted to make explicit the criteria in terms of which the assessment should be made. The major criteria should be the objectives the associate companies and headquarters had set themselves. The conference should consider these in the light of the themes that had been chosen and the reactions of competitors. The central advertising manager wanted to use syndicate methods again, in view of the success that had attended these at the previous conference in thrashing out problems. He wanted to base the conference largely on what the advertising managers wanted. He would carry out an agenda-building exercise beforehand. He also wanted the content of the conference to take adequate account of what leading people at headquarters wanted from the companies. He felt that his branch was not in a position to instruct the advertising managers to do anything. He wanted the structure of the conference and the way his branch behaved to communicate their role as collection of information on the needs of marketing associates in response to those needs.

The second international conference was held in November 1963. In his statement on conference objectives, the central advertising manager said that the aims were "to provide as much information on what may happen in 1964 as is possible; to discuss the requirements for effective advertising and promotion in 1964 and possibly thereafter."

He told delegates that this conference was in many ways a direct follow-up to the problems that had been studied last year, and he restated "the three principal objectives of that last meeting." He said, "Firstly, we aimed to give delegates at firsthand all the available information on the new product. In addition we sought to establish a list of problems to be resolved with marketing management prior to the initiation of campaign preparation. Our third objective was to decide what material it was necessary for head office branches both to collect and collate for the forthcoming campaign."

It is notable how much these objectives now stated for the 1962 conference differ from those with which he had started eighteen months earlier and how the central advertising manager had now accepted the objectives dictated by what the organizational process had redefined as having priority.

The 1963 conference was attended by thirty-one delegates from associate companies (mainly advertising managers and market research men) and, as before, by representatives of several headquarters branches and departments.

The first day of the conference (a five-day event in this case) was devoted to presentations of their Intro campaigns. They depicted the market/advertising situation in which the companies had found themselves at the time of the launch, the problems with which they had been confronted, and the way they had dealt with them. On the next day the research results for each country were examined and compared, so that lessons could be learned from the success or otherwise of the various approaches described. Various branches then assessed from the headquarters point of view how sales had gone in the past year and what was hoped for in the next. Syndicate discussions and plenary reports followed.

At this point (two and one-half days after the conference started) participants divided into two groups. One considered, with the help of Alpha's design consultants, the extent to which national designs should be uniform or be allowed to vary. The other discussed market research achievements and prospects.

Discussion: Decision-Making
as a Social Process

The case described shows, firstly, that a human organization or sub-organization is constrained by its history, existing culture, and social environment from optimizing solutions to new problems that arise.

Historical constraints include the results of past personnel deployments and formal and informal structural arrangements. While the conference was a social event deliberately segregated from normal colleague interaction, it could not start with a blank sheet. Whatever the intention and design of the conference it manifested the characteristic existing behavior and attitudes of members of the organization, for instance the assumption that policy was made at headquarters, that the center was the major source of knowledge and skill, and that the main function of national units was to see that central policies were implemented as closely as possible, local conditions being expected only to modify marginally the details of execution.

Each phase of the conference planning left residues persisting into the next phase, helping to determine what would happen next. It was in this way that the syndicate method introduced as a training device persisted into an operational event: it would probably not have been designed into it had the organizers anticipated the direction of events, that is, the emergence of the syndicates as strong pressure groups. In this case, the accidental residual component contributed to the success of the operation as judged by the management. Presumably the opposite often occurs and residues of earlier decisions reduce the prospects of optimization for those that are made later.

Constraints are contemporaneous as well as historical. From quite early in the planning phase of the conference until its conclusion the aims and methods of the conference and the decisions it took were continuously modified by forces which, from the point of view of the department formally responsible for the conference, were environmental.

The case illustrates, secondly, that decision-making is a continuous process. The aims and nature of the conference shifted not only from the time of the inception of the idea but also, to some extent, during the conference itself. As originally conceived, the main business of the conference was, first, to help in the decision about marketing Intro and, secondly, to consider the nature, function, and techniques of advertising and the role of advertising management within the company's organization. The conference was at first meant to be policy contributing, informative, and educational; insofar as Intro was to play a part this was to be an appendix to the main business. Emphasis then shifted decisively to the operational. The proposed launch of Intro was decided before the conference and not by participants in the conference. The manner of the launching then came to play an increasingly important part, and finally came to dominate the proceedings. The conference finally became the executive vehicle for the Intro launch.

Whether general lessons were learned by participants eventually became irrelevant. We had envisaged use of a practical project on Intro mainly as a vehicle for learning, as a task near enough to real life to grip participants. In the event a real task of considerable urgency was introduced, using our machinery. This was not a business game. It was business.

This is not to say that the original plans had failed. A different set of priorities had been developing in the organization while the plan for a training conference was being formed and these priorities became super-imposed on the arrangements made to implement the original plan.

The case suggests, thirdly, that one reason why decisions and their execution can be only imperfectly rationalized is that so many individuals and groups have a hand in forming and implementing them. Most of the decisions made at the conference were not matters of individual judgment and action or even of one department carrying its plans right through. The shape of the conference, its purpose, its methods, and the results in market-ing action can all be seen to be the result of interplay between individuals and groups, of conflict, collaboration, argument, partial consensus, accom-modation, resignation to being outvoted, and so on. It could, of course, be argued that group interaction of the sort described tends to make in the end for more rational decisions because a wider range of considerations is ad-duced. Consultation takes place with persons who are experienced in the matter at issue who will have to carry cut the decision. I am in no position to say whether the end decisions I describe were better or worse than they would have been without so much interaction—indeed it is impossible to make judgments of this type without controlled experiments. But, better or worse, the decisions that were taken were largely a function of differences in power of the different subgroups within the organization and of the social processes that ensued between conference participants.

Fourthly, the case material highlights the presence in the decision-making process of ambiguity, ignorance, misunderstanding, and confusion. The differences in perception and operating style on the headquarters side and the expectations engendered by the conference structure meant that the function and purposes of the conference and the way delegates were expected to behave at some phases became uncertain. For instance, when the headquarters management invited comments from the floor on a launch-ing date or dates and on the new public relations theme the method was participative. The implication was that the delegates' views might still influ-ence the final decisions. But at other times it seemed that the headquarters men were giving direct instructions.

This sort of confusion and ambiguity is in contrast with the classical writings on organizations which were described in Chapter 8, especially literature of the prescriptive type, which typically emphasizes the need for clarity in role-taking, communications, responsibility, and so on. It might be suggested that these are characteristics of good or proper decision-making and that the elements I describe constitute interference. But a good argument can be made that the ambiguities and uncertainties were in this case functional and may well be so also in other, similar, real-life situations.

To illustrate from events at the conference, it was clear that differences between personnel at the center and the accompanying indecisiveness and uncertainty were not altogether unwelcome to the company representatives. Such phenomena make the man in the local unit less ashamed of the imperfections of his own organization, reassure him that if he needs to seek support for one side rather than another he can locate it, and legitimates use of his own judgment in a situation where he cannot be said to have been given a clear directive. I suggest that it would have been unfortunate if everyone had been clearly told everything and knew exactly what he might or might not do. If one does not know with absolute clarity what one is allowed or expected to do there is a chance that one may be able to use one's discretion creatively.

In the case study freedom for internal entrepreneurship is apparent. The product launch was only partly planned in advance and opportunist advantage was taken of what was originally devised as a training event. By interpreting their responsibilities liberally, members of the central advertising department enabled a platform to be built from which a major new product could be launched. Had the central advertising branch not taken advantage of the looseness of definition of its functions, it is probable that the launch would have got off to a less successful start. Stricter and more formalized definition of roles and of departmental responsibilities would, I think, have blocked the emergence of machinery that proved well adapted to the early phase of launching the new product.

Finally, the case material emphasizes the importance of analyzing organizational decision-making dynamically and sequentially. When social scientists use the concept of "an organization," this usually refers to a set of people in a common task, a range of departments and roles with institutionalized relations between them, an amount of money and equipment with which tasks are performed, and a legal identity that enables this assembly to operate through periods longer than the life span of individual members. To understand organizational behavior in general and organization decision-making in particular we need to examine organizations as flow systems analyzable only through time. I should like to view the roles of individuals or departments less as fixed positions than as loosely defined sets of rights and duties to improvise, innovate, and initiate action and to impinge on colleagues and on the external environment. Certainly one can see in the case described that the conference was not a discrete entity but a sequence of events influencing a larger sequence of events (which we may loosely call the behavior of the Alpha company) and itself being influenced (more correctly, transformed), by the larger sequence. And the conference sequence itself generated its internal changes as it moved along.

A significant part of organizational behavior is to be understood only through close acquaintance with whole successions of interrelated and over-lapping events as they unfold through time. We need a series of firsthand intensive studies that will show how and why it is that one event leads to another and that will provide material for the detection of characteristic sequences, an organizational social psychology of process.

If we are to turn our attention more directly in future to the study of decision as process, we are going to need new types of data, gathered over extensive period by direct observation rather than by the intermittent view-ing and questionnaire completion on which most organizational studies are based.

N O T E S

1. At this stage the intention was to choose those whose firms had shown most interest in marketing innovation and new marketing techniques. This intention changed as objectives of the conference changed.

2. In fact, the majority of participants came with no plans for the launch and some came with no knowledge of the product. The launch was growing unevenly in different parts of the organization from a theoretical possibility into a practical proposition.

3. I deal with this briefly because for the period after the planning stage my in-formation is nearly all secondhand (mainly drawn from records of conference and reports by organizers).

PART VI

Leadership, Change, and Conflict

15 : Leadership

A GOOD deal of what constitutes social science knowledge and opinion on leadership has been anticipated in earlier chapters. Among the main points we have made or implied are the following.

In large contemporary bureaucracies the powers of administrators appointed from above are particularly important. Their powers rest partly on the sanctions they can apply, in the sense of material and symbolic rewards they can bestow or withhold. Their power depends, however, largely on the existence of a value system shared with those whom they are formally entitled to command. That is, the exercise of leadership involves much more than the formal delegation of power from above; it requires the acceptance of the legitimacy of that power and of the fact that it has been delegated to particular persons. This automatically makes the study of leadership, or any other form of organizational control, a study of social structure, of social relationships, and of social interaction. This fact has the further consequence that persons in positions of formal leadership almost invariably seek to induce their subordinates to share their values and objectives.

Attempts at control continue even once an employee has accepted a particular role or agreed set of responsibilities. This is largely because many work roles contain a fair amount of latitude as to the amount and manner of work performed. This can vary from minimal performance just sufficient to retain the post to an enthusiasm that leads the employee to try to expand his contribution.

Formally speaking, managers and supervisors at any given level of the hierarchy are created equal. They do not, however, remain equal. Some are more expert than others or expert in different aspects of the work. Some have a better understanding of people than others. Some are more acceptable to subordinates. Each will have his own distinctive personality and make different assumptions about human nature and about behavior on his part that will evoke cooperation. Even where administrators have equal access to the use of organizational rewards and punishments, they will choose, and need, to use these differently.

In his *Functions of the Executive,* Barnard refined and revised Weber's conceptions of authority by distinguishing between the authority of position and that of leadership. This points to the fact that the success of an influence attempt (willingness to obey) depends in part on superior ability, irrespective of position. This distinction now pervades the literature; it is reflected in the distinction between personal power and power of position and in the distinction between formal and informal aspects of organizations. The most effective control is thought to exist when occupancy of a position of formal leadership is coupled with what may be described as more personal qualities respected or wanted by subordinates. These may include consideration for them and interest in them; having the ear of superiors with regard to wages, promotions, and working conditions; and willingness to protect them against superiors and competitive peer groups.

Leadership is not confined to officials. In some cases the authority of appointed officials is outweighed by the informal influences of others whose views are particularly respected or who are able to influence everyday working cooperation. The direction of influence of the officials and of informal leaders may reinforce or oppose each other.

Ample indication has been provided in earlier chapters of the fact that instructions from a line superior provide only one of several sources of influence on the individual employee. They compete with influence emanating from other superiors whose opinions he respects or who might one day be in a position to grant or deny him things he wants, from peers with whom he has close daily relations, from persons with similar economic interests, from family and from friends. In the literature of industrial sociology particular significance is attached to the influence of peers: one cannot but be aware also of the importance of gatekeepers and opinion leaders who intervene deliberately or otherwise between superiors and subordinates.

When, therefore, we isolate for attention, as we do in this chapter, the role of formal leadership within organizations, we must keep in the center of our minds that we are dealing with only one source of influence. If we want to predict actual outcomes of attempts to exercise power we must take into account the realities of multiple influences, cross-pressures, compromises, and the exercise of personal judgment and autonomy.

Response to the attempted exercise of control will depend on factors that include the power of the would-be controller to grant or withhold significant material and symbolic rewards, the extent to which the employee shares goals with him, his persuasiveness, the existence of employment alternatives, and the felt importance of the work role in the life space of the employee. Response may vary from overt compliance coupled with inner indifference to close identification with seniors. While managements are inclined to believe that the latter is more helpful to their purpose, we know of no systematic data supporting this position. It is indeed conceivable that a high degree of commitment to employers and colleagues can detract from one's contribution, as one's judgment can be blunted by enthusiasm and eagerness to conform.

Functions Performed
by Leaders

Organizations administered on bureaucratic lines have a number of formally designated leaders (managers, supervisors, foremen, and so on) at various hierarchical levels each of whom has certain specific functions.

One set of functions centers on the making and execution of decisions; this includes devising strategies and determining priorities.

A second set of functions consists of the control of persons responsible to him by giving instruction and advice, persuading them to act in particular ways, securing their identification with organizational objectives, manipulating their environments and so on.

A third function, usually implicit, is that of organizational integration. This involves the designated leader in communicating to his subordinates and peers the wishes and intentions of senior management. He has also to make sure that his own superiors appreciate the circumstances, problems, and capacities of his own men and use their resources strategically rather than in some short-term manipulative or exploitative fashion that might damage the relation of the men to himself and the organization.

A fourth set of functions, also usually implicit, may be described as emotional maintenance. This includes keeping interpersonal relations pleasant and friendly; arbitrating in disputes; encouraging people or supporting them through periods of stress or discouragement; calming people down when they appear to be overexcited, overconfident, or careless; and giving minority persons or groups a chance to be heard.

For some purposes it is convenient to refer to the first two sets of functions as control functions or task functions and the second two as system-maintenance functions. The second pair bear directly in the long-run on the continued capacity of the organization to operate. In the long-run the two pairs of functions coincide in the sense that performance cannot be maintained or long-range objectives reached if the way managers go about this disintegrates the necessary group effort.

While the two first-mentioned functions usually receive main emphasis in job-descriptions and at the times when new appointments are made, the significance of system-maintenance becomes more obvious when managerial performance is being assessed or personal crises have arisen.

In large bureaucratic organizations the proportions in which a particular leader combines these functions will be only partly a matter of choice or inclination or ability. This may be largely determined by his level in the hierarchy, his formal job description, the relation of his job to others, and the personal approaches to their jobs of persons whose actions overlap with his own.

Performance of some of these functions appears to reduce capacity to perform others. Bales and his associates have studied the functions of leadership systematically in experimental groups without designated leaders. The experimenters distinguished somewhat as I have done between instrumental activities within these groups (the input of means and their distribution) and expressive activities (having to do with interpersonal relations, norms, rituals, feelings about group membership). They found that these two sets of activities were segregated in group behavior, that is, that different individuals gravitated to the leading roles in these activities. This, they found, was partly because these positions require incompatible role orientations and personal characteristics.[1]

Heinicke and Bales have shown that where such specialization ensues, the effective performance of the group depends on appropriate coordination between the two leadership specialists.[2]

Reviewing the work done by his colleagues and himself,[3] Bales has concluded that task leadership is exercised at the cost of some unpopularity. Conversely, if a leader wants to remain or become popular he loses his effectiveness in task leadership. This difficulty appears to increase over time and there are apparently few people who can combine both roles. The general tendency is for these components of leadership to be split between two persons. In the most stable groups Bales and his colleagues have observed a coalition has in effect been formed between the two leaders. As he remarks, these findings challenge the idea that leadership problems can be solved by identifying individuals as having specific personality attributes. Whether these qualities can be exercised depends on finding a co-leader with complementary qualities. Another factor qualifying the notion of single-person leadership is the tendency for information and requests for information to be addressed to the point of an organization where most information is available rather than to the top spot in the chain of command. This separation indicates again that leadership is a joint or multiple affair and that a division of labor occurs in its exercise.

A similar point about sharing the functions of leadership is brought out in a study by Hodgson, Levinson, and Zalenzik.[4] They show in a convincing case study how the top three administrators in a hospital complement, support, and oppose each other in a way that is sufficiently effective and predictable to enable the organization to function effectively. Their theoretical standpoint is that, whatever administrative arrangements are formally made, in practice organizations are always led by groups, never by individuals.

This view is reinforced in the work of such writers as Benne, Sheats, Bradford, and Thelen, who have been associated with group relations training.[5] They hold that work systems can operate effectively when they permit a wide range of persons to contribute. The diversity of institutional requirements requires that several people make leadership inputs of one sort or another and organizational change results in the contributions of any one person varying over time.

Reasoning along these lines, a converging body of social scientists conceive of leadership as a set of group functions or needs that might be performed by one or many members of the group rather than as an activity of a specifically designated person.

Leadership is seen as something (or a number of things) that a group supplies to itself through a variety of people acting in formal or informal capacities, permanently or temporarily, as needs, temper, group membership, and atmosphere change.

Although it is customary to designate one person as "the" leader of each work group, leadership is not in practice one entity carried out by one individual in the working group. It is a mixed set of functions carried out by different individuals. The same person is not always *the* leader even in regard to *one* of the functions, and the leader-follower relationship is liable to intermittent reversal.

Group Leadership in the Large Corporation

I have been discussing the conclusion of social scientists who study small group and organizational processes that whenever people meet to work together a number of leadership needs characteristically emerge; different people tend to respond (usually in complementary fashion) to these needs and this makes leadership a shared activity.

Quite apart from the issue of these apparent sociological and psychological necessities, independent structural forces clearly operate to make leadership of the modern corporation a group affair.

R. A. Gordon has described the situation as follows:

The prevalence of group, instead of individual, action is a striking characteristic of management organization in the large corporation. In many cases, committees of executives have partially supplanted individuals in the formulation and approval of major decisions, and they frequently share with the chief executive the exercise of the final coordinating function . . . Even where formal management committees do not exist, group action frequently takes place through the medium of informal conferences, out of which may emerge decisions which are the product of no single individual . . . The magnitude and complexity of large-scale business leads to the attempt to substitute group for individual responsibility and to a need for the exchange of opinion among specialists and for formal or informal organizations through which such exchange of opinion may crystallize into a group will.[6]

Galbraith argued in his Reith lectures that under conditions of contemporary industrial technology group decision-making becomes inevitable.

He attributes particular importance to the need to share and combine essential specialized information.

Decision comes not from individuals but from groups. The groups are numerous, as often informal as formal, and subject to constant change in composition. Each contains the men possessed of the information, or with access to the information, that bears on the particular decision together with those whose skills consist in extracting and testing this information and obtaining a conclusion. . . . It is through groups that men act successfully on matters where no single one, however exalted or intelligent, has more than a fraction of the necessary knowledge. It is what makes modern business possible, and in other contexts it is what makes modern government possible.[7]

He suggests further that, once power in an organization is exercised by a group, it passes irrevocably into group hands.

If an individual has taken a decision, he can be called before another individual, who is his superior in the hierarchy, his information can be extracted and examined and his decision can then be reversed by the greater wisdom or experience of the superior. But if the decision requires the combined information of a group, it cannot be safely reversed by an individual. He will have to get the judgment of other specialists.

No one should insist, in these matters, or give cases. There will often be instances when an individual has the knowledge to modify or change the finding of a group. But the broad rule holds: if a decision requires the specialized knowledge of a group of men, it is subject to safe review only by the similar knowledge of a similar group. Group decisions, unless acted upon by another group, tend to be absolute.[8]

Problems in Relating
Formal Leadership
to Organizational Needs

The importance of the different functions of leadership will shift over time. At one phase in the history of an organization or a work group concentration on the objective task may be essential for survival; at another communications may have become so strained, or morale may be so low that what is essential is a revitalization of interest in cooperative endeavor. Variations in leadership requirements are evident when one compares the early stages of organizational life (establishment and first development) with more stabilized, institutionalized stages. In the early stages one needs doctrinal loyalty, aggressiveness, and enthusiasm, and personal stars with charismatic qualities. Later one needs quieter, more controlled and regulated, more routinized administrative skills. This change in phase is commonly referred to, after Weber, as "the routinization of charisma."

Because of the multiplicity of functions involved in leadership and the way these change in relative importance over time, no single appointed leader will be able to undertake more than a fraction of the total of actions required for adequate group leadership over any sustained period—and his tenure is likely to be longer than the phase to which his particular type of best contribution is relevant.

One result of this is that the work group will not necessarily receive the leadership it most needs at any particular time. Another can be that it gets led for phases in the wrong direction or emphasis gets placed on the wrong things.

Problems of loyalty to the leader will arise because it will be apparent that he is incapable of meeting all the demands made upon him. Whatever he does well, members of his group will always be able to identify issues he is neglecting or part of his work that he does relatively badly.

Mechanisms will develop for by-passing formal leadership. Informal leaders will become more prominent.

This situation is liable in the long run to be unstable or become a source of tension. Where formal authority and responsibility do not roughly correspond with the real or imagined contributions of colleagues resentment is likely to be expressed and efforts are likely to be made to redress the situation. The informal leaders may well become competitive with the designated leader because they judge the situation of the work group differently or feel strongly enough about it to fight for their own solutions or emphasis. Or the judgments of the informal leaders may be perceived as consistently better than that of the designed leader. In these cases the formal leader will feel insecure and challenged, the informal leaders will feel undervalued and badly guided, and confidence will be sapped in a senior management that appoints poor leaders or lets these rivalries emerge. Sides will be taken within the work group and within the larger organization, factions will form, and energy will be devoted to a fight for power.

Apart from rivalries between leaders—formal and informal—the existence of more than one person prominent in the leadership provides scope for others to manipulate differences to secure advantages for themselves, for example, by providing support to one or other in return for favors.

The practice of appointing single formal leaders poses the work group and the larger organization with problems of how best to change leaders once circumstances change and once the abilities that have contributed to their appointment become less pertinent. A simple communication of a leader's failure and his demotion or dismissal are often out of the question. Superiors will wish to avoid offending or hurting the man concerned, visiting upon him the consequences of their own error in appointing him, or intimating to others that they are arbitrary or inconsiderate. More circumspect strategies are usually involved, such as attempts to influence, advise or retrain him or to move him in a way that does not constitute an obvious demotion.[9]

Apart from superiors, the immediate work subordinates of the formal unsuccessful leader may want him removed. It is difficult for them to act to do so because this is considered inappropriate to their relative position in the hierarchy, presumptuous, revolutionary, and prospectively self-seeking. Some of them will be perceived as wanting the casualty's job. And when they do try to overthrow their leaders, or ease them out, counterattacks tend to be supported by higher authority who see the power system and their judgment as challenged.

Where formal leadership is manifestly inadequate, work group members may collude with this inadequacy, that is, allow themselves lower levels of performance and responsibility, and rationalize this behavior on the basis that the senior management is clearly not seriously interested in efficiency.

Qualities of Leaders

There has always been a considerable popular interest in what personality attributes contribute to successful leadership. The question has received a substantial amount of systematic study since about 1920. Many different kinds of group and context have been involved in the formal studies and the main common theme can perhaps be described as "what sorts of person tends to exercise a disproportionate amount of power when related to a group of colleagues on a common task." [10]

The question does not seem to be likely to be very productive unless one has in mind a particular type of task and, probably, unless one is limiting oneself at the same time to a particular culture, or type of culture, and a particular type of work situation—for instance one of change or one of stability. It also seems to have little meaning unless one can stipulate at the same time what other sort of person is involved in the situation; even if it is possible that one can characterize one sort of person as likely to emerge as a leader, one has to ask the questions, leader in relation to whom? What would happen if there were more people like him in the group? Would some quite different qualities now become important?

For purposes of this book we are particularly interested in the forms of leadership that are exercised within work organizations organized on a bureaucratic model. One celebrated attempt has been made by W. E. Henry to identify the personality traits of business executives. [11] He studied over a hundred of these men in the United States, using with each of them a Thematic Apperception Test, a short undirected interview, and a number of traditional personality tests. They all had a history of continuous promotion and were earning high salaries relative to most business executives. Henry found that all these executives had certain attributes in common. They had a high drive and desire for achievement, anchored to the sheer accomplishment of the work itself. They had strong mobility drives. They saw their superiors as helpful rather than as obstacles. They were able to relate seemingly unconnected events, to organize unstructured situations. They were interested in predicting the future, including the results of their own actions. They were decisive and would force their way to a conclusion. They had a firm sense of self-identity. They were active and aggressive. They had a sense of the perpetually unattained. They were detached toward subordinates. They felt and acted as if they had severed their emotional ties with their parents. They could not be introspective in a leisurely way.

Henry suggested that certain external conditions contributed to the fact that these consistencies were found. A fairly clear understanding existed of the functions of the executive, of the sorts of behavior expected, and of the rewards that went with success. The role in itself demanded certain qualities from the man. Much selection and rejection took place of persons from business management roles and those who lasted had the qualities needed for the role.

Henry was aware that his own results might be limited to organizations in which cooperation and teamwork were valued and independence emphasized only within the framework of company policy. One might well add further important reservations. His study is limited to American businessmen and may not apply closely to English, Italian, or French managers, with Egyptian or African probably even more discrepant. Enormous variability exists in the roles covered by the term "business executive": there might be very little in common between the advertising manager of an international multi-project giant, the works manager of a smallish plant, and the head of a research and development group—even if they receive similar salaries and have similar social status. The success or survival of one executive may depend largely on how he fits with whatever colleagues are at hand: everyone can hardly be bustling and thrusting as they might then succeed mainly in getting in each others' way. Further, it is not clear for what the identified qualities of Henry's business executives were required—were they the qualities necessary to perform the duties of a senior executive office or were they the qualities required to reach that level? [12]

Without going so far as identifying an executive personality, it is, however, possible and useful to point out that the large industrial bureaucracy has certain features likely to bring out or reinforce certain types of behavior in employees with managerial functions and to discourage others. Many operating procedures become standardized and may attain or retain a value because of tradition and predictability rather than current applicability. Much of the work requires close collaboration with colleagues and this tends to put a premium on the man able to cooperate effectively with others, both on established routines or when change is indicated. Substantial emphasis is placed on mobility within the organization and this is conditional upon gaining the approval of one's seniors—doing one's work effectively, without upsetting others and without too much direct disagreement with seniors. The executive has to be positive toward his current tasks and colleagues and yet be prepared to abandon both if new opportunities arise. His loyalties have to be to the organization and its mission rather than to specific persons. He is expected to be ambitious and reasonably self-interested while at the same time prepared to accept a good deal of organizational discipline. Results are usually achieved as a consequence of team effort, so that the executive has to get results only indirectly within his own control. Often these results and his competence or otherwise in his job are matters of judgment by peers and seniors rather than obvious to everyone, and the evaluation has to be based on highly uncertain and possibly shifting criteria. The executive has to bear this uncertainty and to contribute, through his own confidence, to confidence in him by others.

He has a dual set of tasks to perform in getting the work of the organization done at the same time as making a reputation and building relationships that forward his own career.

He has to be able to tolerate intermittent or continuing ambivalence to himself from his juniors for allowing organizational priorities to outweigh consideration for them and from his seniors for being too considerate.

Cross-Pressures in Formal Leadership Positions

Most persons in formal leadership positions in large organizations are themselves subordinates of more senior leaders. That is, they are simultaneously subordinates and leaders. Such positions of intermediacy between groups expose the leader to conflicting influences from both sources: he is apt to experience contrasting pressures and inclinations as to the attitudes he should hold and the way he should behave. The leader is apt to experience demands from above for productivity and related forms of task effectiveness and from below for consideration of the personal feelings and circumstances of subordinates. Gibb describes this as "a basic dilemma of leadership in our democratic society."

If an intermediate officer is to be a real leader, he has a dual role to play. He must accept the norms and values of superior authority, thus serving as an agent of the impersonal and coercive organization of which he is part. To the extent that he does this effectively his superiors regard him highly. At the same time he must win the willing followership of the men under him, so that he wields over them authority that they have themselves given him. He will be rated highly by the men to the extent that he shows "consideration" for them and to the extent that he mingles freely with them and represents them against the cold machine which is the overall organization.[13]

In practice the position of the intermediate level manager is further complicated by the fact that, even though his nominal responsibility may be to one specified person, his work probably brings him into contact with several seniors who will try to influence his behavior and whose good opinion he will value—because of their competence, because he admires them, or because they can influence his subsequent career. It is quite common for them to differ in what they want from him. His subordinates may divide similarly into subcategories with differing expectations and hopes of him. At the same time, of course, his network of organizational relationships will include interaction with peers, with their own sets of attitudes and expectations bearing on him. While this picture emphasizes the position of the leader as recipient or depository of influence, he is, of course, himself necessarily a source of control, influence, and decisions and in a position to some extent to decide for himself which attempts to influence and control him to take into account and which to ignore. Reconciling conflicts, and tolerating the resentment of some of his colleagues are important components of his managerial role.

Helpful research on the cross-pressures accompanying intermediate managerial roles has been undertaken both in the army and in industry. In their wartime studies of the United States army, Stouffer and his colleagues showed that officers and privates had markedly different attitudes in regard to the extent to which a noncommissioned officer should fraternize with the men, how strict he should be as a disciplinarian and how hard he should work them.[14] In general, officers approved of a more "official" point of view on the part of the noncom while the men approved of informal cooperation from him in avoiding the full effect of inconvenient official regulations. On most of these issues the expressed attitude of the noncommissioned officers was intermediate between those of his superiors and subordinates. This suggests a form of conflict resolution that recognizes the importance both of forwarding the formal objectives of the organization and of maintaining the goodwill of those to whom instructions have to be issued.

Essentially the same problems in the relationship of formal leadership to the needs of more senior management and of subordinates has been extensively discussed and researched in terms of the dilemmas, contradictions and conflicts surrounding performance of the foreman's role.[15]

It has been pointed out in these studies that the foreman is the visible manifestation of the power of management, the personal embodiment of a system that makes demands on workers that they may feel to be incompatible with their personal needs and inclinations. Workers feel that the foreman has to push them to get production out so that somebody else does not push him. He is, therefore, prone to become the target for worker aggression. If he relaxes pressure in order to retain his acceptability to the worker side, he is likely to jeopardize his relationship with management.

On the other hand, he is much closer in position and culture to the workers' side and largely dependent on them for satisfactory day-to-day working relations. If he does not relax (or collude) with them, his personal position may become untenable. Further than this, as A. W. Gouldner pointed out, if the foreman relaxes some of the rules, he is in a better position to enforce others that he regards as more central to his official tasks.[16]

It is clear that the tasks of the foreman are problematic. He has to administer a technical system that he has probably had little hand in designing and to enforce rules and carry out policies that originate elsewhere. In the course of doing so he may well have to require people on whom he is dependent for affiliation satisfactions to act in ways that they define as counter to some of their interests. On the other hand, his role, at its highest, involves mediation between the rigidities and impersonalities of command and the infinite varieties of human nature, as provision for and safeguarding of a variable essential for the organization and its participants, i.e., individual human dignity.

Some of the problematic aspects of intermediary managerial roles can be deduced from the literature on the attitudes of line workers towards the possibilities of becoming a foreman. These point to the fact that foremen are resented, especially when they supervise closely and adopt a boss's viewpoint; that they are accused of being inhuman (i.e., as taking on the quality of the system they are responsible for); that they are held accountable by management for mechanical and human contingencies that they cannot control; and that they are continuously distracted by minor emergencies without gaining the satisfaction of closure on problems and processes. The effects on the foreman of increasing specialization has been particularly noted by Roethlisberger. He said that the foreman is surrounded today by a dozen bosses, each a technical or staff man who has taken away a different segment of what used to be his job. The process engineer has taken away the planning of the job, the time standards department the setting-up of the job, the personnel department the hiring and firing of employees. He can no longer rely upon his unchallenged authority to get things done; he must secure the active cooperation of workers. In attempting to perform his double-barreled task (satisfying management and workers) the foreman may find himself caught between pressure from above and from below.

Chinoy reports that most of the workers he interviewed lacked interest in rising to the ranks of supervision and in some cases denied its desirability. This was partly understandable in terms of lack of opportunity and defensiveness but was due partly to the nature of the foreman's job as these workers saw it. They commented on the grief of the foreman in being a middleman, caught between two sides he has to get along with. As they saw it, the foreman was criticized by management when he got on too well with (or was lenient toward) workers; he was ridden by management to get out production and had similarly to ride his workers; he was liable to lose desirable aspects of his personality; he was liable to be harassed by his workers if he made things too difficult for them by enforcing company policy; he was overexposed to the scrutiny of higher management; he was forced to be a yes-man; he lacked the protection of a union. The extra responsibility was thought to be too much for the extra pay offered, and the job was thought to be highly demanding of self-confidence and managerial skill. At the same time the operatives contrasted this with certain satisfactions available in craftwork and (implicitly at least) in the anonymity of the worker role.

We have been discussing the position of the foreman in terms of vertical relationships. Jasinski has pointed out that foremen act as the work group's intermediaries with groups at the same level. In a study he undertook he found that foremen spent more than half their contact time with people outside the work group and that those rated by their superiors as the more effective spent more than that average, especially with other foremen and with staff and service personnel and least time in contact with their own subordinates.

Styles of
Formal Leadership

As we mentioned in the chapter on Lewin, his early work with Lippitt and Whyte showed that the same groups of people behave in distinctly different ways under leaders whose styles differ. Subsequently, many industrial research workers have stressed the efficiency of leadership that emphasizes consideration, mutual identification, and personal influence. Impressive evidence has been mustered in support of this position through a number of studies by staff members of the Institute of Social Research at the University of Michigan. These studies have usually been conducted with operatives or clerks and those in immediate charge of them.

The general style of these studies is to contrast levels of group performance (on comparable tasks) associated with different styles of supervision. The performance criteria used are productivity, turnover, absenteeism, costs, scrap losses, satisfaction derived by group members, and personal motivation.

In one well-known example Kahn and Katz showed in an insurance company that heads of high-producing sections tended disproportionately to exercise "general" rather than "close" supervision. Closeness of supervision was defined as the degree to which the supervisor checked up on the employees—gave them frequent and detailed instructions and limited their freedom to do the job along the lines they chose. Again, in studying the relations of section heads with their own superiors, Kahn and Katz found that the high-producing sections were disproportionately those where

the section head was given freedom by his superiors to handle his own
problems.[17]

There has also been a series of social science experiments and field
descriptions pointing to the importance of explaining the need for change,
of allowing questions to be raised about the negative as well as the positive
implications of the change, of providing opportunities for working through
the difficulties and of involving all key personnel in contributions to the
change. Coch and French contributed an important study in this field,
indicating that

> it is possible for management to modify greatly or to remove completely group
> resistance to changes in methods of work. . . . This change can be accomplished
> by the use of group meetings in which management effectively communicates
> the need for change and stimulates group participation in planning the changes.[18]

Mann, Neff, and their colleagues have summarized much of the work
that has been done on participative styles of leadership in implementing
change.[19] Their main points are as follows. Consultation helps to alleviate
the fears of the members. It may in itself be a positive source of motivation
towards change, increasing and spreading the general awareness of the need
for change, providing a better understanding of all that is entailed, and
bringing organization members closer to the actual planning as they
express their views and suggest new ideas. Moreover, consultation may also
help the management in their present task; they may better perceive the
values, attitudes and perceptions of the organization members; this may be
a first step towards replanning the process of change to avoid future conflicts and impasses. Planning should at first be tentative and flexible, with
constant reviewing and consultation in order to plan the next step. In order
to do this, the total process should be broken up into a series of relatively
simple subgoals. If necessary, the whole strategy of implementing the
change may have to be modified following an unfavorable response to previous stages, as ascertained by consultation. In other words, consultation
should serve to give both management and other members of the organization a realistic picture of what is involved at all stages of the change and
prepare them for the concrete steps involved.

These propositions about the greater effectiveness of participative methods are supported by theoretical formulations of the conditions necessary
for a change in group attitudes. Cartwright has, for instance, pointed out
that much depends on the extent to which there is identification of members with the group, conformity to group norms and ideals, commonly
shared information and a general agreement of the necessity for change.[20]

Apart from the persuasiveness of the empirical evidence and theoretical
formulations, these ideas on the effectiveness of participative forms of
management have the attraction of consistency with contemporary ethics

and industrial democracy. If one managerial approach can be shown or argued to be both economically effective and humanitarian its desirability is doubled.

Likert regards the behavior of the group leader as particularly important in determining the level of group performance.[21] He concludes from his evidence that the importance of the group leader lies in the sorts of structure and pattern of relations he fosters in the group (rather than in one-to-one relations with subordinates). For example, the successful leader develops his group into a solidary social unit which, with his participation, makes better decisions than he can make alone. He helps the group develop efficient communication and reciprocal influence processes that provide it with better information, more technical knowledge, more facts, and more experience for decision-making purposes than the leader himself can provide. Through group decision-making the members feel more fully identified with each decision and highly motivated to execute it fully. The leader encourages others to establish and maintain a supportive atmosphere in the group. Rather than making great play of his rank, he helps the members to become aware of new possibilities.

Corroboration of some of the main results in productivity quoted by Likert has been obtained in England in a study of ninety foremen in eight factories by Argyle and colleagues. It appeared from this study that foremen of high-producing sections exercised general rather than close supervision and were relatively more democratic and non-punitive than foremen of low-producing sections.[22]

This approach, especially as portrayed by Likert, gives weight to the structure of relations as a key to group performance. While Likert sees the formal nomination of individual leaders as virtually irreplaceable—because of the demands for coordination of complex interdependent work processes—he sees leadership as something the leader must share.

Important qualifications have to be made to the proposition that participative styles of leadership are, in general, particularly effective.

First, Likert makes it clear that whether or not a participative structure of relations can exist is only partly dependent upon the leader's inclinations or personal behavior. The characteristics and approach of the designated leader are only one set of elements in the overall social system of the organization. The structure of relations that can exist depends in large part on wider organizational policy, philosophy, and outlook and on the way the leader is himself led by his superiors. Some companies see their responsibility as breaking down the operation into simple component tasks; developing optimum ways of carrying out each of these; hiring people with the appropriate skills to carry out each; training each of them to do the task in the specified way; providing supervision to see that the chosen people are in fact doing what they have been told in the prescribed way. In such a context, a new manager seeking to introduce participative methods may worsen the situation. If the senior managers think authoritarian methods best for running their organization, they may have attracted workers to whom participative methods are not congenial. Organizations are not isolated in space and time. Whether or not a leader can act in a particular style and what constructions are put on his actions are largely dependent on what has gone before in the shape of management, as well as what is expected in the future.

A second qualification is that there can hardly be a "right" sort of leadership irrespective of the activity being controlled. Continuous production systems require close supervision while unit or batch production provide more scope for self-checking and general supervision and indeed for choice in style of supervision.[23] Successful research laboratories require a good deal of independence, permissiveness, and shared authority, while production lines require stricter coordination.[24] Running a railway surely involves a different approach from securing an economically rewarding return from the "creative" branch of an advertising agency.

Thirdly, what constitutes the most appropriate form of leadership will depend on who is involved in the situation. One form of leadership may work with one set of people but not with another. Personalities apart, the form of leadership appropriate at one level of the organization where employees are committed to the objectives of senior management or to their tasks may be inappropriate at another where for most people the work is mainly a means to an end. The form of leadership appropriate to scientists may be inappropriate to executives. The scientists may be most responsive to the collective opinion of peers in the laboratory and executives more responsive to their formal superior.

Finally, what constitutes an appropriate form of leadership will be largely determined by the nature of the larger social system of which the organization is part, by what one may call the enveloping culture. A work organization is not a sealed impermeable entity but rather more of an association, an activity in which people come together for part of the day, bringing their expectations, values, and assumptions. The terms in which organizations are run cannot be grossly discordant from these, at least not for protracted periods. Blau has pointed out that highly bureaucratized forms of administration were probably more appropriate in Weber's Germany than elsewhere.[25] Similarly, as overseas participants in American group dynamic-training programs are apt to point out, ultra-democratic sharing and openness may be confusing rather than helpful to an executive from Holland or Germany. One can expect such discrepancies to matter even more when comparisons are made between Western and non-Western cultures. In African communities, for instance, one would predict that a large part of the managerial problem for organizations trying to maintain high productivity would be to secure increased individuation of employees rather than increased group cooperation; highly participative styles of management there might reinforce those communal values that block economic growth.

How Much Does Leadership Style Matter?

In considering whether social research has managed to identify principles of effective management, we have emphasized the problems and difficulties in generalization. This does not destroy the participative proposition, though we would be inclined to apply it to only a limited range of social situations, technologies, and levels of management (mainly routine manufacturing and clerical operations), and mainly in Western society.

Granted the principle that some methods of leadership or supervision are more effective than others (taking productivity as an obvious measure of effectiveness) the question should be raised of how much difference is made.

Our first clue is that when work is machine paced, as in assembly-line and continuous-process work, the degree to which workers can affect production is limited. So, how far the level of human activity can affect production may depend in the short run mainly on the technology of the process. (Naturally, human activity determines productivity; in the long-run sense it is human beings who design and implement new technologies.)

Homans notes that Argyle's review and his own work point to the conclusion that the differences in productivity in work groups resulting from contrasting methods of supervision are typically small, usually not larger than 15 percent of the total output.[26] Output differences of this level could make an enormous difference to a single department (to which most such studies are confined) or to whole firms. But increases of this order (or even of three or four times this order) are relatively small compared with those that are brought about by investment in new machinery or new sources of power. New approaches in physical work methods probably matter (at least in the short period) much more than changes in supervisory style. Advances in machinery, materials, and engineering tend to reduce the relative variance in production attributable to the operative's immediate efforts.

Homans adduces another reason to account for the fact that the supervisor or changes in supervisory methods appear to make relatively little impact, that is, the fact that the supervisor no longer has much power or authority. He cannot administer negative sanctions because these are in the hands of higher management, the personnel department, and the trade union. He cannot administer positive sanctions because pay and promotion are similarly determined with him acting only as a marginal participant. If injustices are done to his work group as a whole he cannot do much about this because the answer probably lies in some feature of the job evaluation or promotion system that can be corrected only by higher management in association with the union. He lacks an authority resting in technical expertise because, like the men, he is dependent, in an age of rapid technological development, on staff instruction. These considerations underline the point made earlier in our discussion of the impact of differing styles of formal leadership—that much more is involved than one superior per group. In Homans's words:

The factors making for increased production are located increasingly, not in any particular parts of the organization, but in the workings of the organization as a whole.[27]

This is not to say that supervision does not matter but that in considering what supervision styles can and cannot do we should see supervision as emanating from a wider spectrum of persons with authority and influence.

One major reservation should be made in regard to the types of comparison mentioned by Homans and Argyle. Both are assuming normally functioning work systems and broadly similar levels of competence among supervisors. The variations in style of supervision exclude more extreme cases in which supervisors make either technical mistakes, which mean that expensive materials are wasted, or human mistakes, as a result of which large groups of men walk out. In these extreme situations one is reminded that management is the overriding factor in production, including the use or neglect of ingenious technologies.

We should also bear in mind that most studies conducted to date have dealt with *lower* level supervision and repetitive tasks. There is relatively little scope among operatives for varying work methods, for higher material rewards, for achievement, taking of responsibility, or recognition of special promise. Scope for rewards, recognition, and punishment increase as one goes up the scale, where it is likely that more senior people can affect the behavior of immediate juniors much more. This may mean that differences in managerial style have more effect on organizational performance as one moves away from the more junior and more technologically constrained levels. Unfortunately, leadership at the middle levels of organizations has received far less detailed empirical study than at junior levels, and we are unable to quote a substantial number of studies in support of this general proposition. But the point that, in the end, human management matters most to productivity is perhaps obvious when one considers the implications of behavior at the most senior level of management. Top management makes more difference to production than any other single factor because persons at this level decide whether or not to make new capital investment; determine with trade unions wage and promotion policies; and help determine by official policies and their own behavior how the next levels behave in turn toward lower levels. Senior managements shape working environments, and it is to this topic that I now turn.

Institutional Leadership

Leadership is a kind of work done to meet the requirements of a social situation. I want, therefore, to start by considering the social situation with which the organizational leader had to deal, the social field within which he operates.

Selznick offers us a valuable distinction here between what he calls "an organization" and "an institution." [28] As he puts it, the term "organization" suggests a lean, no-nonsense system of consciously coordinated activities; an expendable tool that can be improved, discarded or replaced; a rational instrument specifically engineered to do a particular job, containing tasks and procedures, rules and objectives set out to some officially approved pattern. They are technical instruments, designed as a means to definite goals. They are judged on engineering premises.

An institution is more nearly a natural product of social needs and pressures, a responsive, adaptive system of behavior. Use of the term "institution" implies recognition of the fact that the deliberate design of an organization never accounts for all that participants do, that formal relations coordinate roles or specific actions, not persons, but that in fact men who fill roles interact as many-faceted persons. As human beings they are more than personnel resources for the formal administrative system; they manifest their own needs, some of which sustain and others of which undermine that system. Individual personality and associations of persons, of varying degrees of spontaneity, break through the confines of "rational" organization and procedure.

The term "institution" implies the existence of a set of beliefs and theories among the persons interacting, shared ways of defining their position and of looking at the world.

It also suggests a historical dimension, the fact that the organization is not starting *de novo* but has experienced a variety of developments, setbacks, and changes that have induced certain characteristic frames of mind, a culture specific to the social entity being considered.

We have the distinction then, essentially between the large organization considered as an administrative instrument and as a group of living human beings, a distinction between designed and responsive, emergent behavior. In practice most living work associations are mixtures, blends, compromises, amalgams of these two aspects, of both designed and responsive behavior. A living association blends technical aims and procedures with personal desires and group interests.

The administrative aspects of the enterprise are the more susceptible to scrutiny by the criterion of efficiency and provide more opportunity for clear-cut management devoted to relating known goals to available resources and methods. This is possible because one has rather clearly defined operating responsibilities, a limited range of possible directions to move in, set communication channels and sure positions in the command structure. In practice this sort of efficiency is attainable only at the junior levels of the enterprise; as one's focus of attention shifts upwards one sees less certainty about what the task actually is or should be, about whether one's unit should be doing the job it is doing, about whether anyone should be doing it, about the functions of the organization and its position in its environment.

Organizations are distinctive structures and distinctive cultures that have developed through time and have evolved their own distinctive forms, with new patterns emerging and declining in response to unpredicted exigencies and to largely unplanned responses to new situations. I emphasize the historical aspect because of the effect of lasting association with an enterprise upon its participant members, upon its stability and upon its capacity for change. As Selznick says, the more fully developed the social structure of the enterprise, the more existing ways and modes of behavior become valued for themselves, not as expendable tools for getting a job done but as fulfillments also of group and personal aspirations and integrity. Ways of behaving become infused with values beyond the technical requirements of the task in hand. Personnel become committed in several senses. They become committed to the continuation of existing ways, they commit the care of themselves and their ambitions to the care of the enterprise, they subscribe to the self-image of the organization and build something of this image into their own personal identities.

On the positive side, these processes of commitment aid communication and order, provide the organization with forces toward self-maintenance, provide meaning for participants and motivate their contributions.

On the other hand, the same identifications may weaken the purely technical resourcefulness of the organization. They bind the organization to specific aims and procedures and limit the freedom of the organization to make new deployments of its resources. As success and survival have taken on symbolic meanings, this supports the claims of internal groupings and individuals to avoid liquidation or transformation on purely technical or economic grounds. Identification with the organization as it has been and now is constitutes resistance to change into what it must now do or may presently become. In other words, personal and group commitments and identifications with the organization may weaken its administrative system and emergent social structure function as expendable tools for attaining organizational goals.

The essence of Selznick's argument is that the executive becomes a statesman of the enterprise as he makes the transition from administrative management to institutional leadership. This, he says, is marked by a concern for the evolution of the organization as a whole, including its changing aims and capabilities.

The overall function of the leader is to define the ends of the existence of the enterprise, to design an enterprise directly adapted to these ends and to see that this design becomes a living reality. It is the task of the leader of the organization to make "character defining" commitments that affect the organization's capacity to control its future behavior, irreversible commitments that set the organization's character. Selznick points out that it is the function of the leader at this level to arrive at policy-making rather than policy-serving decisions, decisions that critically affect what the organization does and what sort of basic arrangements are made for doing this. His problem is to choose key values and to create a social structure that embodies them. Selznick distinguishes the policy-making for which such leadership is responsible from routine policy execution in which the organization remains relatively intact, the goals of the organization are taken as given, and it is managerial and administrative expertise that counts.

NOTES

1. R. Bales and P. Slater, "Role Differentiation in Small Decision-making Groups," in T. Parsons et al, *Family, Socialization and Interaction Process* (Glencoe, Illinois: The Free Press, 1955).

2. C. Heinicke and R. Bales, "Development Trends in the Structure of Small Groups," *Sociometry*, 16 (1953): 7–38.

3. R. F. Bales, "In Conference," *Havard Business Review*, 32, no. 2 (1954): 41–49.

4. R. C. Hodgson, D. J. Levinson, and A. Zaleznik, *The Executive Role Constellation*, (Boston: Harvard University Press, 1965).

5. See K. D. Benne and P. Sheats, "Functional Roles of Group Members," *Journal of Social Issues*, 4, no. 2 (Spring 1948): 41–49; L. P. Bradford, et al., *Explorations in Human Relations Theory*, (Washington: National Training Laboratory in Group Development, 1953); H. Thelen, *Dynamics of Groups at Work*, (Chicago: Chicago University Press.)

6. R. A. Gordon, *Business Leadership in the Large Corporation*, (Berkeley and Los Angeles: University of California Press, 1961), pp. 99 and 105.

7. *The Listener*, 24 (November 1966): 756.

8. J. K. Galbraith, *The Listener*, 24 (November 1966): 757.

9. For a discussion of strategies for handling failure see Sofer, *Men in Mid-Career*, pp. 22–24.

10. For a review of the main findings see C. A. Gibb, "Leadership," in *Handbook of Social Psychology*, G. Lindzey, ed., (Cambridge, Massachusetts: Addison-Wesley, 1954).

11. W. E. Henry, "The Business Executive: The Psychodynamics of a Social Role," *American Journal of Sociology*, 54, no. 4 (1948–1949): 286–291.

12. This echoes the comment of D. Cartwright and A. Zander that "the characteristics that get a person into a position of leadership may be different from those that

make a person an executive leader once he has obtained an office of leadership," *Group Dynamics, Research and Theory* (London: Tavistock, 2nd ed., 1968), p. 303.

13. Gibb, "Leadership," pp. 894 and 895.

14. S. A. Stouffer, et al., *The American Soldier,* 1 (Princeton, New Jersey: Princeton University Press, 1949). See also discussion in B. Berelson and G. A. Steiner, *Human Behavior: An Inventory of Scientific Findings* (New York: Harcourt Brace, 1944).

15. See Chinoy, E., *The Automobile Worker and the American Dream* (New York: Doubleday, 1955); Gouldner, A. W., *Patterns of Industrial Bureaucracy* (Glencoe, Illinois: The Free Press, 1954); Jasinski, F. J., "Foreman Relations Outside the Work Group," *Personnel,* 33 (September 1956), excerpted in Walker, C. R., *Modern Technology and Civilisation* (London: McGraw Hill, 1962); Roethlisberger, F. J., "The Foreman, Master and Victim of Doubletalk," *Harvard Business Review,* 23, no. 3 (April 1945); Walker, C. R. and Guest, R. H., *The Man on the Assembly Line: The Foreman on the Assembly Line* (Cambridge, Massachusetts: Harvard University Press, 1956); Whyte, W. F. and Gardner, B., "The Man in the Middle," *Applied Anthropology* (now *Human Organization*), 4 (Spring 1945): 1–28.

16. A. W. Gouldner, *Patterns of Industrial Bureaucracy* (Glencoe, Illinois: The Free Press, 1949).

17. R. L. Kahn and D. Katz, "Leadership Practices in Relation to Productivity and Morale," in D. Cartwright and A. Zander, eds., *Group Dynamics: Research and Theory* (New York: Harper and Row, 1953).

18. L. Coch and J. R. French, Jr., "Overcoming Resistance to Change," *Human Relations,* 1, no. 4 (1948): 512–531.

19. F. C. Mann and F. W. Neff, *Managing Major Change for Organizations* (Ann Arbor: Foundation for Research on Human Behaviour, 1961).

20. D. Cartwright, "Achieving Change in People: Some Applications of Group Dynamics Theory," *Human Relations,* 4 (November 1951): 381–392.

21. R. Likert, *New Patterns of Management* (New York: McGraw Hill, 1961).

22. Argyle, M., Gardner, G., and Cioffi, F., "Supervisory Methods Related to Productivity, Absenteeism and Labour Turnover," *Human Relations,* 11 (1958): 23–40.

23. J. Woodward, *Management and Technology* (London: Her Majesty's Stationery Office, 1958).

24. T. Burns and G. M. Stalker, *The Management of Innovation* (London: Tavistock, 1969).

25. P. Blau, *The Dynamics of Bureaucracy. A Study of Inter-Personal Relations in Two Government Agencies* (Chicago: University of Chicago Press, 1955), p. 202.

26. G. C. Homans, "Effort, Supervision and Productivity," in R. Dubin, G. C. Homans, F. C. Mann and D. C. Miller, *Leadership and Productivity* (San Francisco: Chandler, 1965).

27. Homans, "Effort, Supervision and Productivity," p. 67.

28. P. Selznick, *Leadership in Administration* (Evanston, Illinois: Row Peterson, 1957).

16 : Organizational Change[1]

THIS chapter examines problems surrounding the introduction of major planned changes, more especially in large-scale industrial organizations or other institutions where managements have considerable scope for choice. These changes inevitably involve the altered deployment of personnel and resources within the enterprise. It is these organizational aspects that concern us here.

Three basic types of change are considered. These are change in the amount of flexibility of the organization; change in the degree of centralization; and change in the lateral distribution of power between different departments. These are not the only types of change, nor do they occur in isolation. But they have particular importance, since any process of change tends to implicate one or more of these aspects. Our procedure is first to contrast organization models with differing degrees of flexibility and of centralization and differing power distributions between departments, and then to consider changes in these variables within one organization over time.

Varying the Extent of Flexibility

In recent years sociologists have become increasingly aware of what are regarded as the shortcomings of highly rationalized approaches to industrial organizations.

In the literature of the past decade what McGregor calls "Theory X,"[2] Argyris "directive leadership,"[3] Gouldner "punishment-centered bureaucracy,"[4] and Shepard and Blake, "mechanistic systems"[5] is presented as a method of management whose general aim is a machine-like efficiency in industrial organizations. Each of these writers explicitly or implicitly contrasts this with approaches that take into more account the personal needs of individuals and what is said to be their greater willingness to cooperate under more flexible conditions. It is argued that the less closely regulated approach is more consistent with notions of democracy and also leads to an efficiency that is better adapted to conditions of change.

Well documented examples given by these writers draw the similar conclusion that a rigid system of administration is liable to produce low efficiency, low productivity, high labor turnover, and high absentee rates. But reactions to a particular type of organization are likely to vary from culture to culture. To take an example, bureaucracies appear to be very inflexible and impersonal: individual members at all levels must give their official duties priority over their personal inclinations or interests so that complex tasks can be efficiently performed through rational, calculated processes. Yet, as Blau [6] has pointed out, such a system is more likely to have been successful and appropriate in Germany in Weber's time than in many other cultures. Elsewhere, systems of bureaucracy less adapted to the particular society or circumstances may be more likely to lead to defensive reactions and withdrawal among those concerned.

At the other extreme we might consider the highly adaptable "organic" type of organization as envisaged for instance, by Shepard and Blake. They have a view of an ideal organization in which there is free interaction, and work group behavior patterns are allowed to modify themselves spontaneously. This is the antithesis of bureaucracy. It almost expressly denies the benefits of a stable, formal system designed to protect members and clients through published and consistently operated rules and relies heavily on the good will and altruistic motives of the working members.

Where the outcome of a situation is not predetermined and where there is much freedom and reliance on goodwill, the stage is set at the same time for the emergence of rival factions and free for all competition which may defeat the formally accepted aims of the organization.

A précis of prevalent views on relatively rigid versus relatively flexible systems appears below.

THE BUREAUCRATIC SYSTEM	THE ADAPTIVE SYSTEM
Impersonal; ascribed roles and rules, rational efficiency, rigid hierarchical structure, mainly vertical communications, specificity of tasks and expectations.	Personal involvement, achievement-oriented, adaptive efficiency, continual adjustment and redefinition of individual tasks to achieve the shared group task, lateral and vertical communications with an emphasis on consultation rather than direction.
(Weber's model, McGregor's "Theory X," Gouldner's "punishment-centered bureaucracy," Argyris's "directive leadership," Shepard's "mechanistic systems.")	(McGregor's "Theory Y," Burns's and Stalker's "organic systems," Gouldner's "mock bureaucracy.")
Effective for handling complex stable processes, dispensing justice to definable classes of persons in identifiably	Effective for coping with change, innovation, and critical situations, and providing a means of personal expres-

similar circumstances and providing secure careers for persons with identifiable qualifications. Essential in public or semipublic sectors of a mass society, as an impartial, efficient instrument of a large number of taxpayers or shareholders. Deficient in adaptability, in flexibility, in tempering policies to particular cases, and in coping with emergencies or unexpected contingencies.

sion and responsibility. In its extreme form may lead to some anxiety for those who find the lack of definition and security a strain, and may encourage dysfunctional opportunism.

CHANGING ORGANIZATIONAL FLEXIBILITY

If an organization is to increase the extent to which it makes innovations, or its capacity to react to environmental changes, it needs also to increase its scope for flexibility. There is, generally speaking, a need for increased flexibility for organizations operating in a world of increasingly turbulent environments.

As Lewin put it,

a successful change includes three aspects: unfreezing the present level, moving to a new level and freezing group life on the new level. Since any level is determined by a force field, permanency implies that the new force field is made relatively secure against change.[7]

In terms of the continuum of flexibility, "unfreezing" precedes a shift towards greater adaptability and "freezing" is a return towards a more rigid system to ensure some degree of stability for the new system.

Discussion about relatively highly structured or relatively flexible forms of organization implies that the model adopted is essentially a matter of choice by the directorate. In fact the determinants are multiple and the directorate is only one source of influence among many. The determinants include the nature of the task: repetitive, predictable operations, such as, for instance, the provision of transport, are naturally amenable to tighter programing than those designed to cope with issues like fires, crimes or weather irregularities. A significant force affecting the extent of rigidity is the form of accountability to which the organization is subject: a college given a more or less predetermined budget on whose spending it must report to a governmental authority will control staff more closely than a private business whose accountability to shareholders is looser and more intermittent.[8] Similarly, the main structures around which Weber built his central conceptions were those with public responsibilities where it is essential to apply clearly understood and uniform rules to cases falling into similar categories and to ensure that the rules are administered by persons whose loyalties and technical competence are clearly segregated from their personal inclinations.

The state of internal management politics may affect the level of structuring, inflexibility, and conservatism in taking advantage of scope for discretion within the existing system. If, for instance, two subgroups of a board of directors are at a stalemate, or if the managing director is due to change within a year, one would expect key personnel to cover themselves by abiding closely by traditional rules and modes.

Apart from anything the senior management may be trying to do, there is a tendency for organizations to drift in a bureaucratic, or at any rate a conservative, direction. The reasons are many. Firstly, those with management responsibilities develop a stake in the positions they have gained and may consciously or unconsciously discourage variation. Secondly, people with responsibilities or special knowledge have, by virtue of their experience and knowledge of the system, the power to protect their vested interests and thereby to perpetuate control over their environment. As Broom and Selznick say, "Leaders can usually meet all but the most determined and well-organized assaults of an aroused membership." [9] Thirdly, the distinction between person and role is often so abstract for persons other than the role incumbent, that people tend to go to the same superiors about the same things even after formal definitions of duty have changed.[10] Fourthly, people are usually quite happy to have someone else performing organizational tasks so long as their own special interests are not visibly threatened. Fifthly, as has vividly been shown by studies of hospitals, certain of the rigidities that get built into institutions function for staff as ways of warding off doubt, uncertainty, and anxiety in tasks that by their very nature arouse these feelings.[11] It is likely that a change in the direction of flexibility within such a system will challenge a much-needed set of defenses and be resisted.

Varying the Amount
of Centralization

By centralization is meant the extent to which organizations concentrate decision-making at the more senior management levels. This is not uniformly coincident with the retention of power at the top of the organization. There are two reasons why these are not necessarily or uniformly coincident. First, as is common knowledge, a management that insists on maximizing the area over which it takes decisions can hamstring itself because it becomes over-preoccupied with trivialities. Secondly, delegation of power very often implies that the persons delegating are doing so to free themselves for more important tasks.

The comparisons that are usually made between relatively centralized and relatively decentralized methods or organization are summarized below:

CENTRALIZED SYSTEM

Concentration of decision-making and what is considered to be the main part of power at the top; enabling effective coordination of activities and direction of tasks.

Effective for complex interrelated activities that require discipline and control, for consistent and experienced decision-making in the hands of the few men at the top.

Owing to remoteness of persons in control and high importance of overworked staff functions, tends to have a deleterious effect on morale within the organization and ultimately on its efficiency.

DECENTRALIZED SYSTEM

Extensive delegation of power to lower levels, leaving senior personnel freer to plan and to assess their external environment.

Effective for loosely structured and geographically dispersed organizations, for situations where specialized or local knowledge is important in these decisions.

Owing to freedom of movement allowed to subordinates, increases the possibility of interdepartmental and interpersonal rivalry which may act against the formally stated aims of the total organization.

CHANGES IN CENTRALIZATION

In recent years, as a reaction against the centralization that has built up in a number of expanding organizations, a process of decentralization through delegating power and responsibility to more junior levels of management has been prevalent in large industrial organizations, especially in the United States.[12] Downward shifts of this kind of overall power or, perhaps more often, selected powers, have been the subject of a number of empirical and analytic studies.

We should distinguish between "decentralization" and "debureaucratization," between a shift towards greater delegation of powers and a shift towards greater flexibility. It is true that changes of both sorts have occurred in recent years as a reaction against what have come to be considered outmoded forms of organization and as means of improving morale and efficiency. It is also true that there is a tendency for organizations to revert to a more bureaucratic form and also to a more centralized form after either type of change.[13] But the two processes are substantially different; and are treated here as two distinct types of organizational change.

Managerial staff faced with a program of decentralization, and hence the loss of certain powers, may be particularly prone to assume that decentralization merely implies improving informal contacts down the line without any real delegation of any of their powers. As Baker and France have shown, such staff they are aware that new forms of behavior are expected of them by their superiors and where they do not wish to relinquish any of their powers, this is an easy way out of the dilemma.[14] A desire to retain power may stem from attitudes which are deeply rooted in men's whole approach to working for an organization; such attitudes prevent them from grasping that decentralization implies *different* rather than *fewer* responsibilities for senior managers.[15] Decentralization entails delegating authority in routine matters to subordinates in order to leave seniors *more* time for *new* responsibilities in assessing the external environment and planning.

Looked at in this way, decentralization involves a discarding only of a selection of the powers of the seniors and their adoption of new powers.

As Selznick sees it, the task of leadership is concerned with critical decisions, planning and inspiring the organization generally with its new goals and values in a constantly changing situation.[16] At a time of rapid organizational change, what have been routine activities may enter the realm of critical decision-making and a need for greater centralization can arise. For example, during periods of relative stability, such aspects as personnel selection and training may be matters of routine performance to be carried out by junior managerial staff, but during times of rapid change these are subject to reappraisal and may well become the concern of more senior managerial staff.

Wherever there is some ambiguity or some latitude for manipulation, there is quite likely to be someone willing to take advantage of the situation. Decentralization must increase the opportunity for many people to work for their own personal ends.

Many studies concentrate on the dilemmas that the delegation of their powers has for senior personnel. There has been less interest in the attitudes and behavior of junior members of an organization faced with a shift towards them of new powers. They also can to some extent manipulate the situation in their favor. Burns and Stalker note the ways in which juniors in an organization may withhold information from their seniors or wait for opportunities to exploit their incompetence in order to further their own ends.[17]

Anxiety is apt to be experienced by organization members given more responsibility than they feel they personally can cope with. It is here that defensive modes of behavior tend to be shown. In the Menzies case quoted the reactions on the part of juniors faced with burdensome responsibility in a situation of strain has actually been to delegate some of these responsibilities to their *seniors*.[18] Favorable circumstances exist for the retention of power by superiors because of the willingness of many subordinates to collude in procedures designed to circumvent delegation.[19]

Junior members of management may be left with less authority after some vertical shift in power downwards has made a double jump and by-passed them. This is frequent after the introduction of some form of joint consultational machinery. Jaques records the opposition of foremen to joint consultation between managers and workers in which they were inadequately represented. The new arrangement formed a two-way channel of communication between the shop floor and management which by-passed them and also reduced the information passed down to them from the management, so that sometimes they heard of new policies and prospects from their own subordinates.[20] Woodward and her colleagues have noted how, among dock workers, trade union activity has tended to weaken the power officially delegated to foremen.[21] As a result the latter resorted to the norms of informal leadership in order to perform their jobs effectively.

Deliberate decentralization or centralization may help an organization to solve some of its major problems. But in so much as these changes also imply a change in the distribution of power in the hands of key personnel they are likely to invoke new conflicts and dilemmas. The ways in which these key personnel react must depend to a large extent on their personalities, values and ambitions. As I have already indicated, there is a general tendency for power to revert to the hands of those at the head of an organization. This may be beneficial in that it helps to ensure coordination, concerted policies, experienced decision-making and diminished rivalry between subordinate departments. But there are a number of disadvantages.[22] In the first place, there is a limit in the extent to which a few people at the top can be aware of all the factors involved in the problems they have to cope with: where specialized or local knowledge is required and where immediate decisions have to be made, a certain degree of delegation of responsibility is necessary. Secondly, if senior managers tackle too many routine matters themselves, they limit the extent to which they can be free to plan and to introduce innovations. Thirdly, there is a point beyond which too much centralization lowers the morale and general interest of those placed too far from the seat of authority. Such factors suggest the need for a certain degree of decentralization. But no organization and no organizational environment is static, and therefore no permanent balance between centralization and decentralization can ever be attained. Power must continually shift up and down the executive hierarchy at all levels, and this must continually present personal and organizational dilemmas.

Varying the Horizontal Distribution of Power

The organization is certain to have a number of coordinated activities in order to fulfill its primary tasks. These activities may be explicitly assigned to different departments and implicitly be given varying degrees of priority.

The larger and more enterprising the organization, the more likely it is to have diversified interests, and a continual, if suppressed or undercover, struggle between production, development, research, housekeeping, sales, and other departments. And in so much as each of these is bound to contain specialists it is unlikely that they will see the company policy in quite the same light: production engineers are likely to regard production as the principal aim of the company, the sales force is likely to regard the marketing of its goods as its most important activity, and so on. Economic and social changes are likely to affect the relative power of each of these and determine a continual realignment of priorities at one time in favor of sales, at another time in favor of staff departments, and so on. But the specialists themselves may be less prepared to take this philosophic view.

A good example of the extreme to which interdepartmental rivalry can develop in the absence of effective sanctions is Selznick's study of the Tennessee Valley Authority.[23] Here a program for rural development committed itself to a grass-roots policy, whereby local institutions were invited to participate in its government and implementation. The strongest local faction in the area, the agriculturalists, gained control of the T.V.A. and redefined its aims to suit their own ends at the expense of other interested parties. The organization had been formed along such democratic lines that there was no means of preventing this happening. Instead of the substantial flexibility leading to individuals modifying their own goals to suit those of the organization, as envisaged in the writings of Shepard and Blake, it was the policies and structures of the higher levels that were modified to suit the interests of the strongest faction.

An organization which lacks a centralized structure has a potential weakness. In their analysis of leadership Burns and Stalker emphasize the role of the managing director in ensuring efficient coordination between the various departments, keeping internal politics in check and thereby maintaining the necessary flexibility for the enterprise to be viable.

CHANGES IN THE
RELATIVE POSITIONS
OF DEPARTMENTS

Any realignment of priorities by the senior management must give greater power to some departments at the expense of others. Such realignments may be expressed by alterations in the distribution of personnel, of technical resources, or of finance, or by the redefinition of organization policy. Again this is a field which is never likely to be static, and the distribution of power between the various departments of an enterprise must constantly be subject to change.

In the late 1930s in the Glacier Metal Company, with new managerial ideas, new staff departments developed at the expense of the production departments: financial controls became the province of an accountant acting as company secretary, who gradually formed his own department; and the training and selection of employees was taken over by a personnel manager who also formed his own department. In each of these spheres, the production departments lost some ground in determining company policy.

The period may be viewed as a continuous shift of power away from the production departments towards the "housekeeping" departments. This general trend was confirmed when the accountant became managing director: even the leadership of the enterprise had shifted in favor of the staff departments.[24]

Miller has drawn attention to the realignment of priorities in the course of building a new steel works.[25] At the time of construction the engineers engaged in solving challenging technological problems were dominant; but once production began, their task was to be confined to routine maintenance. This loss in status would coincide with the development of a new production management in charge of running the new works. In developing their organization beforehand the latter impinged on the engineers' plans for the layout of the site and also looked ahead to their own future conflicts when they would be facing one another from different departments: these anticipations colored their present attitudes and decisions.

After the nationalization of hospital services in Britain, Sofer studied a hospital in which the medical department, the nursing side, and the administrative had been deliberately segregated and put on equal level following the provision of the new regulations.[26] The newly elevated administrative side found difficulty in asserting its formal rights and a proportion of the staff insisted on continuing to behave as if no change had in fact been made, more especially to continue to treat the senior doctor as head of the hospital.

Any organizational development that pays greater attention to the grievances and attitudes of junior members and allows them more voice in determining future policies is a vertical shift of power in their favor. But insofar as this is institutionalized and insofar as power is delegated upwards to a few chosen representatives of the workers, such a development is effectively a lateral shift of power where, in effect a new intramural or extramural department with a new voice on organization affairs has come into being. From the point of view of the enterprise as a bounded, vertically structured, autonomous concern, this may seem paradoxical, especially where union representatives do not even belong to the enterprise itself. But from the point of view of the focus of power and of the realignment of priorities, the growth of trade union movements and of joint consultation represents in part a lateral shift at the expense of the traditional notion of an enterprise.

In summary, we see that lateral shifts in power are associated with internal policies and with changes that involve a realignment of an enterprise's priorities between its many tasks. This section and the previous one taken together may be regarded as ways of looking at an enterprise as a structure in which power is constantly being redistributed as each small or major type of change affects its status quo, and in which each shift in power leads in turn to a new series of changes.

Reorganization and Opportunity

We have singled out three basic dimensions of organizational change as of particular importance. These were flexibility, the vertical distribution of power within the organization, and the lateral distribution of power between departments. Each is closely related to organizational change in general. Any program of change can be carried out only if the organization and its members show a certain degree of flexibility and can be consolidated only if some of that flexibility is removed once the program is complete. Again, so far as the vertical distribution of power is concerned, a program of change is seen to involve the top management personally and to entail their handling matters that at other times might be delegated to more junior members of the organization. And thirdly, any program of change inevitably affects the distribution of power between the various departments and brings to a head rivalry between them.

Besides the most important demands for innovation and rethinking, there are usually many subsidiary problems that have been put to one side awaiting a major upheaval. Up to this point, the management may have dealt with many of its day to day problems with ad hoc decisions that have met the immediate problems without necessarily dealing with wider issues of which they are part or without tracking down more fundamental problems of which they are symptoms. With a demand for innovation in one sphere, the more radical managers are likely to see their chance for a general reorganization. This is the type of change that Mann and Neff refer to as a "controlled explosion" [27] as opposed to the piecemeal change that is merely a way of deferring the need to face a major change.

Crozier has indicated that technological changes may gain added favor from management because they provide the opportunity to piggyback on to the technological changes other reforms which, strictly speaking, have little to do with the technological change.[28] To this one might add the consideration that any organization as it goes is apt to accumulate a number of problems, none of which appears at the time separately to be worth direct confrontation. Toleration continues until some crisis is felt by the senior management to be imminent. At that point it becomes widely understood that it is necessary to take a new look at any standing problems such as interdepartmental rivalries and substandard performance and to call into question the tolerance and accommodation that have so far been exercised. Much of the past gets swept away more or less simultaneously in a sort of administrative surgery. There is always a great deal which, by criteria of economic rationality, can justifiably be swept away. This is because no human association pursues such aims indefinitely—and only rarely for protracted periods. So any organization has much about it that is, or appears to be, economically indefensible and is therefore ready for the surgeon's knife.

The Assessment
of Organizational Change

Unless there are adequate techniques for assessing change there can be no certainty that the changes that are made are effective.

As implied in the first part of this chapter, a central problem derives from the unity of change. How can one say that change X in modifying the flexibility of an organization caused behavior Y if in practice a change in flexibility almost always simultaneously involves changes in the degree of centralization and changes in the lateral distribution of power, and if advantage was taken of the opportunity presented by the reorganization to change personnel between jobs? Again, it is difficult to associate change X with change Y as cause and effect, because some intervening variable—such as subordinates' fantasies about top management's motives in introducing change X—may be the crucial factor in producing change Y and because other changes affecting the same outcomes may be proceeding simultaneously.

In the sections that follow, I indicate some of the ways in which problems in this area have been approached by social scientists and some of the possibilities and limitations in these approaches. The best of the studies that have been made teach us a good deal about organizational functioning, about the possibilities and limits of social science in organizational study and about the relation of sociological theory to the untidy and complicated realities of everyday life. The care and thought that have gone into them can provide social scientists and administrators with guidance as to the most practical and workmanlike approaches to adopt in assessing organizational change, given the character of the problem being faced and the present state of our knowledge, art, and craft.

PRODUCTIVITY AS A CRITERION
FOR MEASURING THE SUCCESS
OF A CHANGE

By the success of an organizational change I imply that a management has deliberately and intentionally modified its existing structure or procedures and wishes to examine the state of the organization at some point of time after the change in order to compare that state with the state preceding the change or with the state aimed at. A successful change is then viewed as one which achieves its overt purpose.

At first sight change in productivity seems the obvious criterion for measuring the success of a planned, deliberate organizational change, since it is a reasonable assumption that the purpose of higher management in introducing a change is to increase productivity.

Productivity has, of course, often been used as the criterion of change. Coch and French regarded increase in productivity in a pajama factory as indicative of improved management-worker relations due to the provision of a new channel of communications.[29] Strauss regarded lowered productivity as the effect of restrictive practices by setters who resented having the authority of mechanical specialists over them removed, being put under the charge of production line foremen and having their mobility blocked by new management trainees.[30] Rice contrasted output in experimental loom sheds with other loom sheds in the same organization when he helped to introduce changes in the social organization of the Ahmedabad calico mills.[31]

But the use of productivity as a criterion for successful organization change has defects and limitations, for reasons that appear below.

1. *The purpose of an organization change is not necessarily to increase productivity.* The aim of change may be maintenance or increase of profits rather than increase in productivity. This greatly increases the complexity of assessing organizational change since so many external factors, such as the behavior of suppliers, competitors, consumers, and government, affect profit.

Those initiating change often have objectives additional to productivity and profits. In his introduction to a study about which I will have more to say later, Lawrence reports

The executives involved were planning a concerted effort to "decentralize" their chain of supermarket stores. . . . Their motivation for this change came from two principal sources. First, they believed that the company needed to move in this direction to compete more effectively in its industry. Secondly, they believed that such a move would make their organization a better place to live and work.[32]

At certain critical phases of an organization's history the aim of a change may not be to increase productivity, profitability, or competitive capacity but merely to survive, to perpetuate, or to reproduce itself. The efforts of cigarette companies to diversify illustrate this. Under these circumstances, increase in profitability is not the best criterion of the effectiveness of an organizational change.

2. The question arises of *the most appropriate time period over which to relate changes in productivity to deliberate changes in organization.* Organizational or technological change may lead to a new level of effort by employees, but, until it is definitely known that production has settled down at this level, associating the higher productivity level with the change may be misleading. A shot in the arm may be injected to the long-term disadvantage of the organization. Managements know that it is possible to put a man in charge who achieves a short-run improvement in productivity, effi-

ciency, and profits, but at the cost of eroding the goodwill of employees in a way bound to boomerang in the long run. In such a case, the reliability of a before-and-after measurement depends almost entirely on the point of time chosen for the after measurement.

The possibility that changes in productivity can be achieved which may in the long run prove positively misleading because other effects of the change will by then have had a chance to work themselves out is strongly suggested by the important study by the Institute of Social Research reported by Morse and Reimer.[33] The hypotheses under investigation were (1) that an increased role in the decision-making processes for rank-and-file groups increases their satisfaction (while a decreased role in decision-making reduces satisfaction), and (2) that an increased role in decision-making for rank-and-file groups increases their productivity (while a decreased role in decision-making decreases productivity). Base line measurements were made and were then followed by a six-month program in which two parts of the organization were restructured and training given, in one case designed to increase rank-and-file decision-making and in the other to increase the upper management role in decision-making. Measurements were made during and after the experimental period (at the end of an operational period of a year) for the two experimental programs. Both decision-making systems were found to increase productivity (as measured by clerical costs), with the hierarchically controlled program resulting in a greater increase. However, the individual satisfaction of the members of the work groups concerned had moved in opposite directions, increasing significantly in the more autonomous group and decreasing significantly in the hierarchically controlled program. The latter was evinced in questionnaire responses and in disproportionate turnover among members of the hierarchically controlled program, who made unfavorable comments about pressure, work standards, and so on.

The question arises of how long it would have been before the cost of the consequences of staff dissatisfaction would have exceeded the benefit of the increased productivity. We should also ask whether, under the new system introduced, productivity would continue to be maintained at a higher level. This study underlines the unreliability of productivity (or productivity on its own) as an indicator of an effective organizational change. It also points to the importance of the study of psychological factors such as attitudes, perceptions, and motivations that intervene between organizational decision and subsequent performance and to the importance of understanding the social processes that ensue.

3. We know from the classic Roethlisberger and Dickson studies that *increases in productivity achieved concurrently with organizational change may have little or nothing to do with the desirability or otherwise of the particular organizational changes introduced.* In their case, as reported, the improvements appear to be associated with the conclusion of the workers

that, if management were prepared to allow study and experiment, management must be more interested in workers than they had assumed. So the change in productivity could reasonably be considered to be independent of the specific organization changes attempted and cannot be regarded as indicative of their success or failure. The same point—that the manner or perception of a change may be the causal factor in productivity changes—arises from Strauss's study already referred to, where the entire programme was instituted through indirection and the changeover was made so subtly that few individuals fully perceived its significance.

4. During a period of organizational change *workers may deliberately manipulate production* as a general manifestation of anti-management sentiments, *to secure some end of their own* or to convince management that a particular scheme designed to increase production will not in fact work.[34] If direct manipulation of the index of change as a political weapon is possible, this throws doubt on such indices or, at least, makes it essential to check that the index is not being manipulated for political motives.

5. A reservation about the use of productivity as an index of effective organizational change arises from questions about *the unit whose behavior is to be measured*. Strauss describes a case in which an experimental attempt was made to give female operatives greater control over the pacing of the processes they performed. Production rose, but

along with improved production in the paint room had come a host of embarrassments. The extra production in the paint room had created a pile-up in front and a vacuum behind and both results were unwelcome to the adjoining departments. . . . It is clear from this instance that *local* improvements can often be obtained . . . but it is also clear that they may not lead to benefits for the organization as a whole. Changes in one part of an integrated organization may require widespread changes elsewhere, and the cost of such readjustments may far outbalance the benefits received in the local situation.[35]

6. The instances cited above are mainly cases in which the focus is on the behavior of manual workers. This fact leads us to *the difficulty of measuring the productivity of non-manual workers*. How does one measure the success of an organizational change which it is hoped will lead to improved communications or easier and more penetrating decision-making? In the case of decentralizing a personnel department, say, how does one determine whether the personnel officers decentralized are being more productive in their new positions, contributing more to the sections where they are now stationed, or contributing more to the organization as a whole? Any attempt at a precise index of productivity in such cases would constitute a denial of the diffuse character of executive (including personnel) tasks and of the collective character of most organizational effort, which reduces the possibility of identifying causal connections between individual effort and group performance.

OTHER PERFORMANCE DATA AS CRITERIA

Apart from productivity such other aspects of performance as labor turnover, work stoppage, absenteeism, and reduction of waste have been used to assess the effects of change.[36]

Guest studied a case of apparently outstanding success in organizational change where the appointment of a new manager who introduced more participative methods was followed by an improvement in several performance indices additional to productivity.[37] Between 1953 and 1956 labor costs decreased, quality of work improved, there was quicker readjustment to changing production demands, an improvement in the safety record, a reduction in the number of labor grievances, less absenteeism and lowered labor turnover. Since performance improvements of a similar order of magnitude were not recorded in comparable plants under the same general direction, the plant studied moved from bottom to top in a "league table" of performance indices, and since in this particular plant the manager had changed and the new manager had introduced a radically new style of management it is highly plausible that the performance changes reflected changes in social and psychological factors affecting staff. But what factors? In accounting for the before-and-after difference Guest gives central emphasis to the style in which the new manager operated. The book contains some evidence about the same man's prior managership in a comparable plant which throws doubt on the record of success Guest associates with him and shows that his own former plant also improved aspects of its performance after he left. It is possible that improvement in the main plant studied could be attributed to relief at the departure of the previous manager or to the fact that the new manager was given much more leeway by his own superiors with regard to the way he ran the plant, thus taking pressure off everybody.

Although Guest describes attitudes and interactions before, during, and after the changes, it is not possible from his data to connect specific aspects of the managerial changes with specific changes in attitudes or specific changes in performance. Analytically speaking this is just what we need. Suggestive though this study is, it does not tell us what particular performance changes or what proportion of the total performance change, are attributable to the change of plant manager in itself as distinct from his personality or methods; to the more democratic methods the new man adopted; to the meetings he introduced; to the institution of rotating jobs at the same organizational level; to the new control methods introduced; to the improvements made in physical conditions; to technological innovations during the same period; to euphoria about a change in atmosphere; or to interim news of performance improvements. This is not being ungrateful for one of the few studies that give a really good record of a before situation and an after situation, as well as some account of what happened in between and which yield quantitative data on a change. But what we have here is a report of what looks like a blanket improvement in performance after a blanket change in management. It does not assess specific effects achieved by specific management changes. This is largely because detailed field studies were not conducted during the two-and-a-half years while the key changes were being made. Information dealing with events between those dates is deductive and is based on written records and on information given by informants, not on observation. Dr. Walker, director of the overall series of projects of which this study was part, says in his foreword that Guest "has focused on the process of change itself, the discrete phenomena which made the structure actually move here from Form A to Form B. He has added, in other words, the dimension of duration to a study of organizational behavior undergoing change." Careful though the author was to collect material bearing on the process of the change, he did not in fact observe the change(s) or systematically collect material while it was under way.

Returning to the general theme, it seems legitimate to argue that if several performance variables move in the same direction after a given organizational change this provides evidence of the (positive or negative) effect of the change. But we should not draw the conclusion that they mean the same thing—for instance, in the case of a negative effect, that withdrawal from the organization (absenteeism, labor turnover) is the same as restriction of production. To class them together may be useful if one wants a crude before-and-after association, but reduces the possibility of redressing the trouble. To put this concretely, an organizational change which leads men to look for other jobs is a very different matter from one which leads them to stay put but go-slow. One needs to understand under what circumstances one gets the one result or the other.

I have been discussing circumstances under which all the variables move in the same direction. But I suspect that such cases are rare, that it is more usual, after an effective organizational change, for some performance indices to move in opposite directions. If a firm insisted on greater punctuality one might well get better timekeeping but higher labor turnover, the latter being the result of moves by people for whom employment in the firm is marginal or who decide that it is worth moving to a less demanding firm. Or, in a highly taxed country, new opportunities for higher earnings may well be accompanied by lower unit costs but also by increased absenteeism.

The same general reservation about these indices must be listed as with productivity: the essential difference between *post hoc* and *propter hoc* in such a complex matter as organizational change, where results may come from unanticipated by-products or side-effects of the proposed change, are susceptible to deliberate manipulation for political purposes or do not stabilize over an extended period.

This type of difficulty is compounded by variations in outside circumstances. Firms being open institutions—or at any rate institutions permeable by external forces—behavior within them is always sensitive to changes in bargaining power as affected for instance by varying opportunities for alternative employment. An unpopular change may be stoically borne during a depression, drastically reacted against in a boom. Or what management conceives to be a concession to workers may reduce labor turnover during a depression but not go far enough during a boom.

ATTITUDES AS CRITERIA

Neither structural alterations nor changes in performance variables occur in a vacuum. Each occurs in a social context. If one chooses, say, to decentralize the personnel function, reception to the decision or to the act of decentralization itself will be affected by such socio-psychological factors as the previous history of the organization, its prevailing culture (for example, whether favorable or hostile to change or experiment), the trust that higher management reposes in juniors, the state of management-worker relations and the current profitability of the business. The decision and the act of decentralization are at the same time communications to the staff which they will interpret in the light of their experiences and preoccupations. These reactions will be partly a result of personal psychological propensities. The social science literature on work groups within larger social settings, on the anchoring of opinion within informal groups and on the role of opinion leaders in mediating between management communications and individual reactions alerts us also to the fact that when plans are announced for organizational change or when the changes begin people will confer with those they trust and esteem to decide on the meaning of these events.[38] And they will react as much to these socially determined meanings as to the events themselves.

Largely because of the importance of attitudes as an intervening factor between organizational change and employee behavior, a number of social scientists have directly studied attitude changes associated with organizational modifications. The usual procedure is to collect information from a representative cross-section of the organization before, during, and after a change, using questionnaires, interviews, or a combination of these. Experienced research workers take great care in the design of the questionnaire so that it will cover attitudes pertinent to all main aspects of the change as understood by the investigator. They know that the cost of systematic use of a predetermined set of questions and topics which will yield comparability is limitation in range and possibly sacrifice of opportunities to take up new subjects discovered during the investigation to be preoccupying respondents.

In a study that illustrates the repeated use of questionnaires to explore attitudes at various phases of an organization's history, Lieberman used a questionnaire repeated three times over three years to measure individual reaction to changes in role.[39] The theoretical proposition he wished to test was that a person's attitude will be influenced by the role he occupies in a social system. In 1951 he gave attitude questionnaires to virtually all the workers, foremen, and shop stewards in a plant. The questions dealt mainly with employees' attitudes toward and perceptions of the company, the union and various aspects of their job situation. Over the next year, twenty-three of the workers surveyed were promoted to foremen and thirty-five workers became shop stewards. In December 1952 the same forms that had been filled out by the rank-and-file workers in 1951 were given to these men (designated the experimental groups) and to two control groups of workers (matched for attitudinal, demographic, and motivational variables) who had not changed their roles. The experimental groups revealed changes in attitudes (with the foremen now more favorable to management than they had been as workers and the shop stewards more favorable to the union than they had been as workers) while the control groups underwent no changes or lesser changes. The changes were greater with the foremen. A question that arises is whether the changed attitudes expressed by the new foremen and new shop stewards were relatively stable or relatively ephemeral, to be held only while the men occupied these new roles. An unusual opportunity arose to test this as, a short time after the 1952 resurvey, a national economic depression ensued, as a result of which many rank-and-file workers were laid off in this factory and a number of foremen were returned to non-supervisory jobs. The researchers took the opportunity to return to the plant and re-administer the questionnaires that had been filled out in 1951 and 1952. By comparing the attitude changes among foremen and shop stewards who had left these roles with the attitude changes that occurred among foremen and shop stewards who remained in these roles, the effects of moving out of these roles could be assessed. The results of this phase of the study showed that foremen who were demoted tended to revert to the attitudes they had previously held while in the worker role, but foremen who remained in the foreman role either maintained the attitudes they had had when they first became foremen or moved even further in that direction. The results among shop stewards were less consistent and clear cut. The investigator concluded that the findings supported the proposition that a person's role will have an impact on his attitudes. The Lieberman study illustrates an effective technique for assessing the attitudinal results of either planned or spontaneous changes during a period of organizational change. But he notes that these findings "still leave unanswered the question of what underlying mechanisms are operating here."

In the study of decentralization of a firm with a chain of supermarkets to which I have referred above (on the question of objectives of change), Lawrence devised a way of measuring the types of behavior change sought by its initiators.[40] He obtained an initial measure of behavior during the early stages of the reorganization effort when the first formal and direct steps had recently been taken (1955) and an "after" measure two years later. Lawrence reasoned that the central element of behavior that was intended to change in the reorganization was the way in which district managers interacted with store managers. The measuring device needed to throw light on such matters as the degree of delegation versus domination at interchanges between the two, the extent to which their meetings were devoted to solving problems, and the degree of balance in the flow of information, opinion, and directions. The characteristics of the organization facilitated systematic observations of interaction. The district manager needed to go to each store separately, see the store manager, and complete his business with him. By accompanying the district manager the investigator could observe interactions in a concentrated form with a minimum of the disturbances that are characteristic, for instance, of factory type situations. Each call by a district manager was also a distinct and complete episode that could be compared with other calls. At each call the observer noted the extent to which either participant raised questions, gave information, expressed opinions, made suggestions or gave directions, introduced small talk or commented on what the other said. In categorizing comments the researcher followed the manifest intent of the speaker rather than either the literal interpretation of his words or the way they were perceived by the hearer. The two men who did field scoring on this project practiced independently scoring the same conversations and comparing results until very nearly identical scoring results were achieved. This enabled them to go further than a descriptive statement of how the men changed and to get a quantitative estimate of the extent to which the behavior of the district managers involved had been brought closer to congruence with the desired model. Similar methods were applied to the relations of selected store managers with their own subordinates.

This study used attitude material as an indicator of change, went beyond attitude material to good descriptive behavior data and systematically sampled and measured an aspect of behavior so central to the planned change that we are obliged to connect it with the change. In this study, there was, however, a two-year break between the first set of observations and the second. The reader misses the description of what happened between 1954–56, being back with the author, so far as this period is concerned, in an area of deduction based on secondhand reports and interpolation. In this respect the study is similar to that of Guest.

A central problem even with the best research in this genre—and I have selected two extremely well-conducted studies—is that of interview effect. The interviewer inevitably enters the social field of the respondent, who, whether deliberately or unwittingly, is prone to organize his responses around what he thinks these should be or what the investigator might want. Additionally, as being interviewed, being observed by a research worker, or being asked to complete questionnaires is not part of the respondent's normal work experience, the interview is, in a sense, part of the change and contaminates the objective character of the enquiry. The usual way of dealing with this is for the investigator either to represent the enquiry as more general in intent than the actual focus of his interest (so as to diffuse the impact of study as such) or to try over a protracted period to get his presence or his questionnaires so accepted as to be taken for granted.

While the research strategy we have just referred to attempts to minimize the disturbance created by interviewer effect, alternative approaches exist that attempt explicitly to bring investigator effect into the design of the study. This has been particularly notable in the work of the Michigan Institute of Social Research and the Tavistock Institute.

A distinctive example of active role-taking by the research worker is the previously discussed study reported by Mann.[41] Mann's work stemmed out of the interests of the Institute of Social Research, Michigan, in learning how to report findings from human relations research into organizations so that they would be understood and used in day-to-day operations. Over a period of two years three sets of data were collected and fed back in an organization; (1) data on the attitudes and perceptions of 8,000 non-supervisory employees towards their work, promotion opportunities, supervision, fellow employees, and so on. (2) data on first- and second-line supervisors' feelings, (3) information from intermediate and top levels of management about their supervisory philosophies, roles in policy formation, and problems of organizational integration. Each superior and his immediate subordinates together considered the survey data pertaining to their own group or the subunits for which they were responsible, helped the research workers and the company personnel department to interpret the data, decided what further analyses should be made to help them form their own plans, and planned the introduction of the findings to the next administrative level. At one phase of the study, Mann and his colleagues matched departments in which feedback programs were operated against control groups where they were not, and found a statistically significant difference in favor of the departments with feedback that indicated its effectiveness.

Mann does not claim specifically that it was his preparedness to report data to the groups from whom it had been collected that enabled him to make repeat studies, to attend discussions of the meaning of the data and to experiment with departments. And it is difficult to prove that his data are better or fuller than those of other research workers who participate less with their respondents. But it would probably be a conservative conclusion to draw that unusually active cooperation from respondents about their reactions to organizational changes was associated with unusual forthcomingness on the part of the researchers.

In the Tavistock studies of organizational change, active participation by the research worker in the change has been a central feature of their approach, which is explicitly designed as "collaborative research" or "action research." One feature of this style of research is that it is taken for granted that the presence of the researcher will in itself affect the field of study—that the investigator is himself part of the field under scrutiny. Attempts are made by the investigator to elucidate the character of the disturbance and to relate to current preoccupations the ways in which respondents react to his presence. The investigator interprets the reaction to him. He does not necessarily voice these interpretations to his respondents but treats her reactions and what he considers to be the meanings of their reactions as primary sources of data. A second, connected feature of this style of research as it has in the past been practiced by the Tavistock investigators has been that the investigator has often actually given concrete help to the organization making the changes. The research worker has offered the prospect of help in exchange for the research opportunity, on the assumption that this will give him access to confidences from which investigators working on a more academic model might be barred.

Apart from the advisory or action component, in which they go further than other investigators, the Tavistock workers have usually maintained unusually close contact with their respondents (or action-research partners) over extended time periods. The Tavistock studies have been particularly revealing of emotional difficulties associated with the implementation of change, and the research workers involved would claim that this is connected with the professional responsibility taken for feedback and advice as well as with the intensity of contact. A number of Tavistock studies have attempted quantitative assessment of organizational change. But controlled experiments or quantitative assessments of attitude change have not been so prominent a feature of published Tavistock work as that of the Michigan Institute.

Dilemmas of Assessment

It is apparent that many types of information are useful for those who seek to assess change. But it requires considerable care, experience, and research ingenuity before one can be satisfied that the information genuinely reflects phenomena at the heart of continued successful organizational functioning.

A variety of approaches exist for the assessment of change, each with its own characteristic strengths and weaknesses. To take the defects alone, quantitative questionnaire methods can yield little more than was in the minds of the investigators before they were administered; they cannot tell how event X leads to event Y; and they lack flexibility, debarring the interviewer from switching to new topics which are found to matter more to respondents and exposing the study to the risk that respondents will become

bored and their responses perfunctory. The results of quantitative questionnaire investigations appear to yield general relationships more than
insights. On the other hand, more intensive observational studies, derived
in style from work in anthropology and clinical psychology, are highly
susceptible to variations in the skills and personality of the field investigator,
and do not yield the objectified or measurable data comparable with that
in other fields. On the positive side the questionnaire type investigations
yield hard, objective data familiar to those working with material objects
and the intensive studies can yield insights of considerable complexity and
subtlety. While a sound research design might ideally combine these two
approaches, this is rarely easy to arrange because of temperamental differences between investigators (or managers) attracted to one or other
approach, and because of the expense involved in doing what appears to
be the same exercise in two different ways. Clearly, the choice between
methods or the emphasis given within a research design to one component
rather than another will also depend largely on the central preoccupation
of the management seeking to assess a change, for example, whether they
are primarily interested in whether a change has in fact occurred, or in how
a change is working itself out in the organization, or in how long any
present change is likely to last.

A dilemma exists for external research workers who wish to study organizational change in that, if their study is to be more than superficial, they
need intimate access to their data and it is virtually impossible for them to
obtain that access without affecting the data. Light involvement may make
the data more objective because respondents are less influenced by the
research worker. On the other hand, where the research worker involves
himself closely with respondents he may learn much more about their responses to change but remain uncertain about the effect on them of this
involvement or of the way they would have behaved had he been less close
to them.

A first-class research design must take into account the fact that an
organizational change is a social process, not a discrete once and for all
act. If it is decided, for instance, that a management training scheme is to
be introduced, what is a decision in principle at one level becomes operational at the next and some new emphases, new considerations, new slants
are introduced as the preoccupation of each level and the personalities
involved manifest themselves. The same sort of modification to the program ensues as the scheme is put into operation, sometimes so much so
that the style of execution contradicts the originally defined object of the
exercise. This may be because the executives involved are modifying the
scheme to suit their own ends or because the original plans are really being
found ineffective in practice. Whatever the reason, a scheme decided in
January is a very different one from that being operated by June and it is
highly doubtful what an assessment operation carried out in October will

be measuring—the wisdom of the original decision, the way it is being carried out (with all its ambivalences and modifications), the determination of the personnel department, the intractibility of the market for trainees, or the capacity of lower levels of the organization to redesign the briefs given them by their bosses. The thorough assessment of organizational change requires close acquaintance with a whole succession of events as they unfold. An organizational change can rarely be sufficiently understood through the abstraction of a small number of discrete variables from the complex sequence of interrelated and overlapping events, emotions, atmospheres, and personalities in practice involved.

Where it is desired to assess the success or failure of an organizational change an attempt should be made to build the change into an experimental design. It should be possible to compare one situation or working unit where the change has been attempted with other similar situations which have not been similarly altered, so that a reasonably clear indication can be obtained of the relative efficacies of different types of policy. Apart from the decisiveness of the results that experiments can yield, they force the initiators of change to specify in some detail the effects they are trying to secure, the means that are being adopted and the way these are thought to relate to each other. The use of experimental methods requires, however, a very considerable participation by social scientists in the internal affairs of organizations and much closer and larger scale collaboration with practicing managers than has so far been common.

NOTES

1. This Chapter is adapted from P. Spencer and C. Sofer, "Organizational Change and its Management," *Journal of Management Studies,* 1, no. 1 (March 1964) and C. Sofer, "The Assessment of Organizational Change," *Journal of Management Studies,* 1, no. 2 (September 1964).

2. D. McGregor, *The Human Side of Enterprise* (New York: McGraw-Hill, 1960).

3. C. Argyris, *Understanding Organizational Behaviour* (Homewood, Illinois: Dorsey Press, 1960).

4. A. W. Gouldner, *Patterns of Industrial Bureaucracy* (London: Routledge and Kegan Paul, 1955).

5. H. A. Shepard and R. R. Blake, "Changing Behaviour Through Cognitive Change," *Human Organization* (Special Issue 1962): 88–96.

6. P. M. Blau, *Dynamics of Bureaucracy* (Chicago: University of Chicago Press, 1955).

7. K. Lewin, "Frontiers of Group Dynamics," *Human Relations,* 1, no. 1 (June 1947): 5–41, p. 35.

8. C. Sofer and G. J. Hutton, *New Ways in Management Training* (London: Tavistock, 1958).

9. L. Broom and P. Selznick, *Sociology* (New York: Row Peterson and Co., 3rd ed., 1963), p. 244.

10. C. Sofer illustrates this in a study of British hospitals after nationalization, "Reactions to Administrative Change, A Study of Staff Relations in Three British Hospitals," *Human Relations,* 8, no. 3 (August 1960): 291–316.

11. See I. E. P. Menzies, "A Case Study in the Functioning of Social Systems as a Defence Against Anxiety," *Human Relations,* 13, no. 2 (May 1960): 95–122.

12. For a detailed account of this see A. D. Chandler, Jr., *Strategy and Structure, Chapters in The History of the Industrial Enterprise* (Cambridge, Massachusetts: M.I.T. Press Research Monographs, 1962).

13. These two tendencies are noted by R. Michels in his *Political Parties* (New York: Crowell, 1962).

14. H. Baker and R. R. France, *Centralization and Decentralization in Industrial Relations* (Princeton, New Jersey: Princeton University Press, 1954).

15. E. Ginzberg and E. W. Reilley, *Effecting Change in Large Organization* (New York: Columbia University Press, 1957).

16. P. Selznick, *Leadership and Administration* (Evanston, Illinois: Row, Peterson, 1957).

17. T. Burns and G. M. Stalker, *The Management of Innovation* (London: Tavistock, 1961).

18. Menzies, "A Case Study."

19. Sofer, *Reactions to Administrative Change.*

20. E. Jaques, *The Changing Culture of a Factory* (London: Tavistock, 1951).

21. T. S. Simey, ed., *The Dock Worker* (Liverpool: Liverpool University Press, 1954).

22. See Baker and France, *Centralization.*

23. P. Selznick, *T.V.A. and the Grass Roots* (Berkeley: University of California Press, 1949).

24. Jaques, *The Changing Culture.*

25. E. J. Miller, *Designing and Building a New Organization,* paper read to the British Association for the Advancement of Science, September 1962.

26. Sofer, "Reactions to Administrative Change."

27. F. C. Mann and F. W. Neff, *Managing Major Change for Organizations* (Ann Arbor: Foundation for Research on Human Behaviour, 1961).

28. M. Crozier, *The Bureaucratic Phenomenon* (London: Tavistock, 1964).

29. L. Coch and J. R. P. French, "Overcoming Resistance to Change," *Human Relations,* 1 (1948).

30. G. Strauss, "The Set Up Man: A Case Study of Organizational Change," *Human Organization,* 13, no. 2 (Summer 1954): 17–25.

31. A. K. Rice, *Productivity and Social Organization* (London: Tavistock, 1958).

32. P. R. Lawrence, *The Changing of Organizational Behaviour Patterns: A Case Study of Decentralization* (Boston: Harvard University Graduate School of Business Administration, 1958), p. 3.

33. N. Morse and E. Reimer, "The Experimental Change of a Major Organizational Variable," *Journal of Abnormal and Social Psychology,* 52, no. 1 (1956): 120–129.

34. See C. R. Walker, *Towards the Automatic Factory* (New Haven: Yale University Press, 1957).

35. L. Strauss in W. F. Whyte, *Money and Motivation* (New York, Harper, 1955), pp. 95 and 96.

36. See for instance Coch and French, "Overcoming Resistance"; A. S. H. Sykes, "The Effect of a Supervisory Training Course in Changing Supervisors' Perceptions

and Expectations of the Role of Managements," *Human Relations,* 15, no. 3 (1962); Rice, *Productivity* (1958).

37. R. H. Guest, *Organizational Change* (Homewood, Illinois: Dorsey Press, Irwin, 1962).

38. See for instance, M. Sherif, *The Psychology of Social Norms* (New York: Harper, 1936); L. R. Sayles, "Work Group Behaviour and The Larger Organization," in C. M. Arensberg, S. Barkin, W. E. Chalmers, H. L. Wilensky, J. C. Worthy, B. B. Dennis, *Research in Industrial Human Relations* (New York: Harper, 1957); E. Katz and P. Lazarsfeld. *Personal Influence* (Glencoe, Illinois: The Free Press, 1955).

39. S. Lieberman, "The Effects of Changes in Roles on the Attitudes of Role Occupants," *Human Relations,* 9, no. 4 (1956): 385–402.

40. Lawrence, *The Changing of Organizational Behaviour Patterns.*

41. F. C. Mann in C. M. Arensberg et al (1957).

17 : Conflicts between Management and Workers

INDUSTRIAL organizations are systems of collaboration, associations of persons who contract to contribute a proportion of their effort to a collective endeavor too large for any one person to carry out on his own. Apart from the active collaboration of the persons who do the day-to-day work of the organization, others are collaborating in the organization by investing funds in it. Stability of the cooperative system is normally maintained by the fact that participants receive monetary and other returns, rewards, and gratifications (including personal and social gratifications) that act as inducements for them to continue their contributions. From the point of view of the maintenance of this flow of inducements—and the possibility of their increase—it is clearly desirable for all parties that the organization should function continuously and effectively. Contemporary organizations are nevertheless characterized by a high incidence of various forms of conflict.

The term "conflict" is used in this chapter to refer to that behavior of organization members which is expended in opposition to other members. Conflict is closely related to, and often follows from, competition, but they are analytically distinct from each other.[1] When we speak of two parties competing with each other we mean that if one gains the desideratum both want, the other cannot have it: nothing is thereby implied about their behavior toward each other. Where they are in conflict they directly oppose each other.

We are adopting for purposes of our discussion the definition of conflict suggested by Coser in the tradition of Simmel, Von Wiese, Park, and Burgess:

A struggle over values or claims to status, power and scarce resources, in which the aims of the conflicting parties are not only to gain the desired values but also to neutralize, injure or eliminate their rivals.[2]

We shall also be helped by keeping in mind Coser's distinction between those conflicts that take place "within the basic social consensus" and those that exceed or threaten the limits of that consensus, that is, challenge the very social order within which the parties interact. The former type of conflict can lead to adjustments between the parties and hence to a closer integration of a society (or part of a society) in the sense of bringing behavior, opportunities, rights, and rewards more closely in line with basic, shared social values. But the latter attacks the basic assumptions of collective existence and can split the society into warring camps.

Forms of Conflict

Strikes are the most conspicuous, overt, and dramatic instances of opposition and attempts at damage: they involve face to face confrontations between declared antagonists, they often involve bitter statements of opinion, and they usually represent organized opposition and the organized use of power. Moreover, they seem, at least at first sight, to highlight contrasts in our society between members of different social classes, people with different education, those who tell others what to do and those who are told, managers and workers. But strikes are only one form of organized group conflict between owners and managers on the one hand and workers on the other. Nor are organized conflicts necessarily the most frequent or damaging.

As Kornhauser, Dubin, and Ross have pointed out, vertical conflicts in industry include several other manifestations apart from strikes.[3] Some are like strikes in that they are organized and intergroup affairs. These include lockouts, work limitations, and deliberate slowdowns. Others are less organized, more spontaneous, and sometimes individually-based rather than group-based. These include withholding of effort, waste, inefficiency, labor turnover and absenteeism and, from the management side, overstrict discipline and discriminatory dismissals. The groups and individuals engaged in such activities have roles and platforms outside the organization or industry where they can also pursue their organizational/industrial interests —in trade unions, the press and political parties, and so on. Because of this it is often unduly limiting to study vertical (or other) organizational conflicts solely in organizational terms, as if the persons concerned were isolated from their environments. Each country has its uniquely interwoven pattern between individuals, work organizations, local communities, labor and employer groupings, and government, and this helps to determine the locale and form of industrial conflict.

The two main manifestations of vertical conflict studied by social scientists have been strikes and restriction of output.

Strikes have been defined as collective action in formal organizations by lower level members of those organizations who try to wrest certain advantages from higher level decision makers through suspending their usual tasks or through violence.[4]

The goals of a strike are often multiple. They may succeed each other in the course of time and the different parties may define them differently. Among the immediate reasons given out in modern times for strike action and threats of strikes are (1) a feeling among workers that wages are inadequate or unfair, (2) instability and irregularity in employment, (3) arbitrary and capricious behavior by managements,(4) dissatisfaction with workloads, workshop conditions, hours and fringe benefits (5) felt inadequacy in employee status. Social scientists have suggested that strikes apparently caused by such disputes are often contributed to, or compounded by, other factors, and that wage demands and other objective conditions are merely a rallying cry. These other factors refer to expression or displacement of class warfare, breakdown of primary groups among workers, a need by the workers to express their autonomy, or deprivations of one sort or another on the job. Whatever the precise relations and relative weight of overt causes of strikes and emotional factors or those diagnosed as lying deeper, there is no doubt that workers' deprivations or felt deprivations furnish a reservoir of feeling and emotion that becomes salient at times of disputes. At times these become central, perhaps especially when some change is experienced as a sharp and unfavorable contrast with a previous situation or when performance does not match promises.[5]

An important stream of sociological research has dealt with restriction of output in industrial firms.[6] The first major study of organized restriction of output was the Hawthorne researches. Among other things, the Bank Wiring Observation Room part of this study drew attention to the systematic restriction by a group of colleagues of the number of units produced every day according to an elaborate set of rules. They maintained a straight-line output somewhat below that of which they were capable. There were also systematic procedures among these colleagues for rewarding and punishing those who did not adhere to the production norm. Social and to some extent physical pressures were exerted both against "ratebusters" and "chiselers." The research workers attributed this behavior mainly to what they saw as a conflict between the technical and social organization of the plant, to inadequate communication between management and workers, and to the imposition of changes that deprived the workers of things that gave meaning and significance to their work. In an important British example of such a study Lupton compared two firms—Wye, in which there existed little or no restriction of production, and Jay's, where there was a significant amount of restriction of production.[7] He took more account than Roethlisberger and Dickson of causal factors in restriction of production external to the firm. Lupton came to the conclusion that among the decisive factors were several economic variables and that restriction tended to occur where the market was stable and large: competition was weak between the individual companies in the industry and they colluded on prices; the industry was dominated by a small number of large firms; there was a large, nationally organized and powerful trade union; labor costs were low; the products were capital goods; and a complicated bonus system existed.

Causes of
Management-Worker Conflict

From this point we are not limiting ourselves to strikes or to any particular form of conflict, organized, unorganized, overt, or covert, but follow Kornhauser, Dubin, and Ross in regarding as our object of study "the total range of behavior and attitudes that express opposition and divergent orientations between industrial owners and managers on the one hand and working people and their organizations on the other hand." [8]

Analyses of causal factors in management-worker conflicts have varied considerably in their emphases. We discuss the main categories of explanation below. The main causes discussed have variously emphasized:

personality traits
conflict of economic interests
class conflict
cultural forces
status and power cleavages within the organization
the (alienating) nature of the work environment, the task, and the work process
the effect of isolation on particular groups of workers
psycho-social factors in conflict
conflict between technical and social organization

PERSONALITY TRAITS

One obvious possibility in management-worker conflicts, as in others, is that these are matters of personality and personality clashes. A workers' leader in an industry or in a firm may be particularly militant or the head of an employers' association particularly intransigent, or both contingencies may occur together. Some people are driven more than others by their own personality problems and needs to behave in an aggressive, antagonistic, or militant fashion. They may be liable to create trouble and conflict wherever they are situated. There is a prima facie likelihood that persons whose character inclines them toward a fighting posture against others will gravitate to roles that suit them. A combination of contest-centered person and conflict-concerned role may certainly aggravate and sometimes precipitate strains and crises in working relations.

But there are serious shortcomings in this type of argument. Leadership of either a workers' group or a managerial group requires a capacity for cooperation, mediation, compromise, and negotiation both within one's own group and in transactions with others. Aggressiveness may from time to time be very important but it is by no means essential to the continued exercise of the role functions and may sometimes be a decided handicap. An incapacity to work with others is likely to be detected in the course of a sustained career and to militate against promotion to positions involving responsibility. In addition, the inception and maintenance of an intergroup dispute normally requires shared beliefs and interests on both sides; it is almost inconceivable, for instance, that a strike, lockout, or go-slow could occur if only a workers' leader were inflamed or only a manager or if the only issue were the fact that they did not get on with each other. Both would need colleagues and support.

People do not normally make trouble unless they are themselves troubled by something.[9] In the case of persons in positions of responsibility, the causes of the trouble are typically associated with the nature of their responsibilities. They are likely to be associated with stresses embedded in their roles and relationships and with the representative functions which they have for groups of colleagues. In looking for causes of persisting trouble between managements and workers we will be helped by looking beyond personalities to issues of social situation, social structure and social and economic processes.

CONFLICT OF ECONOMIC INTEREST

Industrial conflict is often represented as basically a struggle between two organized groups competing for their share of a joint product. Conflict can apparently be just as great when the amount fought over is small as when it is great. It can be greater in times of economic security, high production and earnings because the common need to stay in business and keep jobs has already been secured. At least in the short term there is a distinct clash of economic interests in that what is a reward to one side is a cost to the other. Whether management-worker interests are objectively in conflict becomes less clear-cut when a longer time period is considered. Both groups share an interest in the viability of the firm and to that extent their interests coincide. Again, management is interested in higher production as a way of reducing the ratio of cost to output and thereby improving the firm's financial and competitive position. In an expanding market this makes possible the expansion of the company, increased wages, more opportunities for promotion, a larger labor force, and general prosperity both for the business and its employees. But the economic case that interests coincide may not be attractive or convincing to workers, especially when the market is not expanding and demand is near constant or declining. In these circumstances, higher productivity per worker means that fewer are required for the same level of output or that fewer paid hours are worked by the same number of workers. In either of these cases, many workers may lose rather than gain from the increase in productivity.

Some discussions treat management as equivalent with, or representative of, the owners of the enterprise. In fact, management of large industrial enterprises usually consists of "professionals" with no or minimal share-ownership. They mediate between shareholders, government, financiers, suppliers, customers, and employees and, in so doing, they must on some occasions act primarily in the economic interests of constituents other than employees.

Recent discussion even among labor leaders has nevertheless emphasized the identity or complementarity of management-worker economic interests as perceived by trade union leaders. Mr. George Meany, president of the AFL-CIO,[10] recently argued that

where you have a well-established industry and a well-established union, you are getting more and more to the point where a strike doesn't make sense . . . Our members are basically Americans, they basically believe in the American system and maybe they have a greater stake in the system now than they had 15 or 20 years ago because under the system and under our trade union policy, they have become middle class.

They have a greater stake. You can be quite radical if you were involved in a labor dispute where people are getting 30 cents an hour because, if you pull an honest strike, all you lose is 30 cents an hour.[11]

In the same vein, a leading newspaper has commented on Mr. Leonard Woodcock, new president of the United Automobile Workers Union of America, that he

is far too perceptive a man to carry on a vendetta against General Motors. He knows his economics . . . , he knows the state of the U.S. car industry, and he knows that his function is to protect the interests of his members, not to drive General Motors to its knees.[12]

Herbert Marcuse has argued that skilled workers, if they wished,

could disrupt, reorganise and redirect the mode and relationships of production. However, they have neither the interest nor the vital need to do so; they are well integrated and well rewarded.[13]

Summarizing a series of observations of this general type, A. Beichman has concluded that

workers in Western industrial countries are enjoying job security, rising wages, increasing educational opportunities for their children, decent housing, and demonstrating a stubborn resistance to any and all invitations to bring the house down on all of us.[14]

These spokesmen and commentators are not denying that any conflict of economic interest exists. They are implying that, in their view, it is more advantageous (or felt to be more advantageous) for most groups of industrial workers in western Europe, most of the time, to pursue their economic interests within the existing institutional set-up rather than to attempt to disrupt ongoing economic units, to challenge the system frontally, or to try to overthrow it. The focus of management-worker conflict has in any case been displaced from the local shop-floor to the bargaining table where negotiation, bargaining, and diplomacy become the order of the day.

CLASS CONFLICT

The Marxist thesis is that the worker is alienated from the organization and from the industrial system of which it is part by the nature of his position in society: this separates him from ownership of the means of production and from ownership of the product of his work and compels him to sell his labor as a commodity. Even strong opponents of the Marxists viewpoint accept the view that a barrier to cooperation arises from the individual laborer's felt inequality in bargaining. Each worker is likely to be in touch with fewer potential employers than if the same labor force were spread over a large number of smaller firms. The worker's alternative possibility, of setting up in trade for himself, will amount to little when the existing firms have great amounts of capital.

Marx was suggesting that a basic social schism existed because of the differentiation between such a category of the population and a bourgeoisie or set of capitalists who owned the means of production and in whose interests it was to extract as much work as possible for as little pay as possible.

It is difficult to recognize this pattern in the present social context.[15] Our social structure has proved too complex to allow a division of interests and loyalties into only two camps. Power has been dispersed through the checks and balances of a pluralistic society. The equality of men before the law and in the franchise and the extension of educational opportunity have mitigated the inequalities of working life. A rise in standards of living has reduced contrasts in the incomes of men in different occupations. In the field of industrial relations proper there has been a growth of combinations and an increase in the power of working groups as collectivities. With these there has been a development of worker influence, negotiation, and economic power that has greatly attenuated the ability of individual employers to act in an exploitative way or one that pays low regard to worker interest. This has been accompanied by a growth in government preparedness to intervene in management-worker relations. There has been a rise in sheer humanitarian feeling for the industrial employee, coupled with a growing feeling that satisfaction in the job is associated with improved performance. The labor market has been dominated in recent decades by extensions in demand, and the government has accepted full employment as an objective. There has been a dispersion in ownership of capital assets and a separation of ownership from the control of industry, so that there is no longer a clear-cut class of owners and a clear-cut class of employees. Most of the people who run industry today are themselves also basically employees selling their labor as does the wage-earner.

Many students of industrial relations argue that the major industrial conflicts have now been largely removed from the workers' immediate social world.[16] This is said to be associated with the rise of nation-wide bargaining, the greater variety of workers, the complexity and technicalities of collective bargaining agreements, and the inevitable professionalization of negotiations over wages and conditions of service. Wider-spread prosperity and increased state provision appear to have removed much of the impetus of the labor movement. It is argued that political ideology is no longer important and that the worker's mentality has shifted from "collective idealism" to "individual realism," sometimes referred to as "privatization." The implication is that felt differences in political category are unlikely to be an active element today in conflicts between particular groups of managers and their own employees.

In discussions of the class position of the industrial worker, a major current controversy in the sociological literature has centered around the proposition (often referred to as the *embourgeoisement* thesis) that, as a result of a postwar rise in income, large numbers of manual workers are now effectively middle class.[17] This proposition has been contested by two British sociologists, J. H. Goldthorpe and D. Lockwood, first in a theoretical paper [18] and then an empirical study of highly paid automobile workers reported in an "Affluent Worker" series.[19] The work situation, work experience and work attitudes of their respondents could not be described as similar to those which we identify with the middle class. Unlike middle-class workers, these men worked shifts, worked long hours, gained little satisfaction directly from their jobs, and accepted monotony, speed, and fragmentation of their tasks for the sake of high rewards: they viewed their work in an instrumental manner. Few saw their work place as a source of friends or were interested in developing personal relationships with their supervisors or in reducing status-connected barriers at work. Two-thirds of the blue-collar couples with a husband in the sample had no friends in white-collar jobs and three-quarters had none who were not relatives. Unlike middle class families, those studied by Lockwood, Goldthorpe and their colleagues were not particularly concerned to restrict the size of their families. They were certainly interested in acquiring the consumer durables we associate with middle-class standards of living but did not evince a wide range of middle-class attitudes or aspire to be classified as middle class. The authors suggest that these affluent workers reveal a pattern of industrial life which will become far more widespread in the near future.

Reservations can be expressed about both the embourgeoisement thesis and the Goldthorpe/Lockwood refutation. There are many complexities in definition and categorization and many problems in the way of securing representative samples for comparison among occupational, familial, and community subcultures. But the debate implies that, however accommodated Western industrial workers may be to existing social and economic institutions, some important segments of the working population are going to feel their interests best represented by bargaining for high wages in their current type of work, rather than seeking to rise by spiraling their way up through the occupational and class systems.

On the issue of political cleavage as a factor in industrial conflict, recent observers have also been struck by the apparent refusal of industrial workers to identify themselves with dissident groups seeking to overthrow existing economic and political institutions. While the other dissident groups —notably radical students—express their prime interest as revolutionary changes in our methods of production and distribution, the industrial workers appear to defend these. Commentators have cited the recent rejection by American mailmen of the expressed wish of radical students to help them; hostility of workers toward radical students in the London School of Economics troubles; and the refusal of workers to identify themselves with the student movement in the May 1968 "Revolution" in Paris. One reason appears to be the vested interests already mentioned in our discussion of conflict of economic interests. As a writer in the *Sunday Times* (London) put it, vividly if crudely, "the S.D.S. effort to enlist industrial workers has failed so far. They are too fat and conservative." [20] More widely, Beichman has argued in the *Encounter* article already cited, that

the utopian promise is always that things will be *better* for them but the industrial worker has as always grasped with a fine sociological instinct that the revolutionary programme actually means that the average man will not have it better but *worse*.[21]

CULTURAL FORCES

B. Roberts has effectively drawn attention to the importance of "background" national settings in the comparisons he makes between the character of industrial relations in England and the United States. He says that it is commonplace for visitors to America from European countries to remark on the apparently much less friendly relations between unions and management in the United States. They are astonished at the virulent criticism that is expressed during industrial disputes, at the apparent readiness of unions and employers to ignore all other interests but their own. His explanation is:

The turbulent history of America is naturally one of the primary reasons why the relations between unions and employers are manifestly more hostile than in Europe. Industrial relations are an expression of the character of a society and they reflect its principal features. The dynamic growth of America was brought about by those elements from the older civilisation of Europe who had been limited by the bonds of social structure, which made for stable but miserable and frustrating conditions, throwing off these constraints in the New World. A new life could be won only by an aggressive, ruthless determination to succeed. Not surprisingly, industrial relations were bloody. Employers who had built vast enterprises by vigorous, driving ability were hardly likely to take kindly to attempts by unions to limit their freedom to hire and fire, and to give orders and have them executed without question. Except in the settled conditions of the older eastern seaboard towns where the pattern of life and the character of industry and trade closely resembled that of Europe, the unions had to fight grimly for the right to organise. . . .[22]

Roberts goes on to point out that the nature of industrial strife in Britain and the United States is markedly different. Strikes in the United States are mainly associated with changes in management-work contracts which the unions would like made. Strikes in Britain occur mainly over the interpretation and execution of agreements. Since American industrial agreements, unlike British, are binding in law, an American union striking in this manner might find itself facing legal action for damages.

In analyzing causes of strikes it is important to realize that the social and economic environment of an industry, the history of workers' movements and management-worker relations, and the legal framework that has evolved to handle collaboration and conflict are important determinants of the frequency, intensity, and form of industrial conflict.

STATUS AND POWER CLEAVAGES
WITHIN THE ORGANIZATION

This approach deals with the distribution of status and power in the workplace as distinct from the distribution of status and power in society.

The dichotomous arrangement of personnel into labor and management, those who work with their hands and those who work with their heads, can result in the division of the organization into status groups that see themselves as distinct. This point merges with class conflict, since one has here, within the organization, a compounding of social class and internal power differentials that may reinforce each other.

It has been suggested that a basic strain in the employee-employer relationship derives from the fact that the former must put himself under the employer's or the manager's orders.[23] There have to be rules in the workplace and rules must have sanctions, so that the worker, in taking a job, puts himself under the discipline of others. Despite the fact that employees have, by joining the organization, accepted the principle that others shall have authority over them, there seems to be a resistance against the notion of being controlled, of yielding autonomy and self-direction to another. Whatever they say or agree to, most people feel constricted when others are in charge of them.

In a well-known paper, C. Argyris has suggested a collision between personality needs and the manner in which many large organizations are run.[24] This theory is set out by Argyris as follows: Ideally, healthy development in our culture involves growth from being passive as an infant to being active as an adult; from being dependent to being relatively independent; from being in a subordinate position to achieving equal or higher position than friends achieve; from expressing few and shallow abilities to expressing many and deeper abilities. If formal organization is defined by the use of such principles as task specialization, unity of direction, chain of command, and span of control, then employees work in a situation in which they tend to be dependent, subordinate, and passive to a leader. This type of situation may create frustration, conflict, and failure for the employee. He may react by regressing, decreasing his efficiency and creating informal systems against management.

Although Argyris says that he is contrasting two simplified "ideal models," he often writes as if organizations are really like the formal theoretical model. In fact empirical research on actual behavior has shown repeatedly that persisting organizations arrive at an accommodated, institutionalized state for accomplishing both their economic and human purposes and do not necessarily cut across human needs so sharply. One has also to remember that a proportion of the organization's members have careers in which they can experience the growth which he mentions as a personality need. In addition many people may be dependent in personality and be quite content to do as they are told and to work under the protection of persons whom they consider more powerful than themselves. At the same time, we must acknowledge that there may often be a clash between personality needs for growth, spontaneity, self-regulation, variety, association, and the central sorts of control commonly imposed by large organizations.

A specific aspect of superior-subordinate relations that has received attention in the literature is dislike of close supervision.[25] This induces paranoid feelings, runs counter to one's notion of oneself as an independent, reliable adult who has entered a contract he has every intention of honoring, conveys that one is untrustworthy and likely to default on one's obligations, and runs contrary to the dominant democratic ethic of our society. In other words, one aspect of many control systems is the number of implicitly negative communications they contain for the worker in regard to his value as a person, the contributions he makes, his motivations, the value of work in itself, and the attitude management expects him to take to his work.

The need to maintain or gain autonomy may explain the apparent paradox that when incentive schemes are introduced to encourage workers to produce to fuller capacity this sometimes results in them using the opportunity instead to produce less. They prefer to use part of their time for their own purpose. Collins, Dalton, and Roy brought this fact out in their comparison of several groups of men who worked at well under what management considered their capacity when given the opportunity to produce and earn more under an incentive scheme linked with bonus payments.

To these men piecework meant greater freedom to dispose of their work time as they pleased in the face of a society-wide tendency to routinise and standardise worker activities.[26]

Controlling his contribution to the organization appears to give the worker some feeling of power as opposed to that of his managers. As one of Roy's fellow workers put it graphically in addressing himself to supervisors, "What you want and what you are going to get are two different things." [27]

Bureaucratic systems of administration legitimate the unequal distribution of power on the grounds that authority is matched by competence and expertise. But, as they actually operate, such systems tend to foster cleavages and power struggles along status lines. One important reason for this has been pointed out by Gouldner.[28] While it is true, he says, that large-scale organizations make careful attempts to organize on rational grounds, the source of most of the rules and procedures is not the people who must carry them out. Secondly, he says, the rules and procedures may be rational for the organization as a whole, and for the suppliers of capital, or shareholders, or even the ranks of management, but it does not necessarily follow that these are rational in terms of the goals of all the subgroups in the organization. Or at any rate, even if they are rational for them they may not perceive them as such.

Crozier has pointed out the divisive consequences of the fact that bureaucracies institutionalize social distance between juniors and the more senior ranks.[29] While the purpose of this is to help the seniors maintain objectivity and independence in decisions involving the lower ranks, it also suggests to the latter that nobody is interested in them except other people at the same level.

ALIENATING NATURE OF TASK
AND WORK ENVIRONMENT

The essential argument here is that the modern organization of production strips work of its meaning for the shopfloor worker and that this leads to apathy toward the organization or provides a basis for active dissatisfaction and conflict. It is suggested that work is often so subdivided and the productive process so fragmented that each worker's labor becomes repetitive and monotonous. The worker has little conception of the work process considered as a whole and his contributions to it are meaningless to him. It has been pointed out by Baldamus and others that certain jobs deprive the worker of the opportunity to work to a natural, personal rhythm.[30] One feature brought out by Walker and Guest in their study of automobile workers was that there were virtually no social groups on the job; another that workers felt dominated by the pace of the machine (assembly belt) which they came to define as their enemy.[31] A strain was said to exist because the worker had to adjust to the pace of another, in particular to the pace of a nonhuman object. Friedmann comments on the technical nature of the environment, the lack of response of the technical environment to the worker, and the lack of interaction between the worker and his technical environment.[32] He describes "de-skilling" connected with the declining necessity for the worker to have specialist knowledge of the material with which he is working (leather, wood, glass, etc.). Anyone, he says, can acquire enough knowledge of the materials and what has to be done with them to operate the process after a training involving only months or weeks. Knowledge of the machines is also unnecessary: this is supplied by specialist mechanics, setters, and technical foremen. Lack of opportunity to complete whole tasks is said to create a "Zeigarnick effect" —that is, a feeling of tension because the effort lacks opportunity for completion. The impact, it is said, is that the worker gets none of the satisfactions of problem solving or pride in the job. There is little possibility of satisfaction, let alone pleasure, in getting the work done.

In a well-known work that brings together a good deal of the previous research in this field,[33] Robert Blauner distinguishes four types of alienation often experienced by manual workers in industry. (He alternatively calls these four dimensions of alienation.) What these have in common, he says, is the notion of fragmentation in man's existence and consciousness which impedes the wholeness of experience and activity. What distinguishes the separate dimensions is that they are based on different principles of division or fragmentation. Each alienated state makes it more probable that the person (or worker) "can be used as a thing."

Powerlessness: A person is powerless when he is an object controlled and manipulated by others or by an impersonal system and when he cannot assert himself to change or modify this domination.

Meaninglessness: Individual roles are not seen as fitting into the total system of goals of the organization but are severed from any organic connection with the whole. One's role is so specialised that one is just a "cog" in the organization. One's individual acts seem to have no relation to a broader life-programme.

Isolation: The feeling of being in, but not of, society, a sense of remoteness from the larger social order, an absence of loyalty to intermediate collectivities. Isolation from a community or network of personal relations which would inhibit impersonal treatment.

Self-estrangement: Occupation is not experienced as contributing in an affirmative manner to personal identity and selfhood, but instead is damaging to self-esteem. Activity becomes a means to an end, rather than a fulfilling end, work is monotonous, awareness of time is high between present engagements and future considerations. Work life is separated from other concerns.

Blauner compared four factory industries—printing, textiles, automobiles, and chemicals—and came to this conclusion:

The industry a man works in is *fateful* because the conditions of work and existence in different industrial environments are quite different . . . an employee's industry decides the nature of the work he performs eight hours a day and affects the meaning which that work has for him. It greatly influences the extent to which he is free in his work life and the extent to which he is controlled by technology or supervision. It also influences his opportunity for personal growth and development—to learn, to advance, to take on responsibility.[34]

Looking at alienation in the factory in historical perspective, he suggests that industrialization caused this phenomenon to increase, culminating in the assembly-line industries of the twentieth century. In automotive production, for example, the combination of technological, organizational, and economic factors had resulted in the simultaneous intensification of all the dimensions of alienation listed. But Blauner concludes that new automated technologies may halt or reverse this process.

A capital-intensive cost structure means that heightened efficiency, increased output and higher profits can more easily be attained by exploitation of industry rather than the exploitation of the worker. . . . The economic basis of automated technology allows a more enlightened management to view the workers as human beings, as partners in a collective enterprise, who, because of their responsibilities for expensive machinery and processes, must be considered in terms of their own needs and rights. . . .

With automated industry there is a counter-trend, one that we can fortunately expect to become even more important in the future . . . automation increases the worker's control over his work process and checks the further division of labour and growth of large factories. The result is meaningful work in a more cohesive, integrated industrial climate.[35]

Again a qualifying statement comes from Goldthorpe, Lockwood, and their colleagues,[36] who gives less weight to the effects of technology in determining attitudes to work and the structure of work relationships. They emphasize rather changes in working-class life outside work and within the family. They suggest that the working-class conjugal family is assuming a more companionate form and that relations between husband and wife and parents and children are becoming intrinsically more rewarding. Their prediction is therefore that workers without special occupational skills or responsibilities will not regard their workplaces as a milieu in which they are in search of satisfactions of the kind described by Blauner but will increase pressure on their employing organizations for higher economic returns to pursue familial ends. They add that the possibilities of workers' identification with and commitment to their employing enterprises are likely in any case to be reduced by increases in the scale and bureaucratization of industrial enterprises—forms of rationalization that are partly independent of technological change. They expect greater aggressiveness in the field of cash-based bargaining.

THE "ISOLATED MASS" HYPOTHESIS

Kerr and Siegel examined differences between industries on a cross-national basis in regard to their propensity to strike, sought an explanation for these differences, and compared the facts they collected with certain standard theories of management-worker conflict.[37] They were able to classify industries in a scale going from high propensity (mining, maritime and longshore industries), through medium high (lumber, textiles), to low propensity (railroad, agriculture, trade).

They pointed out that miners, sailors, and to some extent textile workers tended to form isolated masses and to live in their own separate communities with their own codes, myths, heroes, and social standards. There are few neutrals to mediate conflicts and "dilute the mass," there is little internal occupational stratification and grievances are shared. "Here is a case where the totality of common grievances, after they have been verbally shared, may be greater than the sum of the individual parts." It is difficult for these workers not only to move up but also (because they are specialists) to move out to other occupations. There are few voluntary associations with mixed memberships as in the multi-industry town. The worker is not usually close to his employer and is not in close touch with the general public. The union becomes a kind of working-class party or even a government for the employees rather than one association among many.

The strike for this isolated mass is a kind of colonial revolt against far-removed authority, an outlet for accumulated tensions, and a substitute for occupational and social mobility . . . the isolated mass in a classless society may become something like the isolated class in a class society, more or less permanently at odds with the community at large.[38]

At the other end of the scale, say Kerr and Siegel, are workers who have an industrial role to play that integrates them better into the general community. They are more likely to live in multi-industry communities, to associate with people whose work experience differs from their own, and to belong to associations with heterogeneous membership: therefore their grievances are less likely to coalesce into a mass grievance which is expressed at the job level. It is easier for them to change their industry or to move up within their own. There is more stratification in their jobs. There is more contact with the employer. The workers "see and feel" the community and in most of these cases the government takes an active interest in maintaining continuity of the work. Where unions exist they are not in many cases in this category as embedded in the lives of the workers, and are not their chosen instrument of protest. The workers are not maintained on the periphery of society.

While the authors place less emphasis on the character of the job than other writers, they are prepared to combine this hypothesis with their own leading theme to the extent that they state that strikes occur most severely in industries which segregate large numbers of persons who have relatively unpleasant jobs. They accept the importance of human relations at the face-to-face level but only insofar as this reflects more fundamental structural factors. As they say, some situations are structured against good face-to-face relations and this structure is "the more basic cause and the source of the more basic changes." Carrying this logic a step further they assert that it is prima facie unlikely that there is more peace in, say, government agencies than on the waterfront because the former are characterized by "superiority in human relations techniques."

Dominant union leaders leave an imprint on an industry, but particular industries appear to have similar records in different countries with or without such leaders. Specific ideologies or belligerent attitudes affect bargaining relationships and the propensity to strike but,

the citadels of union radicalism and the hotbeds of employer reaction are found in the same industries from country to country. . . The selection of good bargaining techniques can prevent conflict but all parties in all industries have available to them the same storehouse of techniques . . . but it is not for lack of bargaining skill that so many strikes have occurred in the coal mines and on the waterfronts of the world.[39]

The writers repeat that the most general explanation of the interindustry propensity to strike is the nature of the industrial environment and, particularly, its tendency to direct workers into isolated masses or to integrate them into the general community. While they say that this hypothesis elucidates the behavior of most of the industries surveyed for most of the time period studied, it goes only a limited way. It does not explain why some industries lie in the middle of the strike-proneness range or why the records of various firms are different. At the level of the firm many more factors than the industrial environment must be studied.

PSYCHO-SOCIAL FACTORS IN CONFLICT

Stagner and Rosen assert that management-labor disputes are often like the legendary iceberg.[40] There is, they say, usually a vast, hidden subsurface bulk that consists of human emotions, aspirations, expectations, and frustrations whose effect is not necessarily revealed in outward decisions, bargaining, contract discussions, or grievance procedures. While they agree that union-management relations require understanding of economics, engineering and sociology, they feel that these do not offer a full analysis.

They describe perception as the fundamental intervening variable between the person and the objective world, and show its connection with his group memberships and organizational role. Man, as they say, behaves in accordance with his image of reality. Their argument is that differing ways of looking at situations and conflicting goals of union and company lead to disputes. Differences in perceived reality result in "the facts" looking different to different groups of participants. These differing perceptions are shared by persons with similar organizational vantage points, who differ also in socio-economic background and education and this accentuates the perceptual differences and their significance. With "the facts" as viewed by each side seeming so different, when they are discussed what ensues is a "dialogue of the deaf."

Stagner and Rosen then point to the importance of motivation (striving for goals). While the employing organization is a coalition which allows the industrial worker to reach some of its goals, it frustrates others. The union may help in the attainment of these (or of other goals barred by the corporation), though size, complexity, and concern with national or industry-wide issues may well divert the union from the idiosyncratic needs of its members. Or the union may in itself become an additional source of demands on its members.

Managements are subject to frustration as their rights to hire and fire and to organize production as they think best are limited by unions or by less organized groups of workers. On the worker's side there are actual or potential frustrations in the insecurity of his job, risks at work, disappointments at not getting raises and promotions and in the way authority is exercised over him. These feelings may lead to aggressive eruptions on either side, escalating as aggression stimulates counter-aggression.

Stagner and Rosen remind us that in an analysis of this sort one cannot reason as if both union and employing organization are monolithic entities, nor persona acting as if they were individual human beings. Both are coalitions of subgroups with varying, often competitive, interests and, by implication, the internal group dynamics of each affects the organizational level behavior of each toward the other. For instance, an insecure union leadership may precipitate industrial action partly because influential members have regarded it as too accommodating.

These authors point out that in many cases strikes and lockouts have ensued, with damage to both parties, which both would have preferred to avoid through a negotiated settlement. In such cases it would appear that emotions have gotten out of hand and that prestige and the pure issue of winning or losing has taken precedence over continuity in production and continued sharing in the flow of benefits. These appear in the process of disagreement, negotiation, dispute, and stoppage, items from a hidden agenda which block economic rationality as this would be perceived by an objective outside person.

CONFLICT BETWEEN TECHNICAL
AND SOCIAL ORGANIZATION
(THE MAYO THESIS)

Roethlisberger and Dickson described what they saw as a conflict between the technical and social organization of the plant. By the technical plan they meant the written arrangements about the way the plant was supposed to operate, the agencies that were supposed to effect the plan, rules for payment, rules about the way in which work was supposed to get done, rules about regulations with superiors, the implicit assumption that men would act to further their social interest. By the social organization they meant the groupings of men associated with each other, the relations within and between these groups, and the feelings of these groups about themselves, each other, their tasks, and the management. One important (and problematic) aspect of the relation between the technical and the social organization of the plant, they said, was the interaction between management and workers in relation to technical innovation. It was the task of management to devise and implement rapid changes. When the orders reached the men who were doing the actual work they had to accommodate themselves to the changes, although they participated least in the technical organization, although they did not share management's preoccupations, and although, typically, little was done to convince them that what they considered important was considered important at the top.

There was not, said Roethlisberger and Dickson, adequate communication in both directions. Furthermore, many of the changes deprived the workers of things that gave meaning and significance to their work—their own ways of doing their jobs, their own traditions of skill, their satisfactions. The changes were said to interfere with group codes and loyalties that had been built up over extended periods as a product of continued routine interaction. The conclusion of this school was that restriction of output in the Bank Wiring Observation Room was an unconscious, automatic effort of the workers to protect themselves against action taken in accordance with the technical organization that tended to break up, through continual change, the routines and human associations that gave work much of its value. The result of the system, it was said, was to incite a blind resistance to all innovations and to provoke the formation of a social organization at a lower level in opposition to the technical organization.

This study and the approach in which it is embedded contrast sharply with the class conflict/economic conflict thesis. The latter gives primacy to the interest of workers in money and the former gives primacy to social relations. Roethlisberger and Dickson actually wrote:

None of the results . . . gave the slightest substantiation to the theory that the worker is primarily motivated by economic interest.[41]

They rest their argument on the fact (1) that the workers were not clear what would happen if production went up; (2) that none of the operatives studied had experienced cuts in piece rates, etc., that they were supposed to be guarding themselves against, and this was contrary to the firm's policy and practices; (3) that the wage system they were sabotaging would in fact have been in their individual economic interest.

This thesis has a special importance for two reasons. First, is its actual influence on industrial practice—which has been considerable. Second, consideration of the thesis and its refutation take us distinctly further in our understanding of management-worker conflict and of organizational conflict in general.

When one says that the influence of the Mayo thesis on industrial practice has been considerable, one has to make the qualification that it is largely interpretations of the Harvard Business School investigations rather than what was found out which had an impact. As we saw when discussing the work of Mayo and his colleagues, some of his writings lay more in the sphere of citizenship or social philosophy than social science. At times his prescriptions went beyond the actual research into value judgments on what action Mayo felt was now indicated. Certainly his and later popularizations oversimplified the results and went beyond the more cautious conclusions of the actual research workers. As we have shown, it is possible to discover in the writings of Roethlisberger, Dickson, Lombard, and Fox acknowledgments of the importance of structural forces outside the workplace. They also acknowledge conflict between management's drive for technical innovation and increased efficiency and the system of prestige groups among the occupational categories of the labor force. They realized that management-worker conflicts were not purely emotional and could not be cleared up by more efficient communication. We have also to recognize that in industrial practice the ideas deriving from the Mayo group (or believed to derive from them) became mingled with those of Lewin and his colleagues, or, to be accurate again, with derivations of those ideas. The Lewinian derivatives had to do again with emotion and expressive aspects of human interaction, apparently implying that democratic supportive forms of leadership, particularly involving consultation of subordinates and group decision-making, is more effective than authoritarian behavior in getting tasks done. In this case one has, once more, somewhat bolder interpretations than those to which the original research workers would subscribe, although, as we saw, Lewin himself did not directly confront these problems adequately in his work on conflict resolution. In both cases, moreover, one has to reckon with the fact that the apparent action implications of the researchers entered into organizational practice before continued investigations had refined and qualified the first sets of conclusions.

The second issue, the correctness or otherwise of the central ideas sometimes referred to as "neo-human relations" can best be illuminated by referring to a case study and discussion by J. H. Goldthorpe in the British mining industry.[42]

Goldthorpe describes the continuation, indeed increased frequency, of localized unofficial strikes in the mining industry after the nationalization of mines in 1947. He describes the importance attached by the leaders of the industry to preventing or reducing such strikes and to avoiding attitudes that would be conducive to the eruption of disputes. His analysis of the human relations training programs of supervisors shows that the colliery is represented as a collective enterprise in which all grades and occupational groupings perform essential functions and are reciprocally inter-dependent. The objectives of the enterprise are indicated to be economic (production combined with earning opportunities) but also social, that is, concerned with satisfaction to the human beings involved. The attainment of these aims is said to depend on a spirit of cooperation, or harmonious teamwork. The key role of the work group supervisor is emphasized as leader, captain of a team, whose direction and coordination will bring the group success. Supervisors are warned to act in a democratic way, to take into account the views of their men, to try to win support. The training courses emphasized that no difficulty should exist in reconciling produc-tive efficiency with democratic supervision. Efficient operation was in the interest of workers as well as supervisor and the latter should be able to communicate this; for example, to explain why an unpopular task must be carried out.

This approach implied that conflict arises mainly out of psychological problems in interpersonal relations, failures in communication, irrational attitudes, personality clashes, and so on. It was an important part of the supervisors' task to diagnose and deal with these as emotional issues, in-cluding their own personal contributions to the problems.

Goldthorpe points out that in this approach conflict is being defined as pathological, a deviation from a normal state, that can, if the correct methods are adopted, be reduced or eliminated. He criticizes the Coal Board approach on several grounds. The enterprise is more than a system of division of labor: it is also a system of authority in which some have the right to command and others the duty of compliance. Since wages represent income for labor and costs to management, management must, says Goldthorpe, tend to take a partial view and maintain its own interests, as does labor. For management, a high standard of discipline among the labor force means predictability and efficiency in the productive process; for the workers it can mean loss of autonomy. At this point the argument appears to have weakened since it can be persuasively put that both com-petitive labor costs and operating efficiency are in everyone's interest since they protect the viability of the industry. But Goldthorpe is on firm ground in next pointing to the conflicts that arise between supervisors and men because of the physical environment of mining—because physical condi-tions change often, wages must be partly fixed on an *ad hoc* basis and without reference to clear standards. The supervisor will want to keep costs down and the operatives to argue the rate up.

Goldthorpe concludes that there are genuine divergences of interest be-tween the parties, that these are built into the structure of the enterprise and cannot be reduced or dissolved. And, he adds, reluctance to accept the existence of "real" or objective conflict within the enterprise must mean that too little attention is being given to the problem of developing pro-cedures for the effective *regulation* of this conflict.

B. Roberts has pointed out that managerial distinctions are customarily drawn in Europe between managerial decisions that are of direct concern to the unions since they affect immediate conditions of employment and those that are of indirect concern, that will affect conditions of employment sooner or later but that are not normally subject to collective bargaining. But, he says, these distinctions embody value judgments. There is no immutable distribution of the product of enterprise between the factors of production. Nor is there any unchangeable law governing the prerogatives of management.[43] The implication is that there is no objectively correct settlement in either set of issues and that since they involve differences in sectional interests and differences in judgment and values they must, in a democratic society, be subject to indefinite struggle. The same reasoning applies to other standing issues, such as the amount of access unions or other bodies of workers can have to information on the affairs of a company, the ways in which production is to be achieved, and the human costs it justifies.

The Typical Strike
in Britain

Because of the work of the Royal Commission on Trade Unions and Employers' Associations [44] and a series of empirical studies of small-scale stoppages we are able to set out a recent comprehensive analysis of the causes of management-worker conflict and to illustrate these from actual stoppages.

The report of the Royal Commission begins from the fact that official statistics relating to causes of disputes must be used with caution. They relate to the immediate issue which gave rise to a stoppage and this may not be the fundamental underlying cause. Even the immediately apparent causes may be mixed and it may not be easy to decide which preponderate. Most major strikes in Britain are official (that is, sanctioned or ratified by the unions concerned) and concern pay or hours of work or both, but unofficial strikes form some 95 percent of all strikes. The latter tend to involve about 300 workers and to last two to three days.

About half of all unofficial strikes during the period 1964–66 concerned wages. This pattern was general throughout industry. The next most prolific immediate causes of dispute were "working arrangements, rules and discipline" (29 percent) and "redundancy, dismissal, suspension, etc." (15 percent). Ten percent of all unofficial strikes took place over disciplinary issues.

The commission decided to investigate more fully the causes of unofficial strikes in the motor manufacturing industry. They chose this industry because of its exceptional strike-proneness in Britain and were able to draw, among other sources, on the research of a Cambridge University group on this subject.[45] The Commission examined and rejected certain explanations of the industry's strike record that are sometimes suggested. They did not accept the hypothesis that unofficial strikes are "fomented by shop stewards bent on destruction" and quote H. A. Turner and his colleagues to the effect that

strikes have been as common in plants where the stewards' organization is weak and divided as where it is strong: and there is more to suggest that serious stewards attempt to control the development of disputes and are pushed into stoppages from behind than that they lead workers into such crises.[46]

They doubt whether the dull and repetitive character of the work is important, pointing to the lack of complaints and representations on this issue made to the industry's Joint Labour Council. They think boredom may be an indirect cause of disputes by affecting workers' attitudes without their being aware of this—on the other hand, the same industry is not especially strike-prone in other countries. Labor is not particularly raw: labor turnover is lower than in similar industries and periods of expanded recruiting have not coincided particularly with strikes. The commission assigns some weight to inadequate discipline by management, but points out that, unless managements respond flexibly, large parts of a plant can be brought to a standstill: "Great power lies in the hands of relatively small groups of workers because of the close interdependence of the various processes of production." For different reasons, unions may also be unable to influence the workplace situation sufficiently: this is partly because of the readiness of managements to deal with shop stewards rather than full-time union officials and partly because of the multiplicity of unions active in the factories.

The commission points particularly to the industry's wage structure as a cause of strikes.

It is plain that employees' actual earnings are not determined by the negotiations conducted at industry level . . . a crucial part is played by workplace negotiations . . . considerable difficulties are encountered both in maintaining fair relativities between different groups of workers and in keeping a reasonable amount of control over wage levels. In addition it is clear that workers' pay is subject to considerable fluctuations as a result of variations in the flow of work due to factors beyond their control. . . . In these circumstances the seeds of dispute in matters of pay are present in abundance.[47]

Referring to causes of disputes other than wages, the commission concludes that these reflect in part the insecurity of the industry and in part the increased power and readiness of workers, under conditions of full employment, to resist unwelcome disciplinary or other managerial decisions by their employers.

The report asserts that the motor industry's particular difficulties over strikes arise not so much from factors peculiar to the industry as from factors present in many industries, though to a less marked degree. Looking at coal mining, docks, shipbuilding, and ship repairing as well as the motor industry, they say that in all of these work groups organization is exceptionally strong, fragmented bargaining has been the rule, and the wage structure is archaic in some instances, failing to change to take sufficient account of the effects of changing technology on the relative importance of different workers in the production process.

As already mentioned, the commission drew on the studies of Turner, Clack, and Roberts. The commission's analysis can helpfully be expanded by considering Clack's own comments on his firsthand studies of stoppages. He collected this material while working himself on the shop floor of a car factory. In one of his own reports [48] he begins by criticizing certain popular explanations of strikes, including those that emphasize negative attitudes of workers connected with assembly-line work. Somewhat like the Goldthorpe-Lockwood team, he points out that assembly-line work is attractive because of the opportunity for relatively high earnings. Nor, in his opinion, were the strikes attributable to the car workers being older than average (and therefore irritable), or inexperienced. The shop stewards and union convenors were not particularly militant and were concerned to go about things in a constitutional way. There appeared to be some distance between the workers and the union organization—much as Stagner and Ross and others have suggested—and the relevance of officials to workplace seems to have been only tenuously perceived. A number of unions were represented in the firm, but there seemed to be little concern at the factory as to which union a man belonged to, though interunion rivalry did matter at higher levels of union organization. Clack came to the conclusion that the most important factors in rendering the factory strike prone lay (1) in the wage structure and pay system (complicated bonus schemes that were easily misunderstood, allocations of overtime pay between workers that were regarded as inequitable, changes in rates for jobs that distorted established differences between categories of workers); (2) insecurity of job rights and earnings (associated with cyclical and seasonal fluctuations in the general demand for cars as well as variations in the fortunes of the firm's models); (3) ambivalent attitudes and erratic behavior in connection with the activities of labor organizations in the plant, expressed, for example, in the absence of a senior industrial relations specialist and the sporadic intervention of the senior executive at the plant and in restriction of facilities for union officials; (4) confusion about the correct use of the grievance procedure and an anxiety among workers that anything other than local expressions and settlements of disputes would result in their being lost or merged with other issues.

The actual social processes involved emerge more clearly from a separate report by Clack of one stoppage, presumably in the same plant.[49] His account was from the perspective of a participant-observer. As he describes the series of events, the "downer" took shape in the minds of half-a-dozen storemen as they ceased work. There had been a sharp drop in earnings, resulting in discontent, and they had just seen an announcement of what could be expected in pay packets next day. In the morning a small group told a shop steward they wanted an immediate meeting and walked out on the job, calling to others to join in. Although unauthorized meetings in work hours were a breach of disputes procedure, within five minutes all sixty in the department gathered outside. A shop steward tried to persuade them to return to work until a union convenor would be available. This was opposed by two of the original strikers, who said that they should stay out to demonstrate their sincerity, otherwise nothing would be achieved. By general assent the group stayed. It became clear, says Clack, that not everyone knew, or was agreed on, the aims of the strike, though speculation was rife and connection was made with previous protests against the workings of the bonus system: experience in these protests and in attempts to change the bonus methods had evidently left a legacy of ill-feeling. After an hour and a half the convenor arrived and a discussion ensued on past representations and recommendations and what should now be done. Side issues were being introduced, and the meeting was becoming mainly a means of relieving pent-up emotions. A resolution calling for a return to work was then moved and passed unanimously. Repeat performances brought work-study engineers into the department within a few weeks and hastened a report from them. Clack describes the attitudes of the strikers as cynical rather than hot-blooded and emphasizes the effects of "sheer muddle."

Generalizing in the same paper about another series of strikes in the same plant, Clack remarks on the way in which meaning may be lost as issues move away from their locus of origin.

Somewhat similar conclusions were reached by Paterson and Willett during a study of a mine and mining community in Scotland in the course of which they saw a strike start and proceed.[50] There were background stresses in the situation of the miners. The nationalization of the industry had not, as many believed it would, changed life radically for the better, there was little change in the attitudes of management to men, the sheer size of the new national body made it an impersonal abstraction, there had been a drive for lower costs, and mechanization of the pits had disrupted traditional group systems of working. In the colliery studied there were a number of grievances about pay, conditions, and the time taken to examine complaints, a deficiency in underground transport for hauling coal, and time lost because of this. A group of men had been transferred to the colliery at a wage lower than they had received before. The observers noted sporadic outbursts of "wanton destruction" to light fittings and knew of short stoppages or attempted stoppages aborted by the union. Just before one afternoon shift, the group of men gathering to start work began to criticize the transferred workers and their attitudes to local conditions, one subgroup recalled a claim they had themselves made (presumably unsuccessfully) and a discussion ensued on what could be done about it. A remark was made about the fine weather and the men immediately and unanimously decided they would not go underground that afternoon. The group stayed where they were and were joined by newcomers, some coming off the morning shift. Pairs of men began shouting and using aggressive gestures. There was now a general demand for a higher rate for the shift, and for pay comparable with the higher English rate; one element wanted a return to work, another wanted to strike there and then. When it was technically speaking too late for the afternoon shift to start, representatives of management arrived and stated that the pit would be left open for ten minutes, that those now ready could go to work and that the manager would receive a deputation in the morning. The management group left and a couple of speakers addressed the crowd to the effect that if any started work now this would result in others being victimized. They decided to go home and have an evening meeting. At the meeting they were addressed by union representatives holding rather different views, one dissociating himself from the national agreement now governing wage-rates. Loud arguments were shouted back and forth, particularly between locals and immigrants. With some dissentients it was agreed to return to work and to send a deputation to management, though it was agreed from the platform that the demonstration they had made was in itself valuable as an expression of opinion. Next day work was resumed almost normally, though there was some residual feeling that the workers had been misled by their Union leaders and that "strikers got angry instead of smart and then got out-smarted."

Such empirical studies of actual strikes make it clear that conflicts between management and workers are complex in their causation and perpetuation. We have already mentioned contributory causes associated with economic, political, sociological, psychological, organizational, and technological variables. Different factors may be the key to different subgroups and individuals. As B. Roberts says, "In few situations will everybody be agreed on the fundamental thing that he is striking for." [51] It has also become apparent that actual disputes cannot be understood except in the institutional context in which they occur. These include national agreements for wage settlements and collective bargaining and involve close interaction between single unions and employing organizations, federations of these, and central government. When organizations and persons interact they do so in the context of established rules, in this case often heavily weighed with traditions concerned with citizenship, fair play, and distributive justice. Flanders, a well-known British student of industrial relations, has put the issue in the following way:

The drawback of relying on the theory of any one of the several disciplines that have impinged on industrial relations is that it was never intended to offer an integrated view of the whole complex of institutions in this field. Theoretically speaking, these disciplines tear the subject apart by concentrating attention on some of its aspects to the exclusion or comparative neglect of others. And a partial view of anything, accurate as it may be within its limits, must of necessity be a distorted one.[52]

Effects of
Management-Worker Conflicts

On the negative side, strikes and lockouts constitute interruptions in the continuity of tasks, expectations, and normal operations. Real injury and loss can be inflicted on managements, labor and the consumer public. With today's technology and interdependence, conflicts of these sorts ramify far and wide in their effects on other companies and industries. Absenteeism, wastage, restriction of production, and so on clearly reduce the amount that could theoretically be produced and create bitterness in the people whose job it is to maintain levels of production. People engaged in conflict often experience hostile emotions towards the other party that persist after the crisis has been surmounted. Each party threatens and can create disorder on the other side.

But industrial conflict also has its positive side. Looked at in an organizational context, such conflict can help groups to secure a share of the joint product appropriate to their contribution. It allows tensions and differences to come to the surface where some kind of resolution can be achieved. Conflict may help both sides to clarify what is in their separate and common interest. It may stretch managements to consider whether they could pay more if they ran the business better or could substitute other factors of production for labor.[53] It can influence workers to consider how far higher productivity could be made to accompany higher rewards. Conflict may bring grievances to light and attract public interest in poor conditions of work or unjust acts by employers. It may result in improved rules of the game for relations between management and workers.

Looked at nationally, management-worker conflict bring issues into the open where they become sensitive to public opinion and subject to social control (cases getting tested publicly). It provides vitality in the economic system. It clarifies the identity of power-holding groups at various points of the social structure. Industrial conflict helps define the place of management and labor in society. Industrial conflicts may benefit the nation by balancing union power against management power.

Where conflict is institutionalized into collective bargaining procedures, it permits the formulation of specific issues amenable to resolution rather than maintaining a mere dichotomy of principle; it allows a new basis for order to be achieved; it allows for orderly social change.

A balanced view of industrial conflict as experienced in contemporary Western countries suggests that it is not a pathological phenomenon to be understood as the desperate efforts of a deprived and discontented people but a normal aspect of "antagonistic cooperation" [54] in a competitive society in which groups cooperate but at the same time use their power to influence the outcomes of that cooperation to their greater benefit. To return to the formulations of Roberts, trade unions in a democratic society are an expression of the right of persons to organize themselves to protect and promote their interests by collective action. In a democratic society power is diffused through a number of agencies, each free to exercise its pressures on political and economic systems. It is only a totalitarian state that exercises power in a monolithic way that excludes competition and conflict and that assumes an automatic and continuous identity of interest between those who govern or manage and other sectional groups.

Unitary versus
Pluralistic Frame
of Reference

Our opening, expository chapters made it clear that a substantial defect in the work of Taylor, Myers, Mayo, and most of the managers and consultants who tried to set out principles of organization and management was their neglect of conflict. Where conflict was acknowledged to exist, this was regarded as peripheral to the functioning of the enterprise—a form of friction; a consequence of misunderstanding, ignorance, or failure of communication; something that could be overcome by persuasion, explanation, or more rational forms of organization.

The viewpoint presented in this book, on the other hand, is that organizational conflict in the industrial firm is normal and usual, an integral aspect of the enterprise that cannot be removed or eradicated from the system. The industrial organization is an area of conflict as well as collaboration, a coalition of individuals and subgroups simultaneously united by the prospect of common benefits derivable from the enterprise and divided by conflicts of interest, definition and perception.

The former approach is still widely prevalent in managerial and public circles today and has associated with it a characteristic set of assumptions and ideology. Fox has described this approach as centered on the notion that the organization is a unitary system analogous to a team.[55] He has distinguished this from the concept of the organization as a pluralistic system, a coalition of interests that in some respects are divergent. As he says, the importance of this distinction resides in the fact that our frame of reference determines the way in which we expect people to behave and believe they ought to beha e; the way in which we react to people's actual behavior; and the methods we choose when we want to change their behavior.

Fox suggests that the conception of the enterprise as a unitary system includes the idea that this contains one source of authority and one focus of loyalty. Each member is expected to strive toward a common objective, to accept his place and function, and to follow his appointed leader and no other. Morale and success are closely connected and rest heavily on personal relations. Fox suggests that the closest analogy is to a professional football team, in which team spirit together with undivided managerial authority are conceived to coexist to the benefit of all. With this concept is associated an ideology of inspired leadership, of harmony of purpose, of loyalty and esprit de corps. This outlook is exemplified even by such sophisticated firms as the two major British companies I describe in *Men in Mid-Career*. Autoline, the motor manufacturing company, includes in its literature the statement:

We need to work together as a cohesive team dedicated to the concept of complete co-ordination and co-operation.[56]

A speech by the chairman of Novoplast states the same theme, though there is recognition here that the needs of others are also involved.

I believe that the needs of the Company and the needs of individuals are interdependent . . . all of us benefit twice—by increased personal satisfaction and by the increased prosperity of the Company—which in turn will enable us to measure up more fully to our other inescapable responsibilities—to customers, to shareholders and to the nation itself.[57]

Along the same lines a Dutch industrialist asserts that

the trade union becomes superfluous and even harmful if, in representing the firm's employees, it disrupts the working community by suggesting a conflict of interest.[58]

Fox indicates that such ideologies serve three important functions. They reassure managements that a basic harmony of purpose exists and that demonstrations to the contrary are due to the shortcomings of others, to outdated class rancor, or to inability to grasp basic principles of economics. They serve as instruments of persuasion, for insofar as managers can persuade employees and the public that industrial enterprises should not be disrupted, internal control is made easier and challenges are easier to repudiate. Thirdly, the propagation of the idea that the interest of managers and managed are identical helps to confer legitimacy on the regime.

Despite the prevalence of this type of ideology, managements participate daily in an elaborate institutional apparatus of collective bargaining, dispute settlement, and consultation, which reflect the reality of the contrasting conflict-based view of society and of industrial organizations. Fox points out that ideology and structural realities sit oddly with each other and that this disjunction helps to explain the persistence of irrational elements in the system. One important irrationality is that managements concede the rights of groups of workers to exercise their market power in the determination of the economic terms and conditions on which they are hired but not their rights to participate in internal operations after wages and contracts have been decided. Another important irrationality he mentions had to do with the restrictive practices and resistances to change to which I have repeatedly referred in this book. In Fox's words:

Viewed within a pluralistic framework they are neither irrational nor illogical. A management which fully accepts the reality of work-group interests which conflict quite legitimately with their own will seek honestly and patiently to understand the causes of particular group practices and processes in the full awareness that imaginative understanding is a pre-condition of success in modifying behaviour.[59]

Fox concludes that a pluralistic frame of reference is necessary for the development of more sophisticated bargaining techniques at a higher level of mutual advantage.

NOTES

1. This distinction is well established in the literature of sociology. See, for instance, the discussion in E. E. Eubank, *Concepts of Sociology* (Boston: Heath, 1932).

2. L. Coser, "Social Aspects of Conflict," *International Encyclopaedia of the Social Sciences,* 3 (New York: Macmillan, 1968), p. 232.

3. A. Kornhauser, A. P. Dubin, and A. M. Ross, eds., *Industrial Conflict* (New York: McGraw-Hill, 1954).

4. They are distinguished in this way from attempts to change power relationships by substituting a new leadership. See C. J. Lammers, "Strikes and Mutinies. A Comparative Study of Organizational Conflicts" (Institute of Sociology, University of Leiden: Unpublished paper presented at International Sociological Conference, 1966).

5. A. J. M. Sykes, "The Effect of a Supervisory Training Course in Changing Supervisors' Perceptions and Expectations of the Role of Management," *Human Relations,* 15, no. 3 (1962): 227–243.

6. See F. J. Roethlisberger and W. J. Dickson, *Management and the Worker* (Cambridge, Massachusetts: Harvard University Press, 1939); and discussion by G. C. Homans, "The Western Electric Researchers" in Haslett, Schuyler and Dean, eds., *Human Factors in Management* (New York: Harper, 1951). See also D. Roy, "Quota Restriction and Goldbricking in a Machine Shop," *American Journal of Sociology,* 57, no. 5 (March 1952): 427–442; "Efficiency and 'the Fix,'" *American Journal of Sociology,* 60, no. 3 (1954); "Work Satisfaction and Social Reward in Quota Achievement: An Analysis of Piecework Incentive," *American Sociological Review,* 18 (1953): 507–514; O. Collins, M. Dalton and D. Roy, "Restriction of Output and Social

Cleavage in Industry," *Applied Anthropology*, 5, no. 3 (Summer 1946): 1–14; T. Lupton, *On the Shop Floor* (Oxford: Pergamon, 1963).

7. Lupton, *Shop Floor*.

8. Kornhauser, Dubin, and Ross, *Industrial Conflict*, p. 13.

9. Sanford, "Individual Conflict and Organizational Interaction," in R. L. Kahn and E. Boulding, eds., *Power and Conflict in Organizations* (London: Tavistock, 1964). See also R. L. Kahn, D. M. Wolfe, R. P. Quinn and J. D. Snoek in collaboration with R. A. Rosenthal, *Organizational Stress. Studies in Role Conflict and Ambiguity* (New York: Wiley, 1964).

10. American Federation of Labour—Congress of Industrial Organization.

11. Reported in the *Los Angeles Times* (August 31, 1970).

12. *Financial Times* (London, September 19, 1970).

13. H. Marcuse, *Essay on Liberation* (London: Allen Lane, 1969), p. 55.

14. A. Beichman, "Beware of the Proctors," Encounter, 35, no. 2 (August 1970): p. 56.

15. See discussion in E. H. Phelps-Brown, *The Growth of British Industrial Relations* (London: Macmillan, 1960).

16. See discussion in Mark van de Vall, *Labour Organizations: A Macro- and Micro-Sociological Analysis on a Comparative Basis* (Cambridge: Cambridge University Press, 1970).

17. This argument has, for instance, been presented by Kurt B. Mayer, "Recent Changes in the Class Structure of the United States," *Transactions of the Third World Congress of Sociology, 1956;* "Diminishing Class Differentials in the United States," *Kylos,* 12 (1959): 605–628; "The Changing Shape of the American Class Structure," *Social Research,* 30, no. 4 (Winter 1963): 458–468; G. Lenski, *The Religious Factor* (New York: Doubleday, 1961); and by the U.K. Central Office of Information, *Social Change in Britain* (December 1962).

18. J. H. Goldthorpe and D. Lockwood, "Affluence and the British Class Structure," *The Sociological Review,* 11, no. 2 (July 1963): 133–163.

19. J. H. Goldthorpe, D. Lockwood, F. Bechhofer, and J. Platt, *The Affluent Worker,* Vol. 1 *Industrial Attitudes and Behaviour* (Cambridge: Cambridge University Press, 1968); *The Affluent Worker:* Vol. 2 *Political Attitudes and Behaviour* (Cambridge: Cambridge University Press, 1969); Vol. 3. *The Affluent Worker in the Class Structure* (Cambridge: Cambridge University Press, 1969).

20. H. Brandon, *Sunday Times* (London, May 11, 1969). S.D.S. refers to Students for a Democratic Society.

21. Beichman, "Beware," pp. 56 and 57.

22. B. Roberts, *Trade Unions in a Free Society: Studies in the Organization of Labour in Britain and the U.S.A.* (London: Hutchinsons, 1959), pp. 168 and 169.

23. For instance by Phelps-Brown in *The Growth of British Industrial Relations*.

24. C. Argyris, "The Individual and Organization: Some Problems of Mutual Adjustment," *Administrative Science Quarterly,* 2 (June 1957): 1–24.

25. See A. W. Gouldner, *Patterns of Industrial Bureaucracy* (Glencoe, Illinois: Free Press, 1954).

26. Collins, Dalton and Roy, "Restriction of Output."

27. D. Roy, "Work Satisfaction and Social Reward in Quota Achievement," *American Sociological Review,* 18, no. 5 (October 1953): 507–514.

28. Gouldner, *Patterns*.

29. M. Crozier, *The Bureaucratic Phenomenon* (London: Tavistock, 1964).

30. See T. Baldamus, "Type of Work and Motivation," *British Journal of Sociology,* 2, no. 1 (March 1951): 44–58.

31. C. R. Walker and R. H. Guest, *The Man on the Assembly Line,* (Cambridge, Massachusetts: Harvard University Press, 1952).

32. C. Friedmann, *Industrial Society*, (Glencoe, Illinois: Free Press, 1955); and "Technological Change and Human Relations," *British Journal of Sociology*, 3, no. 2 (June 1952): 95–116.

33. R. Blauner, *Alienation and Freedom: The Factory Worker and His Industry*, (Chicago and London: University of Chicago Press, 1964).

34. Blauner, *Alienation*, p. 166.

35. Blauner, *Alienation*, pp. 180–182.

36. J. H. Goldthorpe, et al, *The Affluent Worker, Industrial Attitudes and Behaviour*, (Cambridge: Cambridge University Press, 1968).

37. C. Kerr and A. Siegel, "The Interindustry Propensity to Strike—An International Comparison," in Kornhauser, Dubin and Ross, *Industrial Conflict*.

38. Kerr and Siegel, "The Interindustry Propensity," p. 193.

39. Kerr and Siegel, "The Interindustry Propensity," p. 201.

40. R. Stagner and H. Rosen, *Psychology of Union-Management Relations*, (London: Tavistock, 1966).

41. Roethlisberger and Dickson, *Management and the Worker*, p. 575.

42. J. H. Goldthorpe, "The Treatment of Conflict in Human Relations Training: A Case Study from the British Coal Mining Industry," (unpublished manuscript, 1961); and "La Conception des Conflits du Travail dans L'Enseignement des Relations Humaines," *Sociologies du Travail*, 3, no. 1 (January–March 1961).

43. Roberts, *Trade Unions*.

44. Report of Royal Commission on Trade Unions and Employers' Associations, 1965–1968: Donovan Commission, (London: Her Majesty's Stationery Office, Cmd. 3623, 1968), pp. 100–108.

45. See H. A. Turner, G. Clack and G. Roberts, *Labour Relations in the Motor Industry: A Study of Industrial Unrest and an International Comparison*, (London: Allen and Unwin, 1967).

46. Report of Royal Commission, pp. 102 and 103.

47. Report of Royal Commission, p. 104.

48. G. Clack, *Industrial Relations in a British Car Factory*, (Cambridge: Occasional Paper, Cambridge University Press, 1967).

49. G. Clack, "How Unofficial Strikes Help Industry," *Business* (July 1965): 42–47.

50. T. T. Paterson and F. J. Willett, "Unofficial Strike," *Sociological Review*, section 4: 57–94.

51. Roberts, *Trade Unions*.

52. A. Flanders, *Industrial Relations: What is Wrong With the System?*, (London: Institute of Personnel Management, 1965), pp. 9 and 10.

53. "By constantly threatening to go on strike to secure higher wages and better living conditions, unions compel employers to seek ways and means of cutting their labour costs. Thus, there is generated a constant force pushing the employer into installing more labour-saving equipment, into reducing costs in other directions. All of this means that labour productivity is greatly increased over the years." Roberts, *Trade Unions*, p. 173.

54. This phrase is derived from W. G. Sumner, who says antagonistic cooperation "consists in the combination of two persons or groups to satisfy a great common interest while minor antagonisms of interest which exist between them are suppressed. . . . It is a high action of the reason to overlook lesser antagonisms in order to work together for great interests." *Folkways*, (Boston: Ginn and Co., 1907), p. 18.

55. A. Fox, *Industrial Sociology and Industrial Relations*, Research Paper no. 3. Royal Commission on Trade Unions and Employer's Associations, (London: Her Majesty's Stationery Office, 1966).

56. Sofer, *Men in Mid-Career*, p. 154.

57. Sofer, *Men in Mid-Career*, p. 167.

58. A. M. Kuylaars, "Onderneming en Vakvereniging, Mens en Onderneming IV" (1950), quoted in M. Van de Vall, *Labour Organizations: A Macro- and Micro-Sociological Analysis on a Comparative Basis* (Cambridge: Cambridge University Press, 1970). Van de Vall comments that "it is expected in such (management) circles that the 'human relations' approach will change the enterprise into a 'Gemeinschaft,' i.e. a community-of-work, whose members share the same economic values and where the ethos of cooperation replaces the doctrine of conflict." p. 66.

59. A. Fox, *Industrial Sociology*, p. 39.

18 : Conflict between Colleague Groups[1]

■■■■■■ WHILE vertical conflicts between managements and workers arouse most public attention, this type of competition, struggle, and opposition is only one of many.

Neither "management" nor "workers" are solidary, monolithic bodies. What we conventionally call "management" is divided into a variety of subcategories and subgroups whose interests, outlook and aspirations differ and compete with each other.

Employees are not a homogeneous general class and it is not useful to picture them as such. They are divided into many varieties of occupation, which struggle against each other for rewards, recognition, and precedence just as much as any of them struggle against what we call "management."

In the large complex modern organization, intergroup conflict is closely connected with division into groups of colleagues each responsible for a share of the total of work to be done.

Functional Subgroups

Functional subsystems within an organization (for example, production departments, advisory groups, and office centers) develop goals and frames of reference of their own that give priority to the optimal performance of their own specialty, less to the needs of the overall organization, and even less to other specialized subsystems (colleague subsystems). The larger, enclosing system and its representatives in the form of senior management are perceived largely as providers of resources or disbursers of rewards, and other subsystems largely as competitors or obstacles to getting the work done.

This type of difficulty is probably less common in small work units, for example, in the repair shop of a garage or in a restaurant, where it is clearer to the staff that their fate in the enterprise is intertwined and where they can see that their specialties are interdependent with each other.

Where organizations grow beyond this point, where everyone is not together at the same time (because they work in different areas or in shifts) or where people specialize in jobs, interdependence is less visible and solidarity across the work force becomes more difficult to develop. The individual begins to experience conflict between his identification with a subgroup and identification with the total organization or to confine his identifications to those with whom he interacts most.

The classic case, much studied by social scientists, of conflict within the higher ranks of industrial organizations is that of relations between professionals or scientists, on the one hand, and administrative colleagues on the other. We have already discussed this in Chapter 13.

In a series of studies conducted over the past few years, Lawrence and Lorsch, of the Harvard Business School, have examined in some depth the problems that ensue when organizations allocate to separate functional sub-units the tasks of dealing with different sectors of the environment.[2] Each unit then deals with a sector which may differ in its stability, rate of change and the time required before feedback on effectiveness can be gained. For instance, research and development units, unlike many operational units, are often confronted with situations combining rapid change, low certainty of information and long-term feedback. Lawrence and Lorsch found systematic differences in outlook between members of these units and characteristic differences also in their internal organization—both sets of differences being related to differences in their situation. Differentiation was required to allow each unit to "do its own thing" but also contained the seeds of problems in achieving united effort. This was because competitive effectiveness depended also on a high degree of integration of the differentiated units. Within any one organization the two states (differentiation and integration) are "basically antagonistic." "The more different two highly interdependent units were, the more difficult it was for their members to communicate with the understanding necessary to achieve satisfactory integration."[3]

An example of intergroup conflict between colleagues at the same organizational level is provided by Macaulay—between those departments concerned with sales and those concerned with finance and administration.[4] As he points out, sales departments are much concerned to earn and retain the goodwill of customers. They are apt to promise rapid deliveries and adaptations of products to customer requirements and to take for granted or de-emphasize exact details of formal completion of contracts and time and methods of payment. These are, however, precisely the details that concern the financial administration most and are for them the heart of the matter. Macaulay cites the different reactions likely to occur when a customer decides against going through with a deal. To the salesman, who wishes to preserve the possibility of future deals, this is a canceled sale, but his administrative colleagues may speak in terms of breach of contract, an expression and point of view likely to sever relations with the customer permanently. Some writers on organizations, such as Kahn and Snoek,[5] would place particular emphasis on the part played in conflict arising from such issues by one party working on the boundary of an organization. It is in fact sometimes the case in such roles that persons occupying them feel only marginally members of their employing organizations and in some respects closer to complementary members of other organizations. A similar set of circumstances is reported by Sofer in a study of the relation of food shopkeepers with consumers. The shopkeepers complained that women assistants were too often "customers in overalls," that is, were apt to identify themselves too closely with the perspectives and needs of the female customer.[6]

Another classic case of a functional method of organization breeding intergroup tensions (this time at worker level) is provided by the Trist and Bamforth study of the conventional Longwall system of coalmining.[7] In the system they studied there were basically three phases of work, divided into shifts. Each task group was associated with a shift and had its own customs and agreements, including separate paynotes, so that each was separated from the other and bound within its own fields of interests. Each type of worker was trained in only one set of skills and spent his life in one occupation. There was thus a system of job breakdown integrated into a technological whole by task sequence but little social or organizational integration of the subtasks. This system resulted in mutual suspicion that bad work by others would increase one's own difficulties, concern of each team with its own responsibilities rather than with the overall task, controversies about (relative) pay, and norms of low productivity.

Conflict between functional groups is often exacerbated or consolidated by what are in effect cultural differences in regard to values, beliefs, outlook, and habits of thinking. Persons grouped together on the basis of similar training, qualifications, or tasks characteristically develop ideologies that emphasize their distinctive contributions to organizational ends and their unique place in the social division of labor. Specialization usually involves a narrowing of outlook and knowledge around particular themes and a concomitant justification of such concentration. Many years of one's life become invested in one's occupational specialization, and its exercise becomes an expression of one's personal identity. Relations between occupational groups are for these reasons often exchanges between participants in distinctly different subcultures characterized not only by the affirmation of their own values but rejection of or indifference to others. In some cases different departments recruit from different social classes and this can exacerbate disputes. In England, for example, works managers probably rise from less educated social classes than those from which sales managers are drawn.[8]

Tensions between functional departments become especially noticeable when new arrangements or methods of work are proposed.

Each department or division in an organization, with its unique tasks and responsibilities, tends to interpret any new idea, technical or administrative, in terms of its potential impact on the well-being of its members.[9]

An example can be given from a study of my own of changes in the organizational structure of British hospitals following their nationalization in 1947.

In one type of hospital, the medical superintendent was now required to reduce his administrative functions to two-elevenths of the time he spent on hospital duties and to relinquish his control over lay administration of the hospital and over the nursing service. Five years after this formal change, full reorganization had still not occurred and staff were ignoring and sometimes sabotaging each others' attempts to exercise their rights in the new system. Commenting at the time, I wrote:

Change is restrained by the fact that the Medical Superintendent, Secretary and Matron are not newcomers making a fresh start, but individuals who have worked together over the many years in capacities and relative statuses other than those now formally assigned to them. . . . In the case of the Medical Superintendent particularly, position and incumbent have become so merged with the passage of years that it has become difficult to detach by administrative measures rights and responsibilities from the individual who has in the past filled the formal role of leader. . . . The Secretary and Matron hesitate to presume upon their new rights and to invoke the informal sanctions of resentment and disapproval surrounding deviations from the old-established and firmly institutionalised distribution of power and authority. . . . A large section of the hospital staff, also, continues to behave as if no formal change has been made, and to route information and decisions via the Medical Superintendent. In part, this seems a deliberate resistance on the part of certain departmental heads to a system under which they and their staffs are, to some extent, subordinate to a "layman" rather than a professional.[10]

Conflict between functional groups may stem significantly from actual or felt violations in the norm of reciprocity. We incur costs in what we do for others on the understanding that in the course of time these will come back to us in what they will do for us. We feel uncomfortable or guilty when we are the recipients of too many benefits from others in relation to what we do for them, and vice versa. Conflict is particularly prone to occur where, over a protracted period, the services rendered by one group to another are not clearly reciprocated by the other group, that is, where people are or feel exploited by their colleagues. Such antagonisms arise, for instance, in relations with research and development departments which fail for protracted periods to produce improved products or processes for their colleagues, to whom they then appear to be an expensive luxury.

Much conflict in organizations stems from defense or advancement of self-interest in regard to scarce resources, for example, money, people, space, power, and status.

Freedom and autonomy resemble power in being scarce resources of which one has more or less only relatively to others. Conflict may ensue out of the attempts of any group to maintain autonomy. This involves warding off the attempts of others to control one's own affairs or attempts to control others in a way that will preserve or increase one's freedom of movement. It is not, of course, only organized functional groups occupying distinctive positions in the division of labor who compete for scarce resources.

I have referred particularly to intergroup conflicts within organizations connected with the presence of formally organized groups of task or occupational specialists but made it clear that other categories of employees may from time to time combine to pursue or defend their differing interests. In a somewhat similar way to the interest groups, there exist at any given time within an organization persons who are not normally grouped or categorized together for organizational purposes but whose community roles give them a commonality which may manifest itself in organizational conflict. Such a spillover is often very evident in multiracial societies where employees are apt to react to each other not only in terms of organizational role but also racial group membership.[11] Latent community roles are apt to become especially important within the organization at times of broad social tension, as has been found, for instance, in large companies in Belgium employing both French-speaking Walloons and Dutch-speaking Flemings, or between Afrikaners and English-speaking persons in South Africa. Sides may actively be taken on racial or religious grounds within the organization even where the management does not deliberately make its internal arrangements on such grounds or where the direct occupational interests of these categories do not divide them. The issues may be national, political, and economic power, including ownership and influence in large concerns—real enough issues—and the specific organization then becomes one of many battlefields.

Having discussed realistic intergroup conflicts connected with functional divisions, interest groupings, and latent social roles, we should refer finally to the part played by interpersonal differences and conflicts. Clearly, some colleagues find that they have little in common with each other or actively dislike each other, and large numbers of individuals are normally in competition with each other for promotion, the most attractive posts, recognition, and so on. Intergroup conflict tends to follow if the persons concerned are formally in charge of subgroups within the organization or have political power derived from high status, special expertise, or esteem. This is largely because organizational fates are linked and what happens to the individual depends to some extent on his relationship with his immediate superior. Persons of high status are in a position to affect the organizational fate of their juniors. This puts them in a position to command loyalties and to influence others to fall in behind them when they are engaged in competition or conflict with peers. In this way, personality conflicts based on objective differences can lead or contribute to intergroup conflict.

Perceptual and
Subjective Aspects
of Conflict

In dealing with management-worker conflicts, and intergroup conflicts, it has become apparent that these conflicts incorporate what may be described as both objective and subjective aspects.

Realistic conflict can be traced to objectively observable imbalances; it would in these cases be clear to a careful external observer that real manifest oppositions of interest, values, or of personalities exist between the groups or categories concerned. The contending parties see themselves as frustrated by each other and feel that they can make gains in their position by directing certain types of action toward those seen as frustrating to, or in rivalry with, them. They want to interact with the contending party in a different way or to eliminate him. There are some real ends to be gained and the other party is an obstacle to them. Hostile feelings are not inevitable in realistic conflict and may be absent, for instance, in labor disputes and the relations between lawyers on different sides of a court case.

On the subjective side, perception clearly plays a central role. Man behaves in accordance with his image of reality. He is guided in his actions by the percepts he has acquired of the objects and people in his environment. A crucial factor in industrial conflicts is, accordingly, the reality of opposed interests *as perceived by the parties.* In social behavior, perceptions of a situation matter as much as the objective facts of the situation and are among the factors influencing the system. Such perceptions are no less potent when they are wrong perceptions. The work of Stagner and Rosen suggests that there is, in a sense, only one reason for group conflict, the perception by at least one group of another as threatening to its goals.[12]

These perceptions are conditioned by the roles in which people find themselves, the ideology to which people adhere, and the past history of each group and past relations between them as well as the current relationships. Perception is, of course, not only a matter of individual viewpoint. With sustained interaction, uniformities of perception develop within groups of people who have shared common experiences and who are in a common situation, or define themselves as being in a common situation. They tend to select the same sorts of facts from those available to them and to interpret them in the same way.

An organization may be perceived quite differently by people who stand in different relations to it. Each individual tends to get a different picture depending on where he stands. This point was dramatically demonstrated by Lieberman, as described in chapter 16.[13]

The importance of perception and belief can be illustrated both from the issue of conflict of economic interests and class identification. In the case of the Bank Wiring Observation Room, Roethlisberger and Dickson argued that the behavior of the workers could not be explained on the basis of their economic interests. The system they were sabotaging would, the research workers said, actually have been in their individual economic interests and they had no experience of rate-cutting. But as later analysts have pointed out, it is irrelevant whether the wage system was, objectively speaking, against their interests. The workers felt that there was something to their detriment that could come from higher output. This belief was widespread elsewhere at the time and was, in fact, connected with actual rate-cutting which had taken place at some places in American industry. It is easy to see how the Hawthorne workers could hold the same view, irrespective of whether it was applicable in their case. Sykes, in particular, has argued convincingly that the Hawthorne evidence indicates that the workers conceived their situation as involving a conflict of economic interest.[14]

Again, in the case of the class conflict approach to the study of management-worker tensions and beliefs, it is irrelevant whether or not western societies are objectively structured on lines of economic class. There is no doubt that the view many people have of society is of the sort described by Marx. They identify themselves strongly with "the working class" and see society as divided basically into two opposed factions that are distinguished in terms of wealth and power. Characteristic of this view of society is the belief that one's plane of living cannot be radically changed by individual effort but only by an increase in the power of one's whole class, which will secure for it a larger share in the economic goods of society. Such an attitude will reduce willingness to contribute in the workplace and may provoke apathy if not hostile, destructive, or noncooperative behavior directed against employers and their representatives. As we know, the things that men perceive as real are real in their consequences.

Subjective, or non-realistic, conflict also has within it protective or defensive reactions, deflection or projection of hostile feelings, and elements of ignorance, mistake, and hangover of past bad experiences. The choice of the party with which one contends is partly fortuitous; another antagonist might also do. The conflict is partly occasioned by, or serves as, tension release and is not necessarily occasioned by the rival ends of the parties.

People develop strong attachments to the key primary working groups of which they are members, particularly, one might assume, if such membership is likely to continue. These attachments seem to follow from close and frequent interaction, from experience of cooperation, from a shared value system and framework of perception and interpretation, and from a sense of shared fate. The individual member is likely to derive part of his identity from his group. He is likely to have made sacrifices for the sake of other members. He may well have conscious reservations about the wisdom of the investments he has made in that group or about whether it has conferred on him as much as he feels he has contributed. Such reservations would be associated with negative feelings about the group, existing side by side with more positive feelings. Even those members feeling most positive about the group may have occasional doubts about the balance of exchange within it; certainly in times of crisis the most deeply committed and most involved can be deeply hurt if there are indications that they are insufficiently appreciated. They have at least potentially negative feelings toward the group.

The free expression of overt antagonism within such groups is characteristically regarded as dangerous and wrong; the negative side of members' feelings is regarded as a danger to the group and is denied or by-passed. Unresolved tensions tend, therefore, to be directed outward. Hostility tends to become displaced, to be directed outside, at parties other than those which originally precipitated it. And disvalued features of the behavior of one's own group are projected outward, attributed to other persons and groups.

At the same time members of a work group are apt to feel a need to protect themselves against current or potential criticism or attack from without. Such a need may be related to insecurity about their own standards, lack of confidence in their own performance, or the fear that others will identify (or invent) vulnerable points in their performance. It seems difficult to avoid such actions, reactions, and anticipations under a system in which colleague groups compete with each other for scarce resources. The case of each rests largely on the superiority of its performance and prospects, and reputation is a crucial bargaining point. Reputations are built partly by deliberate attempts to ensure that successful performance is made evident. But, in addition, criticism of other groups distracts attention from defects in one's own performance and can protect one in advance by focusing attention on the defects of others.

People's ideas about the past are an intrinsic part of the contemporary situation and affect current social relationships. Opposed histories based on differential reconstructions or interpretations of the past may exist between different groups in the same organization. Bitter memories or traditions of negative incidents can poison current relations between groups, sometimes even when the key individuals involved are no longer present.

Historical factors can be key in intergroup tensions because of the special importance of vicious circles or self-fulfilling prophecies in human relations. If members of Group A communicate to Group B their expectation that B will act antagonistically to them, this will increase the likelihood that B will in fact do so. Group A will take defensive precautions in the dealings with Group B that are insulting: Group B will react with anger which reactivates members of A and validates their behavior. For members of Group B to make their own views of themselves tolerable they will need a low opinion of A's judgment, motivation, and competence and will adopt or advertise such a view. In other words, the parties can go on behaving in a reciprocally reinforcing way.

One reason why past conflicts continue into the present is that group members are always anxious to justify, validate, or vindicate their past, present, or future behavior. A group may seize on current incidents to store as ammunition for some future expected conflict of interests. They are estimating that future contingencies may come about for which they should be prepared. In this way the future, uncertain though it may be, can be said to play an important part in contributing to intergroup conflict.

Ignorance of other groups is a further subjective factor that can contribute to conflict. Ignorance provides scope for negative fantasies about others and for the acceptance of negatively toned information about others that one will avoid submitting to the test of reality.

Ignorance may be motivated and functional—for example, it may disturb existing coalitions, relationships, or ideologies to have truth impinge on them.

Maintenance and Reinforcement of Conflict

It follows from what has already been said that, whatever factors have priority in time, subsequent factors (objective and subjective) can come to maintain, reinforce, or even aggravate a conflict. For instance, individuals entering a situation may express their hostility more freely where competition for scarce resources is already acute. The free expression of such hostility then may well add to tensions between the parties, reinforcing the opinion that attempts to reduce friction are not worthwhile. Or disagreement within a group about the best way of coping with a threat from an outside party may result in continued projection onto the outside party of responsibility for trouble and therefore increased retaliation.

Conflicts can be reinforced by the fact that people make their careers by moving up the internal hierarchies of status and esteem within groups and organizations. Junior members may protect their futures by displaying to their leaders their commitment to the dominant group ideology, including that part of group beliefs that disparages outside groups. They may want to show in actual behavior that they can be as tough as anyone in dealing with the threatening outsiders. It is theoretically open to a junior member (or any other) to opt out of the conflict, dissociate himself from part of the group ideology, or remain silent when this is discussed, and declare his neutrality. But this makes both him and others uncomfortable, places him at a distance from his colleagues and attenuates his membership.

A key part appears to be played in the escalation of intergroup conflicts by the patterns of differential association that tend to ensue once a conflict has begun. Even in the absence of conflict, people with initially convergent occupations, interests, tastes, and aspirations are drawn together. They tend to interact with each other more than with others, avoiding in this way those with whom they disagree and elaborating the outlook that unites them and marks them off from others.

As Vilhelm Aubert of the University of Oslo has pointed out, the arguments for one's own side are, cognitively speaking, more conspicuous.[15] One hears them more often, puts them oneself more often, reinforces others and becomes reinforced by those others.

Physical proximity, even without deliberate choice of one's neighbors, is in itself also likely to promote feelings of group solidarity. W. H. Whyte, Jr., has demonstrated in his study of Park Forest, a middle-class housing development, the way in which propinquity fosters neighborliness and the formation of geographical subcultures.[16] Propinquity increases interaction and the need to by-pass interpersonal difficulties and the consequent projection of such difficulties as in fact occur onto other persons. Moreover, the opportunity to see what others actually do reduces scope for the proliferation of unrealistic fantasies about their acts and motives.

Chein has graphically described the prospects and process of cumulation that can occur when occupational specialization, physical proximity of the specialists, and contests for resources and esteem coexist. The site he chooses is a university:

Within many large university departments, not all of the faculty can get to know one another with any degree of intimacy. Increased specialisation also contributes to differential patterns of association, not only directly, but also indirectly, through the location of offices, sharing of facilities, differential patterns of concerns with particular students and so on.

No university department is free of frustrations to its individual members, and one is most likely to find a sympathetic listener among those with whom one is thrown into most intimate contact. Sources of frustration are often differentially distributed along the lines of the fostered differential associations, as in the availability of facilities and the allocation of space. Differential patterns of interpersonal association are, therefore, accentuated by differential patterns of shared grievances, and by advantages perceived as accruing to the others with whom one does not associate. It is not easy to see what relative strangers can possibly be doing to merit their salaries, why they should need as much of the space or facilities as they get, or what possible contribution they can make to the welfare of one's own students.

The social worlds of large university departments become polarised into subgroups, each of which tends to perceive the faculty status of its ingroup members as clearly justified, and of the outgroup members as not. . . . One does not know what others are doing except by rumour and hearsay . . . genuine respect is itself conditional upon knowledge of one another's work such as is largely fostered by association.

The newcomer to a large university department, with all of the insecurities of his uprootedness, is likely to gravitate to the people most like himself and most involved in bringing him to his new job; and he can help maintain stability by continuing his contacts with the people he knew best at the institution he has left. Thus he both reinforces whatever tendencies there are at the new institution toward differential association and enlarges his circle of "ins" across institutions. Moreover, his cross-institutional circle of "ins" tends to become assimilated with the cross-institutional circles of ins already established by his new associates and theirs tend to become assimilated with his. The same happens with the circle of "outs." Pretty soon, the newcomer has a new community with his selected associates at the new institution. They all tend to identify the same sets of people as good and bad.[17]

Apart from illustrating conflict accumulation, Chein is making the important point that conflicts can become reinforced by groupings outside the parties immediately involved. Within an organization any contending department will argue, especially with superiors, its own worth relative to rival departments and the reasons why it should be supported and receive preferential treatment. But apart from this, support from an outside source can increase the determination of the department to fight on. The importance of this source of conflict cumulation immediately becomes obvious when one thinks of the effects of national trade unions or employer's associations giving support to one or other party in a management-worker industrial dispute.

Accommodation and Adjustment to Conflict

We can also expect that a number of accommodative mechanisms will come into play which have the effect of mitigating the conflict, taking the edge off conflict, and reducing the display of overt hostility in face-to-face contact.

Several such mechanisms and processes have been observed in the case of relations between scientists and their colleagues; we have already referred to these in Chapter 13. As we showed, accommodation is a two-way matter. While the employing organization changes the recruited scientist, he in turn changes the organization. The literature reports a history of concrete problems during the opening decades of this century in the association of scientists with large-scale industrial enterprises.[18] But the new large industrial organizations characteristic since the mid-twentieth century have become larger users of scientists, more dependent on them, and more experienced in using them to mutual benefit. Many have provided reasonably satisfying conditions for their work. In some cases great corporations have established laboratories as famous as those at leading universities. There have been modifications in bureaucratic forms of administration to cater better to the diverse needs of the variety of categories of specialist nowadays increasingly required in large enterprises. This appears to be helpful to commercial success. Burns and Stalker have shown how firms in a technologically demanding industry have suffered in comparison with their competitors where they have persisted with an authoritarian type of structure that has not provided a favorable context for innovation.[19]

ACCOMMODATION THROUGH SUBVERSION
OF HIGHER-LEVEL AUTHORITY

Investigators have also identified situations of potential conflict between colleagues where accommodative mechanisms have developed to avoid serious overt difficulties. Roy has shown how machine operatives in one shop received surreptitious assistance from service groups in their subversion of formally instituted rules and procedures.[20] Roy's analysis suggests that this cooperation was given because it was part of a larger system of reciprocal obligations. The data also suggest that the service groups rendered the assistance wanted because this involved less work for them, because they were similarly distrustful of management and resentful of changes, and because refusal would have made face-to-face interactions awkward.

ADJUSTMENT THROUGH PERSONNEL TURNOVER

Changes occur in the relations of parties through personnel turnover. This may be through normal retirement, since organizations persist longer than individuals remain working in them.[21] Commonly also, some individuals who are prominent in a conflict or series of conflicts leave the field. This may be a matter of finding an objectively better work opportunity elsewhere. It may be at least in part a manifestation of the individual's reluctance or inability to face continuing stress in his work situation. In some cases physical illness results in a controversial person leaving the organization—one would think that psychological stress is likely to play a predisposing part in this.

Most writers on conflict agree that the fundamental basis of conflict between groups can rarely be explained by the personality characteristics of the leader of either party or by purely personal differences between them, that is, conflicts cannot persist except as social institutions involving group beliefs on both sides. It follows that the mere resignation or retirement of leading members on one or either side is unlikely to change the situation drastically. At the same time a changeover can provide an occasion for redefining relations, reopening negotiations, exploring possibilities for increased cooperation. A gesture towards the other side may be highly appropriate for a new leader. He suffers little loss of amour propre by renewing discussions; the implication is always present that insofar as his side has sinned, been unreasonable or uncooperative, his predecessor can be blamed by both parties. Nor is any loss incurred if the new negotiation fails, since the parties are not in a significantly worse position than before.

It is not only the occasional individual who leaves the field of conflict. Whole groups sometimes emigrate to other institutions or break away to form independent organizations of their own. The former pattern is fairly common in academic life and the latter in the world of advertising agencies.

HUMOR AS A MEANS
OF DEALING WITH TENSION

Rose Coser's study of humor among psychiatric colleagues in a hospital setting neatly describes the use of jokes in tense situations and relations.[22] At its lowest, humor provides a temporary respite from tension, often a displacement of attention and aggression from their present object. She shows how humor among colleagues often constitutes an appeal to those present to rise above the present difficulty to some more inclusive goal, or to escape from it to some other objective held in common such as capacity to enjoy life, to be philosophic, or take a long view. "In laughter," she says, "all are equal—to laugh with others pre-supposes some degree of common definition of the situation." Since appreciation of a joke depends on people taking the same viewpoint, humor constitutes an appeal for sympathy with the person who makes the joke. ("Perhaps the most serious indicator of hostility against one is the unwillingness of one's hearers to share a joke with one.") It is a means "of socialization—of reconciliation, of teaching and learning, of asking for and giving support, of bridging differences." It is a means for reducing social distance, often initiated by a person who makes himself (or his immediate colleagues) the butt of the joke. Here the joker avoids a joke against the other party that might add fuel to the fire but offers himself as an object of aggression that diverts that aggression to something peripheral to the contested part of the relationship, asserts his harmlessness, appeals to human kinship, and provides a basis for cohesion in expressing the agreement of all that his behavior is ridiculous and in affirming shared criteria of what is ridiculous. Since only those who share common norms and values weep or laugh together, laughter and attempts to provoke laughter constitute an appeal to or reaffirmation of such norms as the parties share and of the fact that they belong to the same collectivity.

Since humor expresses aggression as well as the expression by the humorist that his hearer shares the same moral universe as himself it can be used to provide negative sanctions in such a way that the person(s) attacked can accept this. As Coser says, "humour . . . is especially suited for this task because it combines criticism with support, rejection with acceptance." The target of the humor is informed that his misdemeanor is not all that serious, that everyone can laugh about it together. "Humour permits one simultaneously to attack and to lend support . . . it accuses and reassures, and it does both through consensus marked by laughter."

Coser suggests that since humor reduces social distance by enabling people occupying different positions in the social structure to share social pleasures and "to withdraw their focal attention from serious concerns," it has an equalizing function. "It is especially suited, in formal organizations, for bridging the fissures that tend to be a consequence of the status system and of the division of labor."

Humor permits aggression but does more than deflect hostility, provide a safety valve for it, or relieve the humorous person of it. It is, Coser points out, a means for controlling hostility and handling interaction within a group experiencing tension and conflict.

Coser's analysis is consistent with and elaborates Radcliffe-Brown's,[23] according to which joking and teasing are mechanisms for dealing with relationships that involve both attachment and detachment, both social conjunction and social disjunction. In Coser's words, "humor resolves the conflict between the association of persons deriving from their common concerns and the simultaneous dissociation inherent in the status system."

Multiplicity of Conflicts in the Industrial Organization

We have, so far, concentrated on two main forms of organizational conflict—management-worker conflict and conflict between colleague groups. While analytically distinct, they are not always so in practice: intergroup difficulties in both spill over into clashes with the other and conflicts occur within each about how best to handle the other side.

Nor are the management-worker and interdepartmental distinctions the only ones along which battle lines are drawn.

Some types of employee do not fall neatly into either the management or labor category and have interests (which they tend to pursue) in opposition to large numbers in both of the major groups.

Interest group organization and active struggle over interests is promoted in our society by the determination of occupational and life chances by factors (such as education and, to a lesser extent, class) that are difficult to change once the person has adopted his career; social mobility may then best be achieved through the banding together of persons whose qualifications and status are similar.

Conflict between interest groups is sharpened where one of the groups feels that differentiation of rewards is made on an invidious basis, or is not legitimated by the value structure of the organization or community. Feelings of deprivation arise not so much from absolute differences as from comparisons in which one appears to come out worse. Deprivation, as is now well known, is a relative matter. Such judgments are linked with our work technologies. As Thompson has remarked, "The more complex the division of labour the more difficult the formulation and application of standards for equating inducements and contributions." [24] He points out that technological specialization makes differentiation of members unavoidable and the number of possible categories of distinction large, hence the potential for feelings of relative deprivation is enormous.

The multiple character of industrial cleavages is highlighted when one adds a temporal dimension. In the motor manufacturing firm described in *Men in Mid-Career,* there was a whole generation of men with low formal paper qualifications confronted with an incoming generation of graduates. The older men said that academic studies have limited value in the company, that the work did not require particularly high level education, that knowledge acquired in formal education was hardly used, that the company ran on procedures that could be learned on the job, and that time spent on the shop floor was a better investment than formal training when it comes to handling practical problems. Some put quite explicitly the fact that they experienced or expected conflicts with the incoming, better-educated people of whom they were now in charge and with whom they would have to live for the second half of their careers. On the other hand, younger men entering the firm and allocated to work under this type of man complained about difficulty in learning the ropes, about the reluctance of the older men to teach them.

This cleavage and potential conflict is associated with wide social changes and with increased accessibility to higher education, which makes it necessary for employers to look for new staff among university graduates. It is also associated with the internal technological revolution—the growing necessity for staff to be able to deal with symbols, with paper, and with people.

Technological change is in itself a force for cleavage and factions since skills are continually being made obsolescent by new knowledge, new machinery, new processes and techniques. This means that there are often some groups of employees whose expectations are being disappointed and whose bargaining power is being attenuated and some with whom the reverse process is occurring. This can bring both into conflict with management and with each other.

Conflict as
an Integral Part
of Social Life

Conflict in the sense of the clash of objective interests is an inevitable and integral part of organizational (and wider social) life. It is difficult if not impossible to conceive of collective life (especially in democracies) without accepting that there will be some clashes over values, interests, goals, methods, access to resources, and the distribution of rewards, esteem, and power. Social organizations are not like smoothly running machines with their parts in complete harmony. Clashes and friction are especially evident in times of change when old institutions and new (effectively the people whose behavior embodies these) experience stress in relations with each other. Theoretically speaking, any of the objective issues could be resolved by negotiation, arbitration, or higher-level decision-making, and the interests of a defeated party need suffer only to the extent that they are deprived of the prize which others were also pursuing. This is more accurately described as competition rather than conflict because it does not imply efforts actually directed against an opponent. But in practice even competition that does not obviously present intergroup problems tends to have associated with it at least oblique efforts to put the other party in a disadvantageous position to compete—such as secrecy in the conduct of one's affairs or the disclosure of one's resources, canvassing support for one's own side from superiors and bystanders, or manipulation of the image of one's own group. In practice too, individuals will have closer attachments to some groups than others (particularly with groups whose interests they conceive as similar to their own) and this will structure their identifications, their perceptions, and the expression of their feelings in a way that canalizes critical attitudes and hostility into intergroup relations. While the combination of the conflict and canalization of interests does not necessarily make intergroup relations problematic, some measure of active opposition between the parties is common, and clashes of interests, values, and aims, combined with their associated feelings, provide a continuing source of tension in their relationship.

We do not know, except in a very general way, precisely what circumstances bring intergroup conflict into the category of an acknowledged problem. But it is evident that a major reason why conflict is typically contained in social systems rather than bursting out in its more destructive forms is the fact that the parties usually have other, often overriding, interests in common. The members of a manufacturing department may daily contest the actions of their colleagues in sales and express dislike of their approach, but it is usually against their shared interest to take their differences to an extent that perceptibly damages the capacity of their employing organization to compete with its commercial rivals. In other words, competing or conflicting interests commonly exist side by side with different types of relationships and feelings. As Small said as early as 1905,

in form the social process is incessant reaction of persons prompted by interests that in part conflict with the interests of their fellows, and in part comport with the interests of others.[25]

Small appears to be referring here to conflict in the sense of clash of objective interest. The coexistence of the subjective side of conflict with cooperation, indeed the way this follows from cooperation, was brought out by Malinowski. As he put it, aggression is a by-product of cooperation. The smaller the group involved in cooperation, he says, the more united by common interests and the more they have to live and work with each other day by day, the easier it is for them to be mutually irritated and flare up in anger.[26]

A pithy statement of the view taken of conflict in this book is provided by Gluckman: "Every social system is a field of tension full of ambivalence, of cooperation and contrasting struggle."[27]

There are clearly many cleavages in the industrial system about which actual or potential conflict is oriented. To say that there are many actual or potential cleavages is not to say that conflict is endemic around each cleavage all the time. There is certainly continual pulling and pushing to advance the interests of one's own group over others. But a particular conflict may become acute only once in a whole when some particular issue becomes red-hot or a specially important decision has to be taken. Also, since one belongs to a variety of groups and categories one is not on the same side in every conflict—one cannot be, since some are based on function (side of business), some on skill, some on age, some on trade union membership. This multiplicity of cross-cutting conflicts can, as Simmel and Coser have shown us, help to keep the whole system stable or at least viable —because it prevents one massive line-up of two opposing factions.

The multiplicity of cleavages and tensions leaves a good deal of room for manipulation and for the formation of coalitions—whose subgroupings may change according to the issues involved so that one set of groups is united on one occasion and another set on another.

Another approach leading to essentially similar conclusions is that of Cyert and March.[28] They derive their argument mainly from the existence within any firm of a multiplicity of aspirations and goals. Profit maximization appears in practice to be only one of many goals of the firm or to be a goal of only some members. Other goals of higher management are: maintaining a satisfactory amount of profit; maintaining or increasing share of market; and growth.

Most firms operate on a subgroup basis, and the subgroups press their own interests—for example, in regard to a specific function. Subunit goals develop in some degree independently of the goals of higher management. External demands on the firm come from suppliers, shareholders, unions, and government. These conflicts of goals exist around what the firm should do, who should be rewarded by how much, and how the resources of the organization should be allocated. Even where these various needs, demands, and requirements appear to be shared, definitions and perceptions vary as to what the situation of the firm is and what needs to be done.

Cyert and March suggest that, viewed behaviorally, a firm does not have any single, universal, or organizational goal, that there are continual standing conflicts of interest within organizations. Some of these can be traced to the fact that at any given time the senior management is bound by past commitments to people which may be at variance with current distributions of inclinations, interests, and power.

These considerations lead Cyert and March to view the organization as a coalition: in a business organization the coalition members include managers, workers, shareholders, customers, lawyers, tax collectors and regulatory agencies. In government organizations the members include administrators, workers, appointed officials, legislators, judges, and clients. In the voluntary charitable organization, there are paid officers, volunteers, donors, donees, etc. Drawing the boundaries of an organization coalition once and for all is impossible. Each coalition at any point will include people who are diverse with respect to other latent or active conflicts.

Cyert and March ask how it is that, given the existence of continuous unresolved conflict and continued bargaining in the organization, reasonable continuity in the pursuit of goals is maintained.

Part of the answer lies in the reduction of freedom constituted by past commitments. Another part of the answer lies in the fact that organizations do not pursue all their goals at the same time or with equal effort. They concentrate now on one goal, now on another, swinging somewhat in accordance with pressures from coalition members and from other internal and external social, economic, and technological factors affecting their existence. Different interest group coalitions vary in the amount of time and effort they devote in their attempt to influence the organization. Human beings have limited time and limited capacities to devote to any of their interests and clearly some people have more stake than others in what each organization does. Another part of the answer lies in the complex managerial apparatus for voicing and dealing with conflicts—authority system, status system, interdepartmental meetings, etc.

Effects of Conflict

In discussing management-worker conflicts we referred to some of their effects, both positive and negative. Having reviewed now a wider range of organizational conflicts, we formulate below a more general statement on the consequences of organizational conflict, meant to apply in a general way to all.[29]

The existence of conflict within an organization implies a breakdown of social cooperation, and attempted or actual damage to the capacity of a rival group to make its normal contribution. It diverts energy from the tasks of the organization and substitutes warfare as a motive for association. It may well reduce the capacity of the overall, containing organization to compete with other organizations with less current internal trouble. It encourages the formation of social structures organized for war rather than for the real tasks of the organization. It encourages unrealistic beliefs and theories among contestants about each other. It reinforces self-doubt. It blunts judgments about the behavior of others and one's own group. Where dishonesty or opportunism enter into conflict they are apt to corrupt their users and infect other areas of their behavior.

At the same time what societies term progress emerges characteristically from struggles in which various individuals, groups or associations seek to realize their own idea of good. Conflict provides a means of coming into an active relationship with parties with which a person may previously have had little or no contact. Conflict brings into association the like-minded who feel they can together pursue their shared interests more effectively. Conflict provides a group with a sense of its own identity, encouraging its members to define and strengthen what they have in common. Conflict may (at least in the short term) perform group-maintenance functions by allowing the diversion of hostile impulses outward from the group. Conflict allows a group actively to pursue its interests. (As Coser says, power is necessary as well as merit.) Conflict is stimulating. Conflict can clarify expectations between parties and correct imbalance in reciprocities and in power. Conflict of interests can lead to the modification or creation of law and of judicial or law-enforcing institutions. Conflict forces awareness of difficulties on the higher levels of an organization and may lead to structural resolutions which, whatever they do to the group originally involved, may benefit the organization as a whole. Opposition to a group can lead to diagnosis of what is wrong with it and possibility to a solution. Such "sharpening" effects of conflict between colleague groups were recently brought out in the United States by a presidential panel which had just completed a study of the country's high command and the Defense Department. As the panel described events, when the Army, Navy, and Air Force and their chiefs were battling openly, they often exposed each other's arguments and weak points, sharpening the real issues for their civilian superiors. But now there was a tendency toward avoidance of issues in which the accommodations of conflicting views were impossible. On contentious matters that had reached the Joint Chiefs during 1969, that body made unanimous recommendations on all but eight-tenths of 1 per cent of the issues considered. As a result, the panel reported, the president and the defense secretary cannot "consider all viable options" in making major decisions.[30]

Where multiple conflicts exist within an organization, the energies of its members are mobilized in many directions and will not concentrate on one conflict cutting across all relationships. By crisscrossing each other they prevent a basic cleavage along one axis, the tensions do not cluster around one basic theme, and the many-sided conflict in fact constitutes a binding force.

Conflict can provide an impetus to social progress and can contribute to the common welfare and stability of an organization by diffusing struggles in multiple directions. This is what we mean by the stability of a plural society, that is, one in which no organized body of interests is allowed to dominate the rest.

To say that conflict can benefit an organization or a society does not mean that everybody benefits equally or at all from conflict or its effects. A department in an organization whose budget is cut after representations by their colleagues that they are ineffective is likely to become unhappy and resentful. Their interests have been prejudiced. So when one says that conflict can be beneficial to an organization or the society of which it is part, one means beneficial mainly to those who gained the upper hand, to the majority of members (which excludes those whose interests have been damaged) or to those outside who stand to gain from transaction with it.

The Management
of Intergroup Conflicts

This section deals with managerial institutions for anticipating conflict between colleagues at more or less the same level and for mitigating standing conflicts between such colleagues. It also deals with characteristic management interventions when such conflicts reach the level of organizational crises. Again, while conflict between colleagues is normal and usual, it is rarely practicable to allow expression of all current and potential conflicts within an organization. This may be altogether too disruptive and destructive. Consequently, all organizations develop measures for dealing with rival claims, power contests, or value differences; for mitigating, redistributing, or transforming tensions in such a way that the strains of new tensions are less costly than the old; for intervening in conflicts when they show signs of escalating; and for dealing with crises once they have actually occurred.

STRUCTURAL ARRANGEMENTS
FOR HANDLING ROUTINE
OR ENDEMIC CONFLICTS

Standing institutions for anticipating and handling endemic conflicts are an important aspect of the bureaucratization of administrative procedures. The attempt to exercise organizational control on the basis of knowledge, expertness, and technical competence includes procedures to reduce the incidence of conflict and to deal with such conflicts as do occur on a rational basis and within an accepted value system. Rules that stipulate what is to be done, by whom, for whom, and under what circumstances take a large proportion of such decisions out of the area of debate. The formal allocation of duties to departments, task groups, and roles rather than to individuals in their personal capacities emphasizes their dispassionate distribution. The clear stipulation of boundaries reduces the likelihood of competing claims in a no-man's land. Linking formal authority with particular organizational duties helps to legitimate the distribution of power. Strict accountability for the use of organizational resources combined with detailed written documentation of administrative acts enables a central administration unit to require justification of expenditure and other behavior in terms of organizational purpose rather than the pursuit of departmental or private goals.

The allocation of superior authority to persons in senior positions enables those persons to overrule others who oppose them.[31] As Shepard has pointed out,

An organization chart can be viewed as a (conflict) suppression chart. . . Problems can always be "solved" by activation of the suppression chart . . . suppression remains society's chief instrument for handling conflict, as the importance of policing in the supervisory role . . . attests.[32]

A senior person has the right to decide a large range of issues between subordinate subgroups and individuals in his area of jurisdiction. Even quite small differences in formal status give one man the edge over another and facilitate the acceptances of the senior man's wishes. The senior man knows that high authorities are more likely to support his views and the junior man is inclined to moderate his aspirations accordingly.

Committees are set up to consider and adjudicate between competing demands for money and staff and their decisions are binding on the departments affected. Such committees usually include representatives of each such department so that each can be assured that its case has been fully made and representatives can be put into a position to report back to their constituents that the distribution of resources has been fairly made.

Decisions on budgets and establishment are usually made on an annual basis. As a result, competition for resources in its more acute forms tends to be restricted to the couple of months during which bids are made and considered and all departments are required to accept budgetary and personnel establishment decisions as fixed for the next twelve-month period.

Rationalizing principles in bureaucracies extend to the use of human resources. Senior managements are entitled to screen out from among prospective recruits those whose training and ability do not fit them for organizational roles or who lack qualifications that would make their appointment defensible to others. At the same time managements can check on the values, attitudes, and motives of potential recruits. These help to ensure that an intolerable proportion of entrants will not present later problems of dissidence and uncontrollability. Contracts of formal employment with clearly understood duties and rewards, linked to categories of persons with the same qualifications, help to reduce subsequent argument about correctness in classification. Formality in subsequent assessment and promotion schemes helps to ensure that qualification for a post is a public matter, that applicants from one department are not deliberately favored over another, and that subsequent appointments can be justified on the basis of superior technical ability.

Considerable care is normally taken to explain, in terms of rationality and the protection of shared interests, decisions that are potentially divisive or might result in feelings of inequity. In the allocation of responsibilities, resources, and rewards, pains are characteristically taken to show that this is being done strictly on the basis of technical, economic, or efficiency considerations. When agreed or empirical criteria for allocation are lacking, the senior management may seek legitimacy for its allocations by calling in outside authorities, such as consultants, thus deflecting aggression by transferring or sharing the responsibility for unpopular decisions.[33]

CONFLICT PROPHYLAXIS

Preventive action can be illustrated from personnel policies concerning scientists, especially young scientists new to industry.

Mechanisms for reducing the likelihood of tension and friction are many and varied.

At the *recruitment* phase these include encouraging potential employees to visit the organization and its laboratories, to meet present staff and to discuss with them what it is like to work there. This includes opportunities for undergraduates and research students during university vacations. At the *induction* phase, new scientific employees are shown over the total establishments so that they will be helped to see the relationship of parts of the system to each other and, more particularly, where their contribution fits into the overall operation. The newly employed scientist may be given a number of trial projects to work on in the hope that he will feel that he has been given freedom of choice, can take to whichever he likes, and will adopt it as his own.

Young scientists are exposed to practical problems or to executives from other sides of the business, so as to increase the likelihood that they will develop more interest in practical problems as they brush up against them.

They are sent to appreciation courses about other sides of the organization's work and methods, for example, on the economic position of the company and its accounting methods.

Selected scientific employees may deliberately be rotated through different positions in the organization, for example, from a longterm research laboratory through a research and development section and perhaps a production post back to scientific management.

Established scientific staff are often allowed a proportion of time for their own research (personal work), either by designating a portion of their weekly time for this or by providing a shorter required working year than for other staff.

For the established, senior or distinguished scientist, organizational requirements may be relaxed so that he is (or feels) free to devote himself to whatever work he pleases. The senior management hope that the senior scientist will spontaneously choose a line of work that could benefit the organization; that other scientists will be attracted in the expectation of association with such a prominent person or in the hope that they may eventually win similar freedoms; and that the employment of distinguished scientists will have positive public relations value.

To deal with tensions arising where the scientist feels that he lacks the career opportunities of administrators, special financial awards may be provided for scientists who have produced ideas, product or process improvements that have been of conspicuous economic benefit to the organization.

Attempts are made sometimes to increase acceptance of administrative authority by appointing scientists to general management positions. These scientists then cease directly practicing their profession. But in addition to their particular administrative contribution, their presence in these positions is meant to convey the message that the organization has as many career opportunities for scientists as others and will help with the complaint by scientists that people like themselves lack a say in major organizations' decisions.

Specialized roles are often created for scientists in partially segregated substructures of the organization, for instance in specialized departments for basic or long-term research, development, and application of knowledge or service activities. This creates boundaries between the specialist and his colleagues and helps to create a more favorable culture for the fostering of his work and values.

Some internal variation in administrative arrangements is often provided within departments employing scientists and professionals from those dominant in the organization, for instance by developing project teams whose leadership can be shifted with the needs of the particular task in hand and allowing for a measure of colleague control.[34] This can be combined with the provision of special types of leadership by a professional from the same field as other employees, whose tasks are to combine technical leadership and support with superordinate control and also to mediate between his technical colleagues and executives in other departments. Organizations that employ professionals can usually create opportunities for them to achieve some professional rewards while still serving the primary needs defined by the senior management, including attendances at conferences and publication of selected papers and cooperation with eminent scientists acting as advisors to their firms. Further, some major employers of scientists and professionals have set up dual career channels, one for line executives and one for scientists and professionals, permitting the latter to improve their prestige, income, and facilities without giving up their specialities.

SECONDARY SOCIALIZATION
AS A MEANS OF ANTICIPATING
AND CONTROLLING CONFLICT

The aquisition of newcomers is expensive and their subsequent acceptance of the values and rules of the organization is too important to be left
to chance. Entry into the organization and early contacts and experiences
are therefore usually carefully managed. The work organization has a
mandate to change those who enter it, in the sense of adding skills, teaching
them to identify the situations in which those skills should be applied, and
informing them of the rights and obligations attached to their roles.

Induction procedures and early training instill at the same time as information and skill the theory (ideology) of the organization, the rationale
for its existence and for its current practices as well as its methods. All
teaching in technique and subsequent technical training are accompanied
by explicit or implicit attempts to convey values, including the worthwhile-
ness of contributing to the company, appreciation of the functions of others,
and the importance of competence and cooperativeness.

The existence of specific objectives makes work organizations particularly purposive, with the result that departments and roles within them
have defined sub-purposes or functions systematically related to certain
central aims. Individuals who enter and remain in work organizations accordingly occupy roles which have embedded in them a contribution to
some centrally defined objectives. Either they must accept those objectives
as their own or go through motions consistent with the attainment of those
objectives, a process which tends in itself to turn into the commitment
which it may be originally intended only to imply.

There is much more to the process of accepting and sharing objectives
than merely carrying out an individual role. These roles are positions in
interactive systems between people in complementary roles and there will
be a tendency among those in related roles to support the role behavior
by any one role occupant which is appropriate to that role as a formally
defined part of a work system.

The organization persists for periods longer than the individual work-life
span and consists of people of different generations, many of whom pass
out of the organization during the career of the recruit. This, coupled with
expansions in scale, faces the organization with the more or less constant
need to locate and train successors, so that persistent and deliberate attempts are constantly made to identify potential persons for promotion,
to convince them that this is a proper objective for them, and to encourage
them to acquire the skills and values that will be necessary in the next post
and the next sector of the cooperative subsystem of the firm in which that
post will be embedded.

The process is not a depersonalized one involving the person in a relationship with a company in the form of an abstract entity. He will have formed a link with particular sponsors whom he has impressed who will hold out to him an attractive future if he follows their lead, accepts their advice, joins their circle, and identifies himself with their particular functions or with their attitudes toward organizational affairs—often in a context wider than his immediate sphere.

As well as being a hierarchical structure of persons and roles, the organization is a network of overlapping primary groups variously constituted on bases of geographic proximity, task similarity or complementarity, linked occupational fate and so on. The individual will have multiple memberships of such primary groups and in the course of developing and maintaining such memberships will come particularly to value some of his memberships. In the course of retaining and protecting his membership he absorbs the ideologies of some of the groups and accordingly binds himself to them and to the larger social entity of which they are part.

The person enters the organization predisposed to accept its influence, to be pervaded by its values, to intertwine his fate with it, to make its concerns his own, and to identify himself with it and it with himself. He enters after prolonged exposure to a social system in which he has developed psychological needs to support himself and a family, to perform useful services for others, to occupy an accepted position as a worthwhile member of a community carrying out necessary activities, to occupy himself in a way useful to society and to find significance and meaning in his acts. He feels a need to have an impact on his environment, to struggle toward and reach difficult objectives, and to participate in successful associations and enterprises.

Such attitudes predispose persons to accept influence and opportunities to identify themselves with the fate of the organizations of which they are members and to forfeit in doing so a certain amount of autonomy and self-determination.

MANAGERIAL STYLES
IN HANDLING CONFLICT

Earlier in this chapter we referred to the dilemma posed by Lawrence and Lorsch between differentiation and integration. In their field studies they reviewed the structural devices they saw used for achieving integration. In one highly differential organization there was a complicated array of integrating devices and mechanisms. There were entire departments of integrating personnel, cross-functional teams, paper systems and schedules, all reinforcing the management hierarchy itself. In other cases, lesser degrees of differentiation permitted the integration task to be handled through the managerial hierarchy and through paper scheduling. But they argue that another set of factors is important in achieving a productive balance between differentiation and integration, that is, the patterns of behavior used to manage interdepartmental conflict. A paper by Ruedi and Lawrence refers to three main styles of behavior.[35] These were forcing (the use of authority or power to settle conflicts by overruling dissent); smoothing (the handling of conflict by minimizing differences, postponement, or superficial compromise); and confrontation (the process of sharing relevant facts and opinions and struggling through the disagreements in a problems-solving way). As far as this group of research workers is concerned the favored approach is clearly confrontation. They feel able to support this with a research conclusion, that the firms achieving more effective integration made more extensive use of confrontation with only a secondary use of forcing.

Certain reservations need to be expressed about this formulation. Whatever indices are used, effectiveness of integration is difficult to pinpoint. It suggests, in any case, a consensus of aims and standards that might not exist in the normally differentiated organization: what is effective integration from one department's point of view may be a dismal compromise for another. Then, what exactly is confrontation and what are its limits? Confrontation is surely a matter of degree. It is unlikely that any department will provide another with the full range of the information, opinions and attitudes of its members; these are partly strategic ammunition, and partly private matters which could disrupt collaboration. How much confrontation is being prescribed? Are we dealing here with cause and effect or with a correlation in which we do not know which is cause and which is effect? It is surely as plausible to say that highly integrated organizations can afford confrontation as to say that confrontation brings integration. Finally, to suggest that confrontation helps collaboration implies that these are two independent variables: one would expect, on the contrary, that factors that favor the one will favor the other. To argue that goodwill (sharing) can solve a problem is to by-pass the fact that the essence of the problem is lack of goodwill. On the other hand, Lawrence and Lorsch and their colleagues may be making a central point if their main intention is to argue that difficulties of integration may be viewed as costs of differentiation and that interpersonal acrimony may be softened where it is realized that this follows from a position in a functionally organized structure.

Management Interventions
in Disputes and Crises [36]

If a conflict is acute enough, persistent enough, or is perceived as too costly for the organization to bear, higher management sooner or later intervenes, reacting usually to a particular dispute or crisis. We are concerned in the rest of this chapter with extraordinary steps for handling disputes and crises, that is, with the sorts of steps taken when the normal institutions have failed to cope.

The spontaneous reaction of administrators at the top of organizations is to act in some way that preserves the outline of existing institutional arrangements. This is partly a matter of preserving the power and protecting the interests of those at the top; partly a matter of respecting a system that has allowed one to rise to the top; partly a matter of avoiding radical action that would seem to threaten the whole basis of one's existing behavior. Senior administrators are accordingly tempted at first to resort to remedial, palliative action rather than acknowledge severe conflicts where these exist or to confront themselves with the restructuring and personal rearrangements that may be necessary.

The assumption is characteristically first made that the system is not wrong but that the trouble is that people are not working it properly. This assumption is exemplified in such acts as calling for rationality rather than emotion; appealing for tolerance; trying to persuade people to be cooperative; increasing the flow of information in an attempt to improve communications and increase mutual understanding; and mediating and adjudicating between disputants on rights, resources, and boundaries.

MAKING THE WHOLE ORGANIZATION SALIENT

Meetings and conferences are arranged to make the larger organization more salient as a shared frame of reference. Training events and personnel shifts are attempted in order to widen the experience of individuals and to make them more conscious of the contributions of others and of their own shortcomings. It is, of course, common for the purposes of conflict amelioration to be combined with a different overt task and in some cultures it is only the overt task that can be openly discussed.

LOCALIZING DISPUTES

One strategy of management is to insist that certain types of dispute form part of the structure of delegation; for example, middle-level managers may be asked to settle disputes within their departments themselves rather than referring them upward. One apparent reason for this is to indicate that the problem is too minor for a senior person, ranking low in the hierarchy of problems currently confronting him. Another is the wish to contain conflicts in time, space, or form of expression lest they escalate upward or spread to and contaminate other relationships. The same purpose is sometimes met by removing a conflict from an already inflamed battle area by redefining it as the business of some other sector of the organization, for instance, defining it as a financial matter or technical issue rather than one of interpersonal or intergroup relations.

NEW MACHINERY

If persuasion, mediation, and appeal for cooperation fail, a typical solution to the problem is to set up additional machinery. If two departments are not well coordinated, this might involve adding a coordinator or setting up a committee to which disputes must be referred.

The emphasis here is conflict control rather than conflict eradication. This approach can be helpful in leaving the organization with the functional, stimulating part of conflict. At the same time, the creation of new adjudication machinery can become a stimulus for every small grievance to become a conflict. To avoid this the adjudication process is sometimes made to cost something (even if only prestige, or embarrassment of users).

Thompson has said that

technologies require differentiation and interaction, but . . . organizations have some control over (i) the number of categories, (ii) the pattern of interaction among members of different categories. Hence within limits administrative allocations determine the relative deprivation experienced by organization members, and thereby control potential conflict inherent in modern technologies.[37]

Clearly, if existing categorizations, groupings, and interaction patterns promote conflict, re-allocations of task and personnel can mitigate these conflicts or substitute new conflicts that are in prospect more tolerable.

MULTIPLE GROUP MEMBERSHIP

The sorts of strategies attempted here usually involve attempts to make overall organizational needs the most salient for individuals and groups and to reduce group identification below the point where it is given priority over overall interests, while adequately representing the interests of subgroups.

This can be attempted by providing for multiple-group membership, for example, putting scientific managers on selection boards for all management trainees. The same end can be sought by nominating members for planning committees who report to some top officer rather than their departmental heads. The organization's problem, rather than the specialized interests of competing subgroups becomes the context of the committee's operation and the members assume responsibilities as citizens of the larger structure. A related strategy is to ensure that decisions are taken either at a level above functional specializations or by bodies composed of people from a variety of functional specializations, preferably under someone with general management authority above that of a functional specialization. A decision that is taken within one specialized unit and affects the actions of others is bound to be regarded as designed to increase the power of the deciding unit and neglecting the interests of others.

RESTRUCTURING

Resolving conflicts through restructuring can also be attempted through decentralization, for example, a large company may move people from its central personnel department and place them in functional departments nearer the points where the work is done. This is intended to avoid barriers growing between personnel and operational people, to make the problems of the latter more visible to the former, to make the contributions of the personnel people more obvious to those in operations, and to reduce the fantasies that grow with distance.

On a grander scale, Chandler has reported a tendency for large American companies, as they diversify their products and penetrate new geographical territories, to begin to deal with each major product line through a separate, integrated, autonomous division. This structure succeeds the pattern of operating from functionally divided headquarters where each functional department makes its specialized contribution to a wide range of products. He attributes this trend to a need to rationalize the use of expanding resources, but acknowledges the part played by "an increasingly intolerable strain (placed) on existing administrative structures" by "territorial expansion and to a much greater extent product diversification." [38]

Thompson has made essentially the same point of restructuring to reduce conflict in describing as a defense against conflict in large organizations the establishment of semi-autonomous branches each dealing with one class of environmental element.[39] This can function, as he says, so as to reduce the threat of competing task stimuli and reduce vulnerability to (distant) administrative allocations. In this way, feelings of relative deprivation between heterogeneous branches may be less likely to develop. Decentralization, and concomitant (expected) greater solidarity around a task or around overall organizational objectives has, however, always to be balanced around the economies of scale and specialization in accounting, production, advertising, etc.

In the case of conflicts linked with functional specialization, possibilities for restructuring are suggested by Trist and Bamforth's contrast of the composite Longwall system with the conventional system described earlier.[40] The composite system involves a common task and a common paynote. Instead of being divided into several groups with different skills, the work force is constituted into one group whose members are multi-skilled and who are able to carry out most of the operations. The men work together for a shift, taking up the work cycle where they left it at the end of the day. Shift work is rotated, usually by the men themselves. There are task subgroups, but these are interchangeable in membership. Under this system, as described by Trist and Bamforth, all workers have a direct interest in the completion of the cycle and disagreements between subgroups are coped with more effectively and given less importance. As compared with the conventional system, the composite system, though using the same technology, was reported to be more conducive to productive effectiveness, low cost, and work satisfaction. Essentially this system gave a larger work group responsibility for a whole task and showed each person or subgroup the consequences for his immediate colleagues of any work neglected.

Rice worked along similar lines in India, showing that forming larger groups along less specialized lines and giving them wider task responsibility increased both satisfaction and productivity. Rice's studies used the principle that individuals and groups need to be allowed to perform complete tasks. While individuals may perform only part of the task they can identify themselves with the group outcome because they are organized so that they share the same psychological field.[41]

Katz feels that

the use of the group as an extension of individual motivation in this way is limited to the small, face-to-face group of interdependent workers. It is extremely difficult to extend the principle across group lines to the larger organization. Nevertheless it helps reduce conflict in the organization by giving more satisfaction to individual members from the work process itself.[42]

REORGANIZATION

The most drastic forms of restructuring essentially decide disputes in favor of one of the contending parties. They are likely at the same time to involve the dismissal or relocation of personnel. The following two cases, which I had the opportunity to observe while a member of the Tavistock Institute, illustrate this type of administrative action.

Organization A contained a marketing department and an advertising unit. The functions of the former consisted almost entirely of market research. The advertising unit contained a small (but substantial) market research unit. Operational units of the total concern were free to commission research projects by either department. Comparisons were made over a period of years on an informal basis by internal clients between the technical competence of the two units. Occasionally the units worked on more or less the same problems with rather different results. The question began to be raised, mainly outside these units at higher levels of authority, as to whether more fundamental long-range research should be undertaken by the concern and, if so, where this should be located, i.e. in one of these two units, in a different department of the same concern, or should be sub-contracted to an external social research institute. After many months of discussion and argument, it was decided to give the budget to the marketing department with power to sub-contract. The research section of the advertising unit continued to object on the grounds that they were technically superior to the research workers in the marketing unit and that their own staff could do much of the work that had been sub-contracted. After several months the head of the marketing unit had two fairly serious illnesses in close succession and (was) retired. A successor was appointed. During the succeeding

18 months, the successor was criticised on the grounds that he was not running his department as economically as he could, and was not relating the long-term research effectively enough to the needs of the firm. He was asked to resign and an announcement was made that he had done so on health grounds. The two research units were then merged under a new name, a non-specialist from the advertising unit was put in charge, with the senior specialist of the old marketing unit and the specialist from the research section of the advertising unit as his immediate subordinates and at the same level as each other. He was told to exercise immediate and drastic economies and steps were taken to bring the contracted research to an end.

The second case also involved a very large concern.

At the time I came to know the firm its Marketing Department had recently set up two units concerned with market research. One was to be at headquarters and to concern itself with relatively short-term research, mainly oriented toward the needs of headquarters divisions and of operational units in the field associated with the concern. The other, at some distance from headquarters, was to be concerned with strategic, long-range research of a more basic type.

It was not long before the two research units were in difficulties with each other. Each criticised the technical competence of the other; the long-term unit defined itself as the more technical, more concerned with deeper issues, and members were impatient with the eagerness of the men in the other unit to prove themselves of practical use to the concern. For their part, the headquarters personnel thought the leadership at the other unit pretentious, extravagant and impractical and were critical of their apparent reluctance to expose their methods to open discussion. The position was complicated by the fact that the headquarters unit spent part of its budget through the long-range unit on studies which it soon came to criticise. Conflict developed also over relations between the two research units in their contacts with operational units; the headquarters unit was concerned to maintain contact with the market research officers in these units and held conferences with them designed to raise standards and introduce them to headquarters thinking on research. On the other hand, the long-range unit expected the market research officers in the operating units to look toward them rather than headquarters for technical advice and leadership.

During this period of difficulty, the department which contained both units came under fire from top management on the grounds that day-to-day sales were being given insufficient attention. The department was then divided into two sections, one to be concerned with day-to-day sales and the other with long-range marketing development. Both research units were to be within the scope of the latter.

Difficulties between the research units were exacerbated by this split. Both felt less secure in the light of what they took to be an indication of top management's view of new and expensive activities not yielding a demonstrable return.

Shortly afterwards open quarrels took place between leaders of the two units, both of whom complained widely about each other's personal behaviour, about the quality of the other unit's work and about the extent to which the other party was prepared to co-operate. A series of such incidents culminated in a conference with other colleagues at which both felt vindicated in their attitudes by the other's behavior. A couple of weeks after the conference the manager of the short-term unit and his senior assistant were informed that their duties were to be transferred to the other unit and that their services would no longer be required.

Although in the first of these two cases the conflict was deep and sharply fought, little of this was at the direct, face-to-face level. To my knowledge there were few, if any, confrontation incidents. Both parties made their points within their own units, to colleagues at the same level outside their units, and to members of management at a level senior to both. This constituted both an expression of the conflict and an attempt to muster support for their own side against the opposition. In the second case the same process was evident but direct face-to-face confrontations and public scenes took place also. In both cases the public rationale for suppression or modification of the rival party's activities was, as can be expected, the attainment of greater organizational effectiveness.

The two cases point to the fact that intervention by the higher authorities may be prompted by representations made to them by the contending parties. Indeed much of the efforts of the contending parties in intergroup conflicts characteristically goes into trying to win over such authorities to their point of view or soliciting the good opinion and support of third parties in the hope that these parties will report back favorably about them to the management.

Intervention to restructure is often the culminating phase of a continuing organizational political struggle generated at the level of the contestants, a phase at which a judgment has been made that the fallout from conflict outweighs the stimulation of competition.

NOTES

1. On contributory causes of intergroup conflict see R. Williams, *The Reduction of Inter-Group Tensions,* (New York: Social Science Research Council Bulletin 57, 1957); M. and W. Sherif, *Groups in Harmony and Tension,* (New York: Harper, 1953) and *Outline of Social Psychology,* (New York: Harper, 1956); M. Sherif, ed., *Inter-Group Relations and Leadership,* (New York: Wiley, 1962).

2. See P. R. Lawrence and J. W. Lorsch, *Organization and Environment: Managing Differentiation and Integration,* (Cambridge, Massachusetts: Harvard Graduate School of Business Administration, 1967); and P. R. Lawrence, ed., *Studies in Organizational Design,* (Homewood, Illinois: Irwin and Dorsey, 1970).

3. Lawrence and Lorsch, *Organization and Environment,* p. 9.

382 LEADERSHIP, CHANGE, AND CONFLICT

4. S. Macaulay, "Non-Contractual Relations in Business," *American Sociological Review,* 28, no. 1 (February 1963): 55–66.

5. R. L. Kahn, D. M. Wolfe, R. P. Quinn, and J. D. Snoek, *Organizational Stress: Studies in Role Conflict and Ambiguity,* (New York: Wiley, 1964).

6. C. Sofer, "Buying and Selling: A Study in the Sociology of Distribution," *Sociological Review,* 13, no. 2 (July 1965): 183–209.

7. E. L. Trist and K. Bamforth, "Some Social and Psychological Consequences of the Longwall Method of Coal-getting," *Human Relations* 4, no. 1 (February 1951): 3–36.

8. R. V. Clements, *Managers: A Study of their Careers in Industry,* (London: Allen and Unwin, 1958).

9. W. M. Evan, "Organizational Lag," *Human Organization,* 25, no. 1 (Spring, 1966): 51–53.

10. C. Sofer, "Reactions to Administrative Change: A Study of Staff Relations in Three British Hospitals," *Human Relations,* 8, no. 3 (August 1955): 291–316.

11. See C. Sofer, "Urban African Social Structure and Working Group Behaviour," in *Social Implications of Industrialisation and Urbanisation in Africa,* (UNESCO Tensions and Technology Series, 1956). Such phenomena underline the importance of studying organizations as subsystems within larger systems rather than quasi-independent systems.

12. See H. Stagner and H. Rosen, *Psychology of Union-Management Relations,* (London: Tavistock, 1965).

13. S. Lieberman, "The Effects of Change in Roles on the Attitudes of Role Occupants," *Human Relations,* 9, no. 4 (1956): 385–402.

14. A. J. M. Sykes, "Economic Interest and the Hawthorne Researches, A Comment," *Human Relations,* 18, no. 3 (August 1965): 253–264.

15. V. Aubert, in a discussion of an earlier version of this chapter given as a paper at VI World Congress of Sociology (Evian, 1966).

16. W. H. Whyte, Jr., *The Organization Man,* (Garden City, N.Y.: Doubleday Paperback Edition, 1957), chapter 25.

17. I. Chein, "Some Sources of Divisiveness among Psychologists," *American Psychologist,* 21, no. 4 (April 1966): 333–342, and 334.

18. J. J. Beer and W. D. Lewis, "Aspects of the Professionalization of Science," *Daedalus,* 92, no. 4 (Fall 1963): 764–784.

19. T. Burns and G. M. Stalker, *The Management of Innovation,* (London: Tavistock, 1961).

20. D. Roy "Efficiency and 'The Fix'. Inter-group Relations in a Piecework Machine Shop," *American Journal of Sociology,* 60, no. 3 (1954).

21. It is, of course, theoretically possible that impending retirement of a significant figure in a conflict helps to keep that conflict in existence, as people are apt to feel that it is not worth doing anything until he goes.

22. R. Coser, "Laughter Among Colleagues: A Study of the Social Functions of Humour Among the Staff of a Mental Hospital," *Psychiatry,* 23, (February 1966).

23. A. R. Radcliffe-Brown, *Structure and Function in Primitive Society,* (Glencoe, Illinois: Free Press, 1952).

24. J. D. Thompson, "Organizational Management of Conflict," *Administrative Science Quarterly,* 4 (March 1960): 391.

25. A. W. Small, *General Sociology,* (Chicago: University of Chicago Press, 1905), p. 205.

26. B. Malinowski, "An Anthropological Analysis of War," *Magic, Science and Religion,* (Glencoe, Illinois: Free Press, 1948).

27. M. Gluckman, *Rituals of Rebellion in South-East Africa,* (Manchester: Manchester University Press, 1954), p. 21.

28. R. M. Cyert and J. G. March, *A Behavioural Theory of the Firm,* (Englewood Cliffs, New Jersey: Prentice Hall, 1963). See especially chapters 2 and 3.

29. For discussions of negative aspects of conflict see D. Katz, "Approaches to Managing Conflict," and H. A. Shepard, "Responses to Competition and Conflict," both in R. L. Kahn and E. Boulding, *Power and Conflict in Organizations,* (London: Tavistock, 1965). The leading discussion of "positive" or "functional" effects of conflict is contained in L. Coser, *The Functions of Social Conflict,* (Glencoe, Illinois: Free Press, 1956). This is valuable elaboration and commentary on Simmel's classic essay on conflict (Georg Simmel, *Conflict,* trans., K. H. Wolff, (Glencoe, Illinois: Free Press, 1955).

30. Based on leader in *New York Times,* (August 16, 1970).

31. I am indebted to Professor D. Lockwood for discussion of this topic.

32. H. A. Shepard, in R. L. Kahn and E. Boulding, *Power and Conflict in Organizations,* (London: Tavistock, 1964), p. 128.

33. Thompson, "Organizational Management of Conflict," p. 401.

34. See discussion in A. K. Rice and E. J. Miller, *Systems of Organization: the Control of Task and Sentient Boundaries,* (London: Tavistock, 1967).

35. "Organizations in Two Cultures" in Lawrence and Lorsch, *Organization and Environment.*

36. See discussion in D. Katz, "Approaches to Managing Conflict," in R. L. Kahn and E. Boulding, *Power and Conflict in Organizations,* (London: Tavistock, 1964); W. G. Bennis, "A New Role for the Behavioral Sciences: Effecting Organizational Change," *Administrative Science Quarterly* (September 8, 1963): 125–165; P. Spencer and C. Sofer, "Organizational Change and its Management," *Journal of Management Studies,* 1, no. 1 (March 1964): 26–47.

37. Thompson, "Organizational Management of Conflict," p. 392.

38. A. D. Chandler, Jr. *Strategy and Structure. Chapters in the History of the Industrial Enterprise,* (New York: Anchor Books, Doubleday, 1966), p. 53.

39. Thompson, "Organizational Management of Conflict," p. 403.

40. E. L. Trist and K. W. Bamforth, "Some Social and Psychological Consequences of the Longwall Method of Coal-getting," *Human Relations,* IV, no. 1 (1951).

41. A. K. Rice, *Productivity and Social Organization: The Ahmedabad Experiment,* (London: Tavistock, 1958).

42. Katz, "Approaches to Managing Conflict," p. 113.

19 : Professional Interventions in Conflict and Change

METHODS of direct intervention by social scientists in problems of organizational conflict and change have developed in England, in the United States, and, more recently, on the Continent. The first Tavistock work in this genre was by Jaques and his colleagues.[1] A subsequent selection of Tavistock cases and a review of methods and findings was provided by Sofer.[2] W. G. Bennis has compared the ways in which this work is approached in the United States and England and discussed the theoretical assumptions on which it is based.[3] Pages has provided a French viewpoint and approach that converges on the British and American.[4]

In this work a social consultant joins one or more groups within an organization and uses his understanding as a social scientist in their service on an agreed task, usually involving a current interdepartmental crisis or an organizational change in process of introduction.

This type of activity has been variously described as action research, social consultancy, or sociotherapy. It involves the study and treatment of organizations or parts of organizations through methods derived or adapted from sociological/social psychological research and psychiatry.

Professional interventions in organizational problems by social scientists differ in several ways from direct managerial interventions. The social scientist works in close association with line management but is not himself a member of it. His association with the organization is temporary. He pays attention to the forms and processes of social interaction and to perceptions and feelings in addition to the content of the interaction and explicates these forms and processes in collaboration with the client organization. He defines his responsibility as clarification and interpretation of behavior, not as advice on executive action. He concerns himself with the quality of decision-making and the steps taken in reaching decisions rather than with the correctness or otherwise of any particular decisions taken. He questions prevailing institutions and structures rather than regarding himself as obliged to work within the framework they provide. Most social consultants have been staff members of universities or research institutes and have regarded social consultancy as a source of data for teaching and research on social processes and organizational behavior.

The work of the social science consultant overlaps with that of the management consultant. The social consultant is different, however, in his emphasis on social processes (including unconscious motivations and feelings), in his research-centered approach and in his interest in clarifying, interpreting, and studying behavior rather than taking the initiative in recommending specific changes.

Social consultants have normally had the standard training in theory and research of the academic social scientist. Particular theoretical influences derive mainly from Lewin, Freud, and (especially in Britain) W. R. Bion. It is useful to the social consultant to treat his respondents' conceptualizations of their situation, as Lewin did, as part of their life space and to attempt approximations to the major social and personal forces currently bearing on their situations. Social consultants have also been influenced by Lewin's interest in creating more participative (democratic) social systems and by his conviction that applied social research had a special part to play in illuminating basic social processes. Freud's influence is obvious in the assumption that is made that persons are significantly affected by personal motivations of which they are unaware or imperfectly aware. These notions have been underlined in organizational studies by the realization that shared anxieties and unconscious collusions underlie social defenses in social institutions. Lastly, all social consultancy that involves interpretative comments on face-to-face group behavior, whether in committees, project groups, or group relations laboratories, tends to be influenced by Bion's accounts of group process.

Argyris has set out the argument for professional intervention in a recent contribution to the *International Encyclopaedia of the Social Sciences*.[5] He starts from the point that several criteria or requirements exist for organizational effectiveness. One apparently obvious criterion is achievement of formally announced objectives such as profit or efficiency in services provided. But any organization has at the same time to maintain its capacity to solve problems and the willingness of its employees to continue their contributions. While it may be possible in the short run, he says, to emphasize one of these activities at the expense of the others, eventually all must be expressed. There are, he says, nevertheless strong tendencies at the upper levels of management to emphasize activities which neglect or damage the second and third requirements. One of these tendencies is to emphasize behavior and attitudes related directly to getting the job done rather than those that maintain group effectiveness. Another tendency is to devalue the relevance or importance of emotions as against cognitive rationality. A third tendency is to assume that human relationships are most effectively influenced by formal control and sanctions.

Argyris suggests that the consequences of such tendencies in the behavior and attitudes of senior managements are the deliberate or unwitting suppression of interpersonal and emotional aspects of work; displacement of feelings into the form of technical/intellectual problems; restriction to ideas that do not challenge existing norms and practices; reluctance to experiment and take risks; development of a view that senior management is not prepared to change; and executive blindness about the true state of relations with subordinates.

He lists several ways of counteracting these tendencies at middle and lower levels of the organization, and these focus on suggested modifications in technology, controls, and structure. But, he points out, at the upper levels interpersonal relations among the senior executives become more important. The issue he poses is how to change the values and behavior of the senior executives: it is here, he suggests, that the social science trained professional has a special role to play.

In order to consider these matters against a background of concrete descriptions of what happens in this type of work, I describe below a sociotherapeutic case in which I was involved while a staff member of the Tavistock Institute. I refer back from time to time in this chapter both to this case and to the Davidson case described in the earlier chapter on emergent behavior in bureaucracies.[6]

A Case Study in
Social Consultancy:
The James Division

Dr. Andrews, the head of a psychiatric research unit newly established within a division of a large mental hospital, asked me to look over this unit to see if there was anything helpful I could say or do about it. At my first visit his closest colleague, Dr. Butler, the clinical head of the division, was surprised when I arrived, as the request from Dr. Andrews was news to him. He expressed concern at the possible negative effects and implications of my visit and said that a third party, Miss Edwards, in charge of the division's nursing services, would also be affected. I emphasized that I was there only at the request of Dr. Andrews and would abandon my present visit but would come again if all three invited me.

At a meeting with all three, they agreed to invite me to conduct a brief study of social processes and relationships within the division and to announce this invitation to all staff. It would be understood that I would report back to my respondents and to them the main outlines of what I learned; Dr. Andrews, Dr. Butler, and Miss Edwards would remain constituted as a project committee while I did this work. I would meet staff only in groups to avoid having to deal with the ambiguities of semiconfidential personal communications.

Some of the medical staff (whom I then saw) were employed by the hospital, some by the research unit. They said that this meant that they had differing allegiances and loyalties and they were not clearly related to each other in an authority structure. A junior doctor employed by the hospital could, because of his clinical responsibilities, exercise authority over a more senior research man. They complained also that there was a lack of direction from the most senior doctor in the place, the research head.

The laboratory scientists and ward sisters put an essentially similar problem to me, their feeling that colleagues in other wards and in the central administration put too many constraints on the experiments they wished to make in patient care.

My first meeting with nurses at ward level centered around the position of a research nurse who explained that she was responsible to the hospital chief nurse, not the division's own matron. Her duties were to help in the administration of a research project in the division involving the use of group methods of patient care by nurses; to study the attitudes of nurses toward their work; and to advise the hospital chief nurse on the implications for the hospital of nursing experiments in the division.

At reporting sessions with the project committee and respondents I put to them my growing impression that, in their enthusiasm for experiment, many of the staff were denying the significance of the responsibilities to the public of the central hospital administration, responsibilities that compelled caution. There was a risk that innovation would be valued for its own sake. We discussed the position of the research nurse; I suggested that her duties as research administrator must bar her from receiving the communications necessary to her as student of nurse behavior. In regard to the doctors I said that a vacuum had appeared in the level immediately below the top and competition for the number two position had occurred. The younger doctors felt they lacked research supervision; in the circumstances, their research achievments were likely to be modest.

The project group were quick to accept my suggestion that too many negative attitudes were being projected on to the hospital and that this was serving to divert attention from their own internal problems. They seemed to appreciate having their attention drawn to anomalies in the position of the research nurse. Dr. Andrews emphasized the extent to which administrative demands kept him from contact with the medical staff; I connected this with the projection theme.

At my subsequent meetings with the occupational groups I was accompanied by members of the project group. I was now more active. In meeting the nurses I suggested that line responsibility for the proper administration of the research project be moved from the research nurse to the division's matron and then delegated back to the research nurse: this would help everyone to see that research was part of the nurse's job, not a favor the individual nurse was doing the doctors or the research nurse. It would also avoid the danger of the research nurse and divisional matron being played off against each other. Also, if the research nurse wished to study nurses she should do so in another division, since the administrative components of her role would debar her from receiving the necessary confidences of respondents in her own division. These changes were immediately made. At my second meeting with the doctors they referred again to role confusion, ambiguity, and so on: I suggested that this was inevitable and possibly helpful in a new and growing concern and that appeals for clarification from higher authorities took attention off the necessity for individuals to find bases for cooperation among themselves.

There were two final meetings with the project committee. I expressed my conclusion here that the division and research unit were handicapped by the traditional hospital pattern of administration which divided responsibilities in a way that reduced accountability for whole tasks. It might be possible, I said, to rearrange responsibilities for the medical study, clinical care, and nursing of patients in such a way that each individual could experience and try to resolve the conflicts appropriate to his role. The project committee appeared to accept the implication that they should share responsibility for major decisions within the division (in effect become an administrative committee after my departure). But the research director and clinical head rejected my suggestion that the former become clinical head as well and the latter become his deputy on both fronts.

Compliments were paid to me about the manner in which I had worked with these groups and the changes that had resulted. I pointed out that, since the staff knew I was soon to leave, this could provide a rationale for discontinuing the developments and changes in attitude that had started.[7]

Structurally-Centered
Social Consultancy

Another member of the Tavistock group, A. K. Rice, concentrated in his social consultancy on experimental reorganizations of methods of production, sales, and management. The best-known example is his work with the Ahmedabad Calico Mills. In his book *Productivity and Social Organization: the Ahmedabad Experiment* he describes the main phases in the work, involving reorganizations of weaving methods and the creation of new management systems. He started from the basis that

while industrial production systems are, of necessity, designed in accordance with technological demand, there has been a tendency to project the technological into the associated work organization. The assumption is then made that there is only one work organization that will satisfy the conditions of task performance. This has meant treating groups and individuals as though they were machines. . . . Where, as has frequently happened, the resulting work organization has failed to satisfy the social and psychological needs of its members, their attitudes to task performance have inhibited the full realization of technological potential and lowered productivity.[8]

On the advice of Rice, the management made changes in their production system.[9] This involved changes toward a group-centered method of weaving —internally led, more or less autonomous, groups of workers taking responsibility for groups of looms, the groups of workers being themselves largely mutually selected. At management level, the changes included clearer segregation of functions and levels of management and between governing and operating systems; increased delegation; the creation of new roles; movement of personnel between roles; the formalization of new types of executive meetings; and the institution of management conferences. The book refers to the fact that, in cases such as this where family interests predominate, the introduction of new management systems implies stressful changes in family relationships. Although Rice does not say so explicitly in the book, he regarded a measure of help in this sphere as part of his task as consultant.[10] In the changes with which he helped and in the assessment of their effectiveness he took deliberate account of both conscious and unconscious attitudes and processes, including ambivalence toward him, and at some points discussed these with his clients where he thought this would help them to face painful changes.[11]

U.S. Examples

Similar types of intervention in organizations have been undertaken by American social scientists.

Floyd Mann developed a technique in the Detroit Edison company of surveying members' perceptions and attitudes at various levels of the organization, then feeding back the results to the next higher level.[12] He devised a scheme whereby suggestions for organizational change were initiated at successive levels within the organization in a way designed in collaboration with his colleagues and himself. At each level of the organization, members formulated plans for fulfilling their own administrative tasks and discussed them freely with their subordinates. Besides suggesting modifications, the subordinates discussed their own attitudes toward work, promotion, and supervision. The broad aim of this project was to "improve" morale and face-to-face relationships and to provide a better idea of objective and emotional barriers to change.

Argyris, Blake, and Mouton, and others have done work in a similar vein, combining research and reporting back in studies that include changes in behavior among their goals.

Argyris has reported in some detail a study of a board of directors and some of their subordinates in the course of which he combined the approaches of research worker and change agent.[13] He and his colleagues analyzed tape recordings of meetings of the board held over five months and came to the conclusion that their approach to organizational problems was highly directive, excluding personal and emotional issues in favor of formal controls patently related to economic objectives. They presented their report, without interpretative or analytical remarks, to each board member. Argyris attended a series of meetings with the board at which members discussed their reactions to the report with him. They then moved, with help from him, into discussion of their own interaction. His book provides details of several of the key sessions. These appear to show some increase in a tendency among board members to confront interpersonal and emotional issues and a greater interest in the possibilities of changing their behavior. Argyris had also studied in this case the immediate subordinates of the board, who criticized their work environment with particular reference to the behavior of their seniors. Argyris brought the two groups together in a shared feedback session, but reports that this failed, primarily, he conveys, because of the values and behavior of the board and the way these were reflected below. This conclusion appears to have been accepted by the board, who asked Argyris to continue to work with them to help change their interpersonal relations.

Between them they agreed to a series of one-day sessions whose objective was defined as "enhancing interpersonal competence." These sessions centered on tape recordings of board meetings, the executives in effect being required to discuss, with Argyris's help, how they had acted toward each other in the meetings and what the implications might be.

Social scientists associated with the National Training Laboratories, particularly known for conferences at Bethel, Maine, have taken individuals away from their organizational settings and put them in T-groups (training groups) either with colleagues from their own organizations or others. These experiences are designed to increase insight into group processes and to provide the individual participant with information on the way he behaves toward colleagues, and feedback on the impact of his behavior upon them.

The basis of this work is the belief that colleagues in conflict with each other can benefit from protracted opportunities to explore their relations with each other in a sheltered setting, away from their normal work environments. Here they can be helped to confront, acknowledge, and reexamine with professional help their characteristic attitudes and modes of interaction. It is believed, on a clinical psychotherapeutic analogy, that such experiences make individuals more objective about their own behavior and increase their willingness to change it.

Schein and Bennis place particular emphasis on the use of laboratory training methods in changing organizations.[14] While there is no attempt in their book to define laboratory training precisely, what they appear to have in mind is a training event whose essential ingredients are (1) the examination by delegates of their own behavior "in the here and now" as they experience it within training sessions—the delegates become participant observers of the social process to which they contribute; (2) direct feedback to delegates on their own behavior and personal impact so they can check this against their goals; (3) lectures and demonstrations on social science theory that can help to supply "cognitive maps" for delegates and give them some mastery over previously perplexing phenomena.[15] They say, elsewhere, that a core method in laboratory methods is a problem solving approach to conflict by which they mean that "if conflict does exist, it must be recognized and confronted as such instead of being denied, suppressed or compromised."

They describe their rationale for the special place of the laboratory as an opportunity for learning. As they put it, three sets of forces act on the delegate as a result of the special laboratory social structure and training design. First, the customary behavior of the delegate is unfrozen by his separation from his workplace and home and from the social routines and interactions that normally reinforce his patterns. He loses some of his usual self-defining apparatus of status, title, office, business suit, and personal privacy. These losses pose new questions of identity for him. The learner role and scrutiny of interpersonal behavior in T-groups bring his behavior in question so that he is forced to examine it. Secondly, delegates are encouraged to abandon conventional social norms that elude or bypass emotions and the expression of one's feeling about others: this provides them with opportunities to learn about themselves that are not normally available, in a protected setting where the task is discovery, and with opportunities to experiment with new behavior. Thirdly, the learning method helps the delegate relax his defences so that he is less restricted in the communications he accepts from others about what he is like and what effect he has on them, and more prepared to understand what they are trying to convey about themselves.

The heart of their argument so far as organizations are concerned is that "laboratory training provides the instrument whereby the normative goals and improvements set forth by organizational theorists and practitioners of organizations can be achieved." [16]

They cite four well-known examples in which social science theorists have recommended such "goals and improvements" or this is implied in their work. These are (1) Likert's suggestion of personal "linking pins" between colleague groups which might otherwise be in conflict as a device for integrating persons in their work; [17] (2) McGregor's arguments for the replacement of control and coercion with colleagueship; [18] (3) Lewin's demonstrations of the effectiveness of decision-taking procedures that permit participation of those affected; (4) Argyris's emphasis on interpersonal competence as a necessary ingredient in the role of a manager. How, ask Schein and Bennis, can persons leading organizations be induced or helped to carry through policies which would incorporate these operating principles? Ever since the Western Electric studies there has been a flow of criticisms of standard organizational arrangements and also a flow of suggestions and recommendations: the newly developed laboratory methods, they say, provide the means for translating these into practice.

They then go on to consider the relative effectiveness of "change agents" who are members of organizations or external consultants to them. Only the former have the intimate knowledge of the system to be changed and the trust of their colleagues. But the external consultant is more likely to be perceived as an expert with independent knowledge and perspectives. They conclude, reasonably enough, that internal and external change agents working in concert are likely to be most effective.

Although these authors make a point of the special role of laboratory training in changing organizations, they do not give details of exactly how any new learned behavior can be transferred to organizational contexts or maintained there.[19] They say that laboratory training can be introduced either by the organization setting up its own programs or by sending teams to laboratory communities. They add that the aims and methods of laboratory training must be understood and accepted by top management; that the laboratory methods must be installed openly in the same spirit as its training sessions are conducted; that the attendance of delegates must be voluntary; that interpersonal influence within the organization must be accepted; and that the probable effects of the training outside its immediate organizational area of application must be anticipated. They imply also that some national cultures or subcultures may be inappropriate environments for the use of laboratory methods in implementing organizational change.

Schein and Bennis point out that the learning focus of laboratories varies. One type emphasizes personal learning to the relative exclusion of attention to organizational or role relationships and tries to go deeply into personal and interpersonal dynamics. At the other extreme there is training explicitly designed to influence organizational performance. They describe R. R. Blake as one of the foremost innovators in this latter field.

Blake and Mouton contribute an account of their methods to the book edited by Schein and Bennis.[20] This is probably the clearest statement on what American applied social scientists aim to do in the direct work on organizational change. They start with a hypothetical factory faced with problems in one or more of the areas of productivity, wages, profits, interdepartmental conflict, management succession, decision-making and management-union relations.

The question is, "Under what conditions might the operation of this factory be shifted to attain higher production, to achieve union and management relations where the two groups are working together towards accomplishing common goals, to attain effective co-ordination between departments to make better utilization of the ideas available to it, and so on?

The way to attain organizational improvement described here is *not* based on treating symptoms. Rather it is based on a correction of underlying causes of problems that come to the surface as union-management conflict and so forth.

The primary goal is to change *patterns* of relationships between people and groups or between a group and the organization so that more effective problem-solving and greater production effort can occur throughout the entire organization. After this has been achieved, it can be expected that there will be an improvement in the *actual* operation of the factory—through detecting and correcting technical failures, making better economic or business decisions, doing a better job of conducting union or management affairs, or getting greater production.

The approach involves six successive phases. . . .

A learning programme based on behavioural science laboratory experiments is the first phase . . . all managerial members (and operational personnel, where feasible) examine theories of human behaviour and participate in controlled experiments to test these theories.

Team training, in the second phase, involves direct interpersonal feedback among actual work group members. . . . The aim is to examine and to resolve problems of communication, control and decision-making among those whose work requires unity of effort and close cooperation.

[In a] third phase . . . horizontal linking includes people from the same organizational level but from different groups who come into contact with each other in day-to-day activities. They are people who can accomplish their own production goals best when those from other units with whom they work are meshing their efforts with them in a co-ordinated way.

The entire managerial force sets broad organizational improvement goals in the fourth phase. The fifth phase is designed to bring about, in a concrete way, the organizational goals which were set in phase four and to correct the faulty problem-solving actions that were discovered in the earlier phases.

Once the strategy of problem solving and production improvement has been learned, the goal is to insure that it will be applied continuously until it becomes a stable way of organization life. Thus, the sixth and final phase is a stabilization period. . .

The . . . greatest insurance that an organization improvement effort will be successful is possible when all of the phases described are included. . . . In a large industrial plant employing 3,000–5,000, the completion of these phases may require from three to five years, or even longer.[21]

Intervention as
a Therapeutic Technique

My own two cases quoted in this book (the Davidson case and the James Division case) show that my aims were to provide colleagues with an opportunity to review the basis of their interaction; to enable them to check whether their perceptions of each other were accurate; to examine their own behavior as mirrored back through me and to consider its probable implications for the future; to check the extent to which they were using the resources available to them; to discover their anxieties about their situation and to see the relation of their present problems to those anxieties. The last-mentioned point is worth underlining. It became evident to the directors of the Davidson Company that they had appointed and retained substandard supporting staff to make sure that there was a gap in ability between themselves and their immediate subordinates. They may be said to have been defending themselves against possible exposure of their standards to competent people who might criticize them. When examined in the light of day, this hypothetical threat lost much of its force against what now appeared to be the alternative—a loss of competitive business efficiency.

I think it became evident to the hospital staff in the James case that they had invested in an elaborate set of alibis against prospective criticism of their lack of scientific and therapeutic achievement. These alibis were based on the ambivalence of other hospital staff and their own complex internal division of labor. In the project they realized that by dwelling on such attitudes and procedures one is apt to reify and cultivate them so that they do become increasingly real obstacles.

Neither the participants nor I thought in either case that all conflict would be dissipated by our joint work. But it was evident that they were starting to distinguish more clearly between the realistic and subjective aspects of current conflicts and to redefine their collective and individual problems. Collusion to avoid problems and to reduce problems to personal failings were being broken down. My intervention helped participants to analyze their own behavior and to introduce new institutions, both in the formal sense of creating new management structures and in the informal sense of submitting problems to cross-departmental scrutiny. Possibilities of cooperation increased when the parties were able to come to a greater measure of agreement in regard to facts and shared definitions of their situation. To this extent at least the reduction of perceptual distortions was important. No doubt, shame in the presence of an outsider contributed to a shrinkage in the emotional aspects of conflict.

In *The Organization from Within* I described the therapeutic component of this work as (1) the assembly and analysis of facts, and reconceptualization of problems, (2) redefinition of assumptions and expectations, (3) participation in planning and action, (4) introducing, monitoring, and evaluating innovations. The "therapeutic" work of the consultant may be regarded as provision of a special sort of organizational intelligence. In Wilensky's terms, this work is one of the defenses managements operate against the organizational pathologies associated with hierarchy, specialization, and centralization which distort and block the flow of information.[22] While he does not speak of social consultancy in particular, he describes the existence of new types of experts on intelligence, which include "internal-communications specialists." As he writes,

The more the organization depends on the unity and support of persons, groups, factions or parties within its membership for the achievement of its central goals, the more resources it will devote to the intelligence function and the more of those resources will be spent on experts we might call "internal communications specialists." [23]

Wilensky's remarks prompt the reflection that social consultancy provides management with a new or richer variety of data on what happens when they change their organizations and indicates that there are ways of introducing change other than those with which they are already familiar. This may be a better description of social consultancy than the widely used term "change agent" for the social consultancy role. The latter implies that change does not normally take place without external intervention. As Sayles has reminded us, the reverse is the case.[24] It is the core of the task of most senior managements continually to decide what changes are necessary and to implement changes. Nevertheless, as Sayles implies, the social scientist can help to reduce or anticipate some sources of disturbance during change, to identify structural sources and ramifications of instability and stress, and to re-order priorities among changes.

It has been suggested by critics of such work that it aims at reducing tension and reintroducing a more amiable status quo ante.

We know, in fact from the work of Simmel, Coser, and other theorists that tensions are unavoidable. Conflict is inevitable and, as we have explained, often functional for some aspects of the social system in which it occurs. The fact that the social consultant will reveal previously hidden conflicts from which current troubles are displaced will in itself create new conflicts and problems. In the Davidson case, conflict between the secretary and the board was not reduced or halted; it was replaced or moved to another area, that is, conflict between family and firm, between traditional institutions based on kinship and bureaucratic institutions based on economic need. My work with the firm also brought to a head conflict between the two younger directors, which had previously been displaced on to the issues surrounding the secretary.

Such approaches clearly uncover latent hostilities, reveal incompatible attitudes, and raise anxieties among those involved. But as Mann and Neff say, they can lead to a significant change in attitudes.

A major crisis in the planning and execution of a changeover may be necessary to ensure real understanding of the change by key top personnel. Crises can assist in bringing about attitude changes in top level personnel and should be viewed positively as well as negatively.[25]

When crises are precipitated management may for the first time be brought face to face with hitherto unperceived problems. In so much as these generate anxiety, it may be because for the first time they are appraising their situation realistically. These same crises may also bring the need for change to the attention of *other* personnel: such processes need not be confined to top key personnel.[26]

The social consultant would usually aim to encourage the acknowledgement of conflicts and the adoption of a constructive problem-solving approach to them. He would certainly try to intervene where a conflict appeared to be escalating for reasons apparently unrelated to objective conflicts of interest or had entered into a phase of expression of reciprocal paranoia.

Daniel Katz has suggested that socio-therapeutic work is limited because it does not resolve rational structural conflicts.[27] Katz underestimates the extent to which structural changes are in fact made in this type of work. In the hospital case described, the role of the research nurse was appreciably restructured, and a project committee was formed that became a new management group. In the industrial case I have cited, the firm, with my help, instituted a new management selection scheme and an appraisal scheme for middle-level executives, set up a management committee that brought board members and senior executives together under drastically altered conditions, and made new dining arrangements that brought senior executives into the boardroom for meals and informal sharing of management problems. In a technical college case which I reported in *The Organization from Within,* an advisory service for students and new linking structure with industry were introduced. In Rice's work structural changes were massive.

Detailed analysis and working over of the emotional aspects of a problem has been an essential preliminary in social consultancy to the solution of the structural aspects; while its immediate purpose may be to cope with psychological tensions, this has been done not for its own sake but in the pursuit of more radical aims involving structural alterations. This becomes more evident when one asks why fairly obvious structural defects persist unchecked before the socio-therapist sets to work.

This point is demonstrated in Miss Menzies' work in a hospital, in which she points out that certain administratively simple steps were not taken until after her arrival (collection of statistical data bearing on operational and training needs).[28] She links this with the level of anxiety present among staff and with the defensive nature of much of their behavior. The implication is that the staff found it less stressful to bear the confusion of their existing system than to take the rational action that an objective outsider could see was necessary. Until the emotional ground-clearing was done, key rational operational acts could not be taken.[29]

A question may appropriately be raised as to whether the change-agent, therapeutic approach to conflict-resolution, does not overstress the significance of organizational factors against those more clearly stemming from the wider society—the organizational environment. Conflict within an organization might merely be reflections of structural features of the larger society, for example, of class cleavages and differential access to the more valued occupational positions. A work organization is not something separate from the larger society; it is an aspect of the total society, a unit created by the social division of labor, in reciprocal interaction with the outside world, a part of a larger moral order.

In order to diagnose present problems correctly, it can be useful to explore with the client body which elements in their situation can and which cannot be changed, given the constraints imposed by the social framework. A factor to keep in mind is the peace of mind given to troubled people by the realization of what there is in their situation that they cannot appreciably alter. It is possible that they will discover that there are factors in their particular position that they can in fact work effectively on—to gain more collaboration from the particular nurses working in a particular hospital one does not have to change the whole nursing profession. The latter is a counsel of despair that functions to defend participants from doing what is, in fact, possible. As previously mentioned in our chapter on Mayo and his colleagues, members of that group argued cogently that no remedies external to a specific work situation can change a fundamental defect of organization in it; that it is reasonable to expect managements to do what they can to solve those of their problems to which their own behavior and decisions have contributed.

Intervention as Indoctrination

Social consultancy involves the pursuit by the consultant of certain key values. These usually include some of the values of the particular group that has called in the consultant—as well as those of the consultant. The relevant values of the client group may be assumed to relate to economic efficiency and the avoidance of colleague relations which either hamper efficiency or render everyday interaction actively unpleasant. But it is evident from writers in this field that they have a particular outlook that affects the type of work they do.

All are prepared to use their knowledge and skills to help particular organizations with their own problems, whether this involves making profits, government administration, or providing social services. They work within the basic value framework of Western mixed economies rather than, in their applied work, trying to change these fundamental social forms.

All appear to share an interest in putting to some practical purpose formally achieved social research findings and the conceptualizations of social situations which is the core of their professional expertise.

As Argyris points out in his encyclopedia article, there appears to be a common interest in working toward more "organic" styles of management in organizations. This involves emphasis on widespread participation in decision-making, flexibility in organizational structure, the assumption that it is appropriate for persons to be influenced by peers and subordinates as well as by superiors, and a preference for arranging tasks so that they constitute significant wholes and permit collaboration in groups who accept them as their own responsibility. This organic orientation, while shared, is more distinctly characteristic of the American than the British work.

Social consultancy often involves commitment to values concerning proper managerial behavior and candor (openness) in human relationships and efforts to influence managements toward increasing adoption of those values. (This is not to suggest that this is all the social consultant does. Clearly he brings to the attention of management a great deal of knowledge, theory, and investigatory expertise which is new to them and which does not constitute a direct attempt to influence values.)

Attempts to alter values are particularly evident in the case of the American social consultants, though this may merely appear so because they take greater pains than colleagues elsewhere to make these matters explicit.

Argyris includes, for instance, in his description of the organic model quoted above "an emphasis on mutual dependence and co-operation based on trust, confidence" [30] which every social scientist might not think to be a necessary attribute of organizations run on this basis.

A similar value standpoint to that of Argyris is found in the work of Shepard and Blake. In differentiating "mechanical" from "organic" systems of management they make clear their preference for the latter. They couple mechanical systems with inefficiency, cleavage, and strains.[31]

Schein and Bennis argue at one point that

Laboratory training is *not* in the business of suggesting this or that model of organization or *any* action alternative except insofar as these models and alternatives aid the development of learning, diagnosis and inquiry. . . . We view laboratories as controlled learning environments where people learn *not* that democracy or autocracy is a good thing or that cohesive and/or leaderless groups are good or bad (they may be but that is not the point), but that they can study and inquire about the *consequences* of autocracy, democracy, leadership type and cohesiveness. They can then choose with greater knowledge what form or practice might be most appropriate. Clearly it is possible that autocracy might be more appropriate under certain conditions.[32]

At the same time it is difficult to imagine any practitioner in this area actually helping to develop or support an autocratic work culture. Elsewhere, in the same book, these authors describe democratic values (alongside scientific values) as the meta-values of laboratory training. And, like Argyris, they try to encourage more candor and reciprocal confidence among their clients and laboratory delegates.

The conclusion seems inescapable that social consultancy includes attempts to get clients to accept certain key values of the consultant. These center around the values of inquiry and democracy, and include candor in the expression of feelings. While explicated to a lesser extent the Tavistock studies include these values in the same way as the American. Examining social consultancy from a therapeutic point of view one can hardly have reservations about this: surely all forms of therapy and advice-giving imply that the therapist/adviser and the client share the same moral universe and are working together toward agreed ends that both value. It is reasonable to assume that social consultants do not conceal their value orientations and that their clients know what they are asking for: indeed, as our quotations show, consultants are eager to make these clear so that their public is not under any misapprehensions.

At the same time, two questions arise. The first is whether it is in fact therapeutic to client organizations to intervene in the ways described. We have given some examples, in both the English and American work, in which a benefit seems to have been left. But a series of unanswered questions arises of *cui bono*. Has intervention been therapeutic if only members of top management feel that they have received advantages? How does it balance their interests against those of their subordinates? How does one weigh the interests of members of an organization against those outside it but also with stakes in it (consumers, suppliers, potential recruits, the government, the general public)? Are there not distinct possibilities of some persons being influenced against their will in the name of objectives (profit, efficiency, candor) that they do not share? Can one speak of overriding interests of the organization while recognizing that organizations are effectively coalitions of persons whose felt interests partly coincide but also partly collide?

A separate question concerns the relation of therapy to candor. Social consultants do not appear to have taken into sufficient account the potentially disorganizing and demoralizing effects of increased candor between colleagues. As Moore and Tumin have cogently pointed out, ignorance can perform important functions in certain key social relationships.[33] One might be less prepared to continue collaborating with a colleague if one realized the full extent of his hostility toward one or his low opinion of one's contribution. Confrontation with the opinions of others can challenge one's opinions of oneself, shake one's personal security, reduce one's interest in collaboration or one's ambitions, and undermine the defensive rationalizations that one leans on to explain one's personal fate and render it acceptable. Ignorance and ambiguity can be helpful in maintaining morale and effort. It is also conceivable that public expression of what one person thinks of another can reduce the likelihood of change in opinion. Once one expresses an opinion of someone, one is inclined to look for evidence that supports one's assertions. Public expression of an opinion has about it an element of irretrievability. And once one hears a negative opinion of onself by another, one may well be inclined to rule out that person as a credible source of opinions, knowledge, or influence, or resign oneself to the hopelessness of trying to change his impression.

Social Consultancy as
a Research Approach

Interventionist methods are a variety of the "sustained participation" methods of organizational research described by W. R. Scott in his essay on "Field Methods in the Study of Organizations," which itself draws on several earlier discussions of this topic.[34] Scott is concerned to compare "sustained" methods with what he calls "transitory" methods, that is, methods in which the investigator does not remain for a protracted period with the organization he is studying but visits it briefly to obtain information of a limited and specific character, which will be combined with similar data on other organizations.

The sustained researcher is, he says, in a better position than a transitory one to collect a large amount and a great variety of material; to win the confidence necessary for the conduct of experiments; to collect detailed descriptive material on social processes or on what actually happens during a change and to realize the importance of the time factor in organizational processes; to define the "totality" of the situation in which his respondents interact; to observe many aspects of their situation and to trace connections among phenomena, thus preserving the unitary character of the social object being studied; and to make direct observations rather than rely on the reports of respondents or informants.

Scott then describes disadvantages and problems of sustained methods. Participation engenders involvement and some loss of objectivity, thus interfering with the collection of unbiased data. To the extent that the investigator gets drawn into and becomes a participant in the group culture, he runs the risk of overlooking important variables by coming to take for granted what his respondents take for granted. It is difficult to gain acceptance in a variety of groups without becoming identified with one of these. The necessity to gain permission for the work from top officials is liable to prejudice others against him. He will not have equally good relations with all his subjects and will tend to gravitate toward those who make him welcome. Since some members may be very similar to the investigator in social background and personal characteristics, they may be perceived for this reason as being more cooperative, more intelligent, or having a more realistic view of the situation. (Both the last mentioned introduce an undetermined amount of bias into the material.) To stay close to the subject group the research worker must respect its norms. To counteract reactions against intrusion, the research worker may temper his research role with friendliness, helpfulness, or concern for his respondents as persons: in doing this he becomes more of a participant in the situation and loses his objectivity. The research worker may emerge so impressed with the complexity and uniqueness of his case that he has difficulty in thinking abstractly about his materials or generalizing about them. He is more liable to take over the interests and concerns of his subjects, so that his research becomes increasingly guided by their problems. His concern for his subjects and for maintaining good relations with them may interfere in an important way with his collection, interpretation, or reporting of data.

Scott concludes that sustained methods are more appropriate for exploratory or descriptive studies, studies in depth, or studies of patternings of activities and interactions of a limited population, and the transitory approach more appropriate for conducting hypothesis-testing studies focusing on a limited number of subjects and using their reports on their own attitudes and behavior. Both approaches, he says, have their limitations. While the transitory researcher has avoided many of the problems described above because he has restricted himself to a few variables, he must live with the fear that he has not succeeded in his attempt to control all the contaminating influences and that the associations he has found among his key variables are spurious. The two approaches, Scott suggests, should be viewed as complementary.

A. H. Barton appears to see case studies as unlikely to contribute much to organizational theory, particularly if they are one-shot studies.[35] The main contribution, he suggests, derives from comparison with ideal-types. He suggests that the limitations of this method are in part removed when comparisons between organizations are possible.

The general drift of these arguments is that sustained case studies of organizations have their virtues but are limited in scientific contribution. This is certainly correct from the point of view of establishing firm empirical generalizations about organizational phenomena. At the same time Scott and Barton have perhaps not taken adequate account of the importance to social science of the case method. One has only to list the names of Freud, Piaget, and Erikson in psychology and of Malinowski, Radcliffe-Brown, and Levi-Strauss in social anthropology to make the point that crucial contributions have come through case methods. This is, of course, also true in organizational theory, where the important contributions of such sociologists as Homans, Gouldner, Blau, and Selznick can be cited. All have relied heavily on their own case studies, although they have, of course, also used the variety of comparative controls referred to—including comparisons with ideal-type and with other sustained case studies. Particularly in areas of social research where representative sampling is difficult, key contributions to knowledge are made through the case approach, in developing new concepts and theories, throwing doubts on prior conceptualizations, and drawing attention to problems for further investigation.

Sustained research in single organizational communities is essential because of the very nature of the phenomena being studied. As Scott points out, research subjects in organizations differ from many other persons normally included in social study by being closely bound together in a common network of relations. These, of course, constitute the very core of the organization and must be understood if the organization as an entity is to be understood, or if the behavior of individual members is to be accounted for.

Within the range of sustained field approaches to organizational study, social consultancy has its own particular advantages and problems. The advantages center around gaining and maintaining access to organizational behavior and, particularly, access to the study of conflict, change, and resistance to change. This method of work solves the problem of access that dogs empirical sociological study of contemporary society.

Access to positions from which study may be undertaken is difficult to obtain in Western society except in the investigator's own organization, where his study is bound to be grossly distorted by his personal standpoint and interests. One important group of organizations—business firms—exclude observers largely because they see their effectiveness as depending on keeping competitors as ignorant as possible of their operations and plans. But even organizations which do not see their fate as dependent on confidentiality do not normally welcome observers. Observers are felt to invade privacy and get in the way. More important, observation implies the possibility of comparisons that can challenge the rightness and inevitability of existing practices. Much that occurs when people work together is painful, and those concerned are reluctant to have their discomfort witnessed or publicized. One likes to keep to a minimum the people who see or know one's personal conflicts, setbacks, and defeats. A further inhibiting factor is anxiety that the act of making social and personal behavior explicit may destroy the capacity for that behavior. In one approach commonly used to overcome the problem of access, the research worker selects his topic for investigation, decides where he can carry out his field study, enters the field with little or no disclosure of his identity and purpose, and carries out his program; he then withdraws, writes his report, and publishes it with such withholding or disguising of the data as he thinks expedient in the interests of the people studied or of himself. One obvious limitation to this approach is that the observer can rarely assume a role that will lead him to the inner life of the organization. Serious ethical and professional objections can also be made to this mode of operation. Alternatively, it is possible for the investigator openly to define the problem and the area to be studied, and take his research into the public area. He seeks the permission of the appropriate authorities for the right of access to the groups to be studied and undertakes to submit his report for permission to publish, but remains in intention and, as much as possible in practice, a passive observer. This mode of approach is both ethical and productive. It has the limitation, however, that the observer tends to be excluded from the inner councils of the leaders of the organization because they see little overlap between his interests and objectives and their own and do not expect a return from him. He must confine most of his observations to matters of more peripheral concern to them.

In the social consultancy approach, which differs from both of those just described, the prospect of help is exchanged for the research opportunity. It is an explicit part of the contract with the organizations studied that attempts will be made to give them help with some of their problems.

Social consultancy throws light on an important aspect of organizational change—what happens when new information is introduced and what affects its potential use.

The point that knowledge is not (by itself) power is underlined by the experience of many interventionists in feeding back crucial information to persons from whom, or from whose subordinates, it has been collected. Much of the data are characteristically rejected as obvious, untrue, exaggerated, or irrelevant (sometimes all of these at the same time). It is important that social scientists come to understand what determines how much action is taken when correct and apparently essential data about participants and their environment are introduced, what processes typically ensue after the introduction of the data, and what causes underlie these processes.

Social consultancy involves attempts to introduce social changes and confronts the investigator with resistance to change. This means that theoretical light should be thrown on conservative forces in behavior, forces that make for persistence in existing behavior and relationships. These include the collusive, defensive procedures that colleagues develop and that have the effect of warding off anxiety, justifying their present level of performance, and warding off new demands that may be made on them. Just as the key to the understanding of the personality of the individual may lie in comprehending his central anxieties and the means he uses for defending himself against them, so a key to understanding the collective actions that we label organizational behavior may lie in identifying what dangers participants are most preoccupied with and how they strive to protect themselves against these.

Barton has commented on the importance of qualitative case studies that examine time sequences of the behavior of organization members (as my studies and those of several social consultants have done). As he says, such studies can disclose "microprocesses" such as informal pressures that maintain normal equilibrium in the organization. He adds that qualitative studies over long periods, particularly if they cover major organizational changes such as succession, growth, and reorganization, permit derivation of relationships between organizational variables. Such studies also test hypotheses about the functions of various parts of the system by observing what happens when one part is changed. (He adds as a precaution that the fact that such a system of relationships is found to exist in a single case is hardly conclusive evidence that it exists in all cases and that comparative studies of several organizations are necessary to check alternative possibilities and to specify the conditions under which the relationships hold.)

But social consultancy has disadvantages as a research method. In work of this type the investigator finds it difficult to study any problem except the one preoccupying his respondents. His choice of problem is restricted, and this makes it difficult for him to execute a sustained program of research on one topic or to pursue a research interest through to a logical conclusion. He is lucky if he can find a sequence of sufficiently similar or related problems in comparable organizations that will make systematic comparison possible. Nor can he make the most of his opportunities for access. Not knowing what will come up, he cannot formulate the relevant theoretical problem beforehand in the most fruitful way.

A second consequence of the work taking place under the active sponsorship of directorates is that main emphasis tends to be on the needs of the organization as defined by the directorate. In view of the fact that needs differ according to the interests and power of the different groups and categories constituting the organization, a management-centered bias is apt to enter the work.

A third consequence of managerial sponsorship is the temptation for the research workers to concentrate their attention on variables susceptible to manipulation by management. For instance, a problem of "insufficient" involvement of scientists in organizational affairs may be studied mainly in terms of attitudes to the firm and ambivalence toward administrative colleagues, since some managerial action is possible in both these fields. But the explanation for the behavior of the scientists will, in fact, be inadequate if it ignores the importance of professional identification among scientists and the functions of such identification for the maintenance of scientific standard in both basic and applied work.

The risk of "unrepresentativeness," common to all case studies, is underlined in social consultancy by the willingness of the respondents to have themselves and their organizations studied, by the intimacy that grows between organization and consultant, and by the fact that, by definition, the organization will change through the consultant's presence.

Once the work is in motion he forgoes much of his freedom of choice in regard to the order, the timing, and the conditions under which his data will appear. And he cannot isolate and control these in a way that would make possible the checking of his conclusions by other investigators in other organizations.

A certain loss of objectivity occurs through the fact that a degree of emotional identification with the respondents and their activities becomes inevitable. However well trained the investigator, this is likely to distort what he perceives and will wish to report. This is one reason why it is prudent to build into social consultancy projects an arrangement for regular review of the work by at least one uninvolved colleague.

Where payment is received from the client organization, loss of objectivity may also occur for a different reason. If the payment forms a significant proportion of his income, the consultant is bound to be tempted to compromise between his need for information and his need to avoid prejudicing his relationship with his client.

The research limitations placed on the work by the introduction of therapeutic objectives and financial dependence on clients are, of course, shared with medical clinicians. Those placed on the work by observing human beings in their own environments are shared with anthropological field workers. In both spheres, the fact of using single cases and lack of control over the timing of the events which are of interest and the conditions under which they occur have not prevented the emergence of richly suggestive models of behavior, which have contributed a unique understanding of the ways in which different facets of personality and of community life interlock.

There is a general limitation to the research potentialities of social consultancy which is associated with the typical preoccupations and outlook of the applied social research worker.[36]

Problems can often be solved or ameliorated without the full apparatus of a formal explanation of the reasons for their occurrence. It is perfectly feasible, for example, to help an organization deal with problematic relations between managers and workers, line executives and scientists, or graduates and nongraduates by paying greater care in their selection and include in their training the capacity to work with others and to tolerate differences in outlook. At the same time the acknowledgment of such problems and difficulties is not a scientific explanation of why they occur. For this one needs knowledge of the patterns of social stratification in the wider society, the socialization effects of educational experiences and the functions performed by occupational cultures. Social consultants rightly claim to go beyond the symptoms presented by managements to deeper and more extensive diagnoses of problems and causal factors in them. But this extension is usually mainly to the interpersonal dynamics of the local situation or to its current administrative arrangements for getting existing tasks done, because it is economic to limit explanation to variables that the management can manipulate. But if the objective is explanation of the widespread incidence of particular types of organizational problems it is necessary to adduce the societal matrix of interpersonal behavior within organizations as well as that behavior in itself.

NOTES

1. E. Jaques, *The Changing Culture of a Factory*, (London: Tavistock, 1951). Jaques subsequently left the Tavistock but continued to work with the same company on his own along similar lines.

2. C. Sofer, *The Organization from Within*, (London, Tavistock, 1961).

3. W. G. Bennis, "A New Role for the Behavioural Sciences: Effecting Organizational Change," *Administrative Science Quarterly* 8, (September 1963): 125–165.

4. M. Pages, "The Socio-Therapy of the Enterprise: The Conditions of Psycho-

Social Change in Industrial Concerns and the Roles of the Social Psychologist as an Agent of Social Change," *Human Relations,* 12, no. 4 (November 1959): 317–334.

5. C. Argyris, "Organisations: Effectiveness and Planning of Change," *International Encyclopaedia of the Social Sciences,* 11, (New York: Macmillan, 1968), pp. 311–319.

6. A detailed account of the cases, a comparison with others, and a discussion of social consultancy and organizational change appear in C. Sofer, *The Organization from Within.*

7. This study was based on a very brief period of contact and rested almost entirely on one investigatory technique (group discussion). I saw the organization at a critical phase of what was clearly a many-sided evolution that could be fully understood only in its historical context. My material appeared sufficient to provide a basis for discussion and advice, though it could not have done full justice to a complex situation.

8. A. K. Rice, *Productivity and Social Organization: the Ahmedabad Experiment,* (London, Tavistock, 1958), p. 4.

9. Rice has been more inclined than most other social consultants to make direct recommendations to his clients. This was a consequence of his interest as an organizational theorist in designing workable models of organizations and seeing them tested.

10. Personal communication to author.

11. Personal communication to author.

12. F. C. Mann, "Studying and Creating Change: A Means to Understanding Social Organizations," in C. M. Arensberg, ed., *Research in Industrial Human Relations,* (New York: Harper, 1957). See also F. C. Mann, "Changing Superior-Subordinate Relationships," *Journal of Social Issues,* (1951–1952).

13. C. Argyris, *Organization and Innovation,* (Homewood, Illinois: Irwin and Dorsey, 1965).

14. See E. H. Schein and W. G. Bennis, eds., *Personal and Organizational Change Through Group Methods: The Laboratory Approach* (New York: Wiley, 1965, © 1965 by John Wiley & Sons), especially chapter 10. In the case of these two authors their value premises are quite explicit. They speak directly of "the uses of laboratory training in improving social behaviour." ·

15. Schein and Bennis, eds., *Personal and Organizational Change,* p. 34.

16. Schein and Bennis, p. 204. This assertion appears to imply that Schein and Bennis see the conduct of one or other type of laboratory experience as the only medium for the introduction of such changes rather than one among a range of approaches open to senior managements and their social science consultants. Reprinted by permission of John Wiley & Sons.

17. More broadly, this refers to a system advocated by Likert on the basis of organizational research, largely by the Institute of Social Research at Michigan, in which work groups overlap both vertically and horizontally. He argues that this enables influence to be exerted in all directions and the benefits of effective work groups to be widely distributed. See R. Likert, *New Patterns of Management,* (New York: McGraw-Hill, 1961).

18. D. McGregor, *The Human Side of Enterprise* (New York, McGraw Hill, 1960).

19. There is no discussion of the possibly inhibiting effects of colleagues on each other in training group sessions or of the subsequent impact on the person who has returned to his organization of having some colleagues who have come to know him in a more intimate way.

20. R. R. Blake and R. S. Mouton, "A 9.9 Approach for Increasing Organizational Productivity."

21. Blake and Mouton, "A 9.9 Approach," pp. 170–172.

22. H. L. Wilensky, "Organizations: Organizational Intelligence," *International Encyclopaedia of the Social Sciences,* II (New York: Macmillan, 1968).

23. Wilensky, "Organizations," p. 320.

24. L. Sayles, "The Change Process in Organizations: An Applied Anthropology Analysis," *Human Organization,* 21, no. 2 (Summer 1962): 62–67.

25. F. C. Mann and F. W. Neff, *Managing Major Change in Organizations, Report for the Foundation for Research on Human Behaviour,* (Ann Arbor: Broup and Brumfield, Inc., 1961), p. 52.

26. E. Ginzberg and E. W. Reilly, *Effecting Change in Large Organizations* (New York, Columbia University Press, 1957).

27. D. Katz, "Approaches to Managing Conflict," in R. L. Kahn and D. Boulding, eds., *Power and Conflict in Organizations,* (London: Tavistock, 1965).

28. I. E. P. Menzies, "A Case Study in the Functioning of Social Systems as a Defence Against Anxiety," *Human Relations,* 13 (May 1960): 95–121.

29. In a personal communication to me on what should come first in an organizational change project, changes in "interpersonal relations or in structure," C. Argyris argues that it is pointless to proceed with structural changes until and unless the key persons are willing to maintain them.

30. Argyris, *Organization and Innovation,* p. 129.

31. H. R. Shepard and R. R. Blake, "Changing Behaviour Through Cognitive Change," *Human Organization,* 21 (Summer 1962).

32. Schein and Bennis, eds., *Personal and Organizational Change,* p. 328. Reprinted by permission of John Wiley & Sons, Inc.

33. W. E. Moore and M. M. Tumin, "Some Social Functions of Ignorance," *American Sociological Review,* 14 (December 1949): 787–795.

34. In J. G. March, ed., *Handbook of Organizations,* (Chicago: Rand McNally, 1965).

35. A. H. Barton, "Organizations: Methods of Research," *International Encyclopaedia of the Social Sciences,* 11, (New York: Macmillan, 1968): 334–343.

36. A. W. Gouldner has pointed out the "Unlike the pure scientist, who delights in maximizing knowledge either for its own sake or to test hypotheses and extend theories, the applied social scientist will sometimes forgo sources of knowledge, however rich in data they may be, if he fears their use will impede the intended change. . . . The impulse toward change dominates and may be at variance with the impulse to know." A. W. Gouldner, "Theoretical Requirements of the Applied Social Sciences," in W. G. Bennis, K. D. Benne and R. Chin, eds., *The Planning of Change. Readings in the Applied Behavioural Sciences,* (New York: Holt, Rinehart and Wilson, 1961). Gouldner cites as an example the operating principle of Jaques and his colleagues in the Glacier project that no matter would be discussed unless representatives of the group concerned were present or had agreed to the topic being raised. *Changing Culture,* p. 14.

Name Index

Subject Index